Highly Recommended

AF655215

New Edition

OSWAAL BOOKS®

LEARNING MADE SIMPLE

NCERT TEXTBOOK SOLUTIONS

CLASS 11

CHEMISTRY

Strictly based on the Latest NCERT Textbook

Powered by

oswaal.ai
LEARNING MADE SMARTER

Smart guidance that helps you learn, practise and improve.

Your Path to Academic Excellence:

1
100% Updated
with the Latest NCERT Textbook

2
Comprehensive Coverage
with All Concepts & Topics Covered

3
Visual Learning Tools
with Concept Videos

4
Extensive Revision Tools
with Crisp Revision Notes, Mind Maps & Mnemonics

5
Complete Question Coverage
All Questions Fully Solved

OSWAAL BOOKS®
LEARNING MADE SIMPLE

This Edition: 2026

ISBN: 9789359584805

Disclaimer

This publication has been prepared by qualified subject matter experts with rigorous editorial review. Despite our best efforts, errors may exist. Readers are encouraged to report any by scanning the QR code on the Table of Contents page so corrections can reach all users.

This book is a study aid. Examination results depend on multiple factors including individual preparation and the specific examination conducted. No particular outcome is guaranteed.

Links in this book provide access to supplementary content. Accessibility depends on internet connectivity and device compatibility. Third-party content linked herein was verified at the time of printing; however, the Publisher does not guarantee that such content will remain accurate, available, or appropriate over time.

Views expressed by individual contributors are their own and do not represent the Publisher's position. The Publisher does not endorse personal opinions or political statements contained herein.

All maps, boundaries, and diagrams are artistic representations for educational reference only and are not geographically or politically authoritative.

For details on personal data processing, see our Privacy Policy at www.oswaalbooks.com/privacy.
This publication is governed by the laws of India. Disputes shall be subject to the exclusive jurisdiction of courts in Agra, Uttar Pradesh.

Published by: Oswaal Books and Learning Private Limited, Oswaal House, 1/11, Sahitya Kunj, M.G. Road, Agra-282002 (U.P.), India

contact@oswaalbooks.com

+91-562-2857671

Printed at: Upkar Print House Pvt. Ltd., Agra

Contents

Stay Informed: CBSE Updates & Recent Improvements

CBSE Updates

Scan to get the latest syllabus updates & changes

Recent Improvements

Scan to stay updated with important changes in the book!

Learning is fun when you're always up to date! Keep scanning!

PREFACE

"*Education is the passport to the future, for tomorrow belongs to those who prepare for it today.*" – Malcolm X

In the pursuit of academic excellence, the journey often begins with curiosity. As students embark on the path to success in the exams, the Oswaal NCERT Textbook Solutions Book for the latest academic year stands as an invaluable companion, illuminating the way forward.

Success in any exam goes beyond memorization; it involves developing a deep understanding of every concept. The NCERT textbooks provide the essential foundation. Introducing the Oswaal NCERT Textbook Solutions Book, a vital tool to unlock the full potential of every student.

Let's uncover what this book covers for you:

1) **Updated for the latest academic year –** The books are 100% updated for the latest academic year, adhering strictly to the latest NCERT guidelines.

2) **Comprehensive Coverage -** We cover all concepts and topics outlined in the most recent NCERT textbooks.

3) **Visual Learning Aids -** Explore theoretical concepts and concept videos that offer a brief description of the topic and help visualize complex concepts.

4) **Effective Revision Tools -** Benefit from crisp Revision Notes, Mind Maps, and Mnemonics designed to facilitate efficient and effective review.

5) **Complete Question Coverage -** All questions from the NCERT textbooks are covered in our solutions, providing a thorough grasp of the subject matter.

What sets this book apart is the expertise behind its creation. The solutions within are the result of the meticulous efforts of expert faculty, individuals with a profound understanding of the curriculum, and the dedication to maintaining the highest quality standards.

May this book be your guide, encouraging you to not just study but to explore and understand.

Wishing you a fulfilling and successful academic journey.

Team,

Oswaal Books

Order Form

ONE FOR ALL OLYMPIADS (Multicolour)
Classes 1 to 8
Mathematics, English, Reasoning, General Knowledge, Science & Cyber

ONE FOR ALL OLYMPIADS Workbooks
Classes 1 to 8
Mathematics, English, Science

ONE FOR ALL WORKBOOKS (Multicolour)
Classes 1 to 5
Mathematics, English, General Knowledge, EVS, Hindi

NCERT WORKBOOKS (B&W)
Classes 1 to 5
English, Hindi, Mathematics & EVS

NCERT & CBSE One For All Workbooks
Classes 6 to 8
Mathematics, English, Science, Social Science, Hindi & Sanskrit

CBSE Work Books
Classes 9 & 10
English Lang. & Literature, Science, Social Science & Mathematics

CBSE & NCERT Laboratory Manual
Classes 6 to 12
Mathematics, Science, Physics, Chemistry & Biology

CBSE QUESTION BANKS (CHAPTER-WISE & TOPIC-WISE SOLVED PAPERS)
Classes 9 & 10
Hindi-A, Hindi-B, English Lang. & Lit. (With NCERT Workbook), Science, Mathematics, Social Science, Computer Applications, Sanskrit & English Communicative (based on CBSE Textbooks), Information Technology (Class-10th only), Artificial intelligence (Class-10th only)

Classes 11 & 12
Hindi Core (For Class-12 Only), English Core, Mathematics, Chemistry, Applied Mathematics (For Class-12 Only), Biology, Physics, Accountancy, Economics, Business Studies, Geography, History, Political Science, Computer Science, Entrepreneurship (For Class-12 Only), Informatics Practices, Physical Education, Sociology (For Class 12th Only), Psychology (For Class 12th Only)

CBSE Textbook Plus
Classes 10 & 12
English Lang. & Lit., Mathematics, Science, Social Science, English Core, Biology, Physics, Chemistry

CBSE Xcellence 95+
Classes 10 & 12
Sanskrit (शेमुषी), Sanskrit Communicative (मणिका), Physics, Chemistry, English Core

NCERT EXEMPLAR PROBLEMS-SOLUTIONS (Hindi & English Medium)
Classes 9 to 12
Science, Mathematics, Physics, Chemistry, Biology, Mathematics, गणित, विज्ञान, भौतिक विज्ञान, रसायन विज्ञान, जीव विज्ञान

NCERT Textbook Solutions
Classes 6 to 8
Mathematics, English, Hindi, Science, Social Science & Sanskrit

Classes 9 to 12
Science, Mathematics, Physics, Chemistry, Biology

CBSE 10 PREVIOUS YEARS' SOLVED PAPERS
Class 10
Combined: English Lang. & Lit, Science, Social Science,Mathematics Stan.

Class 12
Science (PCM)-(Chemistry, Physics, Mathematics & English Core), **Science (PCB)**-(Chemistry, Physics, English Core & Biology) **Commerce**-(Economics, Accountancy, Business Studies, English Core), **Humanities**-(Geography, History, Political Science & English Core)

CBSE Previous Years' Solved Papers Stand alone Series
Class 10
Hindi-A, Hindi-B, Mathematics Basic, Sanskrit, Computer Applications

Class 12
Applied Mathematics, Mathematics

CBSE RMT FLASH CARDS
Class 10
Mathematics, English Lang. & Lit., Social Science & Science

CBSE ONE FOR ALL
Classes 6 to 8
English, Hindi, Mathematics, Science, Social Science & Sanskrit

Class 10
English Lang. & Lit., Social Science, Science, Hindi-A, Hindi-B, Mathematics (Stand.) & Mathematics Basic

Class 12
English Core, Physics, Chemistry, Mathematics, Biology, Accountancy, Business Studies & Economics

FINAL HUSTLE FOR CBSE
Class 10
Science, Mathematics Standard & Social Science

Class 12
Science (Physics, Chemistry, Mathematics, Biology & English Core), **Commerce** (Accountancy, Business Studies, Economics, Mathematics & English Core), **Humanities** (History, Geography, Political Science & English Core)

CBSE SAMPLE QUESTION PAPERS
Class 9
Science, Mathematics

Class 10
Hindi-A, Hindi-B, English Lang. & Lit., Computer Applications, English Communicative, Mathematics Standard, Mathematics Basic, Science, Social Science, Sanskrit, Samajik Vigyan, Information- Technology, Artificial intelligence, Sanskrit Communicative

Class 12
Hindi Core, Hindi Elective, English Core, Mathematics, Applied Mathematics, Physics, Chemistry, Biology, Accountancy, Economics, Business Studies, Geography, History, Political Science, Computer Science, Informatics Practices, Physical Education, Entrepreneurship, Psychology & Sociology

CBSE 20 Combined Sample Question Papers
Classes 9 to 12
Class- 9 & 10: **Combined Book**
Class- 11 & 12: Science, Commerce & Humanities

CBSE Competency Focused Questions Chapter-wise
Classes 10 & 12
Class 10 :- (Combined Book) Science, Social Science & Mathematics Standard
Class 12 :- Science PCM, Science PCB & Commerce

How To Talk To AI

Crafting the Perfect Prompt

oswaal.ai
LEARNING MADE SMARTER

Think of AI as your super-smart study buddy — **the better you ask, the better it answers.** A **prompt** is simply the question or instruction you give to AI. Master this skill, and you'll unlock a powerful tool for learning.

The Basic Prompt Structure

[Role] + [Task] + [Context] + [Format]

Element	What It Means	Example
Role	Tell it who to be	*"Act as a Subject "........" teacher."*
Task	What you want it to do	*"...explain the concept of..."*
Context	Give background details	*"For Class ...., Chapter ...."*
Format	How you want the answer	*"...using bullet points and a diagram."*

Weak Prompt vs. Strong Prompt

☒ Weak Prompt

Tell me about this topic "..........".

☑ Strong Prompt

"Act as a subject "........" teacher. Explain the topic "........" clearly for school students. Use simple language, include key points, and give one example."

Pro Tips for Better Prompts

Be Specific
Say exactly what you need, not vague requests

Set the Level
Mention your class & board

Ask Examples
Add "with real-life examples" to remember better

Request Format
Ask for tables, flowcharts, or mnemonics

Iterate
Ask follow-ups to simplify or expand

Other Useful AI Tools for Students

ChatGPT
Explains concepts, solves questions, makes notes & projects
chatgpt.com

Google Gemini
Great for diagrams, visuals & numerical explanations
gemini.google.com

Perplexity AI
Research tool with verified info & sources
perplexity.ai

Photomath
Solves Maths problems with step-by-step solutions
photomath.com

Notion AI
Creates notes, organizes syllabus & project structure
notion.so

Quizlet AI
Makes flashcards & quizzes from any chapter
quizlet.com

Canva AI
Makes posters, charts, covers & PPTs easily
canva.com

Otter.ai
Records lectures & converts to written notes
otter.ai

Remember: AI doesn't read minds — it reads prompts. The clearer you are, the more it helps!

Exclusive School Books Suppliers

	KARNATAKA
BANGALORE	Pride Book World, 9448685507, Tanwer Books and Garments, 9916049273, Jipsy, 9620325985
MYSORE	Ragavendra Book Agency, 9591911489
	TELANGANA
HYDERABAD	Shri Sharada store Books & Stationers, 9700768789, Sri Balaji Book Depot, 9676996199, Vishal Book Distributors, 9246333166, Pranavi Publishers, 919948853126, Shri Sharada store Books & Stationers, 9700768789
	TAMIL NADU
CHENNAI	M.K. Stores, 9840030099, Sivaa Book Centre, 9952933315, Kamal Book House, 9841077369
ERODE	Selvam Book Centre, 919843199697
MADURAI	Selvi Book Shoppe, 9345037977, Madurai Book Shop, 9751937519
COIMBATORE CUDDALORE	Indian Book Centre, 9443093053
	MAHARASHTRA
PUNE	Madhusheela Books & Stationers, 7875899892, Pravin Sales, 8888038889
NANDED	Vijay Book Centre, 9822994436
JALNA	Anil Paper Mart, 919422722522
CHHATRAPATI SAMBHAJINAGAR	AARTI BOOK CENTRE, 919422203836
NAGPUR	Sandeep Book Depot, 9371078789
VASAI	Dinvin Books Excellence PVT. LTD. , 9867561128
MUMBAI	New Student Agencies LLP, 8355965098, Ravechi Book Stationery, 9769002371
	ANDHRA PRADESH
VISAKHAPATNAM	VKML Books, 8125168946
NANDYAL	Sathyam Book Store & Fancy, 9052439300
NELLORE	S V S Book Centre, 9347100774
VIJAYAWADA	VKML Books, 9966639957
	HARYANA
ROHTAK	Babu Ram Pradeep Kumar, 9813214692
VIZIANAGARAM	Himamsu Book Distributor, 9493434777
	MADHYA PRADESH
INDORE	Mahesh Book Depot, 9893855543
SHAHDOL	Anjali Book Centre, 917067572992

	JHARKHAND
DEOGHAR	Navyug Sahitya Mandir, 919031917035
BOKARO STEEL CITY	Bokaro Student Friends Pvt. Ltd, 919234628152
	MEGHALAYA
SHILLONG	New Book Centre, 9774088719
	WEST BENGAL
KOLKATA	Oriental Pub. Dist. Pvt. Ltd., 919903879153, United Book House, 9831344622
	UTTAR PRADESH
PRAYAGRAJ	Saraswati book depot, 7706855403
KANPUR	Raj Book, 9235616506
MATHURA	Sapra Traders, 9410076716, Agrawal Book House, 7906527213
GHAZIABAD	Vani Enterprises, 919891276834
	DELHI
DELHI	Mittal Books, 919810133323, Prakash Brothers, 919811179840, R.D. Chawla & Sons, 9810045752, Ameen Global Services, 919716028892, Need Prakashan Pvt Ltd, 9968383261
	GUJARAT
VADODARA	Career Skills Education and Research Foundation, 8469149288
BHARUCH	J.D. Agency, 9099944480
	KERALA
ERNAKULAM	Novel House School Supplies, 8792342807
	ASSAM
GUWAHATI	Central Book Agency, 9954707165
SILCHER	New Book Stall, 919435712617
JORHAT	Bajrang stationery, 9706978968
	RAJASTHAN
ANUPGARH	City Pride Departmental Store, 919414095677
BARMER	Dev Indra Enterprises, 7073282106
	MANIPUR
IMPHAL	Global Agencies, 917641814494
	PUNJAB
TARN TARAN	Sital Di Hatti, 919988206890
KHAMMAM	Sri Nivasa Book Stall, 919948247838
RAIPUR	**CHHATTISGARH**
	Central Book House, 9406016308

Our Distributors

	ANDHRA PRADESH
VISAKHAPA-THAM	Sri Rajeshwari Book Link, 9848036014,
VIJAYAWADA	Sree Vidya Book Depot, 9491830839
	ANDAMAN & NICOBAR ISLAND
PORTBLAIR	Krishna Book Centre, 9474205570
	ARUNACHAL PRADESH
NAHARLAGUN	New Pothi Ghar, 8731832947
	ASSAM
SILCHAR	Book Emporium, 9675972993, 6000763186,
	New Book Stall, 9435712617
GUWAHATI	Kayaan Enterprises, (0361) 2630443,
	BIHAR
PATNA	Nova Publisher & Distributors, (0612) 2666404, Gyan Ganga Limited, 9304826651,
	Rishu Pustak Bhandar, 8294576789, Sri Durga Pustak Mandir, 9334477386,
	Vikas Book Depot, 919504780402,
	Bokaro Student Friends Pvt. Ltd, 7277931285
BIHAR SHARIF	Good Books , 8210685462
MUZAFFARPUR	Pustak Bhandar, 7870834225
	CHATTISGARH
AMBIKAPUR	M.P Department Stores, 9425254264
BOKARO	Bokaro Student Friends Pvt. Ltd, Bokaro, 7277931285
DURG	Bhagwati Bhawani Book Depot, 0788-2327620, 9827473100
RAIPUR	Gupta Pustak Mandir, 7974220323,
BILASPUR	Pustak Bhawan, 9300667909
	DELHI
DELHI	Mittal Books, (011) 23288887, 9899037390, A One Books, New Delhi, 8800497047,
	Batheja Super Store, 9871833924, 9811182352, Zombozone, 9871274082,
	LDS Marketing, 9811182352/9999353491, R.D. Chawla & Sons, 9810045752,
	Janta Book Depot, 9313046321
	Bokaro Student Friends Pvt. Ltd, 7004074900

	GUJARAT
AHMEDABAD	Patel Book Agencies, 9898184248, 9824386112, 9825900335,
	Shalibhadra Stationers, 9904477855
VAPI	Goutam Book Sellers, 9081790813
VADODARA	Shree ji Book Depot, 9824649375, Nilesh Book Centre, 9924458748
	Umakant Book Sellers & Stationer, 6359396370
AHMEDNAGAR	Hira Stationers, 9970150300
	HARYANA
ROHTAK	Swami Kitab Ghar, 9355611088, Babu Ram Pradeep Kumar, 9813214692
GURGAON	Book Care Centre Venture, 9654564783
REWARI	Repro Books Ltd, 8657315914, Annu book depot, 9053246268
	JHARKHAND
BOKARO	Bokaro Student Friends Pvt. Ltd. (0654) 2233094, 7360021503,
	Bharati Bhawan Agencies, 06542-265302, 9431740797
HAZARIBAGH	Khandelwal Book Depot, 9708607489
DEOGHAR	Navyug Sahitya Mandir, 9031917035
RANCHI	Pustak Mandir, 9431115138, Agarwal Book Depot, 9334869210, Jayshree Book House, 8434430311
	Bokaro Student Friends Pvt. Ltd, 7360021508
DHANBAD	Bokaro Student Friends Pvt. Ltd, 6202834756
	KARNATAKA
HUBLI	Renuka Book Distributor, (0836) 2244124,
	Vidyamandir Book Distributors, 9980773976
BANGLORE	Krishna book house, 9739847334,
	Sapna Book House Pvt. Ltd., 9980513242,
	Sree Sai Ram Book Traders, 9738881088
	MADHYA PRADESH
INDORE	Pustak Bhawan, 8982150100, Bhaiya Store, 9425318103
	S.P. & Publication, 7000025933
GWALIOR	Agarwal Book Depot, 9425116210
JABALPUR	Vinay Pustak Sadan, 8962362667,
	Anand Books and Stationers, 9425323508
	Akash Book Distributor, 8989111444, Bharat Book House, 9826541542
KATNI	Shri Mahavir Agency, 9425363412

24/01/26

Our Distributors

	MAHARASHTRA
AMRAVATI	Delta Pen House, 9890350073
PUNE	Vikas Book House, 9921331187, Pravin Sales, 9890683475,
	New Saraswati Granth Bhandar, 9422323859
	Sai Book Collection, 9623224343
	Yash Agencies, 9850956542
MUMBAI	New Student Agencies, 7045065799,
	Shivam Books & Stationery, 8619805332
KOLHAPUR	Jai Book Co. 9404671543
NAGPUR	Laxmi Pustakalay and Stationers, (0712) 2727354, Vijay Book Depot, 9860122094
	Renuka Book Distributor, 9765406133, Novelty Book Depot, 9657690220,
	Shree Mahalaxmi Pustakalaya, 7507099360
DHULE	Navjeevan Book Stall, 7020525561
YAVATMAL	Shri Ganesh Pustkalaya, 9423131275
NASHIK	Vishal Book Centre, Nashik - 8208249434
VASAI	Prime Book Centre, Vasai, 9890293662
	ODISHA
CUTTACK	A. K. Mishra Agencies, 9437025991, 9437081319
BHUBANESHWAR	M/s Pragnya, 8847888616, 9437943777, Padmalaya, 9437026922,
KEONJHAR	Students Corner, 7008435418
KORAPUT	Ambica Book Centre, 7008585008
	PUNJAB
AMBALA	Bharat Book Depot, 7988455354
PATIALA	Goel Sons, 9463619978,
	Adarsh Enterprises, 9814347613
JALANDHAR	Cheap Book Store, 9872223458, 9878258592, City Book Shop, 9417440753,
	Subhash Book Depot, 9876453625,
	Gaurav Book world, 9478821183
LUDHIANA	Amit Book Depot, 9815807871,
	Bhatia Book Centre, 9815277131, Gupta Brothers, 9888200206
CHANDIGARH	Mohindra Book Depot, 9814920226
BATHINDA	Goyal Sons , 9464478362, Bhagwati Book Depot, 9463120564
	RAJASTHAN
AJMER	Laxmi General Store, Ajmer, 0145- 2428942 9460652197
KOTA	Raj Traders, 9309232829
BHILWARA	Nakoda Book Depot, (01482) 243653, 9214983594,
JAIPUR	Saraswati Book House, (0141) 2610823, 9829811155,
	Goyal Book Distt., 9460983939, 9414782130
JODHPUR	Kitab Mahal, 9460957875
	TRIPURA
AGARTALA	Books Corner, 8794894165, 8984657146
	TAMIL NADU
COIMBATORE	Majestic Book House, 9791966665
CHENNAI	M.R. Book Store (044) 25364596,
	Kalaimagal Store, (044) 5544072, 9940619404, Vijaya Stores, 9381037417,
	Bookmark It-Books & Stat. Store, 7305151653,
	M.K. Stores, 9840030099, Tiger Books Pvt. Ltd., 9710447000,
MADURAI	Selvi Book Shoppe, 9843057435
	KERALA
ERNAKULAM	Academic Book House, (0484) 2376613, H & C Store, 9864196344
KOTTAYAM	Asad Book Centre, (0481) 2566992
CALICUT	Aman Book Stall, (0495) 2721282,
KOZHIKODE	T.B.S. Publishers Distributors, 7559822223
	TELANGANA
HYDERABAD	Sri Balaji Book Depot, (040) 27613300, 9866355473
	Vishal Book Distributors, 9246333166
	UTTARAKHAND
DEHRADUN	Inder Book Agencies, 9634045280
	Brothers Pustak Bhandar, 9897833882
	UTTAR PRADESH
AGRA	Sparsh Book Agency, 9412257817,
	Sanjay Publication, 8126699922 Arti book centre, 8630128856,
	Om Pustak Mandir, (0562) 2464014, 9319117771
	Panchsheel Books, 9412257962, 9412257961
	Manav Book World, 9760316933
MATHURA	Sapra Traders, 9410076716
PRAYAGRAJ	Mehrotra Book Agency, (0532) 2266865, 9415636890
AZAMGARH	Sasta Sahitya Bhandar, 9450029674
ALIGARH	K.B.C.L. Agarwal, 9897124960,
NAJIBABAD	Gupta News Agency, 8868932500
KANPUR	Radha News Agency, 8957247427,
	Raj Book Dist., 9235616506,
	H K Book Distributors, 9506033137/9935146730
GORAKHPUR	Vidyarthi Sahitya Bhandar, 6394026706
LUCKNOW	Om Book Depot, 7705871398, Azad Book Depot Pvt. Ltd., 7317000250,
	Ashirwad Book Depot, 9235501197, Book.com, 7458922755, Universal Books,
	9450302161, Sheetla Book Agency, 9235832418, Vidyarthi Kendra Publisher & Distributor Pvt Ltd, 9554967415, Tripathi Book House, 9415425943,
	Navyug Book Agencies, 8073564410, Pustak Vatika, 7905317119
MEERUT	Ideal Book Depot, (0121) 4059252, 9837066307
NOIDA	Goyal Books Overseas Pvt.Ltd., 1204655555, 9873387003
PRAYAGRAJ	Kanhaiya Pustak Bhawan, 9415317109
RENUKOOT	Om Stationers, 7007326732
VARANASI	Bokaro Student Friends Pvt. Ltd , 9798050654
	WEST BENGAL
KOLKATA	Oriental Publishers & Distributor (033) 40628367, Katha 'O' Kahini, (033)
	22196313, 22419071, Saha Book House, (033), 22193671, 9333416484,
	United Book House, 9831344622, Bijay Pustak Bhandar, 8961260603,
NORTH DINAJPUR	Sarkar Book Suppliers, 9830949359
COOCH BEHAR	S.B. Book Distributor, Cooch Behar, 9002670771
KHARAGPUR	Subhani Book Store, 9046891334
SINGRAULI	Ambedkar Book Depot, 9826115292
KANPUR	Lamba Book Stall, 9839024277
KARNAL	Chopra Book Store, 8950322681

24/01/26

SCAN TO FIND OUR DISTRIBUTORS' LOCATIONS

SOME BASIC CONCEPTS OF CHEMISTRY

CHAPTER 1

Importance of Chemistry and Nature of Matter

- Chemistry is the branch of science that deals with the composition, structure and properties of matter.
- **Nature of matter:** Matter is anything that has mass and occupies space.
- Matter exist mainly in three physical states viz, solid, liquid and gas. The other two less common states of matter are Plasma and Bose-Einstein condensate state.
- **Classification of matter:** Matter can be categorised as:

Matter
- Mixtures
  - Homogeneous mixture
  - Heterogeneous mixture
- Pure Substances
  - Elements
  - Compounds

- The matter which contains two or more substances is called **mixture.**
- The mixture in which the composition is uniform throughout the mixture is called homogeneous mixture. e.g., sugar solution in water.
- The mixture in which the composition is not uniform throughout the mixture and sometimes different components are visible is called heterogeneous mixture. e.g., mixture of salt and sugar.
- Pure substances have fixed composition. These can be classified into elements and compounds.
- An **element** contains only one type of particles. These particles may be atoms or molecules.
- A **compound** is a combination of two or more atoms of different elements in a definite ratio.
- Solids have definite volume and definite shape.
- Liquids have definite volume but do not have definite shape.
- Gases have neither definite volume nor definite shape.
- The three states of matter are inter-convertible into each other by changing the conditions of temperature and pressure.

$$\text{Solid} \underset{\text{cool}}{\overset{\text{heat}}{\rightleftharpoons}} \text{Liquid} \underset{\text{cool}}{\overset{\text{heat}}{\rightleftharpoons}} \text{Gas}$$

Properties of Matter and their Measurement

- The general properties of matter are categorised into two types:
  (i) Physical properties
  (ii) Chemical properties
- **Some Physical Quantities:**

(a) Mass and Weight

(i) Mass: The standard unit of mass in the International System of Units (SI) is kilogram (kg).

(ii) Weight: In the International System of Units (SI), weight can be expressed in terms of the force, i.e., Newton (N).

$$\boxed{W = m \times g}$$

where, m = mass, g = gravitational force

Note: The mass of substance is constant, whereas, its weight may vary from one place to another due to change in gravity.

(b) Volume: SI unit of volume is m^3.

(c) Density:

$$\text{Density} = \text{Mass/ Volume}$$
$$d = m/V$$

- SI unit of density is kg m^{-3}.

(d) The three common scales are used to measure temperature:
[e.g., Kelvin (K), degree Celsius (°C), degree Fahrenheit (°F)].

(e) Length:

- Length is expressed in Angstrom (Å), nanometre (nm) and picometre (pm). These are related to the SI unit as follows:

$$1\ \text{Å} = 10^{-10}\ \text{m},$$
$$1\ \text{nm} = 10^{-9}\ \text{m},$$
$$1\ \text{pm} = 10^{-12}\ \text{m}.$$

- There are certain rules used for determining significant figures:

(i) All non-zero digits are significant.
(ii) Zero preceding to first non-zero digit are not significant.
(iii) Zero between two non-zero digits are significant.

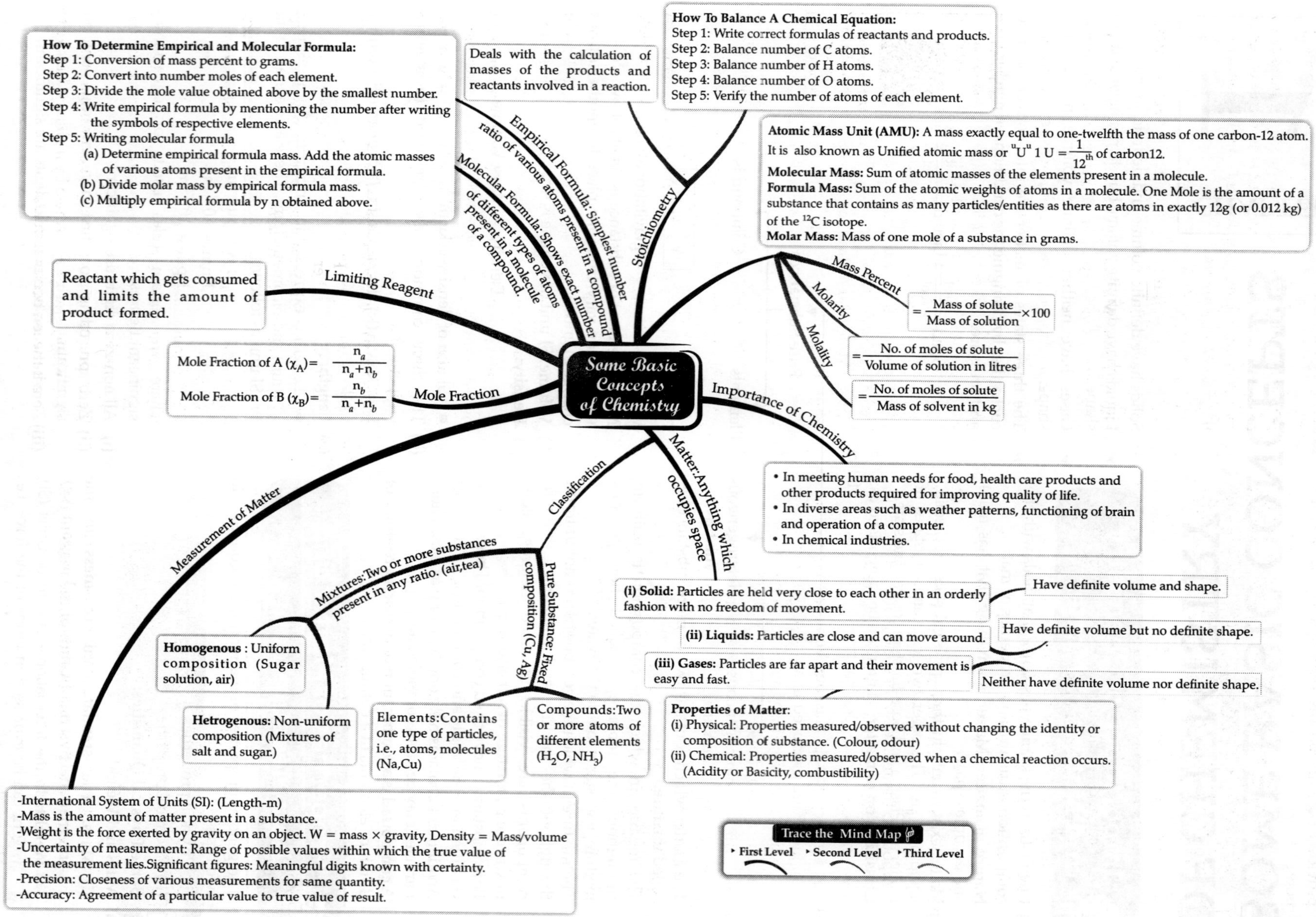
Some Basic Concepts of Chemistry
Stoichiometry
Deals with the calculation of masses of the products and reactants involved in a reaction.
How To Balance A Chemical Equation:
Step 1: Write correct formulas of reactants and products.
Step 2: Balance number of C atoms.
Step 3: Balance number of H atoms.
Step 4: Balance number of O atoms.
Step 5: Verify the number of atoms of each element.
Atomic Mass Unit (AMU): A mass exactly equal to one-twelfth the mass of one carbon-12 atom.
It is also known as Unified atomic mass or "U" 1 U = $\frac{1}{12^{th}}$ of carbon12.
Molecular Mass: Sum of atomic masses of the elements present in a molecule.
Formula Mass: Sum of the atomic weights of atoms in a molecule. One Mole is the amount of a substance that contains as many particles/entities as there are atoms in exactly 12g (or 0.012 kg) of the ^{12}C isotope.
Molar Mass: Mass of one mole of a substance in grams.
Mass Percent
$= \frac{\text{Mass of solute}}{\text{Mass of solution}} \times 100$
Molarity
$= \frac{\text{No. of moles of solute}}{\text{Volume of solution in litres}}$
Molality
$= \frac{\text{No. of moles of solute}}{\text{Mass of solvent in kg}}$
Importance of Chemistry
• In meeting human needs for food, health care products and other products required for improving quality of life.
• In diverse areas such as weather patterns, functioning of brain and operation of a computer.
• In chemical industries.
Matter:Anything which occupies space
(i) Solid: Particles are held very close to each other in an orderly fashion with no freedom of movement.
Have definite volume and shape.
(ii) Liquids: Particles are close and can move around.
Have definite volume but no definite shape.
(iii) Gases: Particles are far apart and their movement is easy and fast.
Neither have definite volume nor definite shape.
Properties of Matter:
(i) Physical: Properties measured/observed without changing the identity or composition of substance. (Colour, odour)
(ii) Chemical: Properties measured/observed when a chemical reaction occurs. (Acidity or Basicity, combustibility)
Classification
Pure Substance: Fixed composition (Cu, Ag)
Elements:Contains one type of particles, i.e., atoms, molecules (Na,Cu)
Compounds:Two or more atoms of different elements (H_2O, NH_3)
Mixtures:Two or more substances present in any ratio. (air,tea)
Homogenous : Uniform composition (Sugar solution, air)
Hetrogenous: Non-uniform composition (Mixtures of salt and sugar.)
Measurement of Matter
-International System of Units (SI): (Length-m)
-Mass is the amount of matter present in a substance.
-Weight is the force exerted by gravity on an object. W = mass × gravity, Density = Mass/volume
-Uncertainty of measurement: Range of possible values within which the true value of the measurement lies.Significant figures: Meaningful digits known with certainty.
-Precision: Closeness of various measurements for same quantity.
-Accuracy: Agreement of a particular value to true value of result.
Mole Fraction
Mole Fraction of A (χ_A)= $\frac{n_a}{n_a+n_b}$
Mole Fraction of B (χ_B)= $\frac{n_b}{n_a+n_b}$
Limiting Reagent
Reactant which gets consumed and limits the amount of product formed.
Empirical Formula: Simplest number ratio of various atoms present in a compound
Molecular Formula: Shows exact number of different types of atoms present in a molecule of a compound.
How To Determine Empirical and Molecular Formula:
Step 1: Conversion of mass percent to grams.
Step 2: Convert into number moles of each element.
Step 3: Divide the mole value obtained above by the smallest number.
Step 4: Write empirical formula by mentioning the number after writing the symbols of respective elements.
Step 5: Writing molecular formula
(a) Determine empirical formula mass. Add the atomic masses of various atoms present in the empirical formula.
(b) Divide molar mass by empirical formula mass.
(c) Multiply empirical formula by n obtained above.
Trace the Mind Map
First Level
Second Level
Third Level

(iv) Zeros at the end or right of a number are significant, provided they are on the right side of the decimal point.

Laws of Chemical Combinations

- Elements combine to form compounds in accordance with the following five basic laws, called the laws of chemical combinations.

Scan to know more about this topic

Law of Multiple Proportions

(i) **Law of Conservation of Mass:** Mass can neither be created nor destroyed.

(ii) **Law of Definite Proportions/ Composition:** A given compound always contains exactly the same proportion of elements by weight.

(iii) **Law of Multiple Proportions:** When two elements combine with each other to form more than one compound, the masses of one element that combine with a fixed mass of the other element, are in the ratio of small whole numbers.

(iv) **Gay Lussac's Law of Gaseous Volumes:** When gases combine or are produced in a chemical reaction they do so in a simple ratio by volume, provided all the gases are at same temperature and pressure.

(v) **Avogadro's Law:** At the same temperature and pressure, equal volume of all gases should contain equal number of molecules.

Dalton's Atomic Theory

- Matter consists of tiny indivisible particles.
- Atoms are indestructible and cannot be divided into smaller particles.
- All atoms of a given element have identical properties, including identical mass. Atoms of different elements differ in mass.
- When atoms of different elements react to form compounds, their atoms combine a simple fixed ratio.
- Chemical reactions involve reorganisation of atoms. These are neither created nor destroyed in a chemical reaction.

- **Drawbacks of Dalton's Atomic Theory:**
- Theory does not explain the occurrence of allotropes.
- Atom can be further divided into sub-parts i.e., Electron, proton, neutron.
- The theory fails to explain how atoms combine with different elements to form a group.

Atomic and Molecular Masses

- **Atomic Mass:** One atomic mass unit is defined as a mass exactly equal to one-twelfth of the mass of one carbon-12 atom.

$$\text{Relative Atomic Mass} = \frac{\text{Average mass of an atom} \times 12}{\text{Mass of an atom of carbon-12}}$$

- **Average Atomic Mass:** The average atomic mass of an element refers to the atomic masses of the isotopes of the element, taking into account the abundances of the element's isotopes.

Average Atomic Mass =

$$\frac{\Sigma(\text{Mass of isotopes} \times \%\ \text{natural abundance})}{100}$$

- **Gram Atomic Mass:** Gram atomic mass is the mass, in grams, of one mole of atoms in a monoatomic chemical element.

Gram Atomic Mass = Atomic mass expressed in grams

- **Molecular Mass:** Molecular mass or molecular weight refers to the mass of a molecule. It is calculated as the sum of the mass of each constituent atom multiplied by the number of atoms of that element in the molecular formula.

Scan to know more about this topic

Determining Empirical and Molecular Formula

- **Gram Molecular Mass or Gram Molecule:** Gram molecular mass is the mass in grams of one mole of a molecular substance.
- **Formula Mass:** The formula mass of a molecule is the sum of the atomic weights of the atoms in the empirical formula of the compound.
- **Mole Concept and Molar Mass:** Mole is a fundamental unit in the system. Molar mass is the mass of one mole of any substance, i.e., element or compound.
- **Percentage Composition:** Percentage composition of a compound is the ratio of the amount of each element to the total amount of individual elements present in a compound multiplied by 100.
- **Empirical Formula:** A formula that gives the simplest whole number ratio of various atoms in a compound.
- **Molecular Formula:** It is a formula in which the exact number of different types of atoms present in a molecule of a compound.
- **Steps for writing molecular formula:**

(i) Conversion of mass percent to grams.

(ii) Convert into number moles of each element.

(iii) Divide each of the mole values obtained above by the smallest number amongst them.

(iv) Write down the empirical formula by mentioning the numbers after writing the symbols of respective elements.

(v) **Writing molecular formula:**

(a) Determine empirical formula mass by adding the atomic masses of various atoms present in the empirical formula.

(b) Divide molar mass by empirical formula mass.

(c) Multiply empirical formula by *n* obtained above to get the molecular formula.

Stoichiometry and Stoichiometric Calculations

- **Chemical Equation:** A chemical equation is the symbolic representation of a chemical reaction.

$$\underbrace{AgNO_3 + NaCl}_{\text{Reactants}} \longrightarrow \underbrace{AgCl + NaNO_3}_{\text{Products}}$$

- Stoichiometry is the calculation of masses (sometimes volumes also) of the reactants and products involved in a chemical reaction.

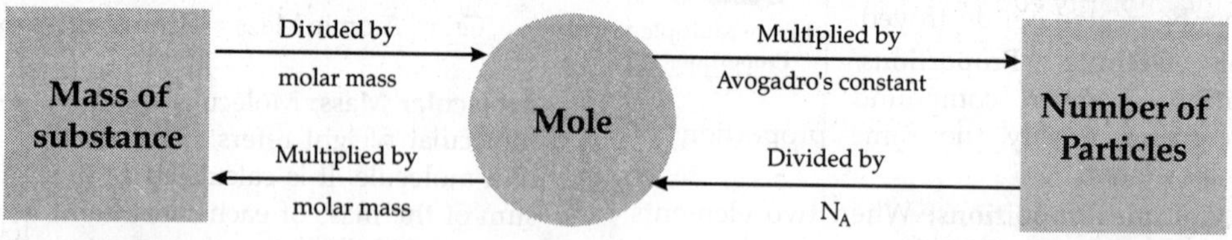

- **Limiting Reagent:** The reactant which gets consumed first, limits the amount of product formed and is, called the limiting reagent. It is present in smaller amount.

Scan to know more about this topic

Mole Conversions

- **Mole Fraction of component:** The ratio of the number of moles of a given component of a mixture to the total number of moles of all the components.

Two components A and B

Mole fraction of A

$$x_A = \frac{\text{Number of moles of A}}{\text{Number of moles of solution}} = \frac{n_A}{n_A + n_B}$$

n_A and n_B are the mole of A and B respectively.

Mole fraction of B,

$$x_B = \frac{\text{Number of moles of B}}{\text{Number of moles of solution}} = \frac{n_B}{n_A + n_B}$$

Also, remember that $x_A + x_B = 1$

- **Molarity:** It is defined as the number of moles of solute dissolve per 1000g or 1 kg of solvent

$$m = \frac{W_B \times 1000}{M_B \times W_A}$$

- **Modes of expressing concentration of solution:**
  - **Mass Percent:**

$$\text{Mass percent} = \frac{\text{Mass of solute}}{\text{Mass of solution}} \times 100$$

- **Molality:** The number of moles of solute per kilogram of solvent. Unit is mol kg^{-1} or m (molal).

$$\text{Molality } (m) = \frac{\text{Number of moles of solute}}{\text{Mass of solvent in kg}}$$

$$m = \frac{\text{Mass of solute} \times 1000}{\text{Molar mass of solute} \times \text{mass of solvent (in g)}}$$

- **Strength of Solution:** It is defined as the amount of solute dissolved per litre of solution.

Strength = M × Molecular weight

M = Molarity

- **Normally:** It is defined as number of gram equivalents of solute dissolved per litre of solution

$$N = \frac{W_B \times 1000}{E_B \times V}$$

- Balancing a chemical equation:

Step 1: Write down the chemical equation using correct formulas of the reactants and products.

Step 2: Write down the number of atoms per element.

Step 3: Start balancing with single element one by one.

Step 4: Verify that the number of atoms of each element is balanced in the final equation.

- **Mass-Mole Number Relationship:**

$$\text{Number of Moles} = \frac{\text{Mass of g}}{\text{Molar mass in g mol}^{-1}}$$

Key Formulae

- $\text{Number of moles of atoms} = \frac{\text{Mass of element}}{\text{Atomic mass}}$
- $\text{Number of moles of molecules} = \frac{\text{Mass of molecules}}{\text{Molecular mass}}$
- $\text{Number of moles of gas} = \frac{\text{Volume of the gas (STP)}}{22.4 \text{ L}}$

Number of molecules = Number of moles × N_A

- Where, N_A = Avogadro's number = 6.022×10^{23}
- Number of atoms = Number of molecules × Atomicity
- $\text{Mass percentage} = \frac{\text{Total mass of element}}{\text{Molar mass}} \times 100$
- **Percentage Composition:**

Mass % of the element =

$$\frac{\text{Mass of element in a molecule of the compound}}{\text{Molecular mass of the compound}} \times 100$$

- **Relationship between Empirical and Molecular Formulae:**

Molecular Formula = n × Empirical formula

$$\text{where } n = \frac{\text{Molar mass}}{\text{Empirical formula mass}}$$

- $\% \text{ by}\left(\frac{v}{V}\right)\text{strength} = \frac{\text{Volume of solute}}{\text{Volume of solution}} \times 100$
- $\% \text{ by}\left(\frac{w}{V}\right)\text{strength} = \frac{\text{Weight of solute}}{\text{Volume of solution}} \times 100$

- $M = \dfrac{\% \text{ Strength} \times \text{density} \times 10}{\text{Molecular weight of solute}}$
- $M = \dfrac{1000 \times M}{M \times \text{Molar mass of solute} - 1000\,d}$

  where, d = density
  M = Molarity
  m = molality
- Specific gravity = $\dfrac{\text{Mass of liquid}}{\text{Vol. of liquid}}$
- Molecular weight = 2 × Vapour density
- For dilution, molarity equation is:

  $$M_1V_1 = M_2V_2$$

  Where, M_1 = initial molarity, V_1 = initial volume, M_2 = final molarity and V_2 = final volume.

Key Equations

- **Density** = $\dfrac{\text{Mass}}{\text{Volume}}$
- **Temperature: K = °C + 273.15;**

  $$°F = \frac{9}{5}(°C) + 32$$

Key Term

- **Molar Volume (V_m):** It is the volume occupied by one mole of any substance.
- **Limiting Reagent:** It is the reactant which gets consumed first or limits the amount of product formed.
- **Mass Percent:** It is the mass of the solute in grams per 100 grams of the solution.

  $$\text{Mass \%} = \frac{\text{Mass of solute in g} \times 100}{\text{Mass of solution in g}}$$
- **Parts per million (ppm).** If a solute is present in trace quantities, the concentration of the solution is expressed in parts per million (ppm).

  $$\text{ppm} = \frac{\text{Weight of solute} \times 10^6}{\text{Weight of solution}}$$

Key Facts

- **The International System of Units (SI):** The SI system has seven base units.
- **Volume:** $V = 1\ dm^3 = 10^3\ cm^3 = 10^{-3}\ m^3$.
- **Standard Temperature Pressure (STP):** 0 °C (273.15 K) temperature and 1 atmosphere pressure.
- **Normal Temperature Pressure (NTP):** 20 °C (293.15 K) temperature and 1 atmosphere pressure.
- **Standard Ambient Temperature Pressure (SATP):** 25 °C (298.15 K) temperature and 1 atmosphere pressure.
- 1 amu = 1.66056×10^{-24} g
- Mass of hydrogen atom in terms of amu

  $$= \frac{1.6736 \times 10^{-24}\ g}{1.66056 \times 10^{-24}\ g/amu}$$

  = 1.0078 amu
- Now, 'amu' has been replaced by 'u' which is called unified mass.
- 1 mole of a substance = Molar mass of substance = Avogadro's number of chemical units = 22.4 L volume at STP of gaseous substance

  e.g., 1 mole of CH_4 = 16 g of CH_4 = 6.022×10^{23} molecules of CH_4 = 22.4 L at STP

  $$n = \frac{w_g}{M_m} = \frac{V_L(\text{at STP})}{22.4\ L} = \frac{x \text{ particles}}{N_A} = \frac{MV}{1000}$$
- Molar volume of gas = 22.4 L at STP (273K, 1 atm) or 22.7 L at SATP (273 K, 1 bar)

  Calculating Molar Volume : PV = nRT

  $$\therefore V = \frac{nRT}{P} = \frac{1\ mol \times 0.0821\ L\ atm\ K^{-1}\ mol^{-1} \times 273\ K}{1\ atm}$$

  = 22.4 L

Mnemonics

Concept Name: Metric System
Mnemonics: The Great Morning King Henry
Mnemonics: Doesn't Usually Drink chocolate Milk
Mnemonics: Mixed with Natural Powder
Interpretation
The: Tera ($\times 10^{12}$)
Great: Giga ($\times 10^9$)
Morning: Mega ($\times 10^6$)
King: Kilo ($\times 10^3$)
Henry: Hecto ($\times 10^2$)
Doesn't: Deca ($\times 10$)
Usually: Unit ($\times 1$)
Drink: Deci ($\times 10^{-1}$)
Chocolate: Centi ($\times 10^{-2}$)
Milk: Milli ($\times 10^{-3}$)
Mixed with: Micro ($\times 10^{-6}$)
Natural: Nano ($\times 10^{-9}$)
Powder: Pico ($\times 10^{-12}$)
Concept: Law of conservation of mass
Mnemonics: BESABS
Interpretation: Balanced chemical equation has Same number of Atoms on Both Sides
Concept: Strength of solution in terms of molarity
Mnemonics: SSMM
Interpretation: Strength of Solution is Molarity into Molecular weight

NCERT CORNER

Q. 1. Calculate the molar mass of the following compounds:

[NCERT Ex. Q. 1.1, Page 25]

(i) H_2O (ii) CO_2 (iii) CH_4

Ans. (i)Molar mass of H_2O

= (2 × atomic mass of hydrogen) + (1 × atomic mass of oxygen)

= 2 (1.008 u) + 1(16.00 u)

= 18.02 u

(ii) Molar mass of CO_2

= 1 × atomic mass of carbon + 2 × atomic mass of oxygen

= 12.011 u + 2 (16.00 u)

= 44.01 u

(iii) Molar mass of CH_4

= 1 × atomic mass of carbon + 4 × atomic mass of hydrogen

= 12.011 u + 4 (1.008 u)

= 16.043 u

Q. 2. Calculate the mass percent of different elements present in sodium sulphate (Na_2SO_4).

[NCERT Ex. Q. 1.2, Page 25]

Ans. Molar mass of Na_2SO_4 = 2 (23.0) + 32.066 + 4(16.0) = 142.006 g

$$\text{Mass \% of an element} = \frac{\text{Mass of that element in the compound}}{\text{Molar mass of the compound}} \times 100$$

$$\text{Mass \% of sodium (Na)} = \frac{46}{142.066} \times 100 = 32.39\% \approx 32.4\%$$

$$\text{Mass \% of sulphur (S)} = \frac{32.066}{142.066} \times 100 = 22.57\% \approx 22.6\ \%$$

$$\text{Mass \% of oxygen (O)} = \frac{64}{142.066} \times 100 = 45.05\% \approx 45.05\%$$

Commonly Made Error

► Students often calculate without mentioning the formula applied.

Answering Tip

► Always mention the working formula followed by substitution of values in it.

Q. 3. Determine the empirical formula of on oxide of from which has 69.9% iron and 30.1% dioxygen by mass?

[NCERT Ex. Q. 1.3, Page 25]

Ans. For determining the empirical formula of an oxide of iron simplest whole number molar ratio of iron and oxygen is determined by using percentage of elements by mass as follows:

Element	Symbol	% by Mass	Atomic mass	No. of moles of element	Simplest molar ratio	Simplest number molar ratio
Iron	Fe	69.9	55.85	$\frac{69}{55.85} = 1.25$	$\frac{1.25}{1.25} = 1$	2
Oxygen	0	30%	16	$\frac{30.1}{16} = 1.88$	$\frac{1.88}{1.25} = 1.5$	3

∴ Empirical formula of oxide of iron = Fe_2O_3

Q. 4. Calculate the amount of carbon dioxied that could be produced when:

(i) 1 mole of carbon is burnt in air.

(ii) 1 mole of carbon is burnt in 16 g of dioxygen.

(iii) 2 moles of carbon are burnt in 16 g of dioxygen.

[NCERT Ex. Q. 1.4, Page 25]

Ans. (i) $\underset{\substack{1\text{ mole} \\ 12\text{ g}}}{C_{(s)}} + \underset{\substack{1\text{ mole} \\ 32\text{ g}}}{O_{2(g)}} \longrightarrow \underset{\substack{1\text{ mole} \\ 44\text{ g}}}{CO_{2(g)}}$

1 mole of carbon on burning in air produces 44 g of CO_2.

(ii) If 1 male of carbon is burnt in 16 g of dioxygen then 22 g of CO_2 is produced.

Dioxygen is a limiting reagent.

∵ 32 g of O_2 gives = 44 g or CO_2

∴ 16 g of O_2 will gives = $\frac{44}{32} \times 16 = 22$ g

Q. 5. Calculate the mass of sodium acetate (CH_3COONa) required to make 500 mL of 0.375 molar aqueous solution. Molar mass of sodium acetate is 82.0245 g mol^{-1}.

[NCERT Ex. Q. 1.5, Page 25]

Ans. Given, Molarity = 0.375M

Molar mass of solute (m) = 82.0245 g mol^{-1}

Volume of solution = 500 ml

Mass of solute = ?

$$\because \quad \text{Molarity} = \frac{w \times 1000}{m \times \text{Volume of solution (mL)}}$$

$$\text{Mass of solute (w)} = \frac{\text{Molarity} \times m \times \text{Volume}}{1000}$$

$$= \frac{0.375 \times 82.0245 \times 500}{1000}$$

= 15.379 g

= 15.38 g

Q. 6. Calculate the concentration of nitric acid in mol per litre in a sample which has a density, 1.41 g mL^{-1} and the mass per cent of nitric acid in it being 69%.

[NCERT Ex. Q. 1.6, Page 26]

Ans. Given, density (d) = 1.41 g mL^{-1}

Mass % of nitric acid = 69%

69% HNO_3 means 100 g of its solution contains 69 g HNO_3.

Mass of HNO_3 = 69 g

∴ Molar Mass of

$$HNO_3 = 1.008 + 14.007 + 3\,(16.00) = 63.015 \text{ g mol}^{-1}$$

$$\text{Density} = \frac{\text{mass}}{\text{volume}}$$

or

$$\text{Volume} = \frac{\text{mass}}{\text{density}} = \frac{100}{1.41} = 70.92 \text{ ml}$$

$$\text{Molarity} = \frac{w \times 1000}{m \times \text{Volume of solution (in mL)}} = \frac{69 \times 1000}{63.015 \times 70.92} = \frac{69000}{4469.0238} = 15.439\text{ M} \approx 15.44 \text{ mol/L}$$

Q. 7. How much copper can be obtained from 100 g of copper sulphate ($CuSO_4$)? [NCERT Ex. Q. 1.7, Page 26]

Ans. Molar mass of $CuSO_4$ = 63.5 + 32 + 4 (16) = 159.5 g mol^{-1}

1 mole of $CuSO_4$ contains 1 mole of Cu.

∵ 159.5 g of $CuSO_4$ forms = 63.5 g of Cu

∴ 100 g of $CuSO_4$ will form $= \frac{63.5}{159.5} \times 100$ g = 39.81 g of Cu

Q. 8. Determine the molecular formula of an oxide of iron in which the mass per cent of iron and oxygen are 69.9 and 30.1 respectively. Given that the molar mass of the oxide is 154.69 g mol^{-1}. **[NCERT Ex. Q. 1.8, Page 26]**

Ans.

Element	Symbol	% by mass	Atomic mass	Number of moles of element	Simplest molar ratio	Simplest whole number molar ratio
Iron	Fe	69.9	55.85	$\frac{69.9}{55.85} = 1.25$	$\frac{1.25}{1.25} = 1$	2
Oxygen	O	30.1	16.0	$\frac{30.1}{16} = 1.88$	$\frac{1.88}{1.25} = 1.5$	3

Empirical formula mass of Fe_2O_3

$= 2 \times 55.85 + 3 \times 16.00 = 159.7$ g mol^{-1}

Molar mass of Fe_2O_3 = 159.8 g

$$n = \frac{\text{Molar mass}}{\text{Empirical formula mass}} = \frac{159.8}{159.7} = 1$$

Hence, molecular formula of oxide of iron is same as that of empirical formula *i.e.* Fe_2O_3.

Q. 9. Calculate the atomic mass (average) of chlorine using the following data:

	% Natural Abundance	**Molar Mass**
^{35}Cl	75.77	34.9689
^{37}Cl	24.23	36.9659

[NCERT Ex. Q. 1.9, Page 26]

Ans. Average atomic mass of an element is the sum of the products of fractional abundances of the isotopes and their corresponding molar masses.

Isotope	% Natural Abundance	Fractional Abundance	Molar mass
^{35}Cl	75.77	$\frac{75.77}{100} = 0.7577$	34.9689
^{37}Cl	24.23	$\frac{24.23}{100} = 0.2423$	36.9659

Average atomic mass of chlorine

$= 0.7577 \times 34.9689 + 0.2423 \times 36.9659$
$= 26.4959 + 8.9568$
$= 35.4527$ u

Q. 10. In three moles of ethane (C_2H_6), calculate the following:
(i) Number of moles of carbon atoms
(ii) Number of moles of hydrogen atoms
(iii) Number of molecules of ethane

[NCERT Ex. Q. 1.10, Page 26]

Ans. (i) 1 mole of ethane (C_2H_6) contains 2 moles of carbon atoms.

So, 3 moles of C_2H_6 will contain = 2 × 3 = 6 mol of carbon atoms.

(ii) 1 mole of C_2H_6 contains 6 moles of hydrogen atoms.

So, 3 moles of C_2H_6 will contain = 6 × 3 = 18 mol of hydrogen atoms

(iii) 1 mole of C_2H_6 contains 6.022×10^{23} molecules of ethane.

So, 3 moles of C_2H_6 will contain

$= 3 \times 6.022 \times 10^{23}$
$= 18.066 \times 10^{23}$ molecules
$= 1.8066 \times 10^{24}$ molecules

Q. 11. What is the concentration of sugar ($C_{12}H_{22}O_{11}$) in mol L^{-1} if its 20 g are dissolved in enough water to make a final volume upto 2 L?

[NCERT Ex. Q. 1.11, Page 26]

Ans. w = 20 g
V = 2 L

Molar mass of sugar ($C_{12}H_{22}O_{11}$)

$= 12 (12) + 22 (1) + 11 (16) = 342$

$$\text{Molarity} = \frac{w}{m \times V \text{ (in litre)}}$$

$$= \frac{20}{342 \times 2}$$

$= 0.0292 \text{ mol L}^{-1}$

Q. 12. If the density of methanol is 0.793 kg L^{-1}, what is its volume needed for making 2.5 L of its 0.25 M solution? **[NCERT Ex. Q. 1.12, Page 26]**

Ans. Given, density (D) = 0.793 kg L^{-1}

$= 0.793 \times 10^3 \text{ g L}^{-1}$

Final volume (V_2) = 2.5 L

Initial volume (V_1) = ?

Final molarity (M_2) = 0.25 M

Initial molarity (M_1) = ?

Molar mass of methanol (CH_3OH)

$= 1 (12) + 4(1) + 16$

$\simeq 32$

$$\text{Molarity} = \frac{\rho}{\text{Molar mass}} = \frac{0.793 \times 10^3 \text{ g L}^{-1}}{32 \text{ g mol}^{-1}}$$

$= 24.78 \text{ mol L}^{-1}$

$M_1V_1 = M_2V_2$

$24.781 \times V_1 = 0.25 \times 2.5$

$$V_1 = \frac{0.25 \times 2.5}{24.781}$$

$= 0.02522 \text{ L}$

$= 25.22 \text{ mL}$

Q. 13. Pressure is determined as force per unit area of the surface. The SI unit of pressure, pascal is as shown below:

1 Pa = 1 Nm^{-2}

If mass of air at sea level is 1034 g cm^{-2}, calculate the pressure in pascal. **[NCERT Ex. Q. 1.13, Page 26]**

Ans. Mass of air at sea level = 1034 g cm^{-2}

Acceleration due to gravity, $g = 9.8 \text{ ms}^{-2}$

$$\text{Pressure of air} = \frac{1034}{1000} \times 9.8 \times 100 \times 100$$

$= 1.01332 \times 10^5 \text{ pa}$

Q. 14. What is the SI unit of mass ? How is it defined? **[NCERT Ex. Q. 1.14, Page 26]**

Ans. The S.I. unit of mass is kilogram. The One kilogram is defined as the mass equal to the mass of the international prototype of kilogram.

Q. 15. Match the following prefixes with their multiples:

Prefixes	**Multiples**
(i) micro	**10^6**
(ii) deca	**10^9**
(iii) mega	**10^{-6}**
(iv) giga	**10^{-15}**
(v) femto	**10**

[NCERT Ex. Q. 1.15, Page 26]

Ans.

Prefixes	**Multiples**
(i) micro	10^{-6}
(ii) deca	10
(iii) mega	10^6
(iv) giga	10^9
(v) femto	10^{-15}

Q. 16. What do you mean by significant figures? **[NCERT Ex. Q. 1.16, Page 26]**

Ans. The total number of figures in a number including the last digit that represents the uncertainty of the result are called significant figures. *e.g.* 4.09 has three significant figures.

Q. 17. A sample of drinking water was found to be severely contaminated with chloroform, $CHCl_3$, supposed to be carcinogenic in nature. The level of contamination was 15 ppm (by mass)

(i) Express this in percent by mass

(ii) Determine the molality of chloroform in the water sample. **[NCERT Ex. Q. 1.17, Page 26]**

Ans. **(i)** 15 ppm means 15 parts in 10^6 parts

$$\therefore \% \text{ by mass} = \frac{15 \times 100}{10^6} = 1.5 \times 10^{-3} \%$$

(ii) Molar mass of

$CHCl_3 = 12 + 1 + 3(35.5)$

$= 119.5$

1.5×10^{-3} % means 1.5×10^{-3} g chloroform is found in 100 g sample.

$$\text{Molality} = \frac{w \times 1000}{m \times \text{Volume of solvent}}$$

$$= \frac{1.5 \times 10^{-3} \times 1000}{119.5 \times 100}$$

$= 0.000125$

$= 1.25 \times 10^{-4}$ m

Q. 18. Express the following in the scientific notation:

(i) 0.0048 **(ii) 234,000** **(iii) 8008**

(iv) 500.0 **(v) 6.0012**

[NCERT Ex. Q. 1.18, Page 26]

Ans. (i) 4.8×10^{-3} (ii) 2.34×10^5

(iii) 8.008×10^3 (iv) 5.00×10^2

(v) 6.0012

Q. 19. How many significant figures are present in the following?

(i) 0.0025 **(ii) 208** **(iii) 5005**

(iv) 126,000 **(v) 500.0** **(vi) 2.0034**

[NCERT Ex. Q. 1.19, Page 26]

Ans. (i) 2 (ii) 3 (iii) 4

(iv) 3 (v) 4 (vi) 5

Q. 20. Round up the following upto three significant figures:

(i) 34.216 **(ii) 10.4107** **(iii) 0.04597**

(iv) 2808 **[NCERT Ex. Q. 1.20, Page 27]**

Ans. (i) 34.2 (ii) 10.4 (iii) 0.0460

(iv) 2810 or 2.81×10^3

Q. 21. The following data are obtained when dinitrogen and dioxygen react together to form different compounds:

Mass of dinitrogen	**Mass of dioxygen**
(i) 14 g	**16 g**
(ii) 14 g	**32 g**

(iii) 28 g 32 g
(iv) 28 g 80 g

(a) Which law of chemical combination is obeyed by the above experimental data? Give its statement.
(b) Fill in the blanks in the following conversions:
(i) 1 km = ... mm = ... pm
(ii) 1 mg = ... kg = ... ng
(iii) 1 mL = ... L = ... dm^3
[NCERT Ex. Q. 1.21, Page 27]

Ans. (a) The above experimental data obey law of multiple proportions.

Law of Multiple Proportions:

According to this law, "if two elements can combine to form more than one compound, the masses of one element that combine with a fixed mass of the other element, are in the ratio of small whole numbers."

(b) (i) 1 km = 10^6 mm = 10^{15} pm
(ii) 1 mg = 10^{-6} kg = 10^6 ng
(iii) 1 mL = 10^{-3} L = 10^{-3} dm^3

Q. 22. If the speed of light is 3.0 ×10^8 m/s, calculate the distance covered by light in 2.00 ns?
[NCERT Ex. Q. 1.22, Page 27]

Ans. Speed of light = $3.0 \times 10^8\ ms^{-1}$
Time = 2.00 ns = 2×10^{-9}s
Distance = speed × time
= $3.0 \times 10^8\ ms^{-1} \times 2 \times 10^{-9}$
= 6.00×10^{-1}m
= 0.600 m

Q. 23. In a reaction

$$A + B_2 \longrightarrow AB_2$$

Identify the limiting reagent, if any, in the following reaction mixtures –
(i) 300 atoms of A + 200 molecules of B
(ii) 2 mol A + 3 mol B
(iii) 100 atoms of A + 100 molecules of B
(iv) 5 mol A + 2.5 mol B
(v) 2.5 mol A + 5 mol B [NCERT Ex. Q. 1.23, Page 27]

Ans. $A + B_2 \longrightarrow AB_2$

(i) The above reaction shows that 1 atom of A reacts with 1 molecule of B. So, 200 atoms of A react with 200 molecules of B_2. Hence, in this case, B is the limiting reagent, so A is in excess.

(ii) The above reaction shows that 1 mole of A reacts with 1 mole of B. So, 2 moles of A react with 2 moles of B. In this case, A is the limiting reagent, so B is in excess.

(iii) In this case, as all 100 atoms of A will combine with 100 molecules of B there is no limiting reagent.

(iv) As 1 mol of atom A combines with 1 mol of molecule B, 2.5 moles of A react with 2.5 moles of B. In this case, B is the limiting reagent and A is in excess.

(v) 2.5 moles of A require only 2.5 moles of B for reaction. In this case, A is limiting reagent so, B is in excess.

Q. 24. Dinitrogen and dihydrogen react with each other to produce ammonia according to the following chemical equation –

$$N_2(g) + 3H_2(g) \longrightarrow 2NH_3(g)$$

(i) Calculate the mass of ammonia produced if 2.00 × 10^3 g dinitrogen reacts with 1.00 × 10^3 g of dihydrogen.
(ii) Will any of the two reactants remain unreacted?
(iii) If yes, which one and what would be its mass?
[NCERT Ex. Q. 1.24, Page 27]

Ans. (i) $N_{2(g)} + 3H_{2(g)} \longrightarrow 2NH_{3(g)}$

	$N_{2(g)}$	$3H_{2(g)}$	$2NH_{3(g)}$
	1 mol	3 mol	2 mol
	28 g	6 g	34 g

$\because$ 28 g of N_2 react with 6 g H_2

$\therefore$ 1 g of N_2 reacts with $\frac{6}{28}$ g H_2

$\therefore$ 2000 g N_2 will react with $\frac{6}{28} \times 2000 = 428.57$ g H_2

So, N_2 is the limiting reagent and H_2 is in excess.

N_2 limits the amount of ammonia produced.

$\because$ 28 g of N_2 produces 34 g NH_3

$\therefore$ 2000 g of N_2 will produce = $\frac{34}{28} \times 2000$

= 2428.57g NH_3

(ii) H_2 will remain unreacted because it is in excess.

(iii) Amount of H_2 remain unreacted
= (1000 – 428.57) g
= 571.43 g
or 5.72×10^2 gm

Q. 25. How are 0.50 mol Na_2CO_3 and 0.50 M Na_2CO_3 different? [NCERT Ex. Q. 1.25, Page 27]

Ans. Molar mass of Na_2CO_3 = 2(23) + 12 + 3(16)
= 106 g mol^{-1}

$\because$ 1 mole of Na_2CO_3 means 106 g of Na_2CO_3

$\therefore$ 0.5 mole of Na_2CO_3 means = 0.50 × 106 g
= 53 g of Na_2CO_3

0.50 M Na_2CO_3 means 0.50 mol i.e. 53 g of Na_2CO_3 are present in 1 litre of the solution.

Q. 26. If ten volumes of dihydrogen gas reacts with five volumes of dioxygen gas, how many volumes of water vapour would be produced?
[NCERT Ex. Q. 1.26, Page 27]

Ans. $2H_2(g) + O_2(g) \longrightarrow 2H_2O(g)$

$2H_2$ (g)	O_2 (g)	$2H_2O$ (g)
2 volumes	1 volume	2 volumes
10 volumes	5 volumes	10 volumes

So, the above equation shows that 10 volumes of water vapour will be produced.

Q. 27. Convert the following into basic units:
(i) 28.7 pm (ii) 15.15 pm (iii) 25365 mg
[NCERT Ex. Q. 1.27, Page 27]

Ans. (i) $\therefore$ 1 pm = 10^{-12} m

$\therefore$ 28.7 pm = 28.7×10^{-12} m or 2.87×10^{-11} m

(ii) 1 pm = 10^{-12} m

$\therefore$ 15.15 pm = 15.15×10^{-12} m or 1.515×10^{-11} m

(iii) $\therefore$ 1 mg = 10^{-6} kg

$\therefore$ 25365 mg = 25365×10^{-6} kg
= 2.5365×10^{-2} kg

Q. 28. Which one of the following will have largest number of atoms?
(i) 1 g Au(s) (ii) 1 g Na(s)
(iii) 1 g Li(s) (iv) 1 g of Cl_2(g)
[NCERT Ex. Q. 1.28, Page 28]

Ans. (i) Number of atoms in 1 g $Au_{(s)}$

$= \frac{1}{197} \times 6.022 \times 10^{23}$

$= 3.057 \times 10^{21}$ atoms

(ii) Number of atoms in 1 g Na(s)

$= \frac{1}{23} \times 6.022 \times 10^{23}$

$= 2.618 \times 10^{22}$ atoms

(iii) Number of atoms in 1 g Li(s)

$= \frac{1}{7} \times 6.022 \times 10^{23}$

$= 8.6042 \times 10^{22}$ atoms

(iv) Number of molecules 1 g of $Cl_2(g)$

$= \frac{1}{71} \times 6.022 \times 10^{23}$

$= 8.48 \times 10^{21}$ molecules

As one molecule of Cl_2 contains 2 atoms of Cl.

Number of atoms of Cl $= 2 \times 8.48 \times 10^{21}$

$= 16.96 \times 10^{21}$

Hence, 1 g of Li(s) has largest number of atoms.

Q. 29. Calculate the molarity of a solution of ethanol in water in which the mole fraction of ethanol is 0.040 (assume the density of water to be one)

[NCERT Ex. Q. 1.29, Page 28]

Ans. Molarity means moles of solute (ethanol) in 1 L of the solution.

1 L of ethanol = 1L of water

Number of moles of H_2O in 1 L water $= \frac{1000 \text{ g}}{18}$

$= 55.55$ mol

For a binary solution,

$$X_1 + X_2 = 1$$

$$\therefore \quad X_{H_2O} = 1 - X_{C_2H_5OH}$$

$$= 1 - 0.040$$

$$= 0.96$$

$$X_{H_2O} = \frac{n_{H_2O}}{n_{H_2O} + n_{C_2H_5OH}}$$

$$0.96 = \frac{55.55}{55.55 + n_{C_2H_5OH}}$$

$$53.328 + 0.96\, n_{C_2H_5OH} = 55.55$$

$$0.96\, n_{C_2H_5OH} = 55.55 - 53.328$$

$$= 2.222$$

$$n_{C_2H_5OH} = \frac{2.222}{0.96}$$

$$= 2.3145$$

$$\therefore \quad \text{Molarity} = 2.3145 \text{ mol L}^{-1}$$

Q. 30. What will be the mass of one ^{12}C atom in g?

[NCERT Ex. Q. 1.30, Page 28]

Ans. 1 mole of ^{12}C atoms $= 6.022 \times 10^{23}$ atoms = 12 g of carbon

$\because 6.022 \times 10^{23}$ atoms of ^{12}C have mass = 12 g

$\therefore$ 1 atom of ^{12}C will have mass $= \frac{12}{6.022 \times 10^{23}}$ g

$= 1.9927 \times 10^{-23}$ g (2)

$\approx 1.993 \times 10^{-23}$ g

Q. 31. How many significant figures should be present in the answer of the following calculations?

(i) $\frac{0.02856 \times 298.15 \times 0.112}{0.5785}$

(ii) 5×5.364

(iii) $0.0125 + 0.7864 + 0.0215$

[NCERT Ex. Q. 1.31, Page 28]

Ans. (i) $\frac{0.02856 \times 298.15 \times 0.112}{0.5785}$

Least precise number of calculation = 0.112

Therefore, number of significant numbers in the answer = Number of significant numbers in the least precise number = 3

(ii) 5×5.364

Least precise number of calculation = 5.364

Therefore, number of significant numbers in the answer = Number of significant numbers in 5.364

= 4

(iii) 0.012 + 0.7864 + 0.0215

As the least number of decimal place in each term is 4, the number of significant numbers in the answer is also 4.

Q. 32. Use the data given in the following table to calculate the molar mass of naturally occurring argon isotopes:

Isotope	Isotopic molar mass	Abundance
^{36}Ar	35.96755 g mol^{-1}	0.337%
^{38}Ar	37.96272 g mol^{-1}	0.063%
^{40}Ar	39.9624 g mol^{-1}	99.600%

[NCERT Ex. Q. 1.32, Page 28]

Ans. Molar mass of Ar

$= (0.00337 \times 35.96755) + (0.00063 \times 37.96272) + (0.9960 \times 39.9624)$

$= 0.121 + 0.024 + 39.803$

$= 39.948$ g mol^{-1}

Q. 33. Calculate the number of atoms in each of the following:

(i) 52 moles of Ar **(ii) 104 u of He**

(iii) 52 g of He **[NCERT Ex. Q. 1.33, Page 28]**

Ans. (i) 1 mole of Ar $= 6.022 \times 10^{23}$ atoms

52 moles of Ar $= 52 \times 6.022 \times 10^{23}$ atoms

$= 313.144 \times 10^{25}$ atoms

$= 3.1314 \times 10^{25}$ atoms

(ii) 4 u of He = 1 atom of He

104 u of He $= \frac{1}{4} \times 104$ atoms

= 26 atoms

52 u of He $= \frac{1}{4} \times 52$ atoms

= 13 atoms

(iii) 1 mole of He = 4 g of He $= 6.022 \times 10^{23}$ atoms

52 g of He $= \frac{6.022 \times 10^{23}}{4} \times 52$ atoms

$= 7.8286 \times 10^{24}$ atoms of He

Q. 34. A welding fuel gas contains carbon and hydrogen only. Burning a small sample of it in oxygen gives 3.38 g carbon dioxide, 0.690 g of water and no other products. A volume of 10.0 L (measured at STP) of this welding gas is found to weigh 11.6 g. Calculate (i) empirical formula (ii) molar mass of the gas and (iii) molecular formula. [NCERT Ex. Q. 1.34, Page 28]

Ans. Molar mass of $CO_2 = 12 + 2(16) = 44$

Molar mass of $H_2O = 1(2) + 16 = 18$

(i) $\because$ 44 g of CO_2 contains = 12 g carbon

$\therefore$ 3.38 g of CO_2 will contain

$$= \frac{12}{44} \times 3.38 \text{ g}$$

$$= 0.9218 \text{ g carbon}$$

$\because$ 18 g of H_2O contains = 2 g hydrogen

$\therefore$ 0.690 g of H_2O will contain

$$= \frac{2}{18} \times 0.690 \text{ g}$$

$$= 0.0767 \text{ g hydrogen}$$

Total mass of compound = 0.9218 + 0.0767

= 0.9985 g

$$\% \text{ of C in the compound} = \frac{0.9218}{0.9985} \times 100$$

$$= 92.318 \approx 92.32\%$$

$$\% \text{ of H in the compound} = \frac{0.0767}{0.9985} \times 100$$

$$= 7.68\%$$

Element	% by mass	Atomic mass	No. of moles of element	Simplest molar ratio	Simplest whole number molar ratio
C	92.32	12	$\frac{92.32}{12} = 7.69$	$\frac{7.69}{7.68} = 1$	1
H	7.68	1	$\frac{7.68}{1} = 7.68$	$\frac{7.68}{7.68} = 1$	1

So, empirical formula of compound = CH

(ii) $\because$ 10.0 L of the given gas at STP weight = 11.6 g

$\therefore$ 22.4 L of the given gas at STP will weigh

$$= \frac{11.6 \times 22.4}{10}$$

$$= 25.984 \text{ g}$$

$\therefore$ Molar mass = $25.984 \approx 26$ g

(iii) Empirical formula mass (CH) = 12 + 1 = 13

$$\therefore \quad n = \frac{\text{Molecular mass}}{\text{Empirical formula mass}}$$

$$= \frac{26}{13} = 2$$

$\therefore$ Molecular formula of compound

$= n \times CH = 2 \times CH$

$= C_2H_2$

Q. 35. Calcium carbonate reacts with aqueous HCl to give $CaCl_2$ and CO_2 according to the reaction.

$CaCO_3(s) + 2HCl(aq) \rightarrow CaCl_2(aq) + CO_2(g) + H_2O(l)$

What mass of $CaCO_3$ is required to react completely with 25 mL of 0.75M HCl? [NCERT Ex. Q. 1.35, Page 28]

Ans. Molarity of HCl = 0.75

Volume of HCl = 25 mL

Molecular mass of HCl = 1 + 35.5 = 36.5 g/mol

$$\because \text{Molarity} = \frac{w \times 1000}{m \times \text{Volume (in mL)}}$$

$\therefore$ Mass of HCl (w)

$$= \frac{\text{molarity} \times m \times \text{volume (in mL)}}{1000}$$

$$= \frac{0.75 \times 36.5 \times 25}{1000}$$

$$= 0.6844 \text{ g}$$

$CaCO_3(s) + 2HCl(aq) \rightarrow CaCl_2(aq) + CO_2(g) + H_2O(l)$

100 g $\quad$ 2 × 36.5

= 73 g

According to balanced chemical equation,

$\because$ 73 g HCl completely reacts with 100 g of $CaCO_3$

$\therefore$ 0.6844 g HCl will react with $\frac{100}{73} \times 0.6844$

= 0.9375 g

Q. 36. Chlorine is prepared in the laboratory by treating manganese dioxide (MnO_2) with aqueous hydrochloric acid according to the reaction:

$4HCl(aq) + MnO_2(S) \rightarrow 2H_2O(l) + MnCl_2(aq) + Cl_2(g)$

How many grams of HCl reacts with 5.0 g of manganese dioxide? [NCERT Ex. Q. 1.36, Page 28]

Ans. $4HCl(aq) + MnO_2(s) \rightarrow 2H_2O(l) + MnCl_2(aq) + Cl_2(g)$

4 × 36.5 $\quad$ 87 g

= 146.0 g

According to balanced chemical equation-

$\because$ 87 g of MnO_2 reacts with 146 g of HCl

$\therefore$ 5.0 g of MnO_2 will react with $\frac{146}{87} \times 5$

= 8.39 g ≈ 8.4g HCl

CHAPTER 2

STRUCTURE OF ATOM

Discovery of Sub-Atomic Particles

- **Discovery of electron:** In mid 1850s many scientists mainly Faraday began to study electrical discharge in partially evacuated tubes, known as cathode ray discharge tubes. A cathode ray tube is made of glass containing two thin pieces of metal, called electrodes, sealed in it.

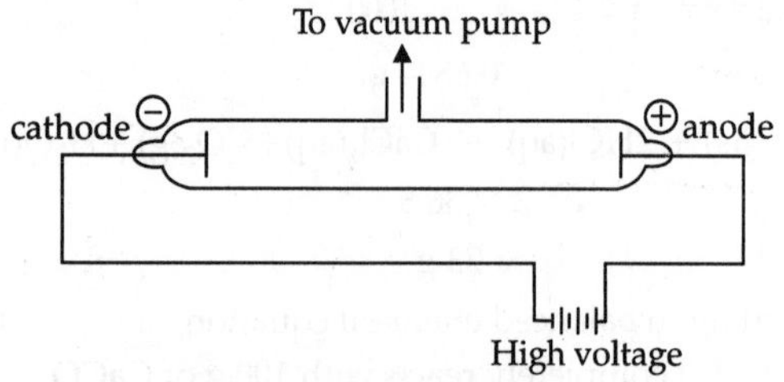

Fig. 1: A cathode ray discharge tube

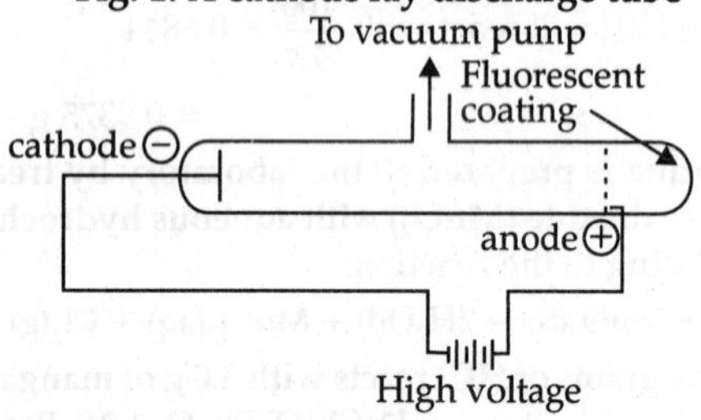

Fig. 2: A cathode ray discharge tube with perforated node and zinc sulphide coating for phosphorescence

The results of these experiments are summarised below:

(i) The cathode rays start from cathode and move towards the anode.

(ii) These rays themselves are not visible but their behaviour can be observed with the help of certain kind of materials (fluorescent or phosphorescent) which glow when hit by them.

(iii) In the absence of electrical or magnetic field, these rays travel in straight lines.

(iv) In the presence of electrical or magnetic field, the behaviour of cathode rays are similar to that expected from negatively charged particles, suggesting that the cathode rays consist of negatively charged particles, called electrons.

(v) The characteristics of cathode rays (electrons) do not depend upon the material of electrodes and the nature of the gas present in the cathode ray tube.

- **Charge to mass ratio:** In 1897, J.J. Thomson measured it by using cathode ray tube and applying electrical and magnetic field perpendicular to each other as well as to the path of electron. Thomson was able to determine the value of e/m_e as 1.758820×10^{11} C kg^{-1}.
- **Charge of electron:** It was determined by R.A. Milikan by oil drop experiment. He found that the charge on the electron to be -1.6×10^{-19} C. The present accepted value of electrical charge is -1.6022×10^{-19} C.
- **Discovery of proton:** Also known as canal rays. They were discovered through electrical discharge carried out in modified cathode ray tube.
- **Discovery of neutron:** These particles were discovered by Chadwick (1932) by bombarding a thin sheet of beryllium by α-particles.

Table 2.1 Properties of Fundamental Particles

Name	Symbol	Absolute charge/C	Relative charge	Mass/kg	Mass/u	Approx. mass/u
Electron	e	-1.602176×10^{19}	–1	9.109382×10^{-31}	0.00054	0
Proton	p	$+1.602176 \times 10^{-19}$	+1	1.676216×10^{-27}	1.00727	1
Neutron	n	0	0	1.674927×10^{-27}	1.00867	1

Atomic Models

- **Thomson Model of Atom:** J. J. Thomson, in 1898, proposed that an atom possesses a spherical shape in which the positive charge is uniformly distributed like plum pudding, raisin pudding or watermelon.
- **Rutherford Nuclear Model of Atom:** Rutherford and his students bombarded very thin gold foil with α–particles.

It was observed that:

(i) Most of the α–particles passed through the gold foil were undeflected.

(ii) A small fraction of the α–particles were deflected by small angles.

Structure of Atom

Mass Number (A)
Number of protons (Z) + number of neutrons (n)

Atomic Number (Z)
Number of protons in nucleus of an atom or Number of electrons in a neutral atom

Isotopes
Atoms of same element having same atomic number but different mass number. (Isotopes of hydrogen Protium $^{1}H_1$, Deuterium $^{2}D_1$ and Tritium $^{3}T_1$).

Isobars:
Atoms of different elements with different atomic number but same mass number. (Ca and Ar)

Discovery of Electron:
By J.J.Thomson Charge to mass ratio of electron $= 1.758820 \times 10^{11}$ C kg^{-1}
Charge an electron $= 1.6022 \times 10^{-19}$C
Mass of electron $= 9.1094 \times 10^{-31}$kg

Discovery of Proton
By Ernest Rutherford
Charge on proton $= +1.6022 \times 10^{-19}$C
Mass of Proton $= 1.672 \times 10^{-27}$ kg

Discovery of Neutron
By James Chadwick
Charge on neutron = 0
Mass of neutron $= 1.675 \times 10^{-27}$ kg

Thomson Model of Atom: (Watermelon Model)
Atom possesses a spherical shape in which the positive charge is uniformly distributed.

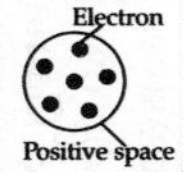

Rutherford's Nuclear Model of Atom
Postulates:
- Positive charge and most of the mass of atoms was densely concentrated in extremely small region i.e., nucleus.
- Nucleus is surrounded by electrons that move around the nucleus with high speed in circular path called orbits.
- Electrons and nucleus are held together by electrostatic forces of attraction.

Drawbacks:
- It cannot explain the stability of an atom.
- It does not say anything about the electronic structure of atoms.

Developments Leading To Bohr's Model of Atom:
Dual nature i.e., wave like and particle like of the electromagnetic radiation.
- Experimental results regarding atomic spectra.
- Wave nature of electromagnetic radiation:

It was given by James Maxwell.
Frequency (n): Number of waves that pass a given point in one second. Unit – Hertz (Hz),
Velocity of light = Frequency × Wavelength
Wave number ($\bar{n}$): Number of wavelengths per unit length. Unit – m^{-1}
- **Particle nature of electromagnetic radiation:**
  Planck's quantum theory: E= hn
  Planck's constant (h) $= 6.626 \times 10^{-34}$ Js

Photoelectric Effect: It was found By H.Hertz
It is the phenomenon of ejection of electrons from the surface of a metal when light of suitable frequency strikes on it.

Energy of orbitals:
Lower the value of $(n+l)$ for an orbital, lower is its energy.

Shapes of orbitals:
s Orbitals: Spherically symmetric Size increases with increase in size in n, i.e., 4s>3s>2s>1s

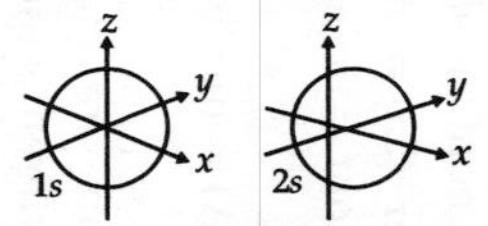

p Orbitals: Each p Orbital consists of two sections called lobes on either side of plane passing through the nucleus.

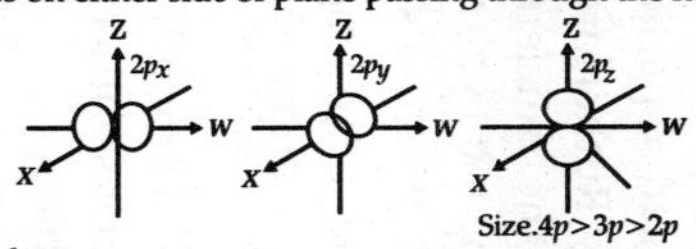

d Orbitals – "Clover leaf" distribution. – Two angular nodes.

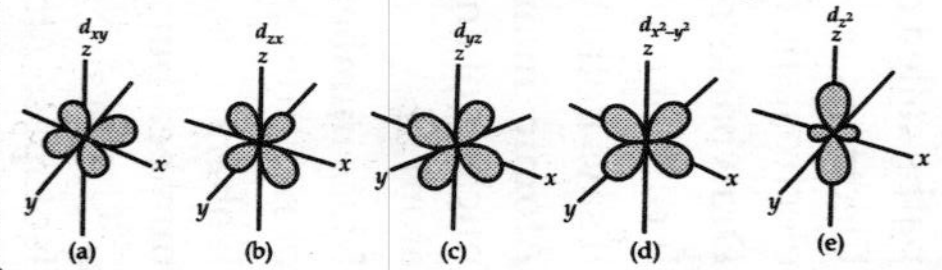

KE of ejected electron $h\nu = h\nu_0 + 1/2\, m_e v^2$

Electronic Configuration of atoms
(i) $s^a p^b d^c$........ notation
(ii) Orbital diagram
□ □□□ □□□□□
s p d

Filling of orbitals in atom
- **Aufbau Principle:** In the ground state of atoms, the orbital's are filled according to increasing energies.
- **Pauli Exclusion Principle:** No two electrons in an atom can have same set of four quantum numbers
- **Hund's rule:** Pairing of electrons in the orbital belonging to same subshell does not take place until each electron belonging to the subshell is singly occupied.

Quantum Numbers
(i) Principal quantum number (n) :n = 1,2,3,4............. Shell = K, L, M, N.......
(ii) Azimuthal Quantum number : For given value of n ,l= 0 to n-1
(iii) Magnetic Quantum number (m) : for subshell with 'l' value m_l=2l+1
(iv) Spin Quantum Number (m_s): $+{}^1/_2$ (↿), $-{}^1/_2$ (⇂)

Schrodinger Equation
Fundamental Equation was developed by Schrodinger as $\hat{H}\psi = E\psi$ where $\hat{H}$= Hamiltonian

Quantum Mechanical Model of Atom:
- Dual behaviour of atom i.e., particle and wavelike. De Broglie equation: $\lambda = \frac{h}{mv} = \frac{h}{p}$
- Heisenberg's Uncertainty Principle: It is impossible to determine simultaneously, the exact position and momentum of an electron

$\Delta x.\ \Delta P_x \geq = \frac{h}{4\pi}$
$\Rightarrow \Delta v.\ \Delta x = \frac{h}{4\pi}$

Bohr's Model for Hydrogen Atom
Postulates:
- Electron in H atom can move around the nucleus in a circular path of fixed radius and energy called as orbits. These orbits are arranged concentrically around the nucleus.
- Each of these orbits has a definite energy known as energy levels or stationary states.
- When an electron jumps from a lower energy level to higher one, some energy is absorbed.
- $\nu = \frac{\Delta E}{h} = \frac{E_2 - E_1}{h}$ Bohr's frequency rule.

Angular momentum of electron: $m_e v_r = n\frac{h}{2\pi}$ n=1,2,3.....

Limitations:
- Unable to account for finer details of H atom. Spectrum observed by sophisticated spectroscopic techniques.
- Could not explain the ability of atoms to form molecules by chemical bonds.

Atomic Spectra
Types:
- **Emission Spectra:** Spectrum of radiation emitted by a substance that has absorbed energy.
- **Absorption Spectra:** It is like photographic negative of an emission spectra.
- **Line / Atomic Spectra:** Emission Spectra which do not show a continuous spread of wavelength from red to violet, rather they emit light only at specific wavelength with dark space between them.

$\bar{\nu} = 109677\left(\frac{1}{n_1^2} - \frac{1}{n_2^2}\right)$ cm^{-1} where

n_1=1,2............n_2=n_1+1, n_1+2.........

Series	n_1	n_2	Spectral Region
Lyman	1	2, 3.........	Ultraviolet
Balmer	2	3, 4.........	Visible
Paschen	3	4, 5.........	Infrared
Brackett	4	5, 6.........	Infrared
Pfund	5	6, 7.........	Infrared

Trace the Mind Map
▸ First Level ▸ Second Level ▸ Third Level

(iii) A very few α–particles (~1 in 20,000) bounced back, that is, were deflected by nearly 180°.

Rutherford drew the following conclusions:

(i) Most of the space in the atom is empty as most of the α–particles passed through the foil undeflected.

(ii) A few positively charged α–particles were deflected. The positive charge has to be concentrated in a very small volume that repelled and deflected the positively charged α–particles.

(iii) Calculations by Rutherford showed that the volume occupied by the nucleus is negligibly small as compared to the total volume of the atom.

According to Rutherford's model of atom:

(i) The positive charge and most of the mass of the atom was densely concentrated in extremely small region called nucleus.

(ii) The nucleus is surrounded by electrons that move around the nucleus with a very high speed in circular paths called orbits.

(iii) Electrons and the nucleus are held together by electrostatic forces of attraction.

Drawbacks of Rutherford's model of atom:

(i) It cannot explain the stability of an atom.

(ii) It says nothing about the electronic structure of atoms.

- **Atomic number (Z)** = number of protons in the nucleus of an atom = number of electrons in a neutral atom
- **Mass number (A)** = number of protons (Z) + number of neutrons (n)
- **Isobars:** Isobars are the atoms with same mass number but different atomic number. For example, ${}_{6}^{14}C$ and ${}_{7}^{14}N$.
- **Isotopes:** Atoms with identical atomic number but different atomic mass number are known as isotopes. For example, protium ${}_{1}^{1}H$, deuterium ${}_{1}^{2}D$ and tritium ${}_{1}^{3}T$.

Developments Leading to the Bohr's Model of Atom

- In order to improve Rutherford's atomic model, two new concepts played a major role, these are:

(i) Dual nature of electromagnetic radiation.

(ii) Experimental results regarding atomic spectra.

- **Wave Nature of Electromagnetic Radiation:** James Maxwell (1870) suggested that when electrically charged particle moves under acceleration, alternating electrical and magnetic fields are produced and transmitted. These fields are transmitted in the form of waves called electromagnetic waves or electro magnetic radiation.
- They do not require any medium for their propagation and can move in vacuum.
- The increasing order of wavelengths of these radiations is given as below :

  Cosmic rays < γ – rays < X – rays < Ultraviolet light < Visible light < Infrared rays < Micro waves < Radio waves.

Mnemonics

Concept: Atomic Spectra

Mnemonics: Ronald McDonald Invented Very

Interpretation: Unusual & eXcellent Gherkins In the order of increasing frequency or decreasing wavelength of electromagnetic waves

Radio waves, Microwaves, Infrared, Visible light, Ultraviolet, X-Rays, Gamma Rays

- **Characteristics of Waves:**
- **Wavelength (λ):** The distance between two successive crests or troughs. Unit: Meter (m).
- **Frequency (υ):** It is defined as the number of waves that pass a given point in one second. Unit: Hertz (Hz) or s^{-1}.
- **Wave number ($\overline{v}$):** The number of wavelengths per unit length. Unit: m^{-1}.
- **Relationship between Wavelength, Wave number, Frequency and Velocity**
- These characteristics are related as:

$$c = \lambda \times \upsilon \quad \text{or} \quad \upsilon = \frac{c}{\lambda} \quad \text{and}$$

$$\frac{1}{\lambda} = \overline{\upsilon} \quad \therefore \quad \nu = c\overline{v}$$

- **Particle Nature of Electromagnetic Radiation:** The phenomenon like diffraction and interference can be explained by wave nature of electromagnetic radiation but it could not explain black body radiation and photoelectric effect.
- **Black Body Radiation and its Explanation:** The ideal body that emits and absorbs radiations of all frequencies, is called black body and the radiation emitted by such a body is called black body radiation.
- According to Planck's quantum theory, atoms and molecules emit (or absorb) energy in the form of small discrete packets of energy, known as quantum. The energy of each quantum is given by the expression:

  $E = h\nu$

  where, h = Planck's constant ($6{\cdot}626 \times 10^{-34}$ J s)

  for n photon $E = nh\nu$

Mnemonics

Concept: Planck's Quantum theory

Mnemonics: Employee's Provident Fund (EPF)

Interpretation: Energy = Planck's constant × Frequency

$\Delta E = h\nu$

- **Photoelectric Effect and its Explanation:**
- The photoelectric effect is the observation that certain metals (e.g., potassium, rubidium, caesium, etc.) emit electrons when light shines upon them. Electrons emitted in this manner can be called photoelectrons.

  Total energy of photon = Work function + Kinetic energy.

$$h\nu = h\nu_0 + \frac{1}{2}mv^2$$

- Electromagnetic radiation shows wave like properties during propagation and shows particle like properties on interaction with matter.

➤ **Dual Nature of Electromagnetic Radiation:** Photoelectric effect shows particle nature of light. Diffraction and interference explain wave nature of light.

The branch of science that deals with the study of spectra is called **spectroscopy.**

Spectra are classified as:

(i) Emission spectra

(ii) Absorption spectra.

➤ **Emission Spectra:** The spectrum of radiation emitted by a substance that has absorbed energy is called an emission spectrum.

➤ **Absorption Spectra:** When the white light is first passed through the substance and the transmitted light is analysed we get absorption spectrum. It consists of dark lines separated by bright bands.

➤ **Line spectra:** The emission spectra of atoms in the gas phase emit light only at specific wavelengths with dark spaces between them. Such spectra are called line spectra or atomic spectra.

➤ **Line Spectrum of Hydrogen**: All series of lines in the hydrogen spectrum can be described by Johannes Rydberg expression:

$$\bar{\upsilon} = 109,677\left(\frac{1}{n_1^2} - \frac{1}{n_2^2}\right)\text{cm}^{-1}$$

where $n_1 = 1, 2,$ .... and $n_2 = n_1 + 1, n_1 + 2,$ ....

➤ **The spectral Lines for Atomic Hydrogen are given as below:**

Series	n_1	n_2	**Spectral region**
Lyman	1	2, 3, ...	Ultraviolet
Balmer	2	3, 4, ...	Visible
Paschen	3	4, 5, ...	Infrared
Brackett	4	5, 6, ...	Infrared
Pfund	5	6, 7, ...	Infrared

➤ From the line spectrum of different elements, it can be concluded that:

(i) Line spectrum of an element is unique.

(ii) There is a regularity in the line spectrum of each element.

Bohr's Model for Hydrogen atom

➤ Neils Bohr (1913) proposed a new model of atom based upon Planck's quantum theory quantitatively explaining the general features of the hydrogen atom structure and its spectrum.

➤ **Postulates of Bohr's Atomic Model:**

- In an atom, the electrons revolve around the nucleus in certain definite circular paths of fixed radius called orbits or shells.
- Each shell or orbit corresponds to a definite energy. Therefore, these circular orbits are also known as energy levels or energy shell.
- Electron can move from one orbital to another either by absorption of energy or by loss of energy.
- The frequency of radiation absorbed or emitted is calculated by Bohr's frequency rule:

$$v = \frac{\Delta E}{h} = \frac{E_1 - E_1}{h}$$

where, E_1 and E_2 are the energies of the lower and higher allowed energy states respectively.

- **The angular momentum of an electron is quantised:** Angular momentum of orbits in which electron revolves must be an integral multiple of $\frac{h}{2\pi}$, where h is Planck's constant ($h = 6.626 \times 10^{-34}$ Js).

$$\therefore \quad m_e = n.\frac{h}{2\pi}$$

where $n = 1, 2, 3,$ ....

➤ **According to Bohr's Theory for Hydrogen Atom:**

(i) The stationary states for electron are numbered n = 1,2,3.......... These integral numbers are known as Principal quantum numbers.

(ii) The radii of stationary states are given by:

$$r_n = n^2 a_0$$

where a_0 = 52·9 pm. As n increases the value of r will increase.

(iii) The energy of stationary state is given by:

$$E_n = -R_H\left(\frac{1}{n^2}\right)$$

where n = 1, 2, 3, ... and R_H (Rydberg constant) = $2{\cdot}18 \times 10^{-18}$ J.

(iv) For hydrogen like ions i.e., one electron system (e.g., He^+, Li^{2+}, Be^{3+}), the radii is given by,

$$r_n = \frac{52.9}{Z}n^2\,\text{pm}$$

and energies of the stationary states are given by:

$$E_n = -2.18 \times 10^{-18}\left(\frac{Z^2}{n^2}\right)$$

(v) It is also possible to calculate the velocities of electrons moving in these orbits.

- If fails to explain zeeman effect (be splitting of spectral line in the presence of magnetic field) and tark effect be slitting of spectral line the presence of electric field.

Scan to know more about this topic

Bohr Model

➤ **Limitations of Bohr's Model:**

- It fails to explain doublet observed in the hydrogen spectrum.
- It fails to explain the ability of atoms to form molecule by chemical bonds.
- It fails to explain Zeeman effect (i.e., splitting of spectral line in the presence of magnetic field) and stark effect (i.e., splitting of spectral line in the presence of electric field)

Towards Quantum Mechanical Model of the Atom

Dual Behaviour of Matter: Einstein had suggested that light can behave as a wave as well as like a particle. i.e., it has dual character.

In 1924, de Broglie suggested that matter like radiations, should also exhibit a dual character – i.e., wave and particle like properties. This means that just as the photon has momentum as well as wavelength, electron should also have both.

According to de-Broglie, the wavelength associated with a particle of mass m, moving with velocity v is given by the relation,

$$\lambda = \frac{h}{mv} = \frac{h}{p}$$

where h = Planck's constant
v = Velocity of particle
($p = mv$) = momentum of the particle.

Heisenberg's Uncertainty Principle

Heisenberg's uncertainty principle states that,
"It is not possible to determine simultaneously both the exact position and momentum (or velocity) of an electron, with absolute accuracy."

Mathematically, this law may be expressed as:

$$\Delta x \times \Delta p_x \geq \frac{h}{4\pi}$$

$$\Delta x.\Delta(mv_x) \geq \frac{h}{4\pi}$$

or $$\Delta x \times \Delta v_x \geq \frac{h}{4\pi m}$$

where,
Δx = uncertainty in position,
Δp_x = uncertainty in momentum,
Δv_x = uncertainty in velocity.

Quantum Mechanical Model of Atom

Quantum mechanics was developed independently by **Heisenberg** and **Schrodinger.**

Schrodinger equation is $\hat{H}\psi = E\psi$ where $\hat{H}$ is a mathematical operator called **Hamiltonian,** E is the total energy of the system and ψ is the wave function.

Scan to know more about this topic

Heisenberg uncertainty principle

Important Features of the Quantum Mechanical Model of Atom

1. The energy of the electrons in atoms is quantized.
2. The existence of quantized electronic energy level is a direct result of the wave like properties of electrons.
3. Both the exact position and exact velocity of an electron in an atom cannot be determined simultaneously. Therefore, only probability of finding an electron at different points is required.
4. An atomic orbital is the wave function ψ for an electron in an atom.
5. The probability of finding an electron at a point within an atom is proportional to the square of the orbital wave function, i.e., $|\psi|^2$ at that point $|\psi|^2$. It is also known as probability density. The value of probable density is always positive.
   From the value of $|\psi|^2$ at different points within an atom, it is possible to predict the region around the nucleus where the electron will most likely be found.

Orbitals and Quantum Numbers

- **Orbitals:** A wave function for an electron in an atom is called an atomic orbital, which describes a region of space in which there is a high probability of finding the electrons. These can be distinguished by their size, shape and orientation.
- **Quantum Numbers:** Electron have only certain permissible values of energy and angular momentum. These permissible states of an electron in any atom are called orbitals which are identified by a set of four numbers. These numbers are called Quantum Numbers.
  The various quantum numbers are:
  (a) Principal quantum number (n)
  (b) Azimuthal or angular momentum quantum number (l).
  (c) Magnetic quantum number (m_l).
  (d) Spin quantum number (m_s).

(a) Principal quantum number (n): This quantum number determines the size energy associated with it. The principal quantum number 'n' is a positive integer with value of n = 1,2,3........ The maximum number of electrons which a shell can accommodate is $2n^2$. All the orbitals of a given value of 'n' constitute a single shell of atom and are represented by the following letters

n = 1 2 3 4 ....
Shell = K L M N ....

(b) Azimuthal or subsidiary or orbital angular quantum number (l): This quantum number defines the three dimensional shape of the orbital. It can have positive integer values from zero to (n – 1) where n is the principal quantum number, i.e., l = 0, 1, 2, 3, ... (n – 1).

Value of n	Value of l	Name of sub-shell	Number of the sub-shells
1	0	1s	one
2	0,1	2s, 2p	two
3	0, 1, 2	3s, 3p, 3d	three
4	0, 1, 2, 3	4s, 4p, 4d, 4f	four

(c) Magnetic Orbital Quantum Number (m_l): This describes the spatial orientation of the orbitals along the standard set of co-ordinate axis. Co-ordinate for a given value of l, the possible values of m_l vary from – l, 0 to + l.

(d) Spin Quantum Number (m_s): This quantum number describes the spin orientation of the electron. Since the electron can spin in only two ways- clockwise or anti-clockwise and, therefore, the spin quantum number can take only two values, +½ or – ½.

Mnemonics

1. Concept: Quantum Numbers
Mnemonics: SPAM
Interpretation:
S – Spin Quantum no. (ms)
P – Principal Quantum no. (n)
A – Azimuthal Quantum no. (l)
M – Magnetic Quantum no. (m)
2. Concept: Sequence of orbitals
Mnemonics: Sober Physicists Don't Find Giraffes Hiding In Kitchen
Interpretation: *s,p,d,f,g,h,i,k*

- **Boundary Surface Diagrams:**
  - **Shape of *s*-orbitals:** *s*-orbitals are non-directional and spherically symmetrical.

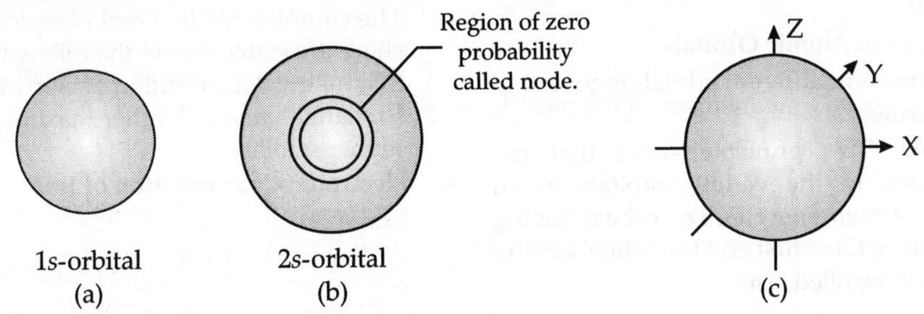

Shape of 1*s* and 2*s* orbitals

- **Shape of *p*-orbitals:** For *p*-orbitals ($l = 1$), there are three possible orientations corresponding to $m_l = -1, 0, +1$ values. This means that there are three *p*-orbitals in each *p*-sub-shell. These are designated as p_x, p_y, and p_z.

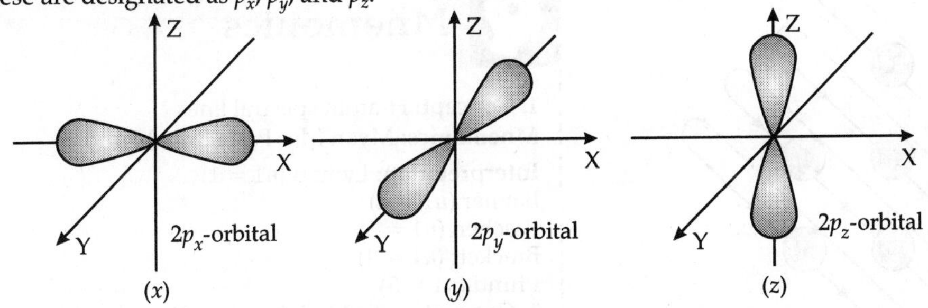

Scan to know more about this topic

The Aufbau principle

Fig. 2.2: Shape of *p*-orbitals

- **Shape of *d*-orbitals:** The five d-orbitals, designated as d_{xy}, d_{yz}, d_{zx}, $d_{x^2-y^2}$, d_{z^2}. The shapes of first four *d*-orbitals are similar to each other, whereas fifth one d_{z^2} is different from others but all the five *d*-orbitals are equivalent in energy, i.e., degenerate.

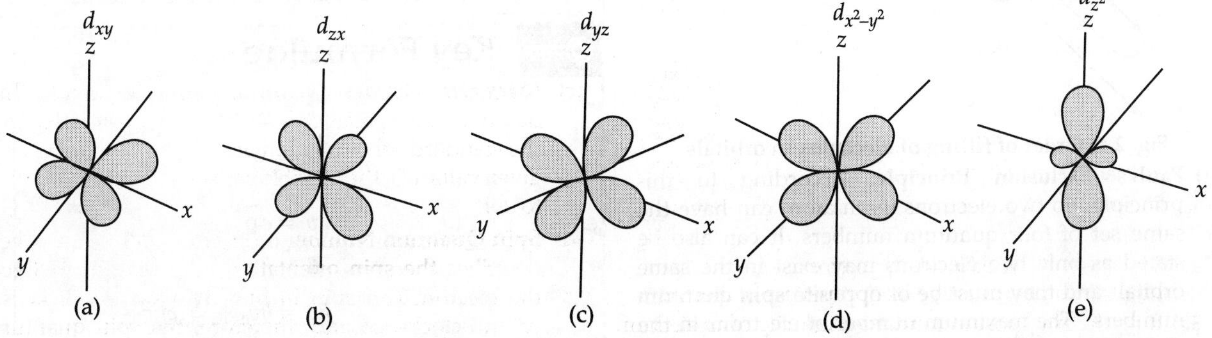

Fig. 2.3: Shape of five *d*-orbitals

The total number of nodes are given by $(n - 1)$, i.e., sum of l angular nodes and $(n - l - 1)$ radial nodes.

- **Nodes and Nodal Planes:** The place or point where probability density function reduces to zero are called nodes or nodal surface.
- **Degenerate Orbitals:** The orbitals with same energy are called degenerate orbitals, e.g., p sub-shell has three degenerate orbitals namely p_x, p_y and p_z.
- **Shielding Effect:** The term shielding effect refers to a decrease in attraction between electrons and the nucleus in an atom. Electrons are highly attracted to the nucleus, because they have a negative charge and the nucleus contains protons, which have a positive charge.
- **$n + l$ Rule:** Orbitals are filled in the order of increasing $n + l$. For equal $n + l$ values, the orbital with the lower n is most often filled first. Here n is the principal quantum number and l is the angular momentum quantum number.
- **Filling of Electrons in Atomic Orbitals:**

The filling of electrons in different orbitals is governed by the following rules:

(i) Aufbau Principle: This principle states that the electrons are filled in the various orbitals in an increasing order of their energies, i.e., orbital having lowest energy will be filled first and the orbital having highest energy will be filled last.

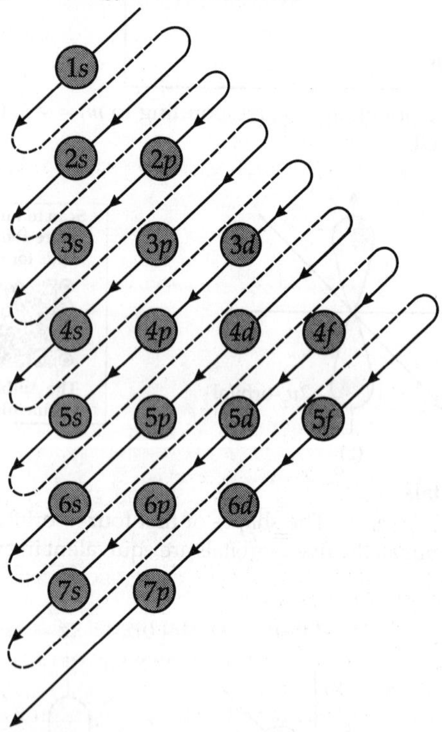

Fig. 2.4: Order of filling of electrons in orbitals

(ii) Pauli's Exclusion Principle: According to this principle, no two electrons in an atom can have the same set of four quantum numbers. It can also be stated as only two electrons may exist in the same orbital and they must be of opposite spin quantum numbers'. The maximum number of electrons in the shell with principal quantum number n is equal to $2n^2$.

(iii) Hund's Rule of Maximum Multiplicity: No electron pairing takes place in p, d and f orbitals until each orbital in the given sub-shell contains one electron having parallel spin, e.g., N_2 (7) has electronic configuration $1s^2$, $2s^2$, $2px^1$, $2py^1$, $2pz^1$ according to Hund's rule:

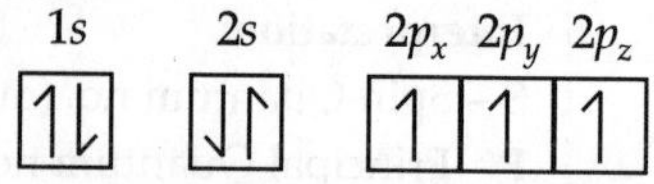

- **Electronic Configuration of Atoms:**

The distribution of electrons in different orbitals is known as electronic configuration of the atom.

- **Significance of Electronic Configuration:** The number of valence electrons in an atom determines how readily an atom will react with other atoms. If it has 7 or 1 valence electron, then it only needs to gain/loss 1 electron which is relatively easier than gaining/losing 3 or 4 electrons.

The completely filled and completely half filled sub-shells are stable due to the following reasons:

1. Symmetrical distribution of electrons
2. Exchange energy: Higher maximum energy leads to higher stability.

- **Electronic Configuration of Ions:**

Examples:

Cl (No. of electrons = 17): $1s^2$, $2s^2$, $2p^6$, $3s^2$, $3p_x^2$, $3p_y^2$, $3p_z^1$

Cl^- (No. of electrons = 18): $1s^2$, $2s^2$, $2p^6$, $3s^2$, $3p_x^2$, $3p_y^2$, $3p_z^2$

Mg (No. of electrons = 12): $1s^2$, $2s^2$, $2p^6$, $3s^2$

Mg^{2+} (No. of electrons = 10): $1s^2$, $2s^2$, $2p^6$

Mnemonics

1. Concept: H-atom spectral lines

Mnemonics: Myan Mer Pasta Bread Fund

Interpretation: Lyman ($n1 = 1$)
Balmer ($n1 = 2$)
Paschen ($n1 = 3$)
Brackett ($n1 = 4$)
Pfund ($n1 = 5$)

2. Concept: Bohr Model of an atom

Mnemonics: Electronic video Recording (EVR)

Interpretation: Energy (E) $\propto$ Z
Velocity (V) $\propto$ Z
Radius (R) $\propto$ n

Key Formulae

$$c = \lambda \times v$$

$$\frac{1}{\lambda} = \bar{\upsilon}$$

$$v = c\bar{\upsilon}$$

$$E = hv$$

$$hv = hv_0 + \frac{1}{2} mv^2$$

- $\bar{v} = 109,677\left(\frac{1}{n_1^2} - \frac{1}{n_2^2}\right)\ \text{cm}^{-1}$
- $v = \frac{\Delta E}{h} = \frac{E_1 - E_1}{h}$
- $m_e vr = n.\frac{h}{2\pi}$
- $r_n = n^2 a_0$
- $E_n = -R_H\left(\frac{1}{n^2}\right)$

Key Terms

- **Electromagnetic Radiation:** Energy emitted from any source in the form of waves in which electric and magnetic fields oscillated perpendicular to each other and travel with a velocity of light is called electromagnetic radiation.
- **Amplitude:** The height of crest or depth of a trough is called amplitude. It is denoted by the symbol 'a'.
- **Velocity:** The distance travelled by a wave in one second is called velocity.
- **Photon:** A packet or particle of light energy is called photon.
- **Photoelectric Effect:** The phenomenon of ejection of electrons from a metal surface when a light radiation of suitable frequency falls on metal surface is called photoelectric effect.
- **Threshold Frequency:** The minimum frequency (v_o) below which photoelectric effect is not observed, is called threshold frequency.
- **Momentum :** The quantity of motion of a moving body measured as a product of its mass and velocity.
- **Uncertainty in position of the particle:** If the velocity of the electron is known precisely [$\Delta(v_x)$ is small], then the position of the electron will be uncertain (Δx will be large), which is called uncertainty in position of the particle.
- **Uncertainty in velocity of the particle:** If the position of the electron is known with high degree of accuracy (Δx is small), then the velocity of the electron will be uncertain [$\Delta(v_x)$ is large], which is called uncertainty in velocity of the particle.
- **Quantum mechanics :** The branch of science that takes into account this dual behavior of matter is called quantum mechanics.
- Effective nuclear charge: It is the net positive charge an electron experiences in an atom with multiple electrons. It may be approximated by the equation

  $Z_{eff} = Z - S$

  where, Z = atomic number

  S = number of shielding electrons

Key Facts

- Energy wise order of electromagnetic radiation :

  Cosmic rays < γ-rays < X-rays < UV light < Visible light < IR rays < Micro waves < Radio waves

  $\longrightarrow$ Wavelength (λ) increases

  $\longrightarrow$ Frequency (v) decreases

  $\longrightarrow$ Wave number ($\bar{v}$) decreases

  $\longrightarrow$ Energy (e) decreases
- The value 109, 677 cm^{-1} is called the Rydberg constant for hydrogen.
- Electrons should have momentum as well as wave length.
- An atomic orbital is the wave function ψ for an electron in an atom.

NCERT CORNER

Q. 1. (i) Calculate the number of electrons which will together weigh one gram.

(ii) Calculate the mass and charge of one mole of electrons. [NCERT Ex. Q. 2.1, Page 69]

Ans. (i) Mass of an electron = 9.1×10^{-28}g

$\therefore$ 9.1×10^{-28}g is the mass of 1 electron

$\therefore$ 1.0 g will be the mass of $\frac{1}{9.1 \times 10^{-28}}$

$= 1.098 \times 10^{27}$ electrons

(ii) $\because$ One mole of electrons = 6.022×10^{23} electrons

Mass of electron = 9.1×10^{-31} kg

Mass of 6.022×10^{23} electrons

$= 9.1 \times 10^{-31} \times 6.022 \times 10^{23}$

$= 5.48 \times 10^{-7}$ kg

$\therefore$ Charge on one electron

$= 1.602 \times 10^{-19}$ coulomb

$\therefore$ Charge on 6.022×10^{23} electrons

$= 1.602 \times 10^{-19} \times 6.022 \times 10^{23}$

$= 9.65 \times 10^{4}$ coulomb

Q. 2. (i) Calculate the total number of electrons present in one mole of methane.

(ii) Find (a) the total number and (b) the total mass of neutrons in 7 mg of ^{14}C. (Assume that mass of a neutron = 1.675×10^{-27} kg)

(iii) Find (a) the total number and (b) the total mass of protons in 34 mg of NH_3 at STP. Will the answer change if the temperature and pressure are changed?

[NCERT Ex. Q. 2.2, Page 69]

Ans. (i) Number of molecules in 1 mole of CH_4 = 6.022×10^{23}

Number of electrons in one molecule of CH_4 = 6 + 4 = 10

$\therefore$ Total number of electrons in 6.022×10^{23} molecules of CH_4

$= 6.022 \times 10^{23} \times 10 = 6.022 \times 10^{24}$ electrons

(ii) (a) Gram atomic mass of carbon (C – 14) = 14 g
$= 14 \times 10^3$ mg
14×10^3 mg of carbon (C – 14) have
$= 6.022 \times 10^{23}$ atoms
∴ 7 mg of carbon (C – 14) have
$$= \frac{6.022 \times 10^{23}}{14 \times 10^3} \times 7$$
$= 3.011 \times 10^{20}$ atoms
Number of neutrons present in one atom of carbon (C – 14)
$= 14 - 6 = 8$
∴ Total number of neutrons present in 3.011×10^{20} atoms of carbon (C–14)
$= 3.011 \times 10^{20} \times 8$
$= 2.408 \times 10^{21}$ neutrons
(b) ∴ Mass of one neutron $= 1.675 \times 10^{-27}$ kg
∴ Total mass of 2.408×10^{21} neutrons
$= 1.675 \times 10^{-27} \times 2.408 \times 10^{21}$
$= 4.033 \times 10^{-6}$ kg
(iii) (a) Gram molecular mass of ammonia (NH_3)
$= 14 + 3 = 17$ g $= 17 \times 10^3$ mg
∴ 17×10^3 mg of NH_3 have $= 6.022 \times 10^{23}$ molecules
∴ 34 mg of NH_3 have $= \dfrac{6.022 \times 10^{23} \times 34}{17 \times 10^3}$
$= 12.044 \times 10^{20}$ molecules
(b) Number of protons present in one molecule of NH_3
$= 7 + 3 = 10$
∴ Total number of protons present in 12.044×10^{20} molecules of $NH_3 = 12.044 \times 10^{20} \times 10 = 1.2044 \times 10^{22}$ protons
∵ Mass of one proton $= 1.67 \times 10^{-27}$kg
Mass of 1.2044×10^{22} protons
$= 1.67 \times 10^{-27} \times 1.2044 \times 10^{22}$
$= 2.01 \times 10^{-5}$ kg

No, the answer will not change upon changing the temperature and pressure because only the number of protons and mass of protons are involved.

Q. 3. How many neutrons and protons are there in the following nuclei?

$^{13}_{6}C$ $^{16}_{8}O$ $^{24}_{12}Mg$ $^{56}_{26}Fe$ $^{88}_{38}Sr$

[NCERT Ex. Q. 2.3, Page 69]

Ans. $^{13}_{6}C$ Number of protons = 6
Number of neutrons = 13 – 6 = 7
$^{16}_{8}O$ Number of protons = 8
Number of neutrons = 16 – 8 = 8
$^{24}_{12}Mg$ Number of protons = 12
Number of neutrons = 24 – 12 = 12
$^{56}_{26}Fe$ Number of protons = 26
Number of neutrons = 56 – 26 = 30
$^{88}_{38}Sr$ Number of protons = 38
Number of neutrons = 88 – 38 = 50

Q. 4. Write the complete symbol for the atom with the given atomic number (Z) and atomic mass (A):
(i) Z = 17, A = 35
(ii) Z = 92, A = 233
(iii) Z = 4, A = 9

[NCERT Ex. Q. 2.4, Page 69]

Ans. (i) Z = 17, A = 35
Symbol: $^{35}_{17}Cl$
(ii) Z = 92, A = 233
Symbol: $^{233}_{92}U$
(iii) Z = 4, A = 9
Symbol: $^{9}_{4}Be$

Q. 5. Yellow light emitted from a sodium lamp has a wavelength (λ) of 580 nm. Calculate the frequency (ν) and wave number ($\bar{\nu}$) of the yellow light.

[NCERT Ex. Q. 2.5, Page 69]

Ans. Given $\lambda = 580$ nm $= 580 \times 10^{-9}$ m

Frequency $\nu = \dfrac{c}{\lambda}$
$$= \frac{3 \times 10^8 \text{ ms}^{-1}}{580 \times 10^{-9} \text{ m}}$$
$= 5.17 \times 10^{14} \text{ s}^{-1}$

Wave number $(\bar{\nu}) = \dfrac{1}{\lambda}$
$$= \frac{1}{580 \times 10^{-9} \text{ m}}$$
$= 1.724 \times 10^6 \text{ m}^{-1}$

Q. 6. Find energy of each of the photons which:
(i) corresponds to light of frequency 3×10^{15} Hz
(ii) have wavelength of 0.50 Å

[NCERT Ex. Q. 2.6, Page 69]

Ans. (i) Given $\nu = 3 \times 10^{15}$ Hz
$E = h\nu$
$= 6.626 \times 10^{-34}$ J s $\times 3 \times 10^{15}\text{s}^{-1}$
$= 1.987 \times 10^{-18}$ J
(ii) Given $\lambda = 0.50$ Å $= 0.5 \times 10^{-10}$m
$$E = \frac{hc}{\lambda} = \frac{6.626 \times 10^{-34} \text{ J s} \times 3 \times 10^8 \text{ ms}^{-1}}{0.5 \times 10^{-10} \text{ m}}$$
$= 3.98 \times 10^{-15}$ J

Q. 7. Calculate the wavelength, frequency and wave number of a light wave whose period is 2.0×10^{-10}s.

[NCERT Ex. Q. 2.7, Page 69]

Ans. Time period $= 2.0 \times 10^{-10}$s

Frequency $(\nu) = \dfrac{1}{\text{Time period}}$
$$= \frac{1}{2.0 \times 10^{-10} \text{ s}}$$
$= 5.0 \times 10^9 \text{ s}^{-1}$

Wavelength $(\lambda) = \dfrac{c}{\nu} = \dfrac{3 \times 10^8 \text{ ms}^{-1}}{5 \times 10^9 \text{ s}^{-1}}$
$= 6 \times 10^{-2}$ m

Wave number $(\bar{\nu}) = \dfrac{1}{\lambda} = \dfrac{1}{6 \times 10^{-2} m} = 16.66 \text{ m}^{-1}$

Q. 8. What is the number of photons of light with a wavelength of 4000 pm that provide 1 J of energy?

[NCERT Ex. Q. 2.8, Page 69]

Ans. Given $\lambda = 4000$ pm $= 4000 \times 10^{-12}$ m $= 4 \times 10^{-9}$ m

Energy of photon $E = \dfrac{hc}{\lambda}$

$$= \frac{6.626\times10^{-34}\,\text{J s}\times3\times10^{8}\,\text{ms}^{-1}}{4\times10^{-9}\,\text{m}}$$

$= 4.969 \times 10^{-17}$ J

$\because$ 4.969×10^{-17} J is the energy of 1 photon

$\therefore$ 1 J is the energy of $= \dfrac{1}{4.969\times10^{-17}}$

$= 2.012 \times 10^{16}$ photons

Q. 9. A photon of wavelength 4×10^{-7}m strikes on metal surface, the work function of the metal being 2.13 eV. Calculate (i) the energy of the photon (ii) the kinetic energy of the emission and (iii) the velocity of the photoelectron. (1 eV = 1.6020×10^{-19} J)

[NCERT Ex. Q. 2.9, Page 69]

Ans. Given $\lambda = 4 \times 10^{-7}$m

Work function = 2.13 eV

(i) Energy of the photon $E = \dfrac{hc}{\lambda}$

$$= \frac{6.626\times10^{-34}\,\text{J s}\times3\times10^{8}\,\text{ms}^{-1}}{4\times10^{-7}\,\text{m}}$$

$= 4.97 \times 10^{-19}$ J

$$= \frac{4.97\times10^{-19}\,\text{eV}}{1.602\times10^{-19}}$$

$= 3.1$ eV

(ii) Kinetic energy of the emission
= Energy of the photon
– work function
= 3.1 – 2.13
= 0.97 eV

(iii) Velocity of photoelectron

$$\text{K.E.} = \frac{1}{2}mv^2$$

$$\therefore \quad v^2 = \frac{2KE}{m}$$

$$v = \sqrt{\frac{2K.E.}{m}}$$

$$= \sqrt{\frac{2\times0.97\times1.602\times10^{-19}\,\text{kg m}^2\text{s}^{-2}}{9.1\times10^{-31}\,\text{kg}}}$$

$= \sqrt{0.341\times10^{12}\,\text{m}^2\text{s}^{-2}}$

$= 0.584 \times 10^{6}$ ms^{-1}

$= 5.84 \times 10^{5}$ ms^{-1}

Q. 10. Electromagnetic radiation of wavelength 242 nm is just sufficient to ionize the sodium atom. Calculate the ionization energy of sodium in kJ mol^{-1}.

[NCERT Ex. Q. 2.10, Page 69]

Ans. Given $\lambda = 242$ nm $= 242 \times 10^{-9}$ m

$$E = \frac{hc}{\lambda} = \frac{6.626\times10^{-34}\,\text{Js}\times3\times10^{8}\,\text{ms}^{-1}}{242\times10^{-9}\,\text{m}}$$

$= 0.0821 \times 10^{-17}$ J

$= 8.21 \times 10^{-19}$ J

Ionization energy of sodium per mol

$$= \frac{8.21\times10^{-19}\,\text{J}\times6.022\times10^{23}\,\text{mol}^{-1}}{1000}$$

$= 49.44 \times 10$ J mol^{-1}

$= 494.4$ kJ mol^{-1}

Q. 11. A 25 watt bulb emits monochromatic yellow light of wavelength of 0.57 μm. Calculate the rate of emission of quanta per second. [NCERT Ex. Q. 2.11, Page 69]

Ans. Given, Power (P) = 25 watt = 25 Js^{-1}

$\lambda = 0.57$ μm $= 0.57 \times 10^{-6}$ m

Energy of photon $E = \dfrac{hc}{\lambda}$

$$= \frac{6.626\times10^{-34}\,\text{J s}\times3\times10^{8}\,\text{ms}^{-1}}{0.57\times10^{-6}\,\text{m}}$$

$= 3.48 \times 10^{-19}$ J

Rate of emission of quanta per second

$$= \frac{\text{Power}}{\text{Energy}}$$

$$= \frac{25}{3.48\times10^{-19}} = 7.18 \times 10^{19}\,\text{s}^{-1}$$

Q. 12. Electrons are emitted with zero velocity from a metal surface when it is exposed to radiation of wavelength 6800Å. Calculate threshold frequency (ν_o) and work function (W_o) of the metal.

[NCERT Ex. Q. 2.12, Page 69]

Ans. Given $\lambda = 6800$ Å $= 6800 \times 10^{-10}$ m $= 68 \times 10^{-8}$ m

$$\text{Frequency } \nu = \frac{c}{\lambda} = \frac{3\times10^{8}\,\text{m s}^{-1}}{68\times10^{-8}\,\text{m}}$$

$= 4.41 \times 10^{14}$ s^{-1}

$\therefore$ Threshold frequency $\nu_0 = 4.41 \times 10^{14}$ sec^{-1}

Work Function $(W_0) = h\nu_0$

$= 6.626 \times 10^{-34}$ J s $\times 4.41 \times 10^{14}$ s^{-1}

$= 2.92 \times 10^{-19}$ J

Q. 13. What is the wavelength of light emitted when the electron in a hydrogen atom undergoes transition from an energy level with $n = 4$ to an energy level with $n = 2$? [NCERT Ex. Q. 2.13, Page 69]

Ans. $n_1 = 2, n_2 = 4$

$$\because \text{Wave number } (\bar{\nu}) = 109677\left[\frac{1}{n_1^2} - \frac{1}{n_2^2}\right]$$

$$= 109677\left[\frac{1}{(2)^2} - \frac{1}{(4)^2}\right]$$

$$= 109677\left[\frac{1}{4} - \frac{1}{16}\right]$$

$$= \frac{109677\times3}{16}$$

$= 20564.43$

$= 2.0564 \times 10^{4}$ cm^{-1}

$$\text{Wavelength } (\lambda) = \frac{1}{\bar{\nu}}$$

$$= \frac{1}{2.0564\times10^{4}\,cm^{-1}}$$

$= 0.486 \times 10^{-4}$ cm

$= 0.486 \times 10^{-6}$ m

$= 486 \times 10^{-9}$ m

$= 486$ nm

Q. 14. How much energy is required to ionise a H-atom if the electron occupies n = 5 orbit? Compare your answer with the ionization enthalpy of H-atom (energy required to remove the electron from n = 1 orbit). [NCERT Ex. Q. 2.14, Page 70]

Ans. Energy for a hydrogen electron present in a particular energy shell

$$En = -\frac{13.12}{n^2} \times 10^5 \text{ J mol}^{-1}$$

$$= \frac{13.12\times10^5}{n^2\times6.022\times10^{23}} \text{J atom}^{-1}$$

$$= \frac{-2.18\times10^{-18}}{n^2} \text{J atom}^{-1}$$

Ionization energy for hydrogen electron present in 5th orbit $n = 5$

$$IE_5 = E_\infty - E_5$$

$$= 0 - \left(\frac{-2.18\times10^{-18}}{25}\right) \text{J atom}^{-1}$$

$$= 8.72 \times 10^{-20} \text{ J atom}^{-1}$$

Ionization energy for hydrogen electron present in 1st orbit $n = 1$

$$IE_1 = E_\infty - E_1$$

$$= 0 - \left(\frac{-2.18\times10^{-18}}{1}\right)$$

$$= 2.18 \times 10^{-18} \text{ J atom}^{-1}$$

$$\therefore \frac{IE_5}{IE_1} = \frac{8.72\times10^{-20} \text{ J atom}^{-1}}{2.18\times10^{-18} \text{ J atom}^{-1}}$$

$$= 0.04$$

$\therefore IE_1$ is 25 times as compared to IE_5.

Q. 15. What is the maximum number of emission lines when the excited electron of a H-atom in n = 6 drops to the ground state? [NCERT Ex. Q. 2.15, Page 70]

Ans. Given $n = 6$

Maximum number of emission lines

$$= \frac{n(n-1)}{2}$$

$$= \frac{6(6-1)}{2}$$

$$= \frac{30}{2} = 15$$

The actual transitions taking place are –

$n = 6$ to $n = 1$	$6 \to 5, 6 \to 4, 6 \to 3, 6 \to 2, 6 \to 1$ (5 lines)
$n = 5$ to $n = 1$	$5 \to 4, 5 \to 3, 5 \to 2, 5 \to 1$ (4 lines)
$n = 4$ to n = 1	$4 \to 3, 4 \to 2, 4 \to 1$ (3 lines)
$n = 3$ to n = 1	$3 \to 2, 3 \to 1$ (2 lines)
$n = 2$	2 (1 line)

Q. 16. (i) The energy associated with the first orbit in the hydrogen atom is -2.18×10^{-18} J atom^{-1}. What is the energy associated with the fifth orbit?

(ii) Calculate the radius of Bohr's fifth orbit for hydrogen atom. [NCERT Ex. Q. 2.16, Page 70]

Ans. (i) $E_1 = -2.18 \times 10^{-18}$ J atom^{-1}, $n_1 = 1$, $n_2 = 5$

For an electron, $\frac{E_1}{E_2} = \left(\frac{n_2}{n_1}\right)^2$

$$\therefore \frac{-2.18\times10^{-18} \text{ J atom}^{-1}}{E_2} = \left(\frac{5}{1}\right)^2 = 25$$

$$E_2 = \frac{-2.18\times10^{-18} \text{ J atom}^{-1}}{25}$$

$$= -8.72 \times 10^{-20} \text{ J}$$

(ii) For H-atom, $r_n = 0.529 \times n^2$ Å

$= 0.529 \times (5)^2$

$= 13.225$ Å $= 1.3225$ nm

Q. 17. Calculate the wave number for the longest wavelength transition in the Balmer series of atomic hydrogen. [NCERT Ex. Q. 2.17, Page 70]

Ans. For Balmer series,

$n_1 = 2$

$n_2 = 3$

According to Balmer formula,

$$(\bar{\nu}) = 109677\left[\frac{1}{n_1^2} - \frac{1}{n_2^2}\right]$$

$$= 109677\left[\frac{1}{(2)^2} - \frac{1}{(3)^2}\right]$$

$$= 109677\left[\frac{1}{4} - \frac{1}{9}\right]$$

$$= 109677\left[\frac{9-4}{36}\right]$$

$$= \frac{109677\times5}{36}$$

$$= 15232 \text{ cm}^{-1}$$

$$= 1.5232 \times 10^4 \text{ cm}^{-1}$$

Q. 18. What is the energy in joules, required to shift the electron of the hydrogen atom from the first Bohr orbit to the fifth Bohr orbit and what is the wavelength of the light emitted when the electron returns to the ground state ? The ground state electron energy is -2.18×10^{-11} ergs. [NCERT Ex. Q. 2.18, Page 70]

Ans. The ground state electron energy is the energy of the electron in the first Bohr's orbit.

$= -2.18 \times 10^{-11}$ ergs (given)

$E_1 = -2.18 \times 10^{-18}$ J [1 J = 10^7 ergs]

E_n = Energy in the nth orbit

$$= \frac{-2.18\times10^{-18}}{n^2}$$

Where n = no. of the orbit

If $n = 5$

$$E_5 = \frac{-2.18 \times 10^{-18}}{5^2}$$

$= 8.72 \times 10^{-20}$ J

Energy has to be absorbed to shift electron from Bohr's first orbit to fifth orbit.

$\therefore \quad \Delta E = E_1 - E_2$

$$= -2.18 \times 10^{-18}\left[\frac{1}{5^2} - \frac{1}{1^2}\right]$$

$$= 2.18 \times 10^{-18}\left[\frac{24}{25}\right]$$

$= 2.08 \times 10^{-18}$ J

$= 2.08 \times 10^{-11}$ ergs

$$\Delta E = \frac{hc}{\lambda} \text{ or } \lambda = \frac{hc}{\Delta E}$$

$$= \frac{6.6 \times 10^{-34} \text{ J s} \times 3 \times 10^8 \text{ ms}^{-1}}{2.08 \times 10^{-18} \text{ J}}$$

$= 951$ Å

Wavelength of the light emitted = 951 Å

Q. 19. The electron energy in hydrogen atom is given by $E_n = (-2.18 \times 10^{-18})/n^2$ J. Calculate the energy required to remove an electron completely from the $n = 2$ orbit. What is the longest wavelength of light in cm that can be used to cause this transition?

[NCERT Ex. Q. 2.19, Page 70]

Ans. Energy required (ΔE) = $E_\infty - E_2$

$$= 0 - \left(-\frac{2.18 \times 10^{-18}}{(2)^2} \text{J}\right)$$

$= 5.45 \times 10^{-19}$ J

$$\therefore \quad \Delta E = \frac{hc}{\lambda}$$

$$\therefore \quad \lambda = \frac{hc}{\Delta E} = \frac{6.626 \times 10^{-34} \text{ J s} \times 3 \times 10^8 \text{ms}^{-1}}{5.45 \times 10^{-19} \text{J}}$$

$= 3.644 \times 10^{-7}$ m

$= 3.644 \times 10^{-5}$ cm

Q. 20. Calculate the wavelength of an electron moving with a velocity of 2.05×10^7 ms^{-1}.

[NCERT Ex. Q. 2.20, Page 70]

Ans. $v = 2.05 \times 10^7$ m/s

According to de-Broglie equation,

$$\lambda = \frac{h}{mv}$$

$$= \frac{6.626 \times 10^{-34} \text{ kg m}^2 \text{ s}^{-1}}{9.1 \times 10^{-31} \text{ kg} \times 2.05 \times 10^7 \text{ ms}^{-1}}$$

$= 3.55 \times 10^{-11}$ m

Q. 21. The mass of an electron is 9.1×10^{-31} kg. If its K.E. is 3.0×10^{-25} J. Calculate its wavelength.

[NCERT Ex. Q. 2.21, Page 70]

Ans. Given, mass of electron (m) = 9.1×10^{-31} kg

K.E. = 3.0×10^{-25} J

$$\text{Kinetic energy} = \frac{1}{2}mv^2$$

$$v^2 = \frac{2K.E.}{m}$$

$$v = \sqrt{\frac{2K.E.}{m}}$$

$$= \sqrt{\frac{2 \times 3.0 \times 10^{-25} \text{kg m}^2 \text{s}^{-2}}{9.1 \times 10^{-31} \text{kg}}}$$

$$= \sqrt{65.9 \times 10^4 \text{m}^2 \text{s}^{-2}}$$

$= 8.12 \times 10^2$ m s^{-1}

Now, according to de-Broglie equation,

$$\lambda = \frac{h}{mv}$$

$$= \frac{6.626 \times 10^{-34} \text{ kg m}^2 \text{s}^{-1}}{9.1 \times 10^{-31} \text{kg} \times 8.12 \times 10^2 \text{ m s}^{-1}}$$

$= 0.08967 \times 10^{-5}$ m

$= 8967 \times 10^{-10}$ m

$= 8967$Å

Q. 22. Which of the following are isoelectronic species i.e. those having the same number of electrons?

Na^+, K^+, Mg^{2+}, Ca^{2+}, S^{2-}, Ar

[NCERT Ex. Q. 2.22, Page 70]

Ans.

Species	**No. of electrons**
Na^+	11 – 1 = 10
K^+	19 – 1 = 18
Mg^{2+}	12 – 2 = 10
Ca^{2+}	20 – 2 =18
S^{2-}	16 + 2 =18
Ar	18

$\therefore$ Na^+ and Mg^{2+} are isoelectronic species, as these have 10 electrons.

K^+, Ca^{2+}, S^{2-} and Ar are isoelectronic species, as these have 18 electrons.

Q. 23. (i) Write the electronic configuration of the following ions-

(a) H^- **(b) Na^+**

(c) O^{2-} **(d) F^-**

(ii) What are the atomic numbers of elements whose outermost electrons are represented by

(a) $3s^1$ **(b) $2p^3$** **(c) $3p^5$**

(iii) Which atoms are indicated by the following configuration?

(a) [He]$2s^1$ **(b) [Ne]$3s^2 3p^3$**

(c) [Ar]$4s^2 3d^1$ **[NCERT Ex. Q. 2.23, Page 70]**

Ans. (i) (a) H^- : No. of electrons = 1 + 1 = 2

$\therefore$ Electronic configuration = $1s^2$

(b) Na^+ : No. of electrons = 11 – 1 = 10

$\therefore$ Electronic configuration = $1s^2, 2s^2\, 2p^6$

(c) O^{2-} : No. of electrons = 8 + 2 = 10

∴ Electronic configuration = $1s^2, 2s^2 2p^6$

(d) F^- : No. of electrons = 9 + 1 = 10

∴ Electronic configuration = $1s^2, 2s^2 2p^6$

(ii) (a) $3s^1$, Atomic number = 11 (Na)

(b) $2p^3$, Atomic number = 7 (N)

(c) $3p^5$, Atomic number = 17 (Cl)

(iii)

Electronic configuration	Atomic number	Atom
(a) $[He]2s^1$	3	Li
(b) $[Ne]3s^2 3p^3$	15	P
(c) $[Ar]4s^2 3d^1$	21	Sc

Q. 24. What is the lowest value of n that allows g orbitals to exist? [NCERT Ex. Q. 2.24, Page 70]

Ans. g-orbitals can exist if the value of l = 4

We know that $l = n - 1$

∴ If $l = 4$ then $n = l + 1 = 4 + 1 = 5$

Hence, the lowest value of '*n*' that allows g-orbitals to exist is 5.

Q. 25. An electron is in one of the 3*d* orbitals. Give the possible values of *n*, *l* and m_l for this electron. [NCERT Ex. Q. 2.25, Page 70]

Ans. For an electron in 3*d* orbital,

$$n = 3$$
$$l = 2$$
$$m_l = -2, -1, 0, +1 + 2$$

Q. 26. An atom of an element contains 29 electrons and 35 Neutrons. Deduce (i) the number of protons and (ii) the electronic configuration of the element? [NCERT Ex. Q. 2.26, Page 70]

Ans. **(i)** Number of electrons = 29

Number of neutrons = 35

∵ Number of protons in a neutral atom = No. of electrons = 29

(ii) Electronic configuration of the element = 2, 8, 18, 1 = $1s^2 2s^2 2p^6 3s^2 3p^6 3d^{10} 4s^1$

Q. 27. Give the number of electrons in the species H_2^+, H_2 and O_2^+. [NCERT Ex. Q. 2.27, Page 70]

Ans.

Species	No. of electrons
H_2^+	2 – 1 = 1
H_2	2
O_2^+	16 – 1 = 15

Q. 28. (i) An atomic orbital has *n* = 3. What are the possible values of l and m_l?

(ii) List the quantum numbers (m_l and *l*) of electrons for 3d orbital.

(iii) Which of two following orbitals are possible?

1p, 2s and 3f [NCERT Ex. Q. 2.28, Page 70]

Ans. (i)

n	*l*	m_l
3	0	0
	1	–1, 0, +1
	2	–2, –1, 0, +1, +2

(ii) For an electron for 3*d* orbital

$$n = 3$$
$$l = 2$$
$$m_l = -2, -1, 0, +1 + 2$$

(iii) 2s, 2p

Q. 29. Using *s*, *p*, *d* notations, describe the orbital with the following quantum numbers –

(a) 1s (c) 4*d*

(b) 3*p* (d) 4*f*

[NCERT Ex. Q. 2.29, Page 70]

Ans.

Quantum numbers	Orbital
(a) $n = 1, l = 0$	(c) $n = 4, l = 2$
(b) $n = 3, l = 1$	(d) $n = 4, l = 3$

Q. 30. Explain, giving reasons which of the following sets of quantum numbers are not possible-

(i)	$n = 0$, l = 0	$m_l = 0$,		$m_s = +½$
(ii)	$n = 1$, l = 0	$m_l = 0$,		$m_s = -½$
(iii)	$n = 1$, l = 1	$m_l = 0$,		$m_s = +½$
(iv)	$n = 2$, l = 1	$m_l = 0$,		$m_s = -½$
(v)	$n = 3$, l = 3	$m_l = -3$,		$m_s = +½$
(vi)	$n = 3$, l = 1	$m_l = 0$,		$m_s = +½$

[NCERT Ex. Q. 2.30, Page 70]

Ans. (i) $n = 0, l = 0.$ $m_l = 0,$ $m_s = +½$

This set of quantum numbers is not possible because the value of n for an atom is never zero.

(ii) $n = 1,$ $l = 0,$ $m_l = 0,$ $m_s = -½$

This set of quantum numbers is possible.

(iii) $n = 1,$ $l = 1,$ $m_l = 0,$ $m_s = +½$

This set of quantum numbers is not possible because if the value of *n* = 1, then *l* cannot be equal to one.

(iv) $n = 2,$ $l = 1,$ $m_l = 0,$ $m_s = -½$

This set of quantum numbers is possible.

(v) $n = 3,$ $l = 3,$ $m_l = -3,$ $m_s = +½$

This set of quantum numbers is not possible because if the value of n = 3, then *l* can not be equal to 3.

(vi) $n = 3,$ $l = 1,$ $m_l = 0,$ $m_s = +½$

This set of quantum numbers is possible.

Q. 31. How many electrons in an atom may have the following quantum numbers?

(a) *n* = 4, $m_s = -½$

(b) *n* = 3, *l* = 0 [NCERT Ex. Q. 2.31, Page 71]

Ans. (a) For *n* = 4

Total number of electrons

$$= 2n^2 = 2(4)^2 = 32$$

Half of these electrons will have

$$m_s = -½$$

∴ Total electrons with m_s (–½) = 16

(b) For

$$n = 3$$
$$l = 0$$
$$m_l = 0$$
$$m_s = +½, -½ \quad \text{(two electrons)}$$

There are two electrons for this set of quantum number.

Q. 32. Show that the circumference of the Bohr orbit for the hydrogen atom is an integral multiple of the de Broglie wavelength associated with the electron revolving around the orbit. [NCERT Ex. Q. 2.32, Page 71]

Ans. According to Bohr's theory,

$$mvr = \frac{nh}{2\pi}$$

or

$$2\pi r = \frac{nh}{mv}$$

or

$$mv = \frac{nh}{2\pi r} \quad ...(i)$$

According to de Broglie equation,

$$\lambda = \frac{h}{mv}$$

or $$mv = \frac{h}{\lambda} \quad ...(ii)$$

From equation (i) and (ii)

$$\frac{nh}{2\pi r} = \frac{h}{\lambda}$$

or $$2\pi r = n\lambda \quad ...(iii)$$

$\because$ Circumference (C) = $2\pi r$

The equation (iii) shows that the circumference of the Bohr orbit for the hydrogen atom is an integral multiple of the de Broglie wavelength.

Q. 33. What transition in the hydrogen spectrum would have the same wavelength as the Balmer transition $n = 4$ to $n = 2$ of He^+ spectrum? [NCERT Ex. Q. 2.33, Page 71]

Ans. For an atom, wave number

$$\bar{v} = \frac{1}{\lambda} = R_H \times (Z)^2 \left[\frac{1}{n_1^2} - \frac{1}{n_2^2}\right]$$

For He^+ spectrum, $Z = 2, n_1 = 2, n_2 = 4$

$$\bar{v} = \frac{1}{\lambda} = R_H \times (2)^2 \left[\frac{1}{(2)^2} - \frac{1}{(4)^2}\right]$$

$$= \frac{3R_H}{4}$$

For hydrogen spectrum,

$$\bar{v} = \frac{3R_H}{4}, Z = 1$$

$$\bar{v} = \frac{1}{\lambda} = R_H \times (1)^2 \left[\frac{1}{n_1^2} - \frac{1}{n_2^2}\right]$$

$$= R_H \left[\frac{1}{n_1^2} - \frac{1}{n_2^2}\right]$$

or $$R_H \left(\frac{1}{n_1^2} - \frac{1}{n_2^2}\right) = \frac{3R_H}{4}$$

or $$\frac{1}{n_1^2} - \frac{1}{n_2^2} = \frac{3}{4}$$

This corresponds to $n_1 = 1, n_2 = 2$ and means that the transition has taken Lyman series from $n = 2$ to $n = 1$. Hence, the transition occurs from n_2 to n_1 in case of hydrogen spectrum.

Q. 34. Calculate the energy required for the process-

$$He^+(g) \longrightarrow He^{2+}(g) + e^-$$

The ionization energy for the H-atom in the ground state is 2.18×10^{-18} J atom^{-1}. [NCERT Ex. Q. 2.34, Page 71]

Ans. Ionization energy of the atom

$$E_n = \frac{2.18 \times 10^{-18} \times Z^2}{n^2} \text{ J atom}^{-1}$$

For H-atom, $Z = 1, n = 1$

$\therefore$ $E_n = 2.18 \times 10^{-18} \times (1)^2$
$= 2.18 \times 10^{-18}$ J atom^{-1}

$\therefore$ For He^+ ion, $z = 2, n = 1$

$E_n = 2.18 \times 10^{-18} \times (2)^2$
$= 8.72 \times 10^{-18}$ J

Q. 35. If the diameter of a carbon atom is 0.15 nm, calculate the number of carbon atoms which can be placed side by side in a straight line across length of scale of length 20 cm long.[NCERT Ex. Q. 2.35, Page 71]

Ans. Length of scale = 20 cm = 20×10^7 nm = 2×10^8 nm

Diameter of carbon atom = 0.15 nm

Number of C-atoms which can be placed side by side in the scale $= \frac{2 \times 10^8}{0.15} = 1.33 \times 10^9$

Q. 36. 2×10^8 atoms of carbon are arranged side by side. Calculate the radius of carbon atom if the length of this arrangement is 2.4 cm. [NCERT Ex. Q. 2.36, Page 71]

Ans. Given, length of the arrangement = 2.4 cm

Total number of C-atoms present = 2×10^8

Diameter of each C–atom $= \frac{2.4 \text{ cm}}{2 \times 10^8}$

$= 1.2 \times 10^{-8}$ cm

$\therefore$ Radius of C-atom $= \frac{1}{2} \times$ diameter of C – atom

$= \frac{1}{2} \times 1.2 \times 10^{-8}$

$= 6.0 \times 10^{-9}$ cm

$= 0.06$ nm

Q. 37. The diameter of zinc atom is 2.6 Å. Calculate (i) radius of zinc atom in pm and (ii) number of atoms present in a length of 1.6 cm if the zinc atoms are arranged side by side lengthwise. [NCERT Ex. Q. 2.37, Page 71]

Ans. Given, diameter of Zn – atom = 2.6 Å

(i) Radius of Zn atom $= \frac{2.6 \text{ Å}}{2} = 1.3$ Å

$= 1.3 \times 10^{-10}$ m

$= 130 \times 10^{-12}$ m

$= 130$ pm

(ii) Length of the scale = 1.6 cm = 1.6×10^{-2} m

$= 1.6 \times 10^{10}$ pm

Diameter of Zn atom = 2.6 Å = 2.6×10^{-10} m

$= 260 \times 10^{-12}$ m = 260 pm

$\therefore$ No. of Zn atoms placed side by side

$= \frac{1.6 \times 10^{10} \text{ pm}}{260 \text{ pm}}$

$= 6.154 \times 10^7$

Q. 38. A certain particle carries 2.5×10^{-16} C of static electric charge. Calculate the number of electrons present in it. [NCERT Ex. Q. 2.38, Page 71]

Ans. Given, Magnitude of charge (q) = 2.5×10^{-16} C

We know that,

Charge on one electron (e) = 1.6022×10^{-19} C

$\therefore$ Number of electrons present in particle

$= \frac{2.5 \times 10^{-16} \text{C}}{1.6022 \times 10^{-19} \text{C}}$

$= 1560$

Q. 39. In Millikan's experiment, static electric charge on the oil drops has been obtained by shining X – rays. If the static electric charge on the oil drop is -1.282×10^{-18}C, calculate the number of electrons present on it. [NCERT Ex. Q. 2.39, Page 71]

Ans. Electric charge on oil drops (q) = -1.282×10^{-18} C

Charge on an electron = -1.6022×10^{-19} C

∴ Number of electrons present on oil drop

$$= \frac{q}{e} = \frac{-1.282 \times 10^{-18}\,C}{-1.6022 \times 10^{-19}\,C} = 8$$

Q. 40. In Rutherford's experiment, generally the thin foil of heavy atoms, like gold, platinum etc. have been used to be bombarded by the α-particles. If the thin foil of light atoms like aluminium etc. is used, what difference would be observed from the above results ? [NCERT Ex. Q. 2.40, Page 71]

Ans. More number of α-particles will pass as the nucleus of the lighter atoms like aluminium is small, smaller number of α-particles will be deflected as the number of positive charges is less on the lighter nuclei.

Q. 41. Symbols $^{79}Br_{35}$ and ^{79}Br can be written, whereas symbol $^{35}_{79}$Br and ^{35}Br are not acceptable. Answer briefly. [NCERT Ex. Q. 2.41, Page 71]

Ans. $^{35}_{79}Br$ is not acceptable because atomic number should be written as subscript, while mass number should be written as superscript. ^{35}Br is not acceptable because atomic number of an element is fixed. However, mass number is not fixed as it depends upon the isotope taken. Hence, it is essential to indicate mass number.

Q. 42. An element with mass number 81 contains 31.7% more neutrons as compared to protons. Assign the atomic symbol. [NCERT Ex. Q. 2.42, Page 71]

Ans. Let the number of protons = x

∴ Number of neutrons = $x + \frac{x \times 31.7}{100}$

$= x + 0.317x$

Mass number of element = 81

∵ Mass number = No. of protons + No. of neutrons

$81 = x + x + 0.317x$

$81 = 2.317x$

∴ $x = \frac{81}{2.317} = 34.958 \approx 35$

∴ Number of protons = 35

Number of neutrons = Mass number – No. of protons

$= 81 - 35$

$= 46$

∵ Atomic number of element = No. of protons

$= 35$

∴ Symbol of atom is $^{81}_{35}$Br (Bromine).

Q. 43. An ion with mass number 37 possesses one unit of negative charge. If the ion contains 11.1% more neutrons than the electrons, find the symbol of the ion. [NCERT Ex. Q. 2.43, Page 71]

Ans. Let the number of electrons in an ion = x

∴ Number of neutrons, $n = x + \frac{11.1}{100}x$

$= 1.111\,x$

(As the number of neutrons are 11.1% more than the number of electrons.)

In the neutral atom, number of electrons,

$e^- = x - 1$

(as the ion carries – 1 charge) Similarly, number of protons, $p = x - 1$

we know that, mass number = $n + p = 37$

$1.111\,x + x - 1 = 37$

$2.111x = 37 + 1$

$2.111x = 38$

$x = \frac{38}{2.111}$

$= 18.0009 \approx 18$

Number of protons = $x - 1$

$= 18 - 1$

$= 17$

Therefore, the symbol of the ion is $^{37}_{17}Cl^-$

Q. 44. An ion with mass number 56 contains 3 units of positive charge and 30.4% more neutrons than electrons. Assign the symbol to this ion. [NCERT Ex. Q. 2.44, Page 71]

Ans. Mass number = 56

Let the number of electrons be x

Number of protons = $x + 3$

[∴ ion has 3 units of positive charge]

Number of neutrons = $x + \frac{30.4}{100}x$

Mass number = No. of protons + No. of neutrons.

$$56 = x + 3 + x + \frac{30.4}{100}x$$

or, $5600 = 200\,x + 300 + 30.4x$

or, $230.4\,x = 5300$

or, $x = \frac{5300}{230.4} = 23$

Number of electrons = 23

Number of protons = 23 + 3 = 26

Atomic Number = 26

Element is Fe

Symbol of ion is $^{56}_{26}Fe^{3+}$

Q. 45. Arrange the following type of radiations in increasing order of frequency: - (a) radiation from microwave oven (b) amber light from traffic signal (c) radiation from FM radio (d) cosmic rays from outer space and (e) X-rays [NCERT Ex. Q. 2.45, Page 71]

Ans. Increasing order of frequency of radiations –

Radiation from FM radio < Radiation from microwave oven < amber light from traffic signal <X- rays < cosmic rays from outer space.

Q. 46. Nitrogen laser produces a radiation at a wavelength of 337.1 nm. If the number of photons emitted is 5.6×10^{24}, calculate the power of this laser. [NCERT Ex. Q. 2.46, Page 71]

Ans. Given λ = 337.1 nm = 337.1×10^{-9}m

Number of photons emitted(N) = 5.6×10^{24}

Power of laser (E) = $\frac{Nhc}{\lambda}$

$$= \frac{5.6 \times 10^{24} \times 6.626 \times 10^{-34} \text{ J s} \times 3 \times 10^{8} \text{ ms}^{-1}}{337.1 \times 10^{-9} \text{ m}}$$

$= 3.3 \times 10^{6}$ J

Q. 47. Neon gas is generally used in the sign boards. If it emits strongly at 616 nm, calculate (a) the frequency of emission, (b) distance travelled by this radiation in 30 s (c) energy of quantum and (d) number of quanta present if it produces 2 J of energy.

[NCERT Ex. Q. 2.47, Page 71]

Ans. (a) Frequency (ν) of emission can be calculated as :

$$c = \nu \times \lambda$$

[where λ = wavelength = 616 nm = 616×10^{-9} m, c = velocity of light $= 3.0 \times 10^{8}$ ms^{-1}]

$$\nu = \frac{c}{\lambda} = \frac{3.0 \times 10^{8}}{616 \times 10^{-9}}$$

$= 4.87 \times 10^{14}$ s^{-1} (2)

(b) Distance travelled in 1 second = 3.0×10^{8} m

Distance travelled in 30 s

$= 30 \times 3.0 \times 10^{8}$ m

$= 9 \times 10^{9}$ m (1)

(c) Energy of the photon (quantum)

$E = h\nu = 6.625 \times 10^{-34} \times 4.87 \times 10^{14}$ J

$= 32.26 \times 10^{-20}$ J

(d) Number of quanta in 2J of energy

$$= \frac{\text{Total energy produced}}{\text{Energy of one quantum}}$$

$$= \frac{2}{32.26 \times 10^{-20}}$$

$= 6.2 \times 10^{18}$ quanta

Q. 48. In astronomical observations, signals observed from the distant stars are generally weak. If the photon detector receives a total of 3.15×10^{-18} J from the radiations of 600 nm, calculate the number of photons received by the detector. [NCERT Ex. Q. 2.48, Page 72]

Ans. Given, total energy received = 3.15×10^{-18} J

λ = 600 nm = 600×10^{-9}m = 6×10^{-7}m

$\therefore$ Energy of one photon $(E) = \frac{hc}{\lambda}$

$$= \frac{6.626 \times 10^{-34} \text{ J s} \times 3.0 \times 10^{8} \text{ m s}^{-1}}{6 \times 10^{-7} \text{ m}}$$

$= 3.313 \times 10^{-19}$ J

$\therefore$ Number of photons received by the detector

$$= \frac{\text{Total energy}}{\text{Energy of one photon}}$$

$$= \frac{3.15 \times 10^{-18} \text{ J}}{3.313 \times 10^{-19} \text{ J}} = 10$$

Q. 49.Lifetimes of the molecules in the excited states are often measured by using pulsed radiation source of duration nearly in the nano second range. If the radiation source has the duration of 2 ns and the number of photons emitted during the pulse source is 2.5×10^{15}, calculate the energy of the source.

[NCERT Ex. Q. 2.49, Page 72]

Ans. Duration of the radiation source = 2 *ns*

$\therefore$ Period = 2×10^{-9}s

$$\text{Frequency } (\nu) = \frac{1}{\text{Period}} = \frac{1}{2 \times 10^{-9}} \text{s}^{-1}$$

$= 0.5 \times 10^{9}$ s^{-1}

No. of photons emitted = 2.5×10^{15}

$\therefore$ Energy of the source = $nh\nu$

$= 2.5 \times 10^{15} \times 6.626 \times 10^{-34}$ J s $\times 0.5 \times 10^{9}$ s^{-1}

$= 8.28 \times 10^{-10}$ J

Q. 50.The longest wavelength doublet absorption transition is observed at 589 and 589.6 nm. Calculate the frequency of each transition and energy difference between two excited states.

[NCERT Ex. Q. 2.50, Page 72]

Ans. To find frequency (ν_1) ; λ_1 = 589 nm = 589×10^{-9} m (given)

To find frequency ν_2 ; λ_2 = 589.6 nm = 589.6×10^{-9} m (given)

$$\nu_1 = \frac{c}{\lambda_1} = \frac{3 \times 10^{8}}{589 \times 10^{-9}}$$

$= 5.0934 \times 10^{14}$ s^{-1}

$$\nu_2 = \frac{c}{\lambda_2} = \frac{3 \times 10^{8}}{589.6 \times 10^{-9}}$$

$= 5.0881 \times 10^{14}$ s^{-1}

Energy = $h\nu$

$E_1 = h\nu_1$

$E_2 = h\nu_2$

$\therefore \Delta E = E_1 - E_2 = h(\nu_1 - \nu_2)$

$= 6.626 \times 10^{-34}$ $(5.0934 \times 10^{14} - 5.0881 \times 10^{14})$

$= 6.626 \times 10^{-34} \times 0.0053 \times 10^{14}$

$= 0.0346 \times 10^{-20}$

$= 3.46 \times 10^{-22}$ J

Q. 51. The work function for caesium atom is 1.9 eV. Calculate (a) the threshold wavelength and (b) the threshold frequency of the radiation. If the caesium element is irradiated with a wavelength 500 nm, calculate the kinetic energy and the velocity of the ejected photoelectron. [NCERT Ex. Q. 2.51, Page 72]

Ans. Given, Work function (W_o) = 1.9 eV

$= 1.9 \times 1.602 \times 10^{-19}$ J

(a) Threshold wavelength $(\lambda_o) = \frac{C}{v}$

$$= \frac{3 \times 10^{8} \text{ m s}^{-1}}{4.59 \times 10^{14} \text{ s}^{-1}}$$

$= 0.6536 \times 10^{-6}$ m

$= 653.6 \times 10^{-9}$ m

$= 653.6$ nm

$\simeq 654$ nm

(b) Threshold frequency $(v) = \frac{W_0}{h}$

$$= \frac{1.9 \times 1.602 \times 10^{-19} \text{ J}}{6.626 \times 10^{-34} \text{ Js}}$$

$= 0.459 \times 10^{15}\ s^{-1}$

$= 4.59 \times 10^{14}\ s^{-1}$

Kinetic energy of photo electron = $h(v - v_0)$

$\because \quad \lambda = 500\ nm = 500 \times 10^{-9}\ m$

$\therefore \quad v = \frac{C}{\lambda} = \frac{3.0\times10^{8}\ ms^{-1}}{500\times10^{-9}\ m}$

$= 6.0 \times 10^{14}\ s^{-1}$

$\therefore$ K.E. $= 6.626 \times 10^{-34}$ Js $(6.0 \times 10^{14}\ s^{-1} - 4.59 \times 10^{14}\ s^{-1})$

$= 9.34 \times 10^{-20}$ J

$\because \quad K.E. = \frac{1}{2}mv^2$

Mass of electron (m) = 9.1×10^{-31} kg

$\therefore \quad V^2 = \frac{2K.E.}{m}$

$V = \sqrt{\frac{2K.E.}{m}}$

$= \sqrt{\frac{2\times9.34\times10^{-20}\ kg\,m^2\,s^{-2}}{9.1\times10^{-31}\ kg}}$

$= \sqrt{20.50\times10^{10}\ m^2\,s^{-2}}$

$V = 4.527 \times 10^{5}\ ms^{-1}$

Q. 52. Following results are observed when sodium metal is irradiated with different wavelengths. Calculate (a) threshold wavelength and (b) Planck's constant.

λ (nm)	**500**	**450**	**400**
$v \times 10^5$ s(cm s^{-1})	**2.55**	**4.35**	**5.35**

[NCERT Ex. Q. 2.52, Page 72]

Ans. Kinetic energy K.E. $= h(v - v_0) = \frac{1}{2}mv^2$

For first experiment,

$\lambda = 500\ nm = 500 \times 10^{-9}\ m$

$v = \frac{C}{\lambda} = \frac{3.0\times10^{8}\ ms^{-1}}{500\times10^{-9}\ m} = 6 \times 10^{14}\ s^{-1}$

$\therefore h(6\times 10^{14}\ s^{-1} - v_o) = \frac{1}{2}\ m\ (2.55 \times 10^{3}\ ms^{-1})^2 \quad \ldots\ldots\ (i)$

For second experiment,

$\lambda = 450\ nm = 450 \times 10^{-9}m$

$\therefore \quad v = \frac{C}{\lambda} = \frac{3.0\times10^{8}\ m\ s^{-1}}{450\times10^{-9}\ m}$

$= 6.67 \times 10^{14}\ s^{-1}$

$\therefore h(6.67 \times 10^{14}\ s^{-1} - v_0) = \frac{1}{2}\ m\ (4.35 \times 10^{3}m\ s^{-1})^2 \quad \ldots\ (ii)$

For third experiment,

$\lambda = 400\ nm = 400 \times 10^{-9}\ m$

$\therefore \quad v = \frac{C}{\lambda} = \frac{3.0\times10^{8}\ m\ s^{-1}}{400\times10^{-19}\ m}$

$= 7.5 \times 10^{14}\ s^{-1}$

$\therefore h(7.5 \times 10^{14}\ s^{-1} - v_o) = \frac{1}{2}\ m\ (5.35 \times 10^{3}m\ s^{-1})^2 \quad \ldots(iii)$

On dividing equation (ii) by equation (i), we get

$\frac{h(6.67\times10^{14}\ s^{-1} - v_o)}{h(6\times10^{14}\ s^{-1} - v_o)} = \frac{\frac{1}{2}m\ (4.35\times10^{3}\ m\ s^{-1})^2}{\frac{1}{2}m\ (2.55\times10^{3}\ m\ s^{-1})^2}$

$\frac{6.67\times10^{14}\ s^{-1} - v_o}{6\times10^{14}\ s^{-1} - v_o} = \frac{(4.35)^2}{(2.55)^2} = 2.91$

$6.67 \times 10^{14}\ s^{-1} - v_o = 2.91\ (6 \times 10^{14}\ s^{-1} - v_o)$

$= 17.46 \times 10^{14}\ s^{-1} - 2.91\ v_o$

$2.91\ v_o - v_o = 17.46 \times 10^{14}\ s^{-1} - 6.67 \times 10^{14}\ s^{-1}$

$1.91\ v_o = 10.79 \times 10^{14}\ s^{-1}$

$\therefore \quad v_o = \frac{10.79\times10^{14}\ s^{-1}}{1.91}$

$= 5.649 \times 10^{14}\ s^{-1}$

$\therefore \quad \lambda_o = \frac{C}{v_o} = \frac{3.0\times10^{8}\ m\ s^{-1}}{5.649\times10^{14}\ s^{-1}}$

$= 5.31 \times 10^{-7}\ m$

$= \frac{h\times(3\times10^{8})}{10^{-9}}\left(\frac{1}{400} - \frac{1}{531}\right)$

$= \frac{1}{2}(9.11\times10^{-31})(5.20\times10^{6})^2$

$= 6.66 \times 10^{-34}$ Js

Q. 53. The ejection of photoelectron from the silver metal in the photoelectric effect experiment can be stopped by applying the voltage of 0.35 V when the radiation 256.7 nm is used. Calculate the work function for silver metal. [NCERT Ex. Q. 2.53, Page 72]

Ans. Voltage applied (V_o) = 0.35V

$\lambda = 256.7\ nm = 256.7 \times 10^{-9}m$

Energy $(E)\ \frac{hc}{\lambda}$

$= \frac{6.626\times10^{-34}\ J\ s\times3.0\times10^{8}\ m\ s^{-1}}{256.7\times10^{-9}\ m}$

$= 7.74 \times 10^{-19}$ J

$= \frac{7.74\times10^{-19}}{1.602\times10^{-19}} = 4.83eV$

Applied voltage gives the kinetic energy to electron

K.E. = e V_0

$= 1.6 \times 10^{-19} \times 0.35$

$= 0.56 \times 10^{19}$ J

$= \frac{0.56\times10^{-19}}{1.602\times10^{-19}} = 0.35eV$

$\therefore$ Work function (W_0) = Energy of incident radiation – Kinetic energy

$= (4.83 - 0.35)$ eV

$= 4.48$ eV

Q. 54. If the photon of the wavelength 150 pm strikes an atom and one of its inner bound electrons is ejected out with a velocity of 1.5 × 10^7 ms^{-1}, calculate the energy with which it is bound to the nucleus.

[NCERT Ex. Q. 2.54, Page 72]

Ans. Wave length of photon (λ) = 150 pm

$= 150 \times 10^{-12}$ m

Velocity (V) $= 1.5 \times 10^7$ m s^{-1}

$$E = \frac{hc}{\lambda} = \frac{6.626\times 10^{-34}\ \text{J.s}\times 3.0\times 10^8\ \text{ms}^{-1}}{150\times 10^{-12}\ \text{m}}$$

$$= 0.1325 \times 10^{-14} = 13.25 \times 10^{-16}\ \text{J}$$

K. E. of ejected electrons $= \frac{1}{2}mv^2$

$$= \frac{1}{2}\times 9.1\times 10^{-31}\ \text{kg}\times(1.5\times 10^7\ \text{m s}^{-1})^2$$

$$= 10.24 \times 10^{-17}\text{J}$$

$$= 1.024 \times 10^{-16}\ \text{J}$$

Work function (W_0) $= hv_0$

$$= hv - \frac{1}{2}mv^2$$

$$= \text{E} - \text{K.E.}$$

$$= 13.25 \times 10^{-16}\text{J} - 1.024 \times 10^{-16}\ \text{J}$$

$$= 12.226 \times 10^{-16}\ \text{J}$$

$$= \frac{12.226\times 10^{-16}}{1.602\times 10^{-19}}\text{eV}$$

$$= 7.63 \times 10^3\ \text{eV}$$

Q. 55. Emission transitions in the Paschen series end at orbit n = 3 and start from orbit n and can be represented as υ = 3.29 × 10^{15} (Hz) [1/3^2 – 1/n^2]
Calculate the value of n if transition is observed at 1285 nm. find the region of the spectrum.

[NCERT Ex. Q. 2.55, Page 72]

Ans. According to the question

$$\upsilon = 3.29 \times 10^{15}\ (\text{Hz})\left[\frac{1}{3^2}-\frac{1}{n^2}\right]$$

But $\upsilon = \frac{c}{\lambda}$

Hence $\frac{c}{\lambda} = 3.29 \times 10^{15}\left[\frac{1}{3^2}-\frac{1}{n^2}\right]$

or $\frac{3.0\times 10^8}{1285\times 10^{-9}} = 3.29 \times 10^{15}\left[\frac{1}{9}-\frac{1}{n^2}\right]$

$$\therefore \frac{1}{9}-\frac{1}{n^2} = \frac{3.0\times 10^8}{1285\times 10^{-9}\times 3.29\times 10^{15}} = 0.07096$$

or $\frac{1}{n^2} = \frac{1}{9} - 0.07096 = 0.401511$

$$\therefore n^2 = \frac{1}{0.0401511} = 24.9059$$

$\therefore$ $n = 5$

$\therefore$ The electron jumps from $n = 5$ to $n = 3$

Since this is a transition occurring in the Paschen series and Paschen series lie in the infrared portion of light.

$\therefore$ Region of the spectrum is infrared, which can also be calculated from the wavelength λ.

Q. 56. Calculate the wavelength for the emission transition if it starts from the orbit having radius 1.3225 nm and ends at 211.6 pm. Name the series to which this transition belongs and the region of the spectrum.

[NCERT Ex. Q. 2.56, Page 72]

Ans. $r_1 = 1.3225$ nm = 1322.5 pm

$r_2 = 211.6$ pm

Radius of nth orbit

$$r_n = \frac{52.9\,n^2}{\text{Z}}\text{pm}$$

$$r_1 = \frac{52.9\times n_1^2}{\text{Z}}$$

$$1322.5 = \frac{52.9\times n_1^2}{\text{Z}} \quad \ldots\ldots.(i)$$

$$r_2 = \frac{52.9\times n_2^2}{\text{Z}}$$

$$211.6 = \frac{52.9\,n_2^2}{\text{Z}} \quad \ldots\ldots.(ii)$$

Divide equation (*i*) from equation (*ii*), we get,

$$\frac{1322.5}{211.6} = \frac{\frac{52.9\,n_1^2}{\text{Z}}}{\frac{52.9\,n_2^2}{\text{Z}}} = \frac{n_1^2}{n_2^2}$$

$$\therefore \frac{n_1^2}{n_2^2} = 6.25$$

or $\frac{n_1}{n_2} = 2.5$

If $n_1 = 2$, $n_2 = 5$, so, the transition is from 5th orbit to 2nd orbit and it belongs to Balmer series

$$\bar{\upsilon} = \frac{1}{\lambda} = 1.09677\times 10^7\left(\frac{1}{n_1^2}-\frac{1}{n_2^2}\right)m^{-1}$$

$$\frac{1}{\lambda} = 1.09677\times 10^7\left(\frac{1}{(2)^2}-\frac{1}{(5)^2}\right)m^{-1}$$

$$= 1.09677 \times 10^7 \times \frac{21}{100}$$

$$= 2.303 \times 10^6\ \text{m}^{-1}$$

$$\lambda = \frac{1}{2.303\times 10^6\ m^{-1}} = 0.43\times 10^{-6}\ m$$

$$= 434.0215 \times 10^{-9}\ \text{m}$$

$$= 434\ \text{nm}$$

It belongs to visible region.

Q. 57. Dual behavior of matter proposed by de Broglie led to the discovery of electron microscope often used for the highly magnified images of biological molecules and other type of material. If the velocity of the electron in this microscope is 1.6 × 10^6 ms^{-1}, calculate de Broglie wavelength associated with this electron.

[NCERT Ex. Q. 2.58, Page 72]

Ans. $V = 1.6 \times 10^6$ m/s

According to de Broglie equation,

$$\lambda = \frac{h}{mv} = \frac{6.626\times10^{-34}\text{ J s}}{9.1\times10^{-31}\text{ kg}\times1.6\times10^{6}\text{ m s}^{-1}}$$

$$= 0.455 \times 10^{-9}\text{ m}$$

$$= 455 \times 10^{-12}\text{ m} = 455\text{ pm}$$

Q. 58. Similar to electron diffraction, neutron diffraction microscope is also used for the determination of the structure of molecules. If the wavelength used here is 800 pm, calculate the characteristic velocity associated with the neutron. [NCERT Ex. Q. 2.58, Page 72]

Ans. $\lambda = 800\text{ pm} = 800 \times 10^{-12}\text{ m}$

Mass of neutron (m) = 1.675×10^{-27} kg

According to de Broglie equation,

$$\lambda = \frac{h}{mv}$$

$$v = \frac{h}{m\lambda}$$

$$= \frac{6.626\times10^{-34}\text{ J s}}{1.675\times10^{-27}\text{ kg}\times800\times10^{-12}\text{ m}}$$

$$= 0.494 \times 10^{3}\text{ ms}^{-1}$$

$$= 4.94 \times 10^{2}\text{ ms}^{-1}$$

Q. 59. If the velocity of the electron in Bohr's first orbit is 2.19 × 10⁶ ms⁻¹, calculate the de Broglie wavelength associated with it. [NCERT Ex. Q. 2.59, Page 72]

Ans. $V = 2.19 \times 10^6$ m/s

Mass of electron (m) = 9.1×10^{-31} kg

According to de Broglie equation,

$$\lambda = \frac{h}{mv}$$

$$= \frac{6.626\times10^{-34}\text{ kg m}^2\text{s}^{-1}}{9.1\times10^{-31}\text{ kg}\times2.19\times10^{6}\text{ ms}^{-1}}$$

$$= 3.32 \times 10^{-10}\text{ m}$$

$$= 332 \times 10^{-10}\text{ m}$$

$$= 332\text{ pm}$$

Q. 60. The velocity associated with a proton moving in a potential difference of 1000 V is 4.37 × 10⁵ ms⁻¹. If the hockey ball of mass 0.1 kg is moving with this velocity, calculate the wavelength associated with this velocity. [NCERT Ex. Q. 2.60, Page 72]

Ans. Velocity (v) of the hockey ball

$$= 4.37 \times 10^5\text{ ms}^{-1}$$

Mass of the ball = 0.1 kg

$$\therefore \quad \lambda\text{ (wavelength)} = \frac{h}{m\times v} = \frac{6.625\times10^{-34}}{0.1\times4.37\times10^{5}}\text{ m}$$

$$= 15.16 \times 10^{-39}\text{m}$$

$$= 1.516 \times 10^{-38}\text{m}$$

Q. 61. If the position of the electron is measured within an accuracy of ± 0.002 nm, calculate the uncertainty in the momentum of the electron. Suppose the momentum of the electron is h /(4 π × 0.05) nm, is there any problem in defining this value ? [NCERT Ex. Q. 2.61, Page 72]

Ans. $\Delta x = 0.002$ nm

$$= 2 \times 10^{-3}\text{ nm}$$

$$= 2 \times 10^{-12}\text{ m}$$

$$\Delta x \times \Delta p = \frac{h}{4\pi}$$

$$\therefore \quad \Delta p = \frac{h}{4\pi\Delta x}$$

$$= \frac{6.626\times10^{-34}\text{ kg m}^2\text{s}^{-1}}{4\times3.14\times(2\times10^{-12}\text{m})}$$

$$= 2.638 \times 10^{-23}\text{ kg ms}^{-1}$$

$$\text{Actual momentum} = \frac{h}{4\pi\times0.05\text{ nm}}$$

$$= \frac{h}{4\pi\times5\times10^{-11}\text{ mn}}$$

$$= \frac{6.626\times10^{-34}\text{ kg m}^2\text{s}^{-1}}{4\times3.14\times5\times10^{-11}\text{m}}$$

$$= 1.055 \times 10^{-24}\text{ kg ms}^{-1}$$

It cannot be defined as the actual magnitude of the momentum is smaller than the uncertainty.

Q. 62. The quantum number of six electrons are given below. Arrange them in order of increasing energies. If any of these combination/s has/have the same energy lists:

(1) n = 4, l = 2, $m_l = -2$, $m_s = -½$
(2) n = 3, l = 2, $m_l = 1$, $m_s = +½$
(3) n = 4, l = 1, $m_l = 0$, $m_s = +½$
(4) n = 3, l = 2, $m_l = -2$, $m_s = -½$
(5) n = 3, l = 1, $m_l = 1$, $m_s = +½$
(6) n = 4, l = 1, $m_l = 0$, $m_s = +½$

[NCERT Ex. Q. 2.62, Page 72]

Ans.

	Quantum number	Sub-shell	$n + l$
(1)	$n = 4, l = 2$, $ml = -2, ms = -½$	4d	4 + 2 = 6
(2)	$n = 3, l = 2$, $ml = 1, ms = +½$	3d	3 + 2 = 5
(3)	$n = 4, l = 1$, $ml = 0, ms = +½$	4p	4 + 1 = 5
(4)	$n = 3, l = 2$, $ml = -2, ms = -½$	3d	3 + 2 = 5
(5)	$n = 3, l = 1$, $ml = -1, ms +½$	3p	3 + 1 = 4
(6)	$n = 4, l = 1$, $ml = 0, ms = +½$	4p	4 + 1 = 5

Increasing order of energies of above orbitals – $3p < 3d = 3d < 4p = 4p < 4d$

Q. 63. The bromine atom possess 35 electrons. It contains 6 electrons in 2p orbital, 6 electrons in 3 p orbital and 5 electrons in 4p orbital. Which of these electron experiences the lowest effective nuclear charge? [NCERT Ex. Q. 2.63, Page 73]

Ans. Br = 2, 8, 18, 7

$$= 1s^2, 2s^2 2p6, 3s^2 3p^6 3d^{10}, 4s^2 4p^5$$

Since, effective nuclear charge decreases as the distance of the orbitals increases from the nucleus.

Therefore, 4p electrons experience the lowest effective nuclear charge.

Q. 64. Among the following pairs of orbitals which orbital will experience the large effective nuclear charge?

(i) 2*s* and 3*s* (ii) 4*d* and 4*f* (iii) 3*d* and 3*p*

[NCERT Ex. Q. 2.64, Page 73]

Ans. Since, the effective nuclear charge decreases as the distance of the orbitals increases from the nucleus.

(i) Since 2*s* is closer to the nucleus than 3*s*, so 2*s*-orbital experiences larger effective nuclear charge than 3*s*.

(ii) Since 4*d* is closer to the nucleus than 4*f*, so 4*d*-orbital experiences larger effective nuclear charge than 4*f*.

(iii) Since 3*p* is closer to the nucleus than 3*d*, so 3*p*-orbital experiences larger effective nuclear charge than 3*d*.

Q. 65. The unpaired electrons in Al are Si are present in 3p orbital. Which electrons will experience more effective nuclear charge from the nucleus?

[NCERT Ex. Q. 2.65, Page 73]

Ans. $_{13}Al = 2, 8, 3 = 1s^2, 2s^22p^6, 3s^23p^1$

$_{14}Si = 2, 8, 4 = 1s^2, 2s^22p^6, 3s^23p^2$

Since Si (+4) has higher nuclear charge than aluminium (+3). Therefore, 3*p* unpaired electrons of Si will experience more effective nuclear charge than Al.

Q. 66. Indicate the number of unpaired electrons in

(a) P (b) Si (c) Cr

(d) Fe and (e) Kr

[NCERT Ex. Q. 2.66, Page 73]

Ans. (a) $_{15}P = 2, 8, 5 = 1s^2, 2s^22p^6, 3s^23p^3$

It has three unpaired electrons. | 1 | 1 | 1 | (3*d*)

(b) $_{14}Si = 2, 8, 4 = 1s^2, 2s^22p^6, 3s^23p^2$

It has two unpaired electrons | 1 | 1 | | (3*d*)

(c) $_{24}Cr = 2, 8, 13, 1$

$= 1s^2, 2s^22p^6, 3s^23p^63d^5, 4s^1$

It has six unpaired electrons.

| 1 | 1 | 1 | 1 | 1 | (3*d*) | 1 | (4*s*)

(d) $_{26}Fe = 2, 8, 14, 2$

$= 1s^2, 2s^22p^6, 3s^23p^6, 3d^64s^2$

It has four unpaired electrons

| ⥮ | 1 | 1 | 1 | 1 | (3*d*)

(e) $_{36}Kr = 2, 8, 18, 8$

$= 1s^2, 2s^22p^6, 3s^23p^63d^{10}, 4s^24p^6$

It has no unpaired electron.

Q. 67. (a) How many sub-shells are associated with $n = 4$?

(b) How many electrons will be present in the sub-shells having m_s value of –½ for $n = 4$?

[NCERT Ex. Q. 2.67, Page 73]

Ans. (a) For $n = 4$

$l = 0$ (*s*-sub shell)

1 (*p*-sub shell)

2 (*d*-sub shell)

3 (*f*-sub shell)

∴ There are four sub-shells associated with $n = 4$. **(1)**

(b) Number of orbitals in 4th shell $= n^2 = (4)^2 = 16$

Maximum number of electrons present in orbital = 2.

Each orbital has one electron with $m_s = -\frac{1}{2}$

So, there are 16 electrons with $m_s = -\frac{1}{2}$

❑❑

CLASSIFICATION OF ELEMENTS AND PERIODICITY IN PROPERTIES

CHAPTER 3

- **Classification of Elements:**
  Arranging the elements in such a way that similar elements are placed together while dissimilar elements are separated from one another is known as classification of elements.
  On the basis of this classification, periodic table may be defined as:
  The arrangement of the known elements according to their properties in a tabular form.

Genesis of Periodic Classification

- **Historical Development of Periodic Table:**
  Some of the earlier important attempts to classify the elements are briefly summed up below:

(i) Dobereiner's triads: In 1829, a German scientist, Johann Dobereiner classified the elements in groups of three elements called **triads.**

The elements in a triad had similar properties and the atomic weight of the middle member of each triad was very close to the arithmetic mean of the other two elements.

DOBEREINER'S TRIADS

Li	Lithium	Ca	Calcium	Cl	Chlorine
Na	Sodium	Sr	Strontium	Br	Bromine
K	Potassium	Ba	Barium	I	Iodine

Elements	**Atomic weight**
Lithium	7
Sodium	23
Potassium	39

Atomic weight of Na $= 23$

Mean of other two elements $= \frac{7+39}{2} = 23$

(ii) Newlands' Law of Octaves: In 1865, John Alexander Newlands gave Law of Octaves which state that "when the elements are arranged in the increasing order of atomic weights, the properties of every eighth element are similar to the first one."

Newlands' called this relation as the law of octaves due to similarity with the musical scale.

Table 3.2 : Newland's Octaves

Element	**Li**	**Be**	**B**	**C**	**N**	**O**	**F**
At. wt.	7	9	11	12	14	16	19
Element	**Na**	**Mg**	**Al**	**Si**	**P**	**S**	**Cl**
At. wt.	23	24	27	29	31	32	35.5
Element	**K**	**Ca**					
At. wt.	39	40					

(iii) Mendeleev's Periodic Law: The physical and chemical properties of elements are periodic function of their atomic weights.

Table 3.3 : Mendeleev's Prediction for the Elements ***Eka-aluminium*** (Gallium) and ***Eka-silicon*** (Germanium)

Property	***Eka-aluminium* (predicated)**	**Gallium (found)**	***Eka-silicon* (predicted)**	**Germanium (found)**
Atomic weight	**68**	**70**	**72**	**72.6**
Density/(g/cm^3)	**5.9**	**5.94**	**5.5**	**5.36**
Melting point /K	**Low**	**302.93**	**High**	**1231**
Formula of oxide	E_2O_3	Ga_2O_3	EO_2	GeO_2
Formula of chloride	ECl_3	$GaCl_3$	ECl_4	$GeCl_4$

- **Characteristics of Mendeleev's Periodic Table:**

(i) Eight vertical columns, called groups: Except for VIII group, each group is further sub-divided in A and B. This sub-division is made on the basis of difference in their properties.

(ii) Seven horizontal rows, called periods.

Significance of Mendeleev's Periodic Table:

(i) Instead of studying properties of elements separately, they can be studied in groups containing elements with same properties. It led to the systematic study of the elements.

Classification of Elements and Periodicity in Properties

Genesis of Periodic Classification

- Law of Triads: Johann Dobereiner (1829)
- Law of Octaves: John Alexander Newlands (1865)
- Periodic Law: Dimitri Mendeleev and Lothar Meyer. It states that the properties of the elements are periodic function of their atomic weights.
- Modern Periodic Law: Henry Moseley (1913) It states that the physical and chemical properties of the elements are periodic functions of their atomic numbers. ; Horizontal rows – Periods – are numbered from 1 to 7 Vertical columns – Groups – are numbered from 1 to 18.

IUPAC Nomenclature of Elements with Atomic numbers > 100:

Derived from the atomic number of element using numerical roots for 0 and numbers 1-9 and "ium" is added at the end.

Properties of Elements based on Electronic Configuration

- Electronic Configuration is the distribution of electrons into orbitals of an atom.
- In periods: Number of elements in each period is twice the number of atomic orbitals available in the energy level that is being filled.
- Group wise: Elements in same group have similar valence shell electronic configurations. Same number of electrons in outer orbitals and similar properties. These are classified into four blocks, i.e., *s*-block, *p*-block, *d*-block and *f*-block.

Periodic Table Classification based on Types of Elements

s-Block Elements

- Group 1 (alkali metals) and Group 2 (alkaline earth metals)
- Outermost configuration is ns^1 or ns^2
- Reactive with low IE.
- Metallic character and reactivity increases down the group.

p-Block elements

- Group 13 to 18.
- Also called as representatives or main group elements
- Outermost configuration varies from $ns^2\ np^1$ to $ns^2\ np^6$
- At the end of period are low reactive noble gases.
- Halogens and Chalcogens have high negative electron gain enthalpies.
- Metallic character increases down the group.

d-Block: Elements

- Group 3-12
- Outer configuration is $(n-1)\ d^{1-10}\ ns^2\ np^6$
- Forms coloured ions.
- Exhibit variable valency, paramagnetism.
- Also called as Transition elements.
- Some are used as catalysts.

f-Block: Elements

- Also called as Inner Transition Elements.
- Contains Lanthanoids and Actinoids.
- Outer configuration ie $(n-2)\ f^{1-14}\ (n-1)\ d^{0-1} ns^2$
- All are metals.
- Actinoids are radioactive.

Purpose

To ease out difficulty in studying individually the chemistry of all the elements and their compounds.

Periodic Trends in Properties of Elements

Properties	Group	Period
(a) Atomic Radius : Distance from the centre of the nucleus to the outermost shell containing electrons.	Increases	Decreases
(b) Electron Gain Enthalpy : Energy released when a neutral isolated gaseous atom accepts an electron from anion.	Becomes less negative	Becomes more negative
(c) Ionization Energy: The minimum amount of energy required to remove the electron from the outermost orbit of an isolated atom in gaseous state.	Decreases	Increases
(d) Electronegativity : Tendency of an atom to attract the shared pair of electrons towards itself.	Decreases	Increases
(e) Electron Affinity	Decreases	Increases
(f) Valency: Number of univalent atoms which combine with an atom of given element.	No Change	Increase from 1 to 4 and then decrease from 4 to 0.
(g) Metallic Character:	Increases	Decreases
(h) Non–Metallic Character:	Decreases	Increases

Trace the Mind Map
- First Level
- Second Level
- Third Level

(ii) Prediction of new elements: At his time, only 56 elements were known. He left blank spaces for unknown elements.

(iii) Mendeleev's periodic table corrected the doubtful atomic weights.

- **Defects in the Mendeleev's Periodic Table:**

(i) Hydrogen was placed in group IA: However, it resembles both group IA elements (alkali metals) and VII A (halogens). Therefore, the position of hydrogen in the periodic table is **anomalous or controversial.**

(ii) Anomalous pairs of elements: Some elements with higher atomic weight like Argon (39.9) precede potassium (39.1) with lower atomic weight.

(iii) Based upon atomic weights, **isotopes of an element could be assigned different groups** but as they are the atoms of same element (with only difference in their molecular mass) they must be in same group.

(iv) Some dissimilar elements are grouped together while some similar elements are placed in different groups. For example, alkali metals in group IA which are highly reactive are in the same group as coinage metals like Cu, Ag, Au of group IB. At the same time, certain chemically similar elements like Cu (group IB) and Hg (group IIB) have been placed in different groups.

(v) Position of elements of group VIII: No proper place was allotted to nine elements of group VIII which have been arranged in three triads without any justification.

Modern Periodic Law

- It states that "The physical and chemical properties of the elements are periodic functions of their atomic number."

  According to the recommendations of IUPAC, the groups are numbered from 1 to 18 replacing the older notation of groups IA ... VIIA, VIII, IB ... VIIB and 0.

  There are 7 periods. The first period contains 2 elements. The subsequent periods contain 8, 8, 18, 18, 32 elements respectively. The 7th period is incomplete and the 6th period would have a theoretical maximum of 32 elements. In this form of periodic table, the elements of both sixth and seventh periods (lanthanoids and actinoids respectively) are placed in separate panels at the bottom.

- **Long Form of Periodic Table:**

  General characteristics of the long form of the periodic table:

(i) There are in all, 18 vertical columns or 18 groups in the long form periodic table.

(ii) These groups are numbered from 1 to 18 starting from the left.

(iii) There are seven horizontal rows called **periods** in the long form of periodic table. Thus, there are seven periods in the long form of periodic table.

First period	**2 elements**	**Shortest period**
Second and Third period	8 elements each	Short period
Fourth and Fifth period	18 elements each	Long period
Sixth period and Seventh period	32 elements each	Longest period

(iv) The elements of group 1, 2 and 13 to 17 are called the **main group elements.** These are also called **typical or representative or normal elements.**

(v) The elements of group 3 to 12 are called **transition elements.**

(vi) Elements with atomic number 58 to 71 (Ce to Lu) occurring after lanthanum (La) are called **Lanthanoids.** Elements with atomic number 90 to 103 (Th to Lr) are called **Actinoids**. These elements are called *f*-block elements and also as inner-transition elements.

- **Defects of long form of the periodic table**

- In periodic table, the position of hydrogen is not clear.
- It is placed in the separate box just above the group I.
- Lanthanoids and actinoids have not been merged with in the main body of the periodic table.

Scan to know more about this topic

Mendeleev's Periodic Table

Nomenclature of Element with Atomic Number Greater than 100

(i) The name is derived directly from the atomic number of the element using the latin numeral roots.

(ii) The symbol of the element is composed of the initial letters of the numeral roots which make up the name.

(iii) The root 'un' is pronounced with a long 'u' to rhyme with 'moon'. In the element names, each root is to be pronounced separately.

Electronic Configuration of Elements and the Periodic Table

- We can classify the elements into four blocks viz, s-block, *p*-block, *d*-block and *f*-block depending on the type of atomic orbitals that are being filled with electrons.

- **Electronic Configuration in Periods:** The period indicates the value of *n* for the outermost or valence shell.

  It can be readily seen that the number of elements in each period is twice the number of atomic orbitals available in the energy level that is being filled.

(i) Elements in first period: The first period (n = 1) starts with the filling of the lowest level (1s) and therefore has two elements – hydrogen (1s^1) and helium (1s^2) when the first shell (K) is completed.

(ii) Elements in second period: There are 8 elements, in the second period $n = 2$ (L shell) starting from lithium $1s^2, 2s^1$ to neon $1s^2, 2s^22p^6$.

(iii) Elements in third period: There are 8 elements in third period $n = 3$ (M shell) starting from Sodium $1s^2$, $2s^2, 2p^6, 3s^1$ to Argon, $1s^2, 2s^2, 2p^6, 3s^2\ 3p^6$

(iv) Elements in fourth period: There are 18 elements in $n = 4$ (N shell) starting from Potassium $1s^2, 2s^2, 2p^6, 3s^2, 3p^6, 4s^1$ to Krypton $1s^2, 2s^2, 2p^6, 3s^2\ 3p^6, 4s^2, 3d^{10}\ 4p^6$.

(v) Elements in fifth period: It starts with Rb (37) with 5s orbital followed by filling of 4*d* orbitals, then 5*p* orbitals and ends at Xe (54), having total 18 elements forming 4*d* transition series.

(vi) Elements in sixth period: It has 32 elements forming lanthanoid series and successive electrons are filled in 6*s*, 4*f*, 5*d* and 6*p* orbitals, in that order.

(vii) Elements in seventh period: This period corresponds to $n = 7$ forming actinoid series and just like sixth period it involves the filling of 7*s*, 5*f*, 6*d* and 7*p*. This period contains synthetic or man-made radioactive elements.

Group-wise Electronic Configuration: Elements in a group have similar electronic configuration, same number of electrons in valence orbitals and similar properties, e.g., Group 1 (alkali) metals have general electronic configuration ns^1.

Position of Helium: The electronic configuration of helium is $1s^2$. So it should be in *s*-block, but it is placed in *p*-block due to the presence of completely filled valence shell ($1s^2$) and similarity in properties with other noble gases.

Position of Hydrogen: Electronic configuration of hydrogen is $1s^1$. Because of the presence of only one electron in *s*-orbital, it can be placed in group 1 with alkali metals and it also achieves the electronic configuration of inert gas so, it can also be placed in 17 group.

Electronic Configurations and Types of Elements

s-Block Elements:

- The elements of group 1 **(alkali metals)** and group 2 **(alkaline earth metals)** which have ns^1 and ns^2 outermost electronic configuration belong to the *s*-block elements.
- They are all reactive metals with low ionization enthalpies. They lose the outermost electron(s) readily to form +1 ion (in the case of alkali metals) or +2 ion (in the case of alkaline earth metals).
- The metallic character and the reactivity increase as we go down the group. Because of high reactivity they are never found pure in nature.
- The compounds of the *s*-block elements, with the exception of those of lithium and beryllium are predominantly ionic.

p-Block Elements:

- The *p*-block elements comprise those belonging to groups 13 to 18 and these together with the *s*-block elements are called the **Representative Elements or Main Group Elements.**
- The outermost electronic configuration varies from ns^2np^1 to ns^2np^6 in each period. At the end of each period is a noble gas element with a closed valence shell ns^2np^6 configuration. All the orbitals in the valence shell of the noble gases are completely filled by electrons and it is very difficult to alter this stable arrangement by the addition or removal of electrons. The noble gases exhibit very low chemical reactivity due to completely filled valence shell.
- Preceding the noble gas family are chemically important groups of non-metals, i.e., chalcogens and halogens.
- The non-metallic character increases as we move from left to right across a period and metallic character increases as we go down the group.

d-Block Elements (Transition Elements):

- These are the elements of Group 3 to 12 in the centre of the Periodic Table.
- These are characterised by the filling of inner $(n-1)$ *d* orbitals by electrons and are therefore referred to as. These elements have the outer electronic configuration $(n-1)d^{1-10}ns^{0-2}$. They are all metals.
- However, Zn, Cd and Hg which have the electronic configuration, $(n-1)d^{10}\ ns^2$ do not show most of the properties of transition elements.

f-Block Elements (Inner-Transition Elements):

- The two rows of elements at the bottom of the Periodic Table, called **Lanthanoids**, Ce (Z = 58) – Lu (Z = 71) and Actinoids, Th (Z = 90) – Lr (Z = 103) are characterised by the outer electronic configuration $(n-2)f^{1-14}\ (n-1)d^{0-1}\ ns^2$.
- They all are metals. The chemistry of the early actinoids is more complicated than the corresponding lanthanoids due to large number of oxidation states.
- Actinoids are radioactive in nature.

Scan to know more about this topic

Periodic Table of Elements

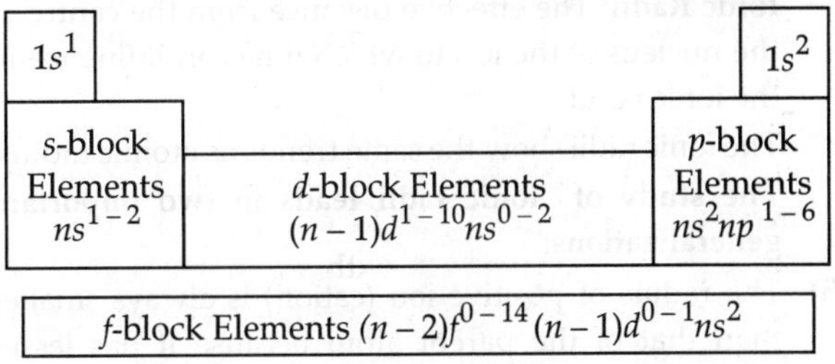

Division of Periodic Table into *s*, *p*, *d*, *f*-Blocks

Metals, Non-metals and Metalloids:

(i) Metals:

- Metals comprise more than 78% of all known elements and appear on the left side of the Periodic Table.
- Metals are usually solid at room temperature (Mercury is an exception ; gallium and caesium also have very low melting point 303 K and 302 K).
- Metals usually have high melting and boiling point except gallium and caesium.

(ii) Non-Metals

- These are present only in *p*-block and appear on the right hand side of the periodic table.
- These can be either solid or gases at room temperature exceptional case is bromine (which is liquid at room temperature).
- Melting and boiling points are very low except boron and carbon.
- They are brittle and neither malleable nor ductile.

(iii) Metalloids: The elements like silicon, germanium, arsenic, antimony and tellurium (Si, Ge, As, Sb, Te) which show properties of both metals and non–metals are called Metalloids.

Periodic Trends in Properties of Elements

- **Atomic Radii:** The term atomic radius means the distance from the centre of the nucleus to the outermost shell of electrons.
- On the basis of the nature of combining atoms, atomic radius can be of following types:
- **Covalent Radius:** Covalent radius may be defined as "one-half of the distance between the centre of nuclei of two similar atoms bonded by a single covalent bond.

For homonuclear molecules,

$$r_{covalent} = \frac{\text{Internuclear distance between two bonded atoms}}{2}$$

- **Metallic Radius:** Metallic radius is taken as one-half of the internuclear distance between the two neighbouring atoms of a metal in a metallic lattice.
- **van der Waals Radius:** Noble gas atoms are held together by weak van der Waals forces of attraction. The van der Waals radius is half of the distance between the centre of nuclei of atoms.

Variation of Atomic Radii in the Periodic Table:

- **Variation in a period:** In general, the atomic radii decrease with increase in atomic number on going from left to right due to the increase of effective nuclear charge.

  For example, in the second period, the atomic radii decrease from Li to Ne through Be, B, C, N, O and F.
- **Variation in a group:** The atomic radii of elements increase from top to bottom in a group. On moving down a group, the effective nuclear charge decreases with increase in atomic number and we expect that the size of atom should increase.

Ionic Radii: The effective distance from the centre of the nucleus of the ion to which it has an influence in the ionic bond.

The ionic radii show the same trends as atomic radius.

The study of ionic radii leads to two important generalizations:

(i) The radius of positive ion (cation) is always smaller than that of the parent atom because it has lesser electrons but same nuclear charge.

(ii) The radius of negative ion (anion) is larger than that of the parent atom because extra electrons are added due to which repulsion among electrons increases and effective nuclear charge decrease.

Isoelectronic Species: These are the atoms or ions having the same number of electrons. e.g., O^{2-}, F^-, Na^+ and Mg^{2+} have 10 electrons.

Ionization Enthalpy: It is defined as the amount of energy required to remove the loosely bound electron from isolated gaseous atom in its ground state.

The first ionization enthalpy (IE_1) is the energy required to remove the most loosely bound electron of the neutral atom and the second ionisation enthalpy (IE_2) is the energy required to remove the second electron from the resulting cation and so on. Thus first ionisation enthalpy of an element (X) may be defined with the reaction represented as :

$$X(g) \xrightarrow{IE_1} X^+(g) + e^-$$

Factors Affecting Ionisation Enthalpy:

- **Size of the atom:** The ionisation enthalpy depends upon the distance between the electron and the nucleus, i.e., size of the atom. It decreases with increase in atomic size.
- **Charge on the nucleus:** With the increase in nuclear charge it becomes more difficult to remove an electron from valence shell and therefore ionization enthalpy increases.
- **Screening effect:** The reduction in force of attraction by the electrons of shells present in between the nucleus and valence electrons is called screening effect or shielding effect. The greater the number of intervening electrons between valence electron and nucleus, the greater will be shielding or screening effect. An increase in the number of inner electrons tends to decrease the ionization enthalpy.
- **Penetration effect of electrons:** *s*-electrons are more penetrating towards the nucleus than *p*-electrons and the penetration power decreases in a given shell in the order.

$$s > p > d > f$$

For the same shell, the ionization enthalpy would be more to remove an *s*-electron than the energy required to remove a *p*-electron, which in turn will be more than that for the removal of a *d*-electron and so-on.

- **Electronic Arrangement:** The ionization enthalpy also depends upon the electronic configuration of the atom.

  For example, half filled and completely filled shells have extra stability associated with them.

(i) The noble gases have the most stable electronic configurations (ns^2np^6) in each period and therefore, have high ionization enthalpies.

(ii) The elements like Be ($1s^2\ 2s^2$) and Mg ($1s^2\ 2s^2\ 2p^6\ 3s^2$) have completely filled orbitals and their ionisation enthalpies are large.

- **Variation down a group:** Within a group, there is a gradual decrease in ionization enthalpy in moving from top to bottom.

  The decrease in ionization enthalpy down a group can be explained as:

- While going from top to bottom in a group, the nuclear charge increases atomic size increases and shielding effect increase.
- There is a gradual increase in atomic size due to an additional main energy shell (n).
- There is increase in shielding effect on the outermost electron due to increase in the number of inner electrons that outweighs the increasing nuclear charge and removal of the outermost electron requires less energy down a group.

- **Variation along a period:** In general, the ionisation enthalpy increases with increasing atomic number in a period.

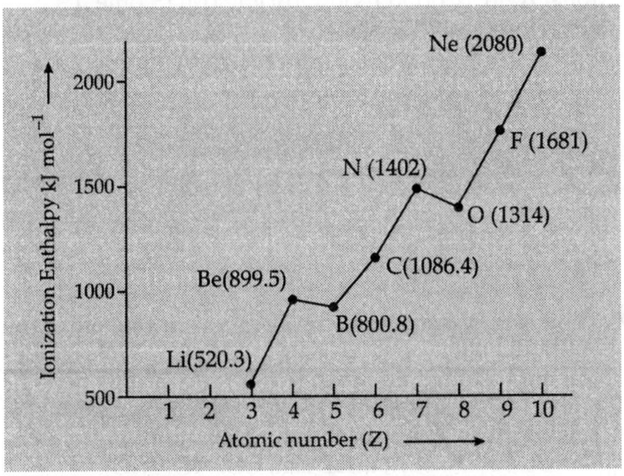

Variation of ionization enthalpy with atomic number in second period

The general Increase of ionisation enthalpy along a period car be explained on the basis of atomic & nuclear change:

(i) On moving across a period from left to right, the effective nuclear charge increases.

(ii) The atomic size decreases along a period though the main energy level remains the same.

- **Successive Ionization Enthalpies:** The energies required to remove subsequent electrons from the atom in the gaseous state are known as successive ionization enthalpies.

  It has been found that

$$IE_1 < IE_2 < IE_3$$

- **Electron Gain Enthalpy ($\Delta_{eg}H$):** It is defined as the enthalpy change, when a neutral gaseous atom takes up extra electrons to form an anion.

$$X(g) + e^- \longrightarrow X^-(g)$$

The value of electron gain enthalpy depends upon atomic size, nuclear charge, etc. With increase in size, the electron gain enthalpy decreases as the nuclear attraction decreases. Thus, electron gain enthalpy generally decreases in moving from top to bottom in a group (F < Cl > Br > I). In a period from left to right, the electron gain enthalpy generally increases due to increase in effective nuclear charge.

- **Factors Affecting Electron Gain Enthalpy:**

- **Nuclear charge:** The electron gain enthalpy becomes more negative as the nuclear charge increases. This is due to greater attraction for the incoming electron if nuclear charge is high.
- **Size of the atom:** With the increase in size of the atom, the distance between the nucleus and the incoming electron increases consequently, the electron gain enthalpy becomes less negative.
- **Electronic configuration:** The elements having stable electronic configuration of half-filled and completely filled valence sub shells show very small tendency to accept additional electron and thus electron gain enthalpies are less negative.

- **Important Trends in Electron Gain Enthalpy:**

- Halogens have the highest negative electron gain enthalpies
- Electron gain enthalpy values of noble gases are positive while those of Be, Mg, N and P are almost zero
- Electron gain enthalpy of fluorine is unexpectedly less negative than of chlorine: However, it is observed that F-atom has unexpectedly less negative electron gain enthalpy than Cl-atom. This is due to the very small size of F-atom. As a consequence of small size, there are strong inter electronic repulsions in the relatively compact $2p$-subshell of fluorine and thus the incoming electron does not feel much attraction.

- **Electronegativity:**

- It is a qualitative measure of the ability of an atom in a chemical compound to attract shared pair of electrons towards itself.
- Pauling scale is generally used on which fluorine (most electronegative element) was assigned a value of 4.0 arbitrarily.

- Electronegativity generally increases on moving across a period because of increase in effective nuclear charge.
- It decreases on moving down a group because of decrease in effective nuclear charge.

► **Summary of the trends in the periodic properties of elements in the periodic table:**

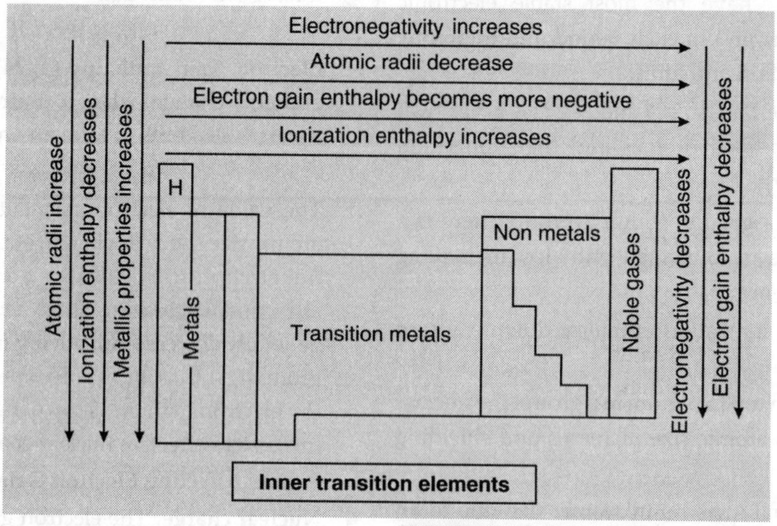

► **Valency:** The electrons present in the outermost shell of an atom are called valence electrons and the number of these electrons determine the valence or the valency of the atom. It is because of this reason that the outermost shell is also called the valence shell of the atom and the orbitals present in the valence shell are called **valence orbitals.**

Mnemonics

Concept: Electronegativity
Mnemonics: First off, cloud now. Bring in some caps, hats and pants
Interpretation: Fluorine > Oxygen > Chlorine > Nitrogen > Bromine > Iodine > Sulfur > Carbon > Hydrogen ≥ Phosphorus
Pronounce: FOCIN BrIS CHP.
(F)irst (O)ff, (Cl)oud (N)ow, (Br)ing (I)n (S)ome (C)aps, (H)ats, and (P)ants

► **Diagonal Relationship:**

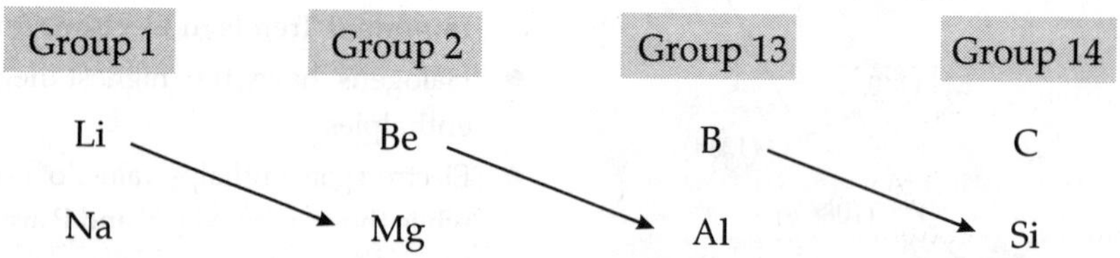

The resemblance of properties of Li with Mg (which is diagonally situated): Be with Al and B with Si is called diagonal relationship. It is due to similar polarising power.

► **Periodic Trends and Chemical Reactivity:**

- The ionization enthalpy of the extreme left element in a period is the least and the electron gain enthalpy of the element on the extreme right is the highest negative (excluding noble gases).
- Alkali metals (at extreme left) has maximum tendency to form cation (by loss of an electron) and halogens (at extreme right) has maximum tendency to form anion (by gain of an electron).
- Metallic character is maximum at the left and non-metallic character is maximum at the right within a period.
- The oxides formed by the elements at the left of the periodic table are basic (e.g., Na_2O) while oxides formed by the elements at the right of the periodic table are acidic (e.g., Cl_2O_7). However, oxides of elements in the centre are either amphoteric (e.g., Al_2O_3, Sb_2O_3) or neutral (e.g., CO, NO, N_2O).
- In transition metals, change in atomic radii is much smaller than representative elements. Their ionization enthalpies are between *s*-and *p*-block elements. Therefore, they are less electropositive than group 1 and 2 metals.

General Trends of Periodic Properties in Periodic Table

Trends of Atomic Radius

► Noble gases have large atomic radius than group 17 elements due to complete filling of electron in outer shell electron-electron repulsion mildly increases.

Trends of Ionization Enthalpy

First Ionization Enthalpy:

Li < B < Be < C < O < N < F <Ar

Second Ionization Enthalpy:

Be <C , B < N < F < O < Ne

- **Metallic Behaviour:** Decreases from left to right in a period due to increase in ionization enthalpy.
- **Non-metallic Behaviour:** Increases from left to right due to more number of electron in outermost shell and added electron goes towards nucleus.
- Radius of Cation< Atomic radius

  It is due to more number of protons than the number of electrons in a cation. Coulombic force increases, size decreases.

  $Mg^{2+} < Mg^{+} < Mg$
- Radius of Anion > Atomic Radius

  It is due to more number of electrons than the number of protons in an anion.

  $N^{3-} > O^{2-} > F^{-}$

  Electron – electron repulsion increases, coulombic force of attraction decreases and size increases.
- **For Isoelectronic Species:**
  - Greater the charge of cation, lesser will be the size.
  - Greater the charge of anion, greater will be the size.

  Eg., $O^{2-} > F^{-} > Na > Na^{+} > Mg^{2+}$

Trends of Electron Gain Enthalpy:

Halogen > Oxygen > Nitrogen > Metal of group 1 and 13 and non-metal of group 14 > Metal of group 2.

- Chlorine has maximum electron gain enthalpy.
- Phosphorus and sulphur have negative electron gain enthalpy then nitrogen and oxygen respectively.

Trends of Electronegativity:

- Highest electronegative atoms in periodic table :

  F > O > N

- Effective nuclear change (Z_{eff}) = Nuclear charge – shielding effect

  Trend : Z_{eff} increases from left to right in a period.

  Z_{eff} decreases from top to bottom in a group.

Mnemonics

Concept: Genesis of Periodic Classification

Mnemonics: **L**ondon and **T**urkey **D**onates **L**ots of **N**uts to **P**eru, **L**ibya and **Ma**laysia but denied to **M**exico, **P**oland, **L**iberia and **M**aldives

Interpretation: Laws of Trieds – Dobereiner

Laws of Octaves – Newland

Periodic Law – Mendeleev

Modern Periodic Law – Moseley

Concept: Classification of Elements and Periodicity in Properties.

1. Elements of Atomic No (1-18)

Mnemonics:

Happy **H**arry **Li**sten **BBC** **N**etwork **O**ver **F**rench **Ne**twork. **Na**tive **M**agpies **Al**ways **Si**t **P**eacefully **S**earching **Cl**ear **Ar**eas

Interpretation:

H, He, Li, Be, B, C, N, O, F, Ne, Na, Al, Si, P, S, Cl, Ar

2. Group I Elements

Little Nasty Kids Rub Cats Fur

Lithium (Li), Sodium (Na), Potassium (K), Rubidium (Rb) Caesium (Cs), Francium (Fr)

3. Group II Elements

Mnemonics: Beer Mugs Can Snap Bar's Reputation

Interpretation: Beryllium (Be), Magnesium (Mg), Calcium (Ca),

Strontium (Sr), Barium (Ba), Radium (Ra)

4. Group III Elements

Mnemonics: BAGIT

Interpretation:

Boron (B), Aluminium (Al), Gallium (Ga), Indium (In), Thallium (Tl)

5. Group IV B Elements

Mnemonics: Can Simple Germans Surprise Public

Interpretation: Carbon (C), Silicon (Si), Germanium (Ge), Tin (Sn), Lead (Pb)

6. Group V B Elements

New Police Assign Subordinate Bikram on Duty

Nitrogen (N), Phosphorus (P), Arsenic (As), Antimony (Sb), Bismuth (Bi)

7. Group VI B Elements

Old Saharanpur Seems Terribly Polluted

Oxygen (O), Sulphur (S), Selenium (Se), Tellurium (Te), Polonium (Po)

8. Group VII B Elements

First Class Biryani In Australia

Fluorine (F), Chlorine (Cl), Bromine (Br), Iodine (I), Astatine (Al)

9. Group VIII B/18 Elements

He never Arrived; Karan exited with Rohan

Helium (He), Neon (Ne), Argon (Ar), Krypton (Kr), Xenon (Ex), Radon (Rn)

10. 3d-Series

Scary Tiny Vicious Creatures are

Mean females come to Night Club Zen

Sc, Ti, V, Cr, Mn, Fe, Co, Ni, Cu, Zn,

11. 4d-Series

Yes S(z)sir Nob. Most Technicians Rub Rod's Pale Silver Cadillac

Y, Zr, Nb>Mo, Tc, Ru, Rh, Pd, Ag, Cd

12. 5d-Series

Late Harry Took Walk, Reached

Office In Pajamas After an Hour

La......., Hf, Ta, W, Re, OS, Ir, Pt, Au, Hg

13. Lanthanides

Ladies Can't Put Needles Properly in

Slot-machines. Every Girl Tries Daily

However, Every Time You'd be lose

La, Ce, Pr, Nd, Pm, Sm, Eu Gd, Tb, Dy, Ho, Er, Tm, Yb, Lu

14. Actinides series
Three Planets: Uranus, Neptune, and Pluto. Amy Cured Berkeley, California. Einstein and Fermi Made NobleLaws.(Ac) Th Pa U Np Pu Am Cm Bk Cf Es Fm Md No Lr
1. Alkali Metals
Concept: Trends in Atomic and physical properties
Mnemonics:
H – Hydrogen-His
Li – Lithium-Last
Na – Sodium-Son
K – Potassium-Plays
Rb – Rubidium-Rugby
Cs – Caesium-Cricket
Fr – Francium-Football
2. Atomic/Ionic radii, metallic, reducing, characteristics (group)
Mnemonics: Like Nadia Kareena likes Rugby & Cricket
Interpretation: Li <Na <K <Rb <Cs
3. Ionisation Energy, melting/boiling points, reactivity with Hydrogen/Halogens, Enthalpy
Mnemonics: Little Naughty Krishna Rules Close friends
Interpretation: Li >Na >K >Rb >Cs
Electronegativity
Mnemonics: Cat Sings Gentle Songs in Public
Interpretation: C < Si = Ge = Sn < Pb

Key Terms

- **Periods:** The horizontal rows in the periodic table are called periods.
- **Groups:** The vertical columns in the periodic table are called groups.

- **Transuranic Elements:** The elements which follow uranium [i.e., neptunium to Uub (Z = 112) of actinoids] in the periodic table are called transuranic or man-made elements. These element do not occur in nature because their half-life periods are so short.

Key Facts

- At present, 118 elements are known.
- In modern periodic table, there are 18 groups.

  Group 1 and 2: *s*-block elements in which last electron entered in *s*-sub shell [ns^1, ns^2].

  Group 3 to 12: *d*-block 'or transition' elements elements in which last electron entered in *d*-sub shell $(n-1)d^{-10}$

  Group 13 to 18: *p*-block elements in which last electron entered in *p*-sub shell [np^1 to np^6].

  Group 18: Noble gases. Group 1-2, 13-17 are known as typical or normal or representative elements.
- In '*s*' and '*p*' – block elements, the last electron enters in the outermost shell.
- In *d*-block elements, the last electron enters in the penultimate shell $(n-1)$.
- In *f*-block elements, the last electron enters in the sub-penultimate shell $(n-2)$.
- Elements with atomic number 58 to 71 (Ce to Lu) occurring after lanthanum (La) are called Lanthanoids. Elements with atomic number 90 to 103 (Th to Lr) are called Actinoids. These elements are called f-block elements and also as inner-transition elements.

NCERT CORNER

Q. 1. What is the basic theme of organisation in the periodic table? [NCERT Ex. Q. 3.1, Page 96]

Ans. The basic theme of organization in the periodic table is the systematic study of physical and chemical properties of all the elements and their compounds. **(1)**

Q. 2. Which important property did Mendeleev use to classify the elements in his periodic table and did he stick to that? [NCERT Ex. Q. 3.2, Page 96]

Ans. Mendeleev used atomic weight to classify the elements in his periodic table. He arranged the elements in periods and groups in order of their increasing atomic weight. He placed the elements with similar properties in the same group. He did not stick to this arrangement, he found that if elements were arranged in order of their increasing atomic weights, then some elements did not fit in his scheme.

Q. 3. What is the basic difference in approach between the Mendeleev's Periodic Law and the Modern Periodic Law? [NCERT Ex. Q. 3.3, Page 96]

Ans. According to Mendeleev's Periodic Law, "The properties of the elements are a periodic function of their atomic weights".

According to Modern Periodic Law, "The properties of the elements are a periodic function of their atomic numbers".

Q. 4. On the basis of quantum numbers, justify that the sixth period of the periodic table should have 32 elements. [NCERT Ex. Q. 3.4, Page 96]

Ans. In the modern periodic table, the sixth period corresponds to sixth shell. For sixth shell, the value of principal quantum number (*n*) is 6. According to Aufbau's principle, the orbitals are filled in order of their increasing energies in the ground state of the atoms. So, in the sixth period, electrons enter in 6*s*, 4*f*, 5*p* and 6*d* subshells.

Therefore, there are a total of sixteen orbitals available. According to Pauli's exclusion principle, each orbital can accommodate a maximum of 2 electrons. The maximum number of electrons which can be present in these subshells is 2 + 14 + 6 + 10 = 32. Since, the number of elements in a period corresponds to the number of electrons in the shells. So, sixth period should accommodate maximum of 32 elements.

Q. 5. In terms of period and group, where would you locate the element with Z = 114?
[NCERT Ex. Q. 3.5, Page 96]

Ans. $_{114}Z = [Rn]\ 7s^2, 5f^{14}, 6d^{10}, 7p^2$

Since, the last electron enters in *p*-subshell of

$n = 7$

∴ This element lies in 7th period and 14th group

[for *p*-block elements, group number = 10 + number of electrons in the valence shell (4)]

Q. 6. Write the atomic number of the element present in the third period and seventeenth group of the periodic table. **[NCERT Ex. Q. 3.6, Page 96]**

Ans. General electronic configuration of 17th group element = ns^2np^5.

For third period, it becomes $3s^23p^5$

∴ Electronic configuration of element

$= 1s^2, 2s^2\ 2p^6, 3s^2, 3p^5$

No. of electrons = 2 + 2 + 6 + 2 + 5 = 17

∴ The atomic number of element = 17

Q. 7. Which element do you think would have been named by :
(i) Lawrence Berkeley Laboratory
(ii) Seaborg's group? **[NCERT Ex. Q. 3.7, Page 96]**

Ans. **(i)** Lawrencium (Lr) with atomic number

Z = 103

And Berkelium (Bk) with atomic number

Z = 97

(ii) Seaborgium (Sg) with atomic number

Z = 106

Q. 8. Why do elements in the same group have similar physical and chemical properties?
[NCERT Ex. Q. 3.8, Page 96]

Ans. The physical and chemical properties of elements depend on the number of valence electrons. The elements in the same group have similar electronic configuration so these elements have similar physical and chemical properties.

Q. 9. What does atomic radius and ionic radius really mean to you? **[NCERT Ex. Q. 3.9, Page 96]**

Ans. Atomic Radius: The distance from the centre of nucleus to the outermost shell of electrons in the atom of any element is known as atomic radius.

If the element is a metal then atomic radius refers to the metallic radius and if element is non-metal it refers to covalent radius.

Ionic Radius : The distance between cations and anions in ionic crystals is called ionic radius.

Q. 10. How do atomic radius vary in a period and in a group? How do you explain the variation?
[NCERT Ex. Q. 3.10, Page 96]

Ans. Atomic radius decreases on moving from left to right in a period. It is due to increase in effective nuclear charge from left to right across a period.

Atomic radius increases on moving down the group. It is due to increase in the number of shells down the group.

Q. 11. What do you understand by isoelectronic species? Name a species that will be isoelectronic with each of the following atoms or ions:
(i) F^- (ii) Ar (iii) Mg^{2+} (iv) Rb^+
[NCERT Ex. Q. 3.11, Page 96]

Ans. Those species (atoms or ions) which have same number of electrons are called isoelectronic species.

(i) F^- and Na^+ are isoelectronic species.
(Number of electrons = 10)

(ii) Ar and Ca^{2+} are isoelectronic species.
(Number of electrons = 18)

(iii) Mg^{2+} and Al^{3+} are isoelectronic species.
(Number of electrons = 10)

(iv) Rb^+ and Sr^{2+} are isoelectronic species.
(Number of electrons = 36)

Q. 12. Consider the following species:
N^{3-}, O^{2-}, F^-, Na^+, Mg^{2+} and Al^{3+}
(a) What is common in them?
(b) Arrange them in the order of increasing ionic radii.
[NCERT Ex. Q. 3.12, Page 96]

Ans. **(a)** Since, all these species have equal number of electrons, i.e., 10 therefore, these are isoelectronic species.

(b) In isoelectronic species, greater the nuclear charge, lesser will be the ionic radius therefore, increasing order of ionic radii :

$Al^{3+} < Mg^{2+} < Na^+ < F^- < O^{2-} < N^{3-}$

Q. 13. Explain why cations are smaller and anions larger in radii than their parent atoms?
[NCERT Ex. Q. 3.13, Page 96]

Ans. Cations are smaller in radii than their parent atoms because effective nuclear charge increases with loss of one or two electrons. As the force of attraction of electrons to the nucleus increases therefore, ionic radii of cations decreases.

Whereas anions are larger in radii than their parent atoms because effective nuclear charge decreases with gain of one or two electrons. As the force of attraction of electrons to the nucleus decreases therefore, ionic radii of anions increases.

Q. 14. What is the significance of the terms 'isolated gaseous atom' and 'ground state' while defining ionization enthalpy and electron gain enthalpy?
[Hint: Requirements for comparison purposes]
[NCERT Ex. Q. 3.14, Page 96]

Ans. In the gaseous state, the atoms are widely separated therefore, interatomic forces are minimum. It is because of this reason the term 'isolated gaseous atom' has been included in definition of ionisation enthalpy and electron gain enthalpy.

The term 'ground state' here means that the atom must be present in the most stable state, i.e., the ground state. Therefore, for comparison purposes, the ionisation enthalpies and electron gain enthalpies of gaseous atoms must be determined in their respective ground states.

Q. 15. Energy of an electron in the ground state of the hydrogen atom is -2.18×10^{-18} J. Calculate the ionization enthalpy of atomic hydrogen in terms of J mol^{-1}.
[Hint: Apply the idea of mole concept to derive the answer] [NCERT Ex. Q. 3.15, Page 96]

Ans. $E_1 = -2.18 \times 10^{-18}$ J

$E_\infty = 0$

$\Delta E = E_\infty - E_1 = 0 - (-2.18 \times 10^{-18}\ J)$
$= 2.18 \times 10^{-18}$ J

Ionization enthalpy per hydrogen atom
$= 2.18 \times 10^{-18}$ J

∴ Ionization enthalpy per mole of hydrogen atoms
$= 2.18 \times 10^{-18} \times 6.022 \times 10^{23}\ J\ mol^{-1}$
$= 13.12 \times 10^5\ J\ mol^{-1}$

Q. 16. (i) Among the second period elements, the actual ionization enthalpies are in the order.
Li < B < Be < C < O < N < F < Ne
Explain why (i) Be has higher $\Delta_i H$ than B
(ii) O has lower $\Delta_i H$ than N and F ?
[NCERT Ex. Q. 3.16, Page 96]

Ans. (i) Be $\longrightarrow 1s^2 2s^2$
B $\longrightarrow 1s^2 2s^2 2p_x^1$

In case of Be, electron has to be removed from *s*-orbital whereas in boron, removal takes from *p*-orbital.
As *s*-orbital is closer to nucleus, hence removal of electron is difficult which raises its ionisation enthalpy.

(ii) O $\longrightarrow 1s^2 2s^2 2p^4$
N $\longrightarrow 1s^2 2s^2 2p^3$
F $\longrightarrow 1s^2 2s^2 2p^5$

Comparing O and N, nitrogen has completely half filled *p*-orbitals, hence, I.E. of nitrogen is greater than oxygen. [Half filled orbitals account for greater stability].
Comparing O and F, F has increased nuclear charge and small size, hence removal of electron is difficult. Therefore, I.E. of F is greater than O.

Q. 17. How would you explain the fact that first ionisation enthalpy of sodium is lower than that of magnesium but its second ionisation enthalpy is higher than that of magnesium? [NCERT Ex. Q. 3.17, Page 97]

Ans. The first electron in both the cases has to be removed from 3s-orbitals, but nuclear charge of Na is less than that of Mg. Hence, I.E. of Na is lower than that of Mg.

Na $= 1s^2, 2s^2 2p^6, 3s^1 \xrightarrow{IE_1} Na^+ (= 1s^2, 2s^2 2p^6)$

Mg $= 1s^2, 2s^2 2p^6, 3s^2 \xrightarrow{IE_1}$
$Mg^+ (= 1s^2, 2s^2 2p^6, 3s^1)$

After the loss of first electron, the electronic configuration of Na^+ is $1s^2, 2s^2 2p^6$, i.e., that of noble gas which is very stable and hence the removal of second electron from Na^+ is very difficult. In the case of Mg, after the loss of first electron, electronic configuration of Mg^+ ions is $1s^2, 2s^2 2p^6, 3s^1$. The second electron to be removed is from 3s orbital which is easier.
Hence, IE_2 of sodium is much larger than IE_2 of Mg.

Q. 18. What are the various factors due to which ionization enthalpy of the main group elements tends to decrease down a group ? [NCERT Ex. Q. 3.18, Page 97]

Ans. (i) Atomic size $\propto \frac{1}{I.E.}$

On moving down the group, atomic size increases, hence ionization energy decreases.

(ii) With the addition of new shells, the number of inner shell electrons which shield the valence electrons from the nucleus increases. In other words, shielding or screening effect increases. As a result, the force of attraction of the nucleus for the valence electron further decreases and hence the ionisation energy decreases.

(iii) Nuclear charge increases down the group with increase in atomic number. As a result, the force of attraction of the nucleus for the valence electrons should increase thus I.E., should increase. The combined effect of the increase in the atomic size and the screening effect compensates the effect of increased nuclear charge.

Q. 19. The first ionization enthalpy values (in kJ/mol) of group 13 elements:

B	**Al**	**Ga**	**In**	**Tl**
801	**577**	**579**	**558**	**589**

How would you explain this deviation from the general trend ? [NCERT Ex. Q. 3.19, Page 97]

Ans. As we move down the group, atomic size increases.

We know I.E. $\propto \frac{1}{\text{Atomic size}}$, hence it is expected that on moving down the group, I.E. should decrease.
The deviation is due to weak screening or shielding effect of d-orbital due to which atomic size decreases and ionisation energy increases.

Q. 20. Which of the following pairs of elements would have a more negative electron gain enthalpy ?
(i) O or F, (ii) F or Cl [NCERT Ex. Q. 3.20, Page 97]

Ans. (i) F ($-$ 328 kJ mol^{-1}) has more negative electron gain enthalpy than O ($-$ 141 kJ mol^{-1}).

(ii) Cl ($-$ 349 kJ mol^{-1}) has more negative electron gain enthalpy than F ($-$ 328 kJ mol^{-1}).

Q. 21. Would you expect the second electron gain enthalpy of O as positive, more negative or less negative than the first ? Justify your answer.
[NCERT Ex. Q. 3.21, Page 97]

Ans. When an electron is added to oxygen atom to form O^- ion, energy is released. But when another electron is added to O^- ion to form O^{2-} ion, energy is absorbed to overcome the strong electrostatic repulsion between the negatively charged O^- ion and the new electron being added. The second electron gain enthalpy of O is positive.

Thus, first electron gain enthalpy:
$O(g) + e^- \rightarrow O^-(g); \Delta_{eg}H = -141\ kJ\ mol^{-1}$
(energy is released)

Second electron gain enthalpy:
$O^-(g) + e^- \rightarrow O^{2-}(g); \Delta_{eg}H = +780\ kJ\ mol^{-1}$
(electrostatic repulsion) (energy is absorbed)

Q. 22. What is the basic difference between the terms electron gain enthalpy and electronegativity ?
[NCERT Ex. Q. 3.22, Page 97]

Ans. Electronegativity differs from electron gain affinity in the sense that the latter is related to atoms in their isolated states, whereas former is a property of an atom in a bonded state, i.e., in a molecule.

Electronegativity is only qualitative and is not a measurable quantity while electron gain enthalpy is quantitative.

Q. 23. How would you react to the statement that the electronegativity of N on Pauling scale is 3.0 in all the nitrogen compounds? [NCERT Ex. Q. 3.23, Page 97]

Ans. On Pauling scale, the electronegativity of nitrogen is 3.0, which indicates that it is sufficiently electronegative. But it is not true that the electronegativity of nitrogen in all the compounds is 3. It depends on type of hybridization in a particular compound. Greater the percentage of s-character, greater will be the electronegativity of the element.

Q. 24. Describe the theory associated with the radius of an atom as it:
(a) gains an electron
(b) loses an electron [NCERT Ex. Q. 3.24, Page 97]

Ans. **(a)** When a neutral atom gains an electron to form an anion, the number of electrons in the anion increases whereas its nuclear charge remains the same as that of the parent atom. Since the same nuclear charge now attracts larger number of electrons, therefore, the force of attraction of the nucleus on the electrons of all shells decreases. This means that the effective nuclear charge decreases and the expansion of the electron cloud occurs. Because of this, the distance between the centre of the nucleus and the last shell increases thereby increasing the ionic radius.

(b) When a neutral atom looses an electron to form a cation, the number of electrons in the cation decreases, whereas its nuclear charge remains the same as that of the parent atom. Since the same nuclear charge now attracts lesser number of electrons, therefore the force of attraction of the nucleus on the electrons of all shell increases. This means that the effective nuclear charge increases and the contraction of the electron cloud occurs. Because of this distance between the centre of the nucleus and the last shell decreases thereby decreasing the ionic radius.

Q. 25. Would you expect the first ionization enthalpies for two isotopes of the same element to be the same or different? Justify your answer.
[NCERT Ex. Q. 3.25, Page 97]

Ans. The first ionization enthalpies for two isotopes of the same element are expected to be same because ionization enthalpy depends upon the electronic configuration and effective nuclear charge. Since, isotopes of an element have same electronic configuration and so possess same nuclear charge and same ionization enthalpies.

Q. 26. What are the major differences between metals and non-metals ? [NCERT Ex. Q. 3.26, Page 97]

Ans. **(I) Physical Properties**

Metals	Non-Metals
(1) State Metals are generally solids at room temperature. They volatilize only at high temperatures.	Non-metals are generally gases or liquids or brittle solids. They volatilize at fairly low temperatures.
(2) Hardness and Lustre Metals are generally hard and possess lustre.	Non-metals are usually soft and do not possess lustre.
(3) Melting and Boiling points They have high melting points.	They have generally low melting points.
(4) Malleability and Ductility Metals are generally malleable and ductile.	Non-metals are generally non-malleable and brittle.
(5) Conductivity They are good conductors of electricity.	They are bad conductors of electricity.

(II) Chemical Properties

Metals	Non-Metals
(1) Oxidising and Reducing action Metals are generally good reducing agents.	Non-metals are generally good oxidising agents.
(2) Nature of Oxides There oxides are generally basic in nature.	These oxides are generally acidic in nature.
(3) Nature of Hydrides Metals usually form unstable hydrides.	Non-metals usually form stable hydrides.
(4) Action with Acids Metals usually dissolve in mineral acids to form salt and liberate hydrogen gas.	Non-metals generally do not react with mineral acids.
(5) Arrangement of Valence electrons Metals have one, two or three valence electrons.	Non-metals usually have 4, 5, 6, 7 valence electrons.

Q. 27. Use the periodic table to answer the following questions ?
(a) Identify an element with five electrons in the outer sub-shell.
(b) Identify an element that would tend to lose two electrons.
(c) Identify an element that would tend to gain two electrons.

(d) Identify group having metal, non-metal, liquid as well as gas at the room temperature.

[NCERT Ex. Q. 3.27, Page 97]

Ans. (a) Fluorine F = $1s^2, 2s^2, 2p^5$, [$5e^-$ in $2p$ subshell]

(b) Calcium Ca = $1s^2, 2s^2, 2p^6, 3s^2, 3p^6, 4s^2$ [It can lose $2e^-$]

(c) Oxygen O = $1s^2, 2s^2, 2p^4$ [It can gain $2e^-$]

(d) Group 17 has metal, non-metal, liquid as well as gas at room temperature.

Q. 28. The increasing order of reactivity among group 1 elements is Li < Na < Rb < Cs whereas that among group 17 elements is F > Cl > Br > I. Explain.

[NCERT Ex. Q. 3.28, Page 97]

Ans. As ionization enthalpy decreases from top to bottom in group 1, therefore, the reactivity increases down the group from Li to Cs.

The group 17 elements are halogens with electronic configuration of ns^2np^5 in their valence shells, they try to become ns^2np^6 by acquiring one electron.

All the halogens are highly reactive elements due to the following reasons:

(i) Low bond dissociation energy: ($X_2 \rightarrow 2X$) Halogens have low bond dissociation energy. F_2 has lowest bond dissociation energy which makes it the most reactive.

(ii) High electron gain enthalpy: Due to high electron gain enthalpy, these elements have a strong tendency to gain an electron and thus are highly reactive.

(iii) High reduction potentials: F_2 has maximum and I_2 has minimum reduction potentials. Hence, order of reactivity is F > Cl > Br > I.

Q. 29. Write the general outer electronic configuration of *s*–, *p*–, *d*– and *f*– block elements.

[NCERT Ex. Q. 3.29, Page 97]

Ans. s – block elements = ns^{1-2} (where $n = 2 - 7$)

p – block elements = ns^2np^{1-6} (where $n = 2 - 6$)

d – block elements = $(n-1)d^{1-10}\,ns^{1-2}$ (where $n = 4 - 7$)

f – block elements = $(n-2)f^{1-14}\,(n-1)d^{0-1}\,ns^2$ (where $n = 6 - 7$)

Q. 30. Assign the position of the element having outer electronic configuration (i) ns^2np^4 for n = 3, (ii) $(n-1)d^2ns^2$ for n = 4 and (iii) $(n-2)f^7(n-1)d^1ns^2$ for n = 6, in the periodic table. **[NCERT Ex. Q. 3.30, Page 97]**

Ans. (i) $ns^2np^4 \rightarrow 3s^23p^4$

Element is sulphur in the 3rd period and group 16.

(ii) $(n-1)d^2\,ns^2$ for $n = 4$

$3d^24s^2$

Element is titanium (atomic number 22) in the 4th period and 4th group.

(iii) $(n-2)f^7\,(n-1)\,d^1ns^2$ for $n = 6$

$4f^75d^16s^2$

It is Gadolinium (Ga).

It is an inner transition element which belongs to lanthanoid series of 4*f* series.

Q. 31. The first (Δ_iH_1) and the second (Δ_iH_2) ionization enthalpies (in kJ mol^{-1}) and the ($\Delta_{eg}H$) electron gain enthalpy (in kJ mol^{-1}) of a few elements are given below:

Elements	Δ_iH_1	Δ_iH_2	$\Delta_{eg}H$
I	520	7300	– 60
II	419	3051	– 48
III	1681	3374	– 328
IV	1008	1846	– 295
V	2372	5251	+ 48
VI	738	1451	– 40

Which of the above element is likely to be :

(i) the least reactive element.

(ii) the most reactive metal.

(iii) the most reactive non-metal.

(iv) the least reactive non-metal.

(v) the metal which can form a stable binary halide of the formula MX² (X = halogen)?

[NCERT Ex. Q. 3.31, Page 98]

Ans. (i) The least reactive element is V. It has no tendency to lose electrons [as is clear from its high Δ_iH_1 and its higher Δ_iH_2], nor can it gain electrons [positive value of electron gain enthalpy – energy has to be absorbed to gain or add an electron].

(ii) The most reactive metal is II. Its Δ_iH_1 is lowest and Δ_iH_2 is very high, i.e., it can lose one electron readily from its valence shell [4th] to become II. It cannot lose 2nd electron readily because of stable noble gas configuration.

(iii) The most reactive non-metal is III whose Δ_iH_1 and Δ_iH_2 are very high, so it cannot lose electrons readily. On the other hand, its electron gain enthalpy has a large negative value indicating it can accept an electron readily.

(iv) The least reactive non-metal is IV. Its Δ_iH_1 and Δ_iH_2 are very high, meaning it cannot lose electrons readily. On the other hand, its electron gain enthalpy has a large negative value (but not as large negative value as F above) indicating that it can accept an electron readily.

(v) The metal which can form a stable binary halide of the formula MX_2 (X = halogen) is VI.

$$Mg + X_2 \rightarrow MgX_2$$

Its Δ_iH_1 and Δ_iH_2 are not very high but its electron gain enthalpy is very small, Δ_iH_2 is not very large as compared to Δ_iH_1.

Because of its electropositive nature and tendency to lose two electrons, it can form a stable binary halide MX_2.

Q. 32. Predict the formulas of the stable binary compounds that would be formed by the combination of the following pairs of elements:

(a) Lithium and oxygen

(b) Magnesium and nitrogen

(c) Aluminium and iodine

(d) Silicon and oxygen

(e) Phosphorus and fluorine

(f) Element 71 and fluorine

[NCERT Ex. Q. 3.32, Page 98]

Ans. (a) Li Group 1, Valence = 1

O Group 16, Valence = 2

Hence, formula would be Lithium oxide (Li_2O)

(b) Mg Group 2, Valence = 2
N Group 15, Valence = 3
Hence, formula would be Magnesium nitride (Mg_3N_2)
(c) Al Group 13, Valence = 3
I Group 17, Valence = 1
Hence, formula would be Aluminium iodide (AlI_3)
(d) Si Group 14, Valence = 4
O Group 16, Valence = 2
Hence, formula would be Silicon dioxide (SiO_2)
(e) P Group 15, Valence = 5
F Group 17, Valence = 1
Hence, formula would be Phosphorus pentafluoride (PF_5)
(f) The element having atomic number 71 referred to as Lutetium (Lu), whose electronic configuration is [Xe] $4f^{14}\,5d^1\,6s^2$
∴ Binary compound of Lu and fluorine is lutetium fluoride (LuF_3).

Q. 33. In the modern periodic table, the period indicates the value of –
(a) atomic number
(b) atomic mass
(c) principal quantum number
(d) azimuthal quantum number
[NCERT Ex. Q. 3.33, Page 98]

Ans. (c) In the modern periodic table, the period indicates the value of principal quantum number (n).

Q. 34. Which of the following statements related to the modern periodic table is incorrect?
(a) The *p*-block has 6 columns, because a maximum of 6 electrons can occupy all the orbitals in a *p*-subshell.
(b) The *d*-block has 8 columns, because a maximum of 8 electrons can occupy all the orbitals in a *d*-subshell.
(c) Each block contains a number of columns equal to the number of electrons that can occupy that subshell.
(d) The block indicates value of azimuthal quantum number (l) for the last subshell that received electrons in building up the electronic configuration.
[NCERT Ex. Q. 3.34, Page 98]

Ans. Statement (b) is incorrect for the modern periodic table. The d-block has 10 columns as maximum of 10 electrons can occupy all the orbitals in a d-subshell.

Q. 35. Anything that influences the valence electrons will affect the chemistry of the element. Which one of the following factors does not affect the valence shell?
(a) Valence principal quantum number (n)
(b) Nuclear charge (Z)
(c) Nuclear mass
(d) Number of core electrons.
[NCERT Ex. Q. 3.35, Page 99]

Ans. (c) Nuclear mass does not affect the valence shell.

Q. 36. The size of isoelectronic species: F^-, Ne and Na^+ is affected by:
(a) nuclear charge (Z).
(b) valence principal quantum number (*n*).
(c) electron-electron interaction in the outer orbitals.
(d) none of the factors because their size is the same.
[NCERT Ex. Q. 3.36, Page 99]

Ans. (a) The size of isoelectronic species is affected by nuclear charge (Z).

Q. 37. Which one of the following statements is incorrect in relation to ionization enthalpy?
(a) Ionization enthalpy increases for each successive electron.
(b) The greatest increase in ionization enthalpy is experienced on removal of electron from core noble gas configuration.
(c) End of valence electrons is marked by a big jump in ionization enthalpy.
(d) Removal of electron from orbitals bearing lower *n* value is easier than from orbital having higher *n* value.
[NCERT Ex. Q. 3.37, Page 99]

Ans. The statement (d) is incorrect in relation to ionization enthalpy.

Q. 38. Considering the elements B, Al, Mg and K, the correct order of their metallic character is:
(a) B > Al > Mg > K
(b) Al > Mg > B > K
(c) Mg > Al > K > B
(d) K > Mg > Al > B [NCERT Ex. Q. 3.38, Page 99]

Ans. The correct order of metallic character is–
(d) K > Mg > Al > B
We know that metallic character decreases on moving from left to right in a period. However, metallic character increases on moving from top to bottom in a group. So, the correct order of metallic character is K > Mg > Al > B.

Q. 39. Considering the elements B, C, N, F and Si, the correct order of their non-metallic character is:
(a) B > C > Si > N > F
(b) Si > C > B > N > F
(c) F > N > C > B > Si
(d) F > N > C > Si > B [NCERT Ex. Q. 3.39, Page 99]

Ans. The correct order of non-metallic character is:
(c) F > N > C > B > Si
We know that non-metallic character increases on moving from left to right in a period. (F > N > C > B). However, non-metallic character decreases from top to bottom in a group (i.e., C is more non-metallic than Si). So, the correct order of non-metallic character is:
F > N > C > B > Si

Q. 40. Considering the elements F, Cl, O and N, the correct order of their chemical reactivity in terms of oxidizing property is :
(a) F > Cl > O > N
(b) F > O > Cl > N
(c) Cl > F > O > N
(d) O > F > N > Cl [NCERT Ex. Q. 3.40, Page 99]

Ans. The correct order of the chemical reactivity in terms of oxidizing property is :
(b) F > O > Cl > N
We know that the oxidizing power of element increases from left to right in a period. As N, O and F lie in same period and possess oxidizing power which decreases in the order : F > O > N.
However, oxidizing power decreases from top to bottom in a group. So F has more oxidizing power than Cl and O is more electronegative than Cl. So, O has more oxidising power than Cl. Hence, the correct order of the chemical reactivity in terms of oxidizing property is F > O > Cl > N.

□□

CHEMICAL BONDING AND MOLECULAR STRUCTURE

CHAPTER 4

- **Chemical Bond:** The attractive force which holds various constituent particles (atoms, ions or molecules) together in a chemical species is known as chemical bond.

KÖSSEL – LEWIS Approach to Chemical Bonding

- **Octet Rule:** The octet rule or the electronic theory of chemical bonding was developed by Kossel and Lewis. According to this rule, atoms can combine either by transfer of valence electrons from one atom to another (gaining or losing) or by sharing their valence electrons. The principle of attaining maximum of eight electrons in the valence shell of atoms is called octet rule. Lewis postulated that atoms achieve to stable octet when they are linked by chemical bonds.
- **Limitations of the Octet Rule:** Some limitations of octet rule are:
  - In periodic table in and beyond the third period (after silicon) this rule is not applied. These elements can "expand their octet" and have more than eight valence electrons around the central atom, e.g., PF_5, SF_6 etc.
  - Molecules with an odd number of electrons such as NO and NO_2 cannot satisfy the octet rule.
  - In some molecules, the central atom cannot possibly have eight valence electrons. For example, LiCl, $BeCl_2$ and BCl_3 do not obey the octet rule.
  - It is based upon the chemical inertness of noble gases. However, some noble gases such as Xenon and Krypton combine to form a number of compounds like XeF_2, KrF_2, $XeOF_2$, etc.
  - This theory does not account for the shape of molecules.
  - It also does not explain the relative stability of the molecules.

Ionic or Electrovalent Bond

- "Ionic bonding is a type of chemical bond that involves the electrostatic attraction between oppositely charged ions together is known as ionic bond and electrovalent bond." Thus, the electrovalence is equal to the number of unit charge on the ion.

  "Electrovalent compounds are those compounds in which constituent particles are ions or positively charged species and they are formed by transfer of electron from a metal to a non-metal.

$$\underset{(2,8,1)}{Na\cdot} + \underset{(2,8,7)}{:\ddot{\underset{..}{Cl}}:} \longrightarrow \underset{(2,8)}{Na^+} + \underset{(2,8,8)}{[:\ddot{\underset{..}{Cl}}:]^-}$$

- **Properties of Ionic Compounds:**
  - Ionic compounds have high melting points and high boiling points.
  - They have higher enthalpies of fusion and vaporization than molecular compounds.
  - They are hard and brittle.
  - These compounds conduct electricity when they are dissolved in water or in molten state.
  - Ionic solids are good insulators.
  - The ionic bond is non-directional. This is because each ion is surrounded by oppositely charged ions uniformly distributed all around the ion.
- **Covalent Bond:** A covalent bond is a chemical bond that involves the sharing of electron pairs between atoms. The stable balance of attractive and repulsive forces between atoms when they share electrons is known as covalent bonding.

$$\dot{H} + \dot{H} \longrightarrow \underset{\text{Sharing of electrons}}{H:H} \quad \text{Or} \quad H—H$$

- **Lewis Structure of Ionic Compounds:**

(i) $(Na^+)(:\ddot{\underset{..}{Cl}}:^-)$ (ii) $(K^+)(:\ddot{\underset{..}{Cl}}:^-)$

(iii) $(Mg^{2+})(:\ddot{\underset{..}{Cl}}:^-)_2$ (iv) $(K^+)_2(:\ddot{\underset{..}{O}}:^{2-})$

(v) $(Mg^{2+})(:\ddot{\underset{..}{O}}:^{2-})$ (vi) $(Ca^{2+})(:\ddot{\underset{..}{O}}:^{2-})$

(vii) $(Na^+)_2(:\ddot{\underset{..}{S}}:^{2-})$ (viii) $(Na^+)_3(:\ddot{\underset{..}{P}}:^{3-})$

(ix) $(Li^+)_2(:\ddot{\underset{..}{O}}:^{2-})$ (x) $(Ca^{2+})_3(:\ddot{\underset{..}{N}}:^{3-})_2$

- **Lewis Structure of Covalent Compounds:**

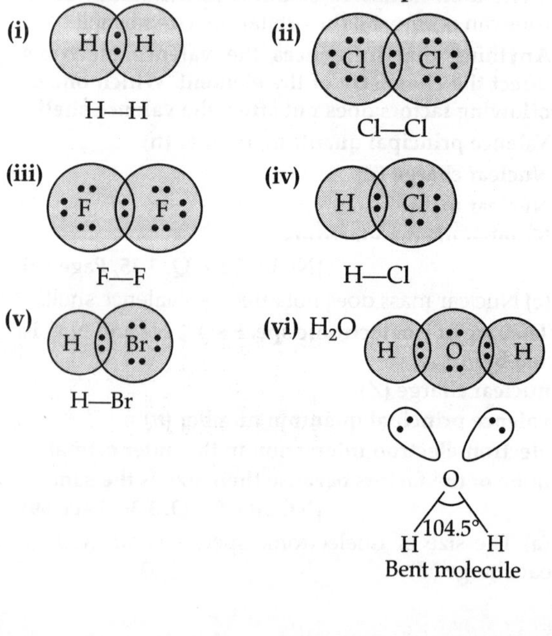

Chemical Bonding and Molecular Structure

Chemical Bond: Attractive forces which hold the various chemical constituents together in different chemical species.

Types:

(i) Covalent Bond: A chemical bond formed between two atoms by mutual sharing of electrons between them to complete their octet.

(ii) Ionic Bond: A chemical bond formed by complete transfer of electrons from one atom to another acquire the stable nearest noble gas configuration.

Lattice Enthalpy

Energy required to completely separate one mole of a solid ionic compound into gaseous constituent ions.

Molecular orbital theory

Postulates:

- Electrons in a molecule are present in various molecular orbitals as electrons are present in atomic orbitals.
- Atomic orbitals of comparable energies and proper symmetry combine.
- Atomic orbitals is monocentric while a molecular orbital is polycentric.
- Number of molecular orbital formed is equal to number of combining molecular orbitals.
- Bonding molecular orbitals has low energy and high stability Types of MO: σ(Sigma), p (Pi), d (Delta)

Chemical Bonding

Kossel Lewis approach to chemical bonding:

- Lewis pictured the atom as a positively charged 'kernel' and the outer shell accommodates a maximum of eight electrons.
- Lewis postulated that atoms achieve the stable octet when linked by chemical bonds.
- Kossel gave following facts:
- In the periodic table, highly electronegative halogens and highly electropositive alkali separated by noble gases.
- Formation of a negative ion from a halogen atom and a positive ion from an alkali metal atom is associated with gain and loss of electron by respective atoms.
- Negative and positive ions formed attains noble gas electronic configuration.
- Negative and positive ions are stabilized by electrostatic attraction.

Octet Rule: Atoms can combine either by transfer of valence electrons from one atom to another or by sharing of valence electrons to complete octet in their valence shells.

Lewis Dot Structure provides a picture of bonding in molecules and ions in terms of the shared pairs of electrons and the octet rule.

How To Write A Lewis Dot Structure:

Step 1: Add the valence electrons of the combining atoms to obtain total number of electrons.

Step 2: For anions, each negative charge means addition of one electron. For cations, each positive charge means subtraction of one electron from total number of valence electrons.

Step 3: Write chemical symbols of combining atoms.

Step 4: Least electronegative atom occupies central position.

Step 5: After accounting for shared pairs of electrons, remaining are either utilized for multiple bonding or remain as lone pairs.

Formal Charge= (Total number of valence electrons in free atom) – (Total number of non-bonding electrons) – 1/2(Total number of bonding electrons)

Limitations Of Octet Rule:

- Shows three types of exceptions i.e. incomplete octet of central atom, odd-electron molecules and expanded octet.
- Does not account for the shape of molecules.
- Fails to explain stability of molecules.

Hydrogen Bond: Formed when the negative end of one molecule attracts the positive end of other.

Types:

(i) Intermolecular: Between two different molecules of same or different substances.

(ii) Intramolecular : H atom is between two highly electronegative atom of same molecule..

Valence Shell Electron Pair Repulsion (VSEPR)

Postulates:

- Shape of molecule depends upon the number of valence shell electron pairs around central atom.
- Pairs of electrons in the valence shell repel one another.
- These pairs of electrons tend to occupy such positions in space that minimize repulsion.
- The valence shell is taken as a sphere with electron pairs localising on spherical surface at maximum distance from one another.
- A multiple bond is treated as if it is a single electron pair and the two or three electron pairs of a multiple bond are treated as a single super pair.
- When one or more resonance structures can represent a molecule, VSEPR model is applicable.
- **Decreasing order of repulsive interaction:** lp – lp > lp – bp > bp – bp

Valence Bond Theory: Given by L Pauling. It explains that a covalent bond is formed between two atoms by overlap of their half-filled valance orbitals, each of which contains one unpaired electron.

Orbital Overlap Concept: Formation of a covalent bond results by pairing of electrons in valence shell with opposite spins.

Types of Overlapping: (i) Sigma (σ) bond – end to end.
(ii) Pi (π) bond – axis remain parallel to each other.

Hybridisation: Process of intermixing of orbitals of different energies resulting in formation of new set of orbitals of equivalent energies and shape.

Types of Hybridisation –(i) *sp* (ii) sp^2 (iii) sp^3

Bonding Molecular Orbitals: Addition of atomic orbitals.

Antibonding Molecular Orbitals: Substraction of atomic orbitals.

Bond Parameters

(I) Bond Length: Equilibrium distance between the nuclei of two bonded atoms in molecule.

(ii) Bond Angle: Angle between the orbitals containing bonding electron pairs around central atom in a molecule complex ion.

(iii) Bond Enthalpy: Amount of energy required to break one mole of bonds of particular type between 2 atoms.

(iv) Bond Order: Number of bonds between the two atoms of a molecule.

(v) Resonance Structures: A set of two or more Lewis structures that collectively describe the electronic bonding a single polyatomic species.

(vi) Dipole Moment: Product of the magnitude of the charge and distance between centres of positive and negative charge. μ = Q x r

Hybridization

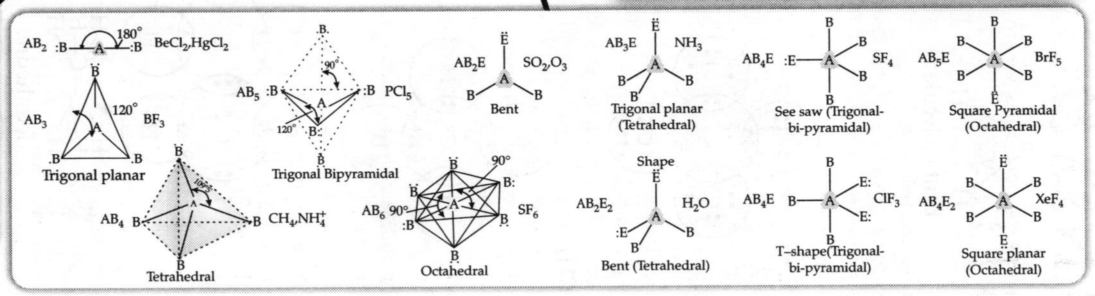

Trace the Mind Map: First Level · Second Level · Third Level

(vii) H_2S

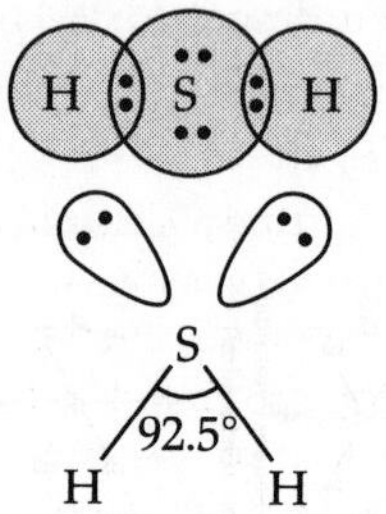

Bent molecule

(viii) NH_3

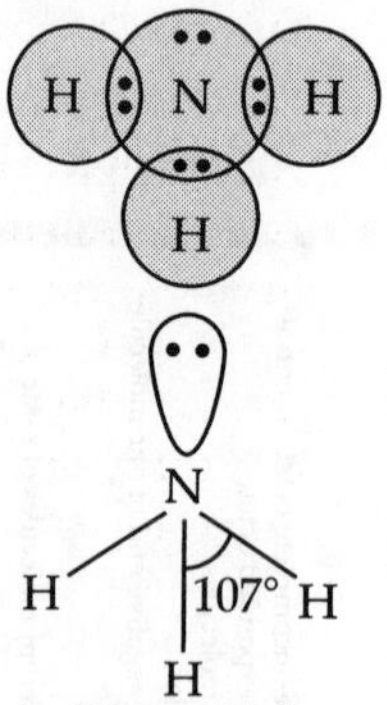

Pyramidal

(ix) CCl_4

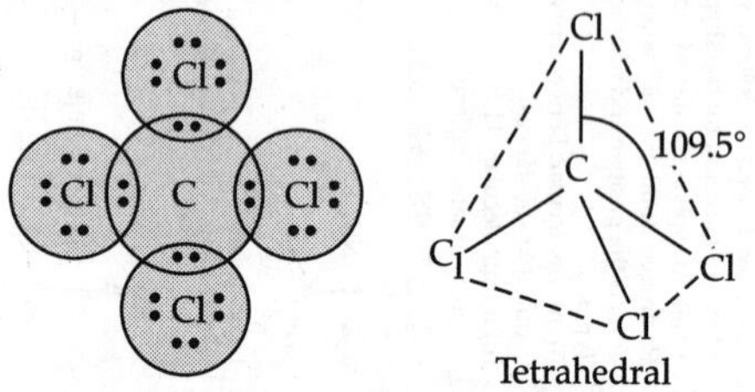

Tetrahedral

(x) CH_4

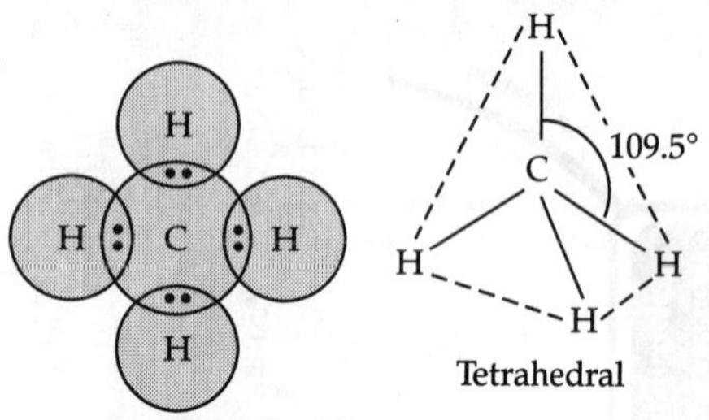

Tetrahedral

(xi) C_2H_6

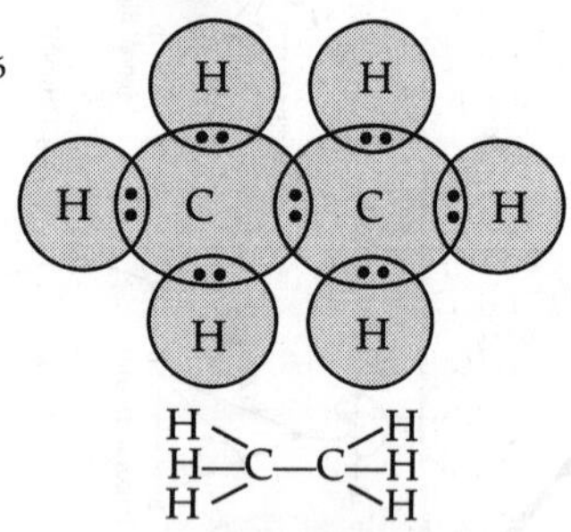

Tetrahedral

(xii) C_2H_4

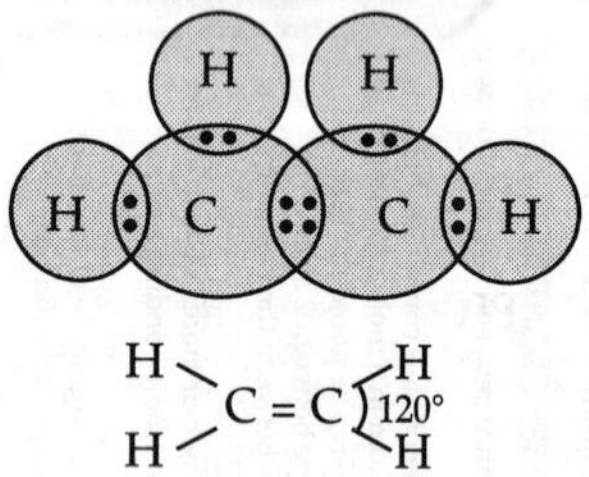

Trigonalplanar

(xiii) C_2H_2

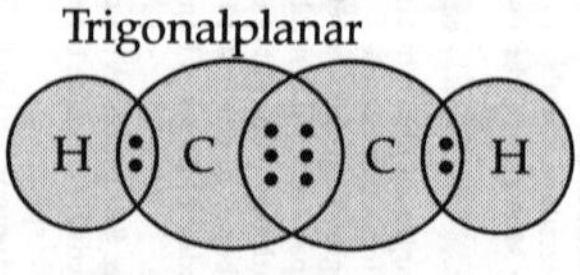

H—C≡C—H

Linear, Bond angle 180°

(xiv) $HgCl_2$

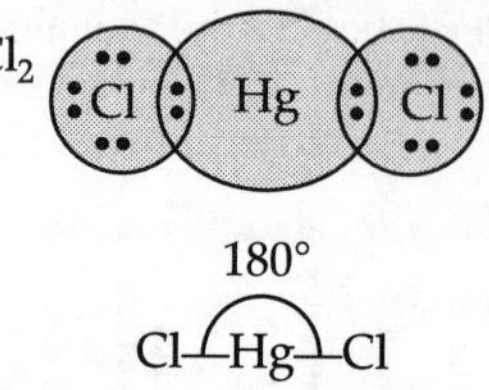

- **Formal Charge:** The formal charge of an atom in a polyatomic ion or molecule is defined as – "The difference between the number of valence electrons in an isolated or free state and the number of electrons assigned to that atom in a Lewis structure."

  It may be expressed as:

  Formal charge on an atom in a Lewis structure = (Total number of valence electrons in free atom) – (Total number of non-bonding (lone pair) electrons) $-\frac{1}{2}$ (Total number of bonding (shared) electrons)

  $$FC = V - L - \frac{1}{2}S$$

  where FC = Formal charge on an atom

  V = Total number of valence electrons in the free atom

  L = Total number of non-bonding (lone pair) electrons

  S = Total number of bonding (shared) electrons.

- **Properties of Covalent Compounds:**

- **Low melting and boiling points:** Covalent compounds consist of molecules held by weak forces. These can be easily overcome by heat.
- **Non-conduction nature:** Covalent compounds do not conduct electricity, i.e., electricity does not pass through the covalent compounds. This is because the covalent compounds do not contain ions or free electrons.
- **Solubility:** Covalent compounds are non-polar and do not dissolve in polar solvents like water. The covalent compounds however, dissolve in non-polar solvents like benzene, toluene, etc.
- **Slow rate of reaction:** The reaction of the covalent compounds are quite slow. The reaction is molecular, and the molecular reactions are slow.

Bond Parameters

- The various characteristic features shown by a bond are called the bond parameters.
- **Bond length:** Bond length is defined as "the equilibrium distance between the centres of the nuclei of two bonded atoms in a molecule." Bond lengths are measured by spectroscopic, X-ray diffraction and electron diffraction techniques.

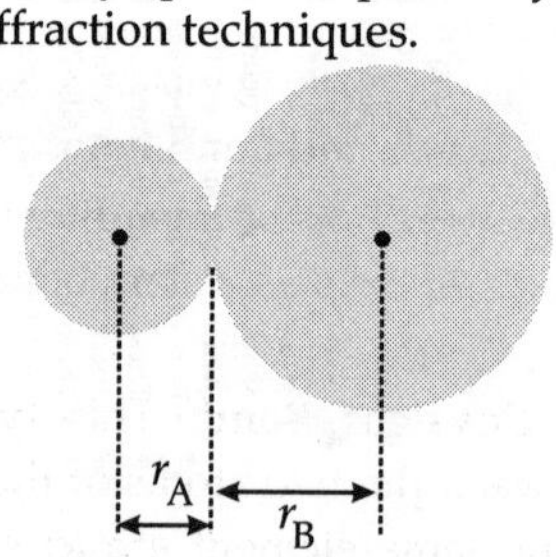

$$R = r_A + r_B$$

In case of covalent bond, the covalent radius is measured as the radius of an atom's core which is in contact with core of an adjacent atom in a bonded situation.

$$\text{Covalent radius} = r_A + r_B = \frac{d}{2} \qquad [\text{if } r_A = r_B]$$

The van der Waals radius represents the overall size of the atom which includes its valence shell in a non-bonded situation.

Single covalent radius decreases from left to right along a period and increases down a group just like atomic radii.

- **Bond angle:** It is defined as the angle between the orbitals containing bonding electron pairs around the central atom in a molecule/complex ion. For example, the bond angle in some compounds can be represented as under:

Scan to know more about this topic

Introduction to Ionic Bonding and Covalent Bonding

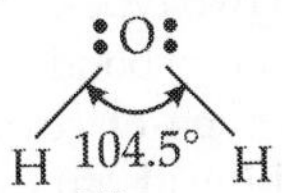

Water
(H_2O)

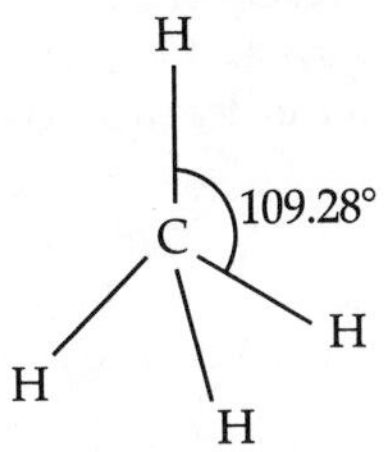

Methane
(CH_4)

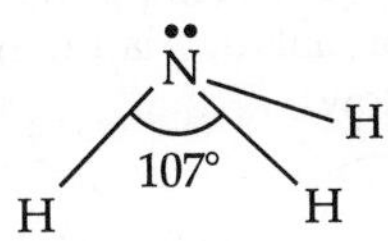

Ammonia
(NH_3)

- **Bond enthalpy:** It is defined as the amount of energy required to break one mole of bonds of a particular type between two atoms in a gaseous state. The unit of bond enthalpy is kJ mol^{-1}. For example H – H bond enthalpy in hydrogen molecule is 435.8 kJ mol^{-1}.

$$H_2(g) \longrightarrow H(g) + H(g)\ ;\ \Delta_a H^\ominus = 435.8 \text{ kJ mol}^{-1}$$

- **Bond order:** In the Lewis description of covalent bond, the bond order is given by the number of bonds between the two atoms in a molecule. Bond order in H_2 is one, in O_2, it is two and in N_2 it is three.

Isoelectronic molecules and ions have identical bond orders. For example F_2 and O_2^{2-} have bond order 1 and N_2, CO and NO^+ have bond order 3.

Thus, the stabilities of molecules can be understood by the statement "**with increase in bond order, bond enthalpy increases and bond length decreases.**"

- **Types of Covalent Bond:** Depending upon the nature of combining atoms, the covalent bonds can be of two types:

- **Non-polar Covalent Bond:** This type of bond is formed between the two atoms of the same element. Atoms of the same element attract electron equally. This type of covalent bond is described as a non-polar covalent bond.

  For example: H_2, O_2 and Cl_2, etc.

- **Polar Covalent Bond:** When two dissimilar atoms, having different electronegativities combined together to form a covalent bond, For example, in case of a heteronuclear molecule like HF, the shared electron pair between the two atoms gets displaced more towards fluorine since the electronegativity of fluorine is far greater than that of hydrogen. The atom with higher affinity for electrons develops a slight negative charge and atom with lesser affinity for electrons develops a slight positive charge. Eg., HCl, H_2O etc.

- **Dipole Moment:** It is defined as "the product of the magnitude of the charge and the distance of separation between the charges."

  Dipole moment (μ) = Charge (Q) × Distance of separation (r)

  It is usually expressed in Debye units (D).

  Dipole moment is also expressed in the units of C m (Coulomb meter):

$$1\text{D} = 3.33564 \times 10^{-30} \text{ C m}$$

The dipole of HF may be represented as:

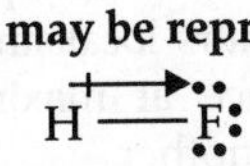

The presence of dipole moment is represented by the crossed arrow (+⟶).

- **Resonance:** When a molecule cannot canonically be represented by a single structure but its characteristic properties; position of nuclei, bonding and non-bonding pairs of electrons can be described by two or more than two canonical structures, then actual structure is said to be a resonance hybrid of these structure. Resonance is represented by a double headed arrow. Some of the examples of resonance structure are O_3 molecule, CO_3^{2-}, CO_2 molecule.

- **Conditions for Writing Resonating Structure:**

- The contributing structures should have same atomic positions, same number of unpaired electrons and nearly same energy.
- The structures should be written such that negative charge is present on an electronegative atom and positive charge is present on an electropositive atom.
- In these structures, the like charges should not reside on adjacent atoms.

- Resonance stabilizes the molecule because the energy of the resonance hybrid is less than the energy of any single canonical structures. Resonance also averages the bond characteristics as a whole.

- **Resonance Energy:** It is the difference between the actual bond energy of the molecule and that of the most stable resonating structures (having least energy). Thus,

Resonance energy = Actual bond energy – Energy of the most stable resonating structure

Valence Shell Electron Pair Repulsion (VSEPR) Theory

- In 1940, Sidgwick and Powell proposed a simple theory based on the repulsive interactions of the electron pairs in the valence shell of the atoms. It was further developed and refined by Nyholm and Gillespie in 1957.

  They suggested that the shapes of molecules can be determined by the number of electron pairs (bonding as well as non-bonding) in the valence shell of the central atom.

- **Postulates of VSEPR Theory:**

- The geometry of a molecule depends upon the total number of valence shell electron pairs (bonded or non-bonded) around the central atom in the molecule.
- Pairs of electrons in the valence shell repel one another since their electron clouds are negatively charged.
- These pairs of electrons tend to occupy such positions in space that minimise repulsion and thus maximise distance between them.
- The valence shell is taken as a sphere with the electron pairs localising on the spherical surface at maximum distance from one another.
- A multiple bond is treated as if it is a single electron pair and the two or three electron pairs of a multiple bond are treated as a single super pair.

Scan to know more about this topic

VSEPR Theory

- Where two or more resonance structures can represent a molecule, the VSEPR model is applicable to any such structure.

Valence Bond Theory by Heitler and London

- **Valence bond Theory by Heitler and London.** According to theory, a covalent bond is formed between the two atoms by the overlap of half filled valence atomic orbitals of each atom containing one unpaired electron.
- The bond is formed when two atoms approach each other in such a way that occupied orbitals with similar energies are able to overlap.
- Greater the overlap, stronger is the bond.
- **Types of overlapping and nature of covalent bonds:** Depending upon the type of overlapping, the covalent bonds may be divided into two types:

  (a) Sigma (σ) bond and **(b)** Pi (π) bond

  (a) Sigma (σ) bond: This type of covalent bond is formed by the end to end (head on) overlapping of bonding orbitals along the internuclear axis. The overlap is known as **head on overlap** or **axial** overlap.

  (i) ***s-s* overlapping:** In this type, two half filled *s*-orbitals overlap along the internuclear axis as shown below.

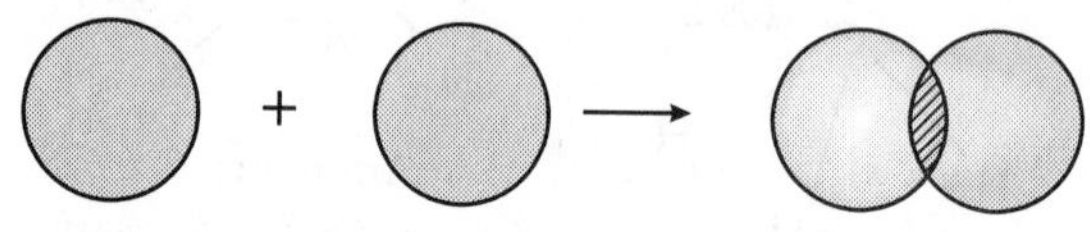

s-orbital *s*-orbital *s-s* overlap

(ii) ***s-p* overlapping:** This type of overlapping between the half filled *s*-orbital of one atom and *p*-orbital of the other atom.

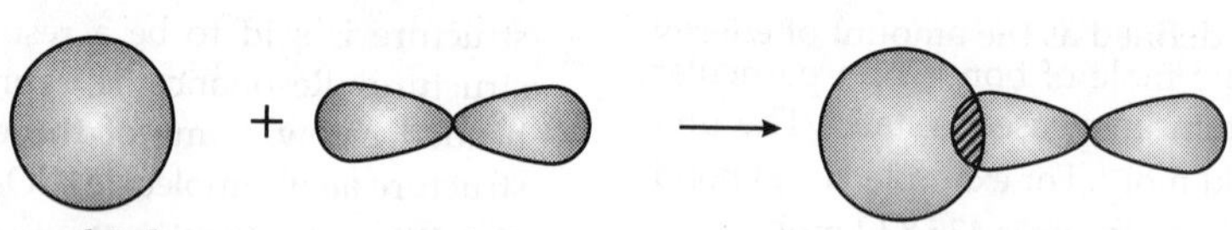

s-orbital *p*-orbital *s-p* overlap

(iii) ***p-p* overlapping:** This type of overlapping occurs between half filled *p*-orbitals of the two approaching atoms.

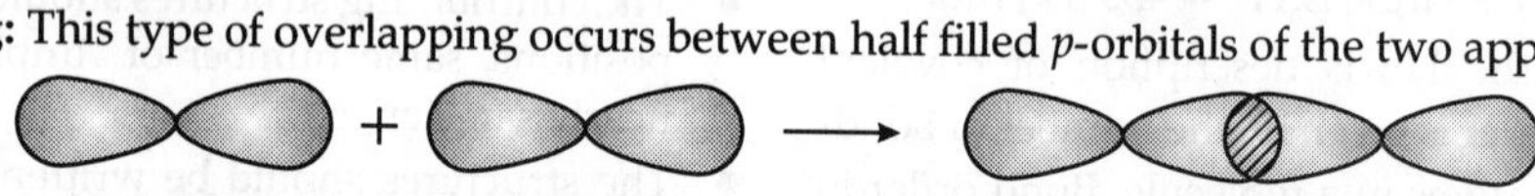

p-orbital *p*-orbital *p-p*-overlap

(b) Pi (π) bond: This type of covalent bond is formed by the sidewise overlapping of the half filled atomic orbitals of bonding atoms. Such an overlap is known as **sidewise** or **lateral overlap.** The atomic orbitals overlap in such a way that their axis remain parallel to each other and perpendicular to the internuclear axis. The orbital obtained as a result of sidewise overlap consists of two saucer type charged clouds above and below the plane of the participating atoms.

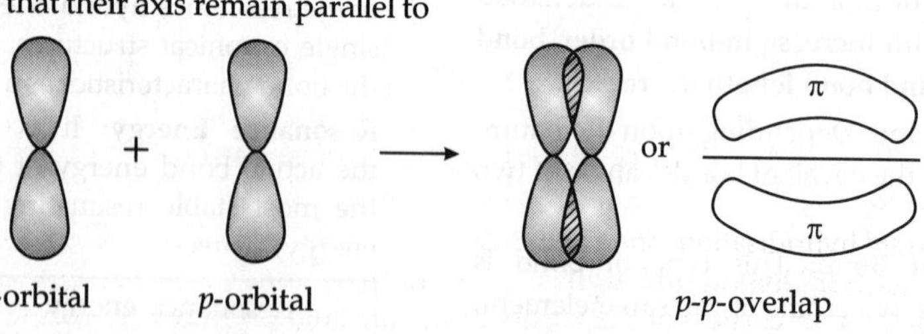

p-orbital *p*-orbital *p-p*-overlap

- **Strength of sigma and pi-bonds:** The strength of a covalent bond depends upon the extent of overlapping of atomic orbitals forming the bond. During the formation of a sigma bond, the overlapping of orbitals takes place to a larger extent.

  On the other hand, during the formation of a pi-bond, the overlapping occur to a smaller extent. Therefore, a sigma bond is strong than a pi-bond.

Hybridisation

- According to Pauling, This may be defined as—
  "The process of intermixing of the orbitals of slightly different energies so as to redistribute their energies resulting in the formation of new set of orbitals of equivalent energies and shape."
- **Characteristics of Hybridisation:**
- The number of hybrid orbitals equals the number of orbitals that become hybridised; also, the hybridised orbitals are always equivalent in energy and shape; additionally, the hybrid orbitals are more efficient at creating stable bonds than the pure atomic orbitals.
- The type of hybridisation indicates the geometry of the molecule.
- **Conditions for Hybridisation:**
- Only the orbitals present in the valence shell of the atom are hybridised.
- The orbitals undergoing hybridisation should have only a small difference in energy, i.e., should have almost equal energy. The orbitals which differ largely in energy cannot take part in hybridisation.
- Promotion of electron is not essential condition prior to hybridisation.
- It is not essential that only half filled orbitals participate in hybridisation. In certain cases, even filled orbitals of valence shell participate in hybridisation.
- **Types of Hybridisation:**
- ***sp* Hybridisation:** In *sp* hybridisation, one *s* and one *p* orbital mix and form two equivalent *sp* hybrid orbitals. The orbitals suitable for *sp* hybridisation are *s* and p_z orbitals, if the hybrid orbitals are to lie along *z*-axis. Each *sp* hybrid orbitals has 50% *s*-character and 50% *p*-character. These two *sp* hybrid orbitals are oriented in opposite direction forming an angle of 180° with linear shape.

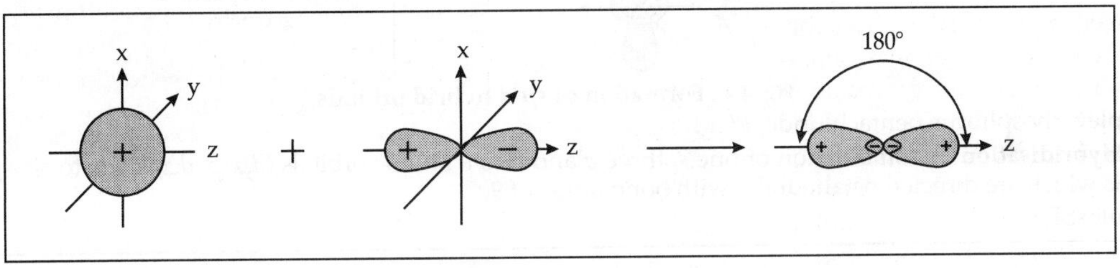

Fig. 4.1 : Formation of *sp* hybrid orbitals

Example: BeF_2, $BeCl_2$, etc.

- **sp^2 Hybridisation:** The combination of one *s* and two *p* orbitals gives rise to three sp^2 hybrid orbitals. These three hybrid orbitals lie in the same plane and are directed towards the three corners of an equilateral triangle in a plane have an angle of 120° and shape trigonal. Each sp^2 hybrid orbital has 33.3% *s*-character and 66.7% *p*-character.

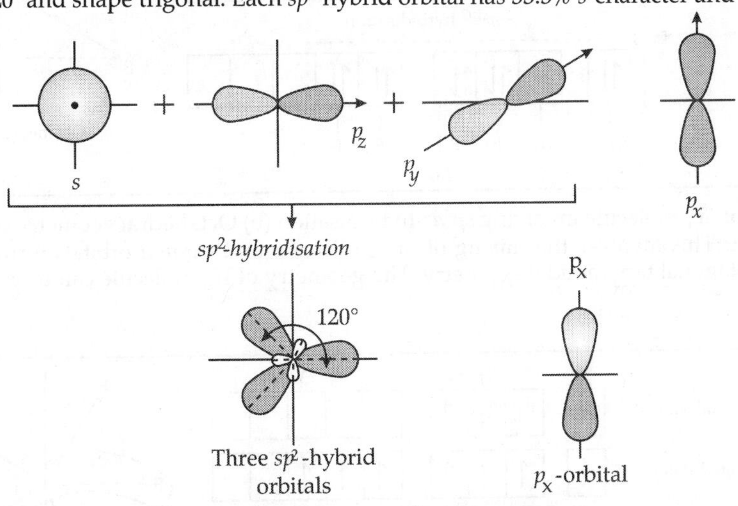

Fig. 4.2 : Formation of sp^2 hybrid orbitals

Example : BCl_3, BF_3, etc.

- **sp^3 Hybridisation:** In sp^3 hybridisation, one *s* and three *p* orbitals mix and form four sp^3 hybrid orbitals of equivalent energies and shape. Each sp^3 hybrid orbitals has 25% *s*-character and 75% *p*-character. The four sp^3 hybrid orbitals are directed towards the four corners of the tetrahedron. The angle between sp^3 hybrid orbital is 109°5′and shape tetrahedron.

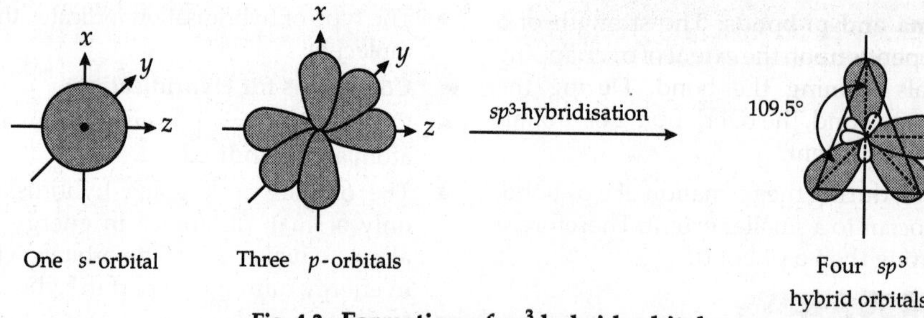

Fig. 4.3 : Formation of sp^3 hybrid orbitals

Example: CH_4, CCl_4, etc.

- ***sp^3d* Hybridisation:** This hybridisation involves the mixing of one *s*, three *p* and one *d*-orbitals. These five orbitals hybridise to form five sp^3d-hybrid orbitals. These hybrid orbitals point towards the corners of a trigonal bipyramidal geometry.

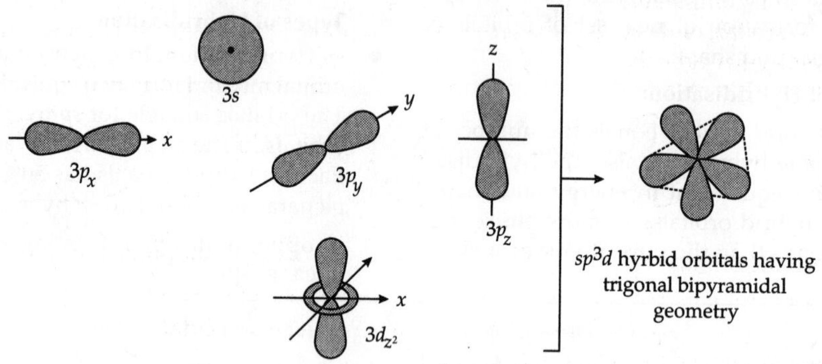

Fig. 4.4 : Formation of sp^3d hybrid orbitals

Example : Phosphorus pentachloride, PCl_5.

- ***sp^3d^2* Hybridisation:** A combination of one *s*, three *p* and two *d* atomic orbitals ($d_{x^2-y^2}$, d_{z^2}) leads to six sp^3d^2 hybrid orbitals which are directed octahedrally with bond angle of 90°.

Example: SF_6

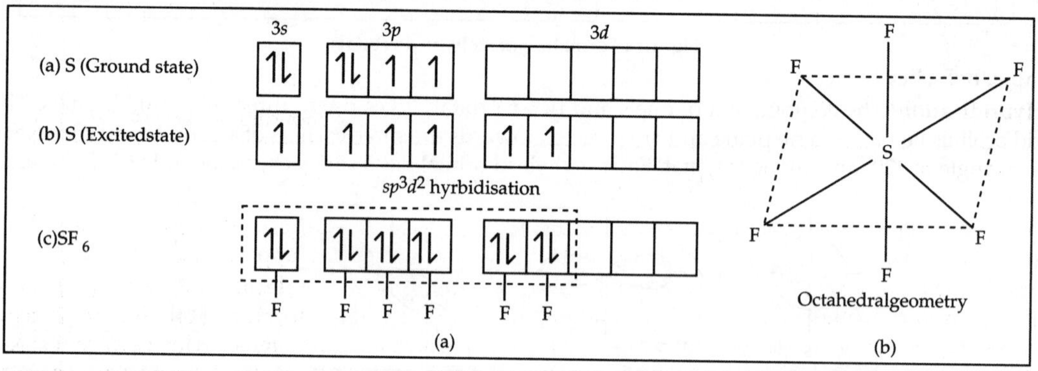

(a) Formation of SF_6 molecule involving sp^3d^2-hybridisation (b) Octahedral geometry of SF_6 molecule

- ***sp^3d^3* Hybridisation:** This involves the mixing of one *s*, three *p* and three *d*-orbitals forming seven sp^3d^3-hybrid orbitals having pentagonal bipyramidal geometry. The geometry of IF_7 molecule can be explained on the basis of sp^3d^3 hybridisation.

Example: IF_7

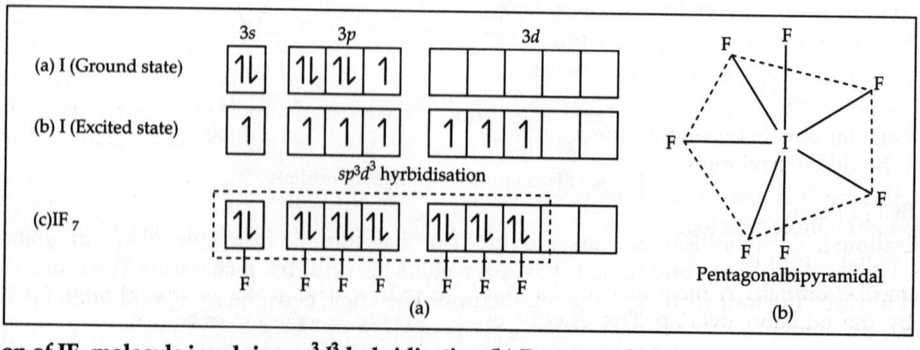

(a) Formation of IF_7 molecule involving sp^3d^3-hybridisation (b) Pentagonal bipyramidal geometry of IF_7 molecule

Molecular Orbital Theory

- Molecular orbital theory was proposed by F. Hund and R.S. Mulliken in 1932.

Salient Features of Molecular Orbital Theory:

- Just like an atom, molecule has orbitals of definite energy levels. Like electrons of atoms are present in atomic orbitals, electrons of a molecule are present in different molecular orbitals.
- Molecular orbitals are formed by the combination of atomic orbitals of proper symmetry and comparable energies. The atomic orbitals of these atoms merge into molecular orbitals.

Scan to know more about this topic

Valence Bond Theory & Hybrid Atomic Orbitals

- An electron in an atomic orbital is under the influence of only one nucleus. However, an electron in a molecular orbital is under the influence of two or more nuclei depending upon the number of atoms present in the molecule.
- The number of molecular orbitals formed is equal to the number of combining atomic orbitals. When two atomic orbitals combine, they form two molecular orbitals. These are called bonding molecular orbital and antibonding molecular orbital.
- The bonding molecular orbital has lower energy and hence greater stability whereas corresponding antibonding molecular orbital has more energy and hence lesser stability.
- The molecular orbital formed by the addition of two atomic orbitals is called bonding molecular orbital.

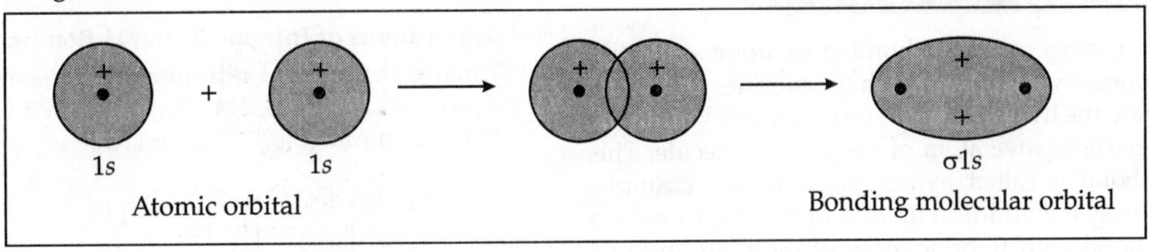

Fig. 4.5 : Formation of bonding molecular orbital

- The molecular orbital formed by the subtraction of two atomic orbitals is called antibonding molecular orbital.

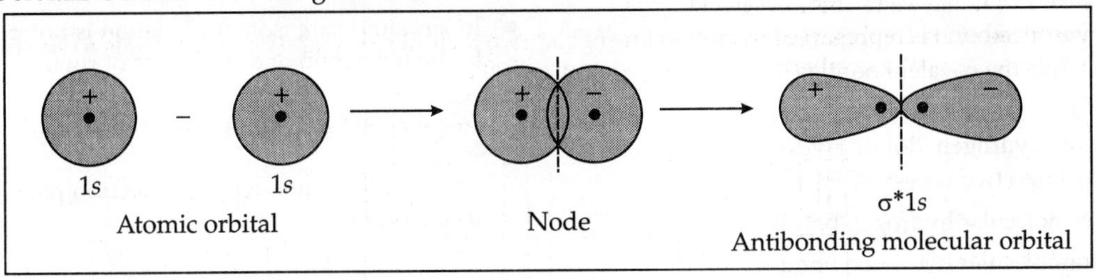

Fig. 4.6 : Formation of antibonding molecular orbital

It is clear from the figure that the electron density in between the two nuclei is practically zero and is concentrated in regions away from each nucleus. In this case, the electron probability densities of two atomic orbitals get cancelled in the centre (by subtraction) so that there is no probability of finding the electron in the region of overlap, i.e. between the nuclei. This situation does not favour the bond formation. Such an orbital is called antibonding molecular orbital. It is designated as σ*1s (called sigma star 1s). The asterisk '*' is used to represent antibonding molecular orbital.

- **Conditions for the Combination of Atomic Orbitals:**

- The combining atomic orbitals must have same or nearly the same energies.
- The extent of overlapping between the atomic orbitals of two atoms should be maximum.
- The combining atomic orbitals must have the same symmetry about the molecular axis.

- **Types of Molecular Orbitals:**

- **Bonding molecular orbitals:** A molecular orbital that is obtained by the addition overlap The energy of bonding molecular orbital is less than that of the constituent overlapping atomic orbitals.
- **Non-bonding molecular orbitals:** They do not play any part in the formation of molecule. When atomic orbitals do not interact with each other, formation of non-bonding molecular orbitals takes place. The reasons for no interaction may be one of the following:

(i) One orbital is far away from other orbital, so overlapping is not possible.
(ii) Symmetries of atomic orbitals are not same.
(iii) Energies of atomic orbitals are not same.

- **Antibonding molecular orbitals**: A molecular orbital that is obtained by the subtraction overlap (i.e., when the lobes of atomic orbitals overlap with the opposite sign) of two atomic orbitals is known as antibonding molecular orbital.

For molecules O_2 onwards, the increasing order of energies for molecular orbitals in which they are filled is as follows :

$\sigma 1s < \sigma^* 1s < \sigma 2s < \sigma^* 2s < \sigma 2p_z < (\pi 2p_z = \pi 2p_y) < (\pi^* 2p_z = \pi^* 2p_y) < \sigma^* 2p_z$

Bonding in Some Homo-nuclear Diatomic Molecules

- However, for homonuclear diatomic molecules of second row elements such as, Li_2, Be_2, B_2, C_2, N_2, the $\sigma 2p_z$ MO is higher in energy than $\pi 2p_x$ and $\pi 2p_y$ MOs. The increasing order of energies order for MOs for their molecules is
$\sigma 1s < \sigma{*}1s < \sigma 2s < \sigma{*}2s < (\pi 2p_x = \pi 2p_y) < \sigma 2p_z < (\pi{*}2p_x = \pi{*}2p_y) < \sigma{*}2p_z$
- Presence of unpaired electron shows that molecule is paramagnetic, however, paired electrons show that it is diamagnetic.

Hydrogen Bonding

- When hydrogen atom is bonded to atoms of highly electronegative elements such as fluorine, oxygen or nitrogen, the hydrogen atom forms a weak bond with the electronegative atom of the other molecule. This weak bond is called hydrogen bond. For example, in hydrogen fluoride, HF, hydrogen atom forms a weak bond with fluorine atom of the high bonding molecule while remaining bonded to its fluorine atom. This may be shown as :

$$........H^{\delta+} — F^{\delta-} .... H^{\delta+} — F^{\delta-} .... H^{\delta+} — F^{\delta-}$$

The hydrogen bond is represented by dotted line (_ _ _ _ _) while the covalent bond is represented by solid line (—).

- **Types of Hydrogen Bond:** Hydrogen bonds can be classified into two types:

(a) Intermolecular hydrogen bond

(b) Intramolecular hydrogen bond

(a) Intermolecular hydrogen bond: Intermolecular hydrogen bond is formed between different molecules of the same or different substances.

For example,

(i) hydrogen bond between the molecules of hydrogen fluoride.

(ii) hydrogen bond in alcohol or water molecules.

(b) Intramolecular hydrogen bond: Intramolecular hydrogen bond is formed when the hydrogen atom is between the two highly electronegative atom (F, O or N) present within the same molecule.

For example,

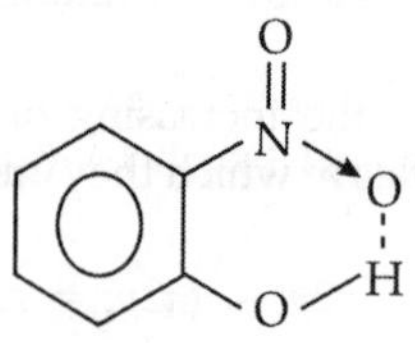

Ortho-nitrophenol

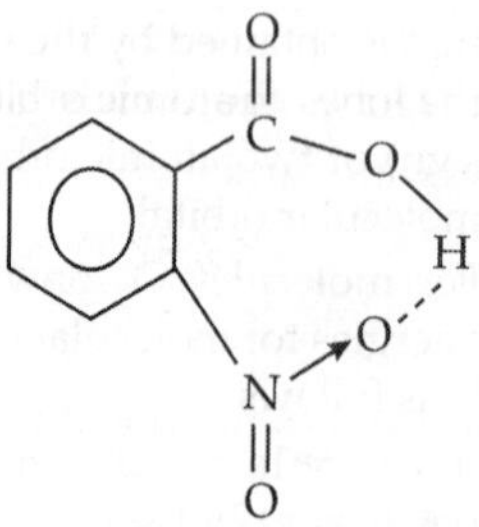

Ortho-nitrobenzoic acid

- **Applications of Intermolecular H-bonding:**
- **Very high Melting point and boiling point of water:** Water has the lowest molecular weight among the hydrides of group 16 elements yet it has the highest melting and boiling points. It is due to intermolecular H–bonding in H_2O.
- **Ice has less density than water:** In crystal structure of ice, every water molecule is associated with four other water molecules by H-bonding in a cage like tetrahedral structure. On melting, H-bonds in the ice are broken and space between water molecules decreases and density of water increases up to 4°C. Above 4°C, more H-bond are broken. The water molecules get apart from each other and the density again decreases. Thus, water has maximum density at 4°C.
- **Applications of Intramolecular H-Bonding:**
- **Volatile character of nitrophenols:** *ortho*-nitrophenol is more volatile (b.p. 214°C) as compared to *meta* (b.p. 290°C) and *para* (b.p. 279°C). It is due to chelation.

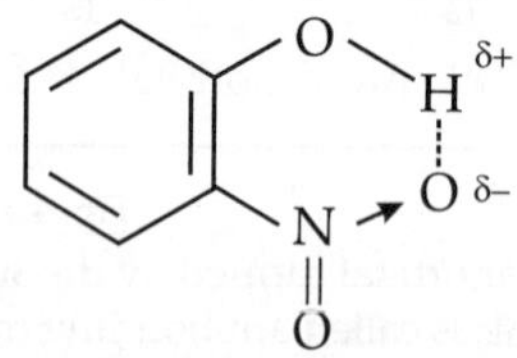

- In *meta* and *para* isomer, chelation is not possible due to the formation of desired size of ring.

Key Facts

- The repulsive interaction of electron pairs decrease in the order –

$$lp – lp > lp – bp > bp – bp$$

(where, *lp* = lone pair, *bp* = bond pair)

The presence of lone pairs in addition to bond pairs will result in certain distortions in the regular geometry of molecules.

- A positive bond order (i.e., $N_b > N_a$) means a stable molecule while a negative (i.e., $N_b < N_a$) or zero (i.e., Nb = Na) bond order means an unstable molecule.

where, N_b = No. of electrons in bonding molecular orbital.

N_a = No of electrons in anti-bonding molecular orbital.

Key Terms

- **Valence Electrons:** The outermost shell electrons which take part in the formation of chemical bond are called valence electrons.
- **Lattice Enthalpy:** The lattice enthalpy of an ionic solid is defined as the energy required to completely separate one mole of a solid ionic compound into gaseous constituent ions.
- **Bond Enthalpy:** It is defined as the amount of energy required to break one mole of bonds of a particular type between two atoms in a gaseous state.

- **Electrovalency:** The valence of an ion, equal to the number of positive or negative charges acquired by an atom through a loss or gain of electrons is known as electrovalency.
- **Covalency:** The bond formed between two atoms by mutual sharing of electrons between them so as to complete their octets is known as covalent bond and number of electrons involved is covalency.
- **Bond Enthalpy:** It is defined as the amount of energy required to break one mole of bonds of a particular type between two atoms in a gaseous state.

- **Electrovalency:** The valence of an ion, equal to the number of positive or negative charges acquired by an atom through a loss or gain of electrons is known as electrovalency.
- **Covalency:** The bond formed between two atoms by mutual sharing of electrons between them so as to complete their octets is known as covalent bond and number of electrons involved is covalency.

- **Bond Order:** It is defined as one half the difference between the number of electrons present in the bonding and the anti bonding orbitals. [Bond order $= \frac{1}{2}(N_b - N_a)$]

Mnemonics

Concept: Chemical Bond Strength

I can't Handle Dirty Vans

Ionic > Covalent > H–bonds > Dipole > van Der Waal

5. Bond Polarity

SNAP

Symmetrical → Non Polar

Asymmetrical → Polar

1. Concept: Formal Charge

Mnemonics: For Very Lovely Son!

Interpretation: [Formal Charge (F.C) = Valence e– in free state (V.E) – Lone pair (l.p) –1/2 × Shared e–(S.E)]

2. Concept: Hydrogen

Mnemonics: H-bonding is FON (Fun)!

Interpretation: Fluorine, Oxygen, Nitrogen

NCERT CORNER

Q. 1. Explain the formation of a chemical bond.

[NCERT Ex. Q. 4.1, Page 133]

Ans. A chemical bond between atoms can be formed due to following reasons:

(i) Lowering of energy of combining atoms.

(ii) Lewis octet rule.

The formation of chemical compounds takes place as a result of combination of atoms of various elements in different ways. In order to explain the formation of chemical bond in terms of electrons, Kossel and Lewis were the first to provide explanation of valence which was based on the inertness of noble gases.

Lewis postulated that atoms achieve the stable octet when they are linked by chemical bonds. In the formation of a molecule, only the outer shell electrons take part in chemical combination and these are called valence electrons. Atoms combine with one another in different ways, i.e., by transfer of electrons (from an ionic bond) or by sharing of electrons (from a covalent bond), etc.

Q. 2. Write Lewis dot symbols for atoms of the following elements:

Mg, Na, B, O , N, Br **[NCERT Ex. Q. 4.2, Page 133]**

Ans.

Atoms	Electronic Configuration	Lewis dot symbol
$_{12}Mg$	2, 8, 2	$\ddot{Mg}$
$_{11}Na$	2, 8, 1	$\dot{Na}$
$_{5}B$	2, 3	$\cdot\dot{B}\cdot$
$_{8}O$	2, 6	$:\ddot{O}:$
$_{35}Br$	2, 8, 18, 7	$:\ddot{\underset{..}{Br}}\cdot$
$_{7}N$	2, 5	$:\dot{N}:$

Q. 3. Write Lewis symbols for the following atoms and ions: S and S^{2-}; Al and Al^{3+}, H and H^-

[NCERT Ex. Q. 4.3, Page 133]

Ans.

Atoms/ Ions	No. of Electronic	Electrons Configuration	Lewis dot symbol
S	16	2, 8, 6	$:\ddot{S}:$
S^{2-}	16+2=18	2, 8, 8	$[:\ddot{\underset{..}{S}}:]^{2-}$
Al	13	2, 8, 3	$\dot{Al}\cdot$
Al^{3+}	13–3=10	2, 8	$[Al]^{3+}$
H	1	1	$\dot{H}$
H^-	1+1=2	2	$[\ddot{H}]^-$

Q. 4. Draw the Lewis structures for the following molecules and ions:

H_2S, $SiCl_4$, BeF_2, CO_3^{2-}, HCOOH

[NCERT Ex. Q. 4.4, Page 133]

Ans. Lewis structure of H_2S:

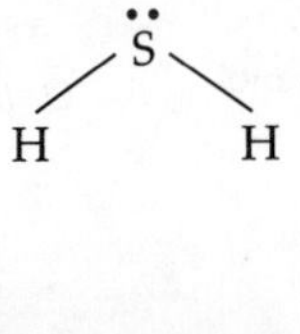

Lewis structure of $SiCl_4$:

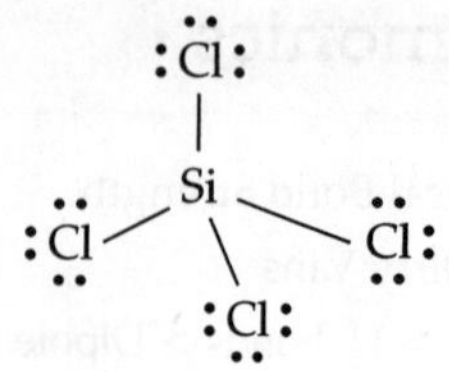

Lewis structure of BeF_2:

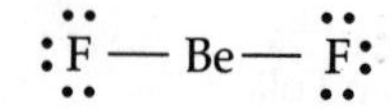

Lewis structure of CO_3^{2-}:

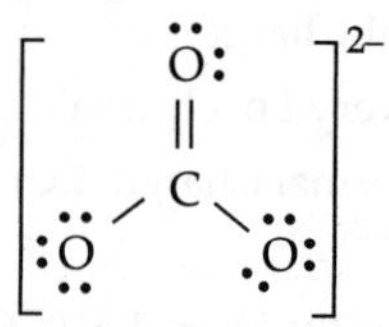

Lewis structure of HCOOH:

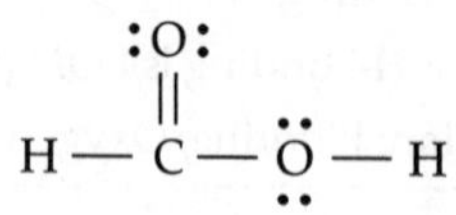

Q. 5. Define octet rule. Write its significance and limitations. [NCERT Ex. Q. 4.5, Page 133]

Ans. Octet Rule: This rule states that elements gain or lose electrons to attain an electronic configuration of the nearest noble gas, i.e., eight electrons in the valence shell (two for hydrogen atoms).

Significance of Octet Rule:

1. It helps to explain the combination of different atoms with each other to form a chemical bond.
2. It explains the structure of chemical compounds.

Limitations of Octet Rule:

(i) Incomplete octet of the central atom:

In some compounds, the number of electrons surrounding the central atom is less than eight. This is especially the case with elements having less than four valence electrons.

e.g. LiCl	BeH_2	BCl_3
		Cl
Li : Cl	H : Be : H	Cl : $\ddot{B}$: Cl

Li, Be and B have 1, 2 and 3 valence electrons only.

(ii) Odd-electron molecules :

In molecules with an odd number of electrons like nitric oxide (NO) and nitrogen dioxide (NO_2), the octet rule is not satisfied for all the atoms.

(iii) The expanded octet :

In some compounds, there are more than eight valence electrons around the central atom.

e.g., PF_5, SF_6, etc.

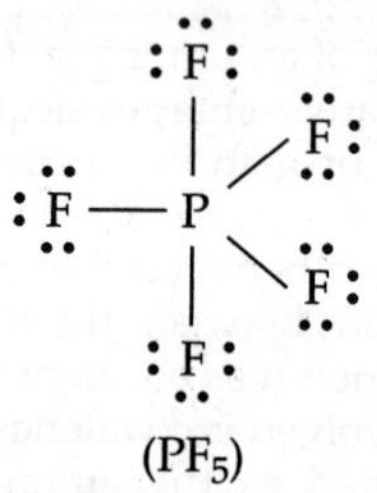

(PF_5)
(10 electrons around the P-atom)

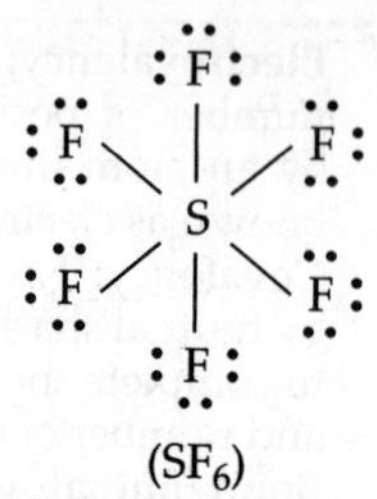

(SF_6)
(12 electrons around the S-atom)

Q. 6. Write the favourable factors for the formation of ionic bond. [NCERT Ex. Q. 4.6, Page 134]

Ans. Following are the favourable factors for the formation of ionic bond:

(i) Low ionization energy of the element forming cation.
(ii) High electron affinity (more negative electron gain enthalpy) of the element forming anion.
(iii) High lattice energy of the ionic compound formed.

Q. 7. Discuss the shape of the following molecules using the VSEPR model: [NCERT Ex. Q. 4.7, Page 134]

$BeCl_2$, BCl_3, $SiCl_4$, AsF_5, H_2S, PH_3

Ans. According to VSEPR theory, the shape of a molecule depends upon the number of valence shell electron pairs (bonded or non-bonded) around the central atom and lone pairs.

$BeCl_2$: Cl : Be : Cl
Bond pairs = 2
Lone pairs = 0
Geometry = Linear

BCl_3:

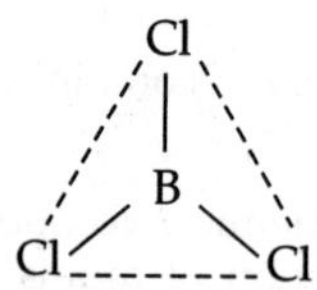

Bond pairs = 3
Lone pairs = 0
Geometry = Trigonal planar

$SiCl_4$:

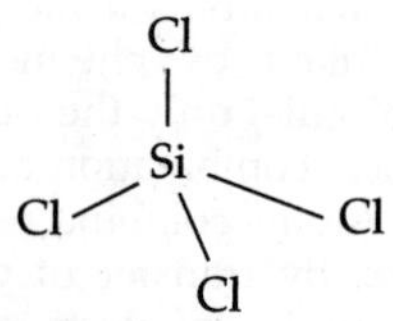

Bond pairs = 4
Lone pairs = 0
Geometry = Tetrahedral

AsF_5:

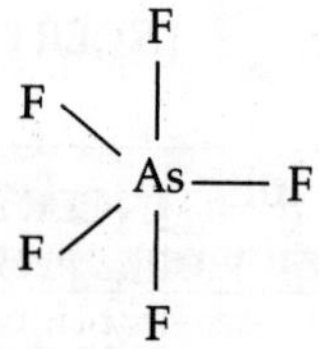

Bond pairs = 5
Lone pairs = 0
Geometry = Trigonal bipyramidal

H_2S :

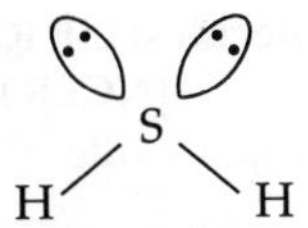

Bond pairs = 2
Lone pairs = 2
Geometry = Angular or bent shape

PH_3:

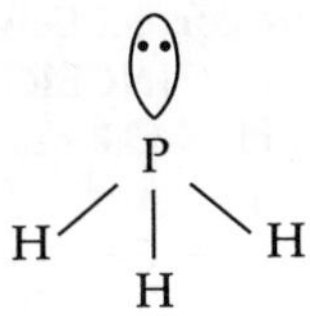

Bond pairs = 3
Lone pair = 1
Geometry = Trigonal bipyramidal

Q. 8. Although geometries of NH_3 and H_2O molecules are distorted tetrahedral, bond angle in water is less than that of ammonia. Discuss.

[NCERT Ex. Q. 4.8, Page 134]

Ans. According to VSEPR theory, the structures of NH_3 and H_2O molecules are given as below :

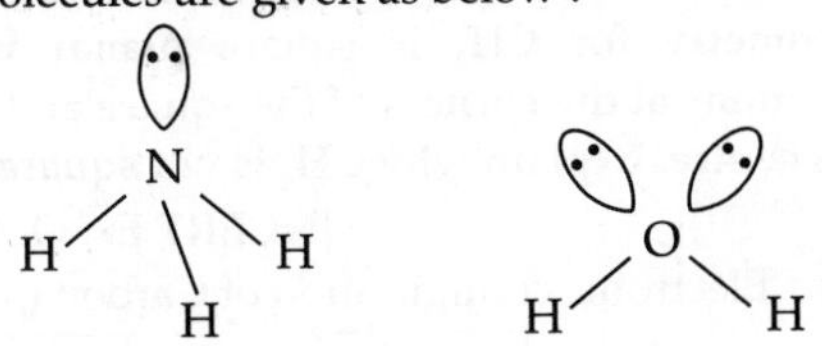

NH_3 $\begin{Bmatrix} bp = 3 \\ lp = 1 \end{Bmatrix}$ H_2O $\begin{Bmatrix} bp = 2 \\ lp = 2 \end{Bmatrix}$

bond angle = 107.5°   bond angle = 104.5°

In H_2O, oxygen has two lone pairs and in NH_3, nitrogen has only one lone pair. In H_2O, two lone pairs on oxygen repel each other than the bonded pairs more strongly and cause them to come closer thereby decreasing the bond angle. [$lp \sim lp$ repulsion > $bp \sim lp$ repulsion]

Q. 9. How do you express the bond strength in terms of bond order? [NCERT Ex. Q. 4.9, Page 134]

Ans. Bond order is directly proportional to the bond strength.

Bond order $\propto$ bond strength

Greater the bond order of molecule or ion, greater will be the bond strength. Because, bond enthalpy increases with increase in bond order. Hence, bond strength is also high.

Q. 10. Define the bond length.

[NCERT Ex. Q. 4.10, Page 134]

Ans. It is defined as the equilibrium distance between the nuclei of two bonded atoms in a molecule.

OR

It is defined as the average distance between the centres of the nuclei of the two bonded atoms in a molecule.

Bond length (R) = $r_A + r_B$

where r_A = Covalent radius of atom A
r_B = Covalent radius of atom B

Q. 11. Explain the important aspects of resonance with reference to the CO_3^{2-} ion. [NCERT Ex. Q. 4.11, Page 134]

Ans. The single Lewis structure based on the presence of two single bonds and one double bond between carbon and oxygen atoms is inadequate to represent the molecule accurately as it represents unequal bonds. According to the experimental findings, all carbon to oxygen bonds in CO_3^{2-} are equivalent. So, the carbonate ion is best described as a resonance hybrid of the canonical forms I, II and III shown below :

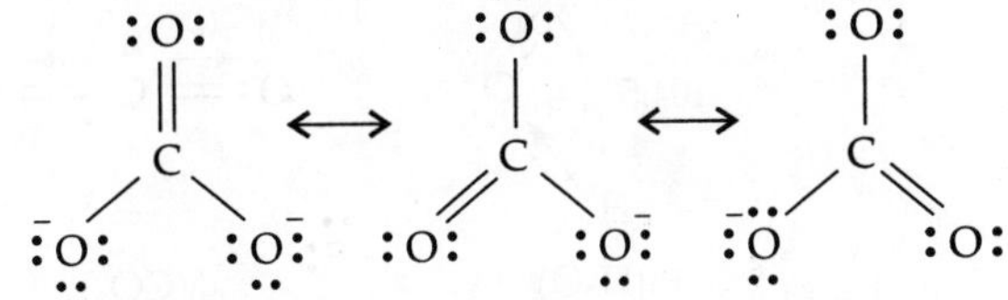

(I) (II) (III)

Q. 12. H_3PO_3 can be represented by structures 1 and 2 shown below. Can these two structures be taken as the canonical forms of the resonance hybrid representing H_3PO_3? If not, give reasons for the same.

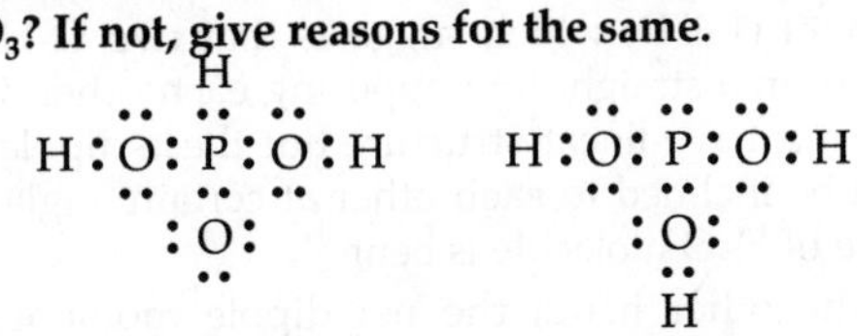

(1) (2)

[NCERT Ex. Q. 4.12, Page 134]

Ans. These two structures of H_3PO_3 cannot be called as canonical forms because relative position of hydrogen is changed. In resonance, canonical forms should differ only in the position of electrons and not in the position of atoms.

Q. 13. Write the resonance structures for SO_3, NO_2 and NO_3^-. [NCERT Ex. Q. 4.13, Page 134]

Ans. Resonance structures of SO_3

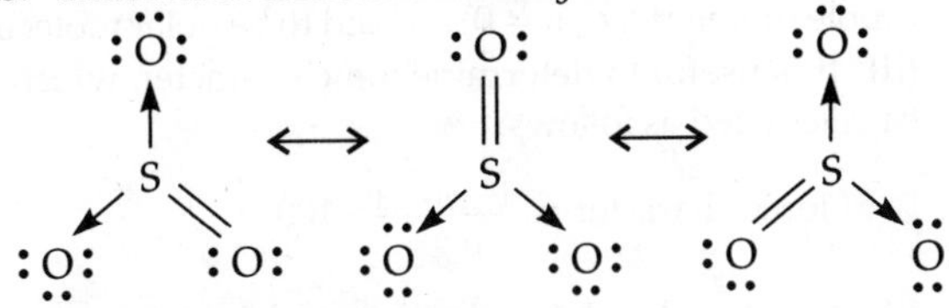

Resonance structures of NO_2 :

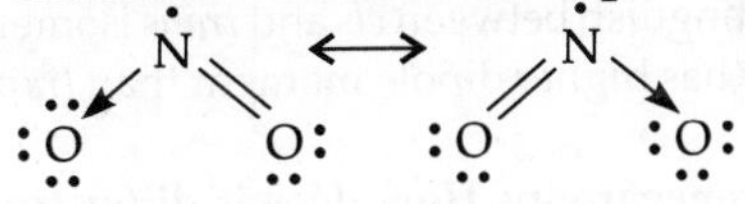

Resonance structures of NO_3^-:

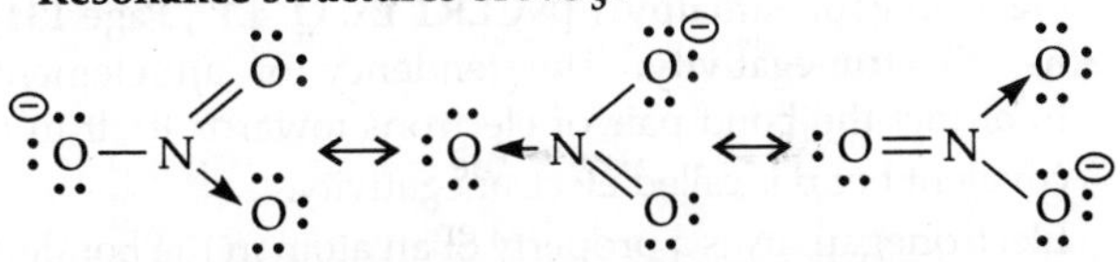

Q. 14. Use Lewis symbols to show electron transfer between the following atoms to form cations and anions:

(a) K and S (b) Ca and O (c) Al and N

[NCERT Ex. Q. 4.14, Page 134]

Ans. (a) $2\,K^{\cdot} + \ddot{S}: \rightarrow 2K^+[:\ddot{S}:]^{2-}$ or K_2S

(2, 8, 8, 1) (2, 8, 6)

(b) $Ca: + \ddot{O}: \rightarrow Ca^{2+}[:\ddot{O}:]^{2-}$ or CaO

(2, 8, 8, 2) (2, 6)

(c) $\dot{Al}\cdot + \dot{N}: \rightarrow Al^{3+}[:\ddot{N}:]^{3-}$ or AlN

(2, 8, 3) (2, 5)

Q. 15. Although both CO_2 and H_2O are triatomic molecules, the shape of H_2O molecule is bent while that of CO_2 is linear. Explain this on the basis of dipole moment. **[NCERT Ex. Q. 4.15, Page 134]**

Ans.

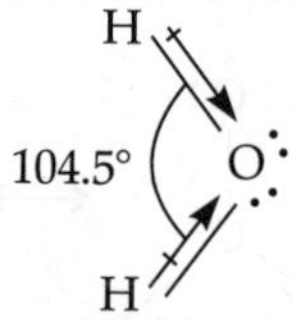

(H_2O)	(CO_2)
Shape = Bent	Shape = Linear
Dipole moment	Dipole moment
(μ) = 1.85 D	(μ) = 0 (zero)

Since, the H_2O molecule is found to have a net dipole moment (1.85D) which suggests that two O-H dipoles are not in a straight line opposing each other, i.e., H_2O does not have linear structure but these dipoles (O–H) must be inclined to each other at certain angle. So, the shape of H_2O molecule is bent.

On the other hand, the net dipole moment of CO_2 molecule is zero. This is due to the fact that the two equal bond dipoles ($\overset{\delta+}{C} - \overset{\delta-}{O}$) point in opposite directions and cancel the effect of each other. So, the shape of CO_2 molecule is linear. (3)

Q. 16. Write the significance/applications of dipole moment. **[NCERT Ex. Q. 4.16, Page 134]**

Ans. Following are the applications of dipole moment:

(i) The dipole moment is useful to predict the polarity of the molecule. Molecules having zero dipole moment are said to be non-polar molecules and those having net dipole moment (i.e., $\mu \neq 0$) are said to be polar molecules.

(ii) It is useful to determine ionic character, which can be calculated as follows:

$$\% \text{ of ionic character} = \frac{\mu_{observed}}{\mu_{ionic}} \times 100$$

(iii) It is useful to determine geometry of the molecules.

(iv) It helps to distinguish between *cis* and *trans* isomers. Usually *cis*-isomer has higher dipole moment than *trans*-isomer.

Q. 17. Define electronegativity. How does it differ from electron gain enthalpy? **[NCERT Ex. Q. 4.17, Page 134]**

Ans. Electronegativity: The tendency of an element to attract the bond pair of electrons towards itself in a covalent bond is called electronegativity.

Electronegativity is a property of an atom in the bonded state which is not constant while electron gain enthalpy relates to atoms in their isolated gaseous states. It can be negative or positive depending upon whether electron is added or removed.

Q. 18. Explain with the help of suitable example, polar covalent bond. **[NCERT Ex. Q. 4.18, Page 134]**

Ans. In a heteronuclear molecule, the shared pair of electrons between the two atoms gets displaced more towards more electronegative atom. In such molecule, the resultant covalent bond is known as polar covalent bond.

For example: HF

$$H : \ddot{\underset{..}{F}} : \quad \text{or} \quad \overset{\delta+}{H} - \overset{\delta-}{F}$$

Q. 19. Arrange the bonds in order of increasing ionic character in the molecules: LiF K_2O, N_2, SO_2 and ClF_3 **[NCERT Ex. Q. 4.19, Page 134]**

Ans. According to Fajan's rule, the increasing order of ionic character:

$N_2 < SO_2 < ClF_3 < K_2O < LiF$

Q. 20. The skeletal structure of CH_3COOH as shown below is correct, but some of the bonds are shown incorrectly. Write the correct Lewis structure for acetic acid. **[NCERT Ex. Q. 4.20, Page 134]**

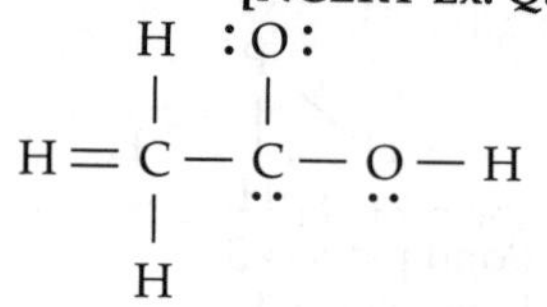

Ans. The correct Lewis structure for acetic acid is –

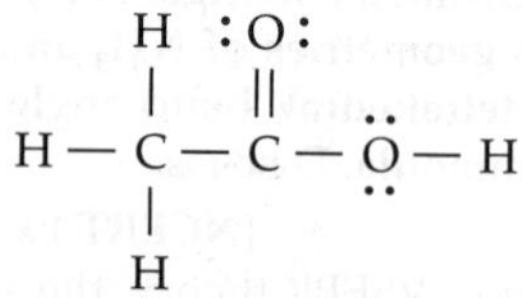

Q. 21. Apart from tetrahedral geometry, another possible geometry for CH_4 is square planar with the four H-atoms at the corners of the square and the C-atom at its centre. Explain why CH_4 is not square planar? **[NCERT Ex. Q. 4.21, Page 134]**

Ans. Electronic configuration of Carbon ($_6C$)

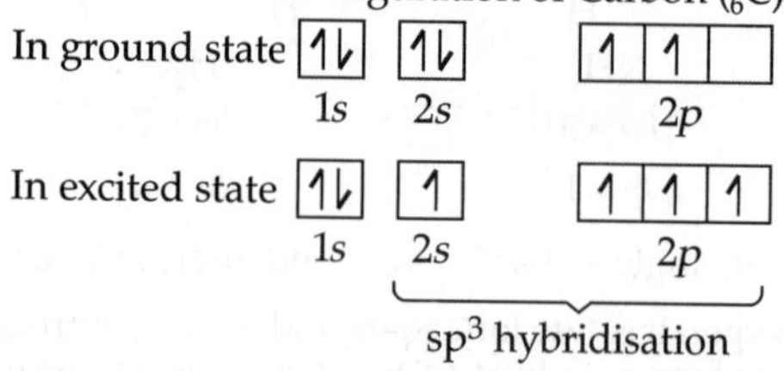

Since, sp^3 hybridisation occurs in CH_4 molecule. So, it is tetrahedral in shape. For square planar geometry, dsp^2 hybridisation is required, which is not possible in carbon due to absence of *d*-orbitals. Moreover, according to VSEPR theory, only bond pairs of electrons are present in CH_4 but no lone pair, so its geometry is tetrahedral (i.e., four bonded electron pairs around carbon atom arranged themselves in a regular tetrahedron geometry) and bond angle is 109°28′. While in square planar structure, the bond angle is 90°. Hence, it is clear that CH_4 is not square planar.

Q. 22. Explain why BeH_2 molecule has a zero dipole moment although the Be–H bonds are polar? **[NCERT Ex. Q. 4.22, Page 134]**

Ans. BeH_2 is a linear molecule.

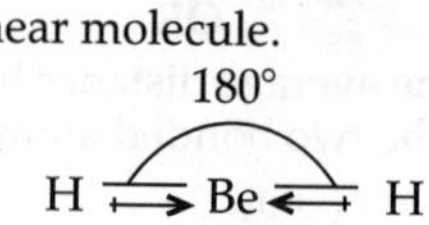

In this molecule, the two equal bond dipoles point in opposite directions and cancel the effect of each other. Hence, BeH_2 molecule has a zero dipole moment (μ = 0).

Q. 23. Which out of NH_3 and NF_3 has higher dipole moment and why? **[NCERT Ex. Q. 4.23, Page 134]**

Ans. The dipole moment of NH_3 is higher than NF_3, although both the molecules are pyramidal in shape.

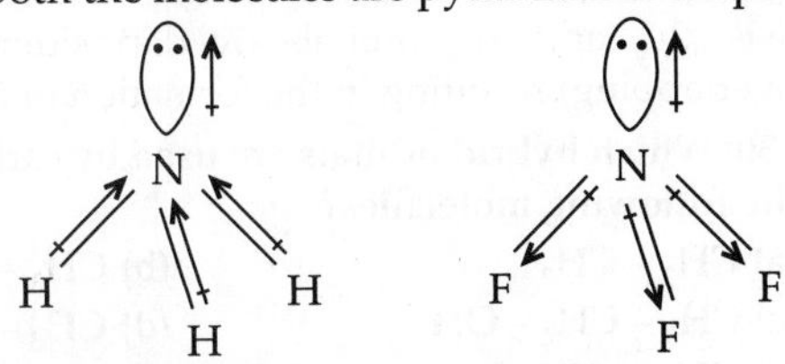

(NH_3) (NF_3)

($\mu = 4.90 \times 10^{-30}$ C m) ($\mu = 0.80 \times 10^{-30}$ C m)

According to structure of both molecules, in NH_3, the orbital dipole due to lone pair is in the same direction as the resultant dipole moment of the three N – H bonds, while in NF_3, the orbital dipole due to lone pair is in the opposite direction to the resultant dipole moment of three N – F bonds. Hence, the resultant dipole of NH_3 is higher than NF_3.

Q. 24. What is meant by hybridisation of atomic orbitals? Describe the shapes of *sp*, sp^2, sp^3 hybrid orbitals.

[NCERT Ex. Q. 4.24, Page 134]

Ans. Hybridisation: It is defined as a process of intermixing of the orbitals of slightly different energies so as to redistribute their energies, resulting in the formation of new set of orbitals of equivalent energies and shape.

***sp* hybridisation:**

Such a molecule in which the central atom is *sp*-hybridised possessing linear geometry with bond angle 180°.

e.g., $BeCl_2$.

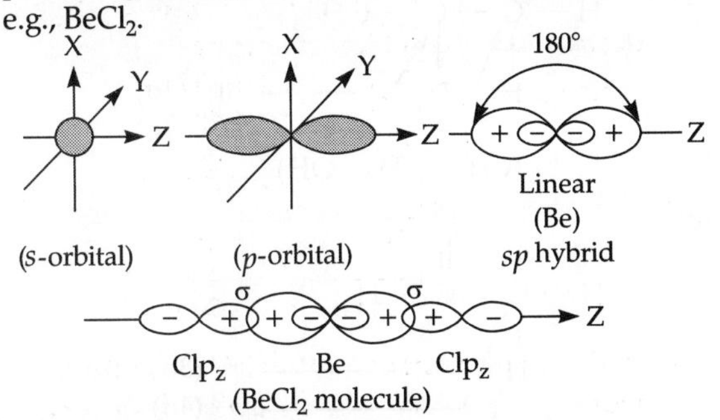

Formation of *sp* hybrid orbitals in $BeCl_2$ molecule

sp^2 hybridisation:

Such a molecule in which the central atom is sp^2 hybridised possessing trigonal planar geometry with bond angle 120°.

eg., BCl_3

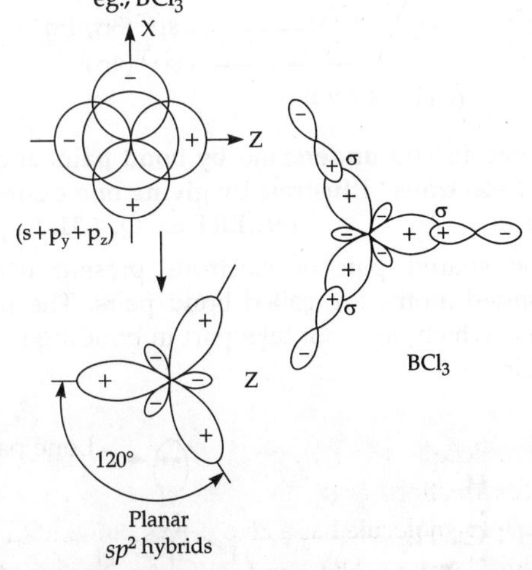

Formation of sp^2 hybrid orbitals in BCl_3 molecule

sp^3 hybridisation:

Such a molecule in which the central atom is sp^3 hybridised possessing tetrahedral geometry with bond angle 109.5°.

e.g., CH_4

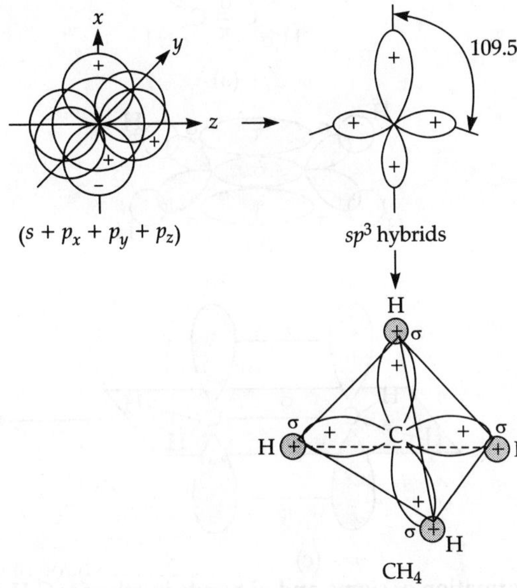

Formation of sp^3 hybrid orbitals in CH_4 molecule

Q. 25. Describe the change in hybridisation (if any) of the Al atom in the following reaction:

$$AlCl_3 + Cl^- \longrightarrow AlCl_4^-$$

[NCERT Ex. Q. 4.25, Page 134]

Ans. Electronic configuration of $_{13}Al$ = 2, 8, 3

In ground state [↿⇂] [↿⇂] [↿⇂|↿⇂|↿⇂] [↿⇂] [↿| |]
1s 2s 2p 3s 3p

In excited state [↿⇂] [↿⇂] [↿⇂|↿⇂|↿⇂] [↿] [↿|↿|]
1s 2s 2p 3s 3p
($3s$, $3p$: sp^2)

∴ In the formation of $AlCl_3$, Al undergoes sp^2 hybridisation and possesses trigonal planar geometry.

While in case of $AlCl_4^-$

Electronic configuration of Al in excited state [↿⇂] [↿⇂] [↿⇂|↿⇂|↿⇂] [↿] [↿|↿|↿]
1s 2s 2p 3s 3p
($3s$, $3p$: sp^3)

∴ In the formation of $AlCl_4^-$, Al undergoes sp^3 hybridisation and possesses tetrahedral geometry.

Q. 26. Is there any change in the hybridisation of B and N atoms as a result of the following reaction?

$$BF_3 + NH_3 \longrightarrow F_3B.NH_3$$

[NCERT Ex. Q. 4.26, Page 135]

Ans. In BF_3, the central atom B is sp^2 hybridised as it contains 3 bond pairs and 0 lone pairs. While in NH_3, the central atom N is sp^3 hybridised as it contains 3 bond pairs and 1 lone pair.

After the reaction, hybridisation of B in BF_3 changes from sp^2 to sp^3 hybridisation whereas hybridization of nitrogen in NH_3 remains same because N shares its lone pair with electron deficient B.

Q. 27. Draw diagrams showing the formation of a double bond and a triple bond between carbon atoms in C_2H_4 and C_2H_2 molecules. **[NCERT Ex. Q. 4.27, Page 135]**

Ans. Formation of sigma and pi bonds in ethene (C_2H_4)

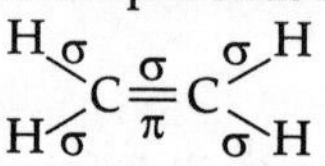

(a)

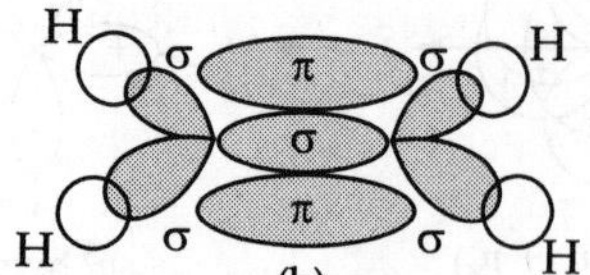

(b)

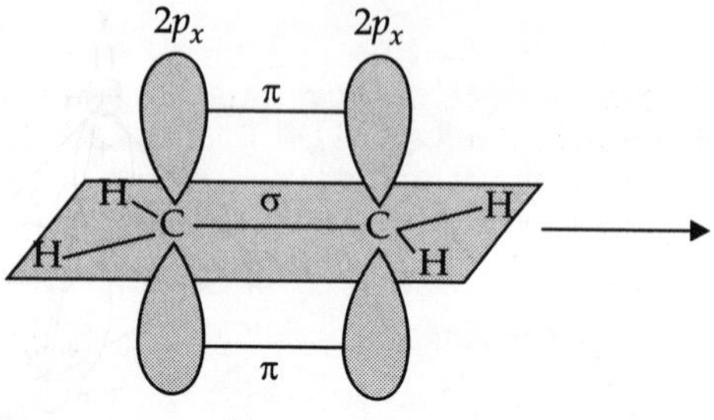

(c)

Formation of sigma and pi bonds in ethyne (C_2H_2)

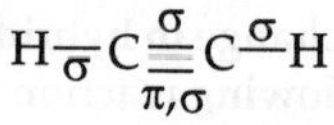

(a)

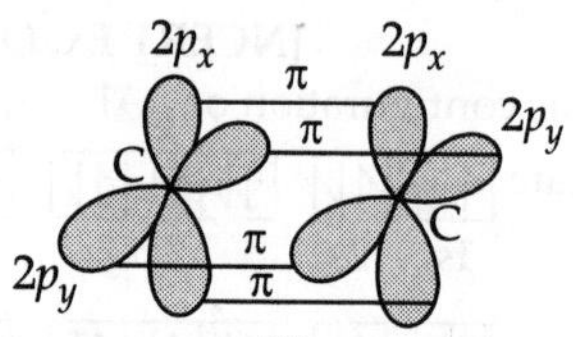

(b)

Q. 28. What is the total number of sigma and pi bonds in the following molecules?

(a) C_2H_2 **(b) C_2H_4**

[NCERT Ex. Q. 4.28, Page 135]

Ans. (a) C_2H_2

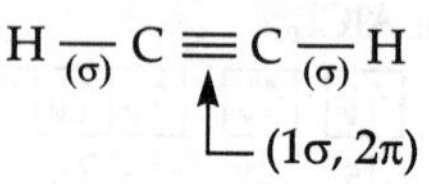

∴ It contains 3σ and 2π bonds.

(b) C_2H_4

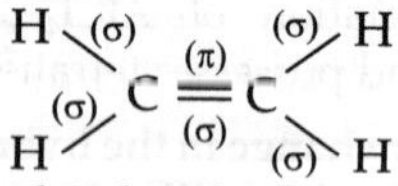

∴ It contains 5σ and 1π bonds.

Q. 29. Considering *x*-axis as the internuclear axis which out of the following will not form a sigma bond and why?

(a) 1*s* and 1*s* **(b) 1*s* and 2p_x**

(c) 2p_y and 2p_y **(d) 1*s* and 2*s***

[NCERT Ex. Q. 4.29, Page 135]

Ans. The option (c) 2p_y and 2p_y will not form a sigma bond because on considering *x*-axis as the internuclear axis, 2p_y and 2p_y orbitals overlap sideways (lateral overlapping) resulting in the formation of a pi-bond.

Q. 30. Which hybrid orbitals are used by carbon atoms in the following molecules?

(a) $CH_3 - CH_3$ **(b) $CH_3 - CH = CH_2$**

(c) $CH_3 - CH_2 - OH$ **(d) $CH_3 - CHO$**

(e) $CH_3 - COOH$ **[NCERT Ex. Q. 4.30, Page 135]**

Ans. (a)

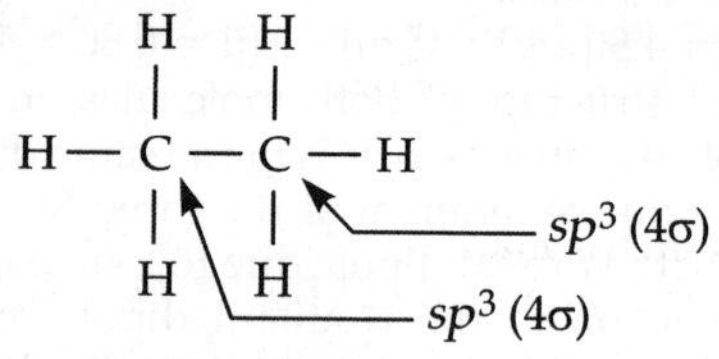

($CH_3 - CH_3$)

(b)

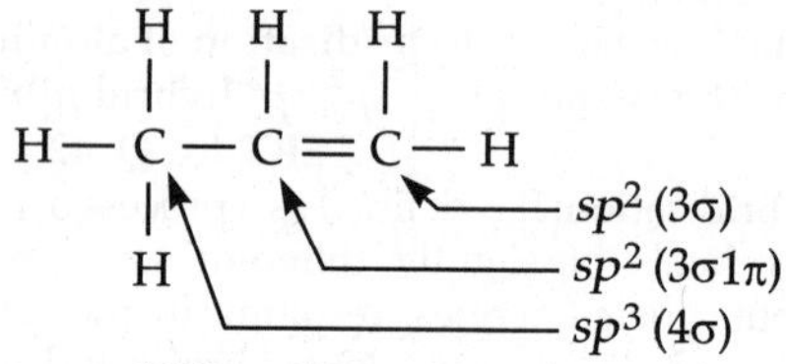

($CH_3 - CH = CH_2$)

(c)

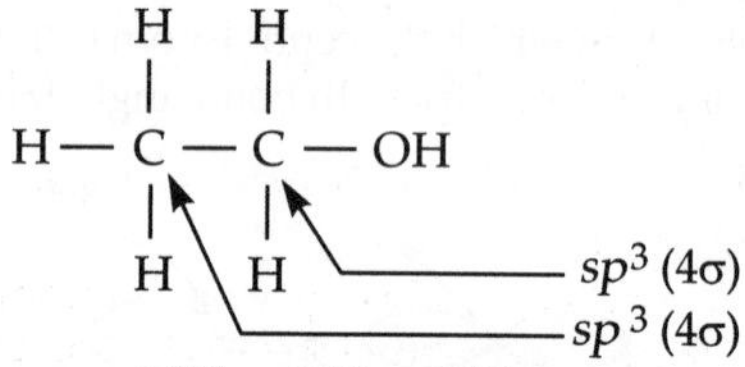

($CH_3 - CH_2 - OH$)

(d)

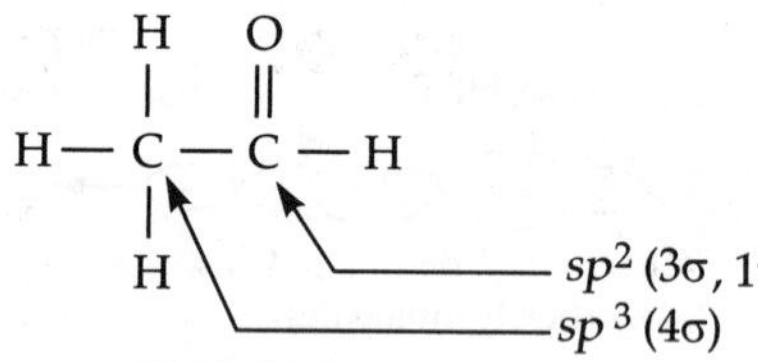

(CH_3CHO)

(e)

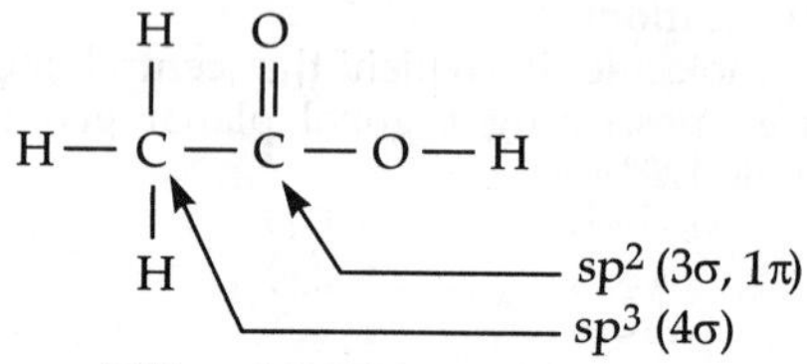

($CH_3 - COOH$)

Q. 31. What do you understand by bond pairs and lone pairs of electrons? Illustrate by giving one example of each type. **[NCERT Ex. Q. 4.31, Page 135]**

Ans. The shared pair of electrons present between the bonded atoms are called bond pairs. The pair of electrons which does not take part in bonding is called lone pair.

e.g.,

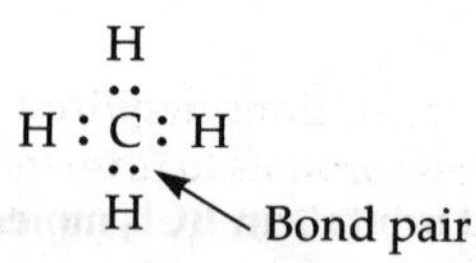

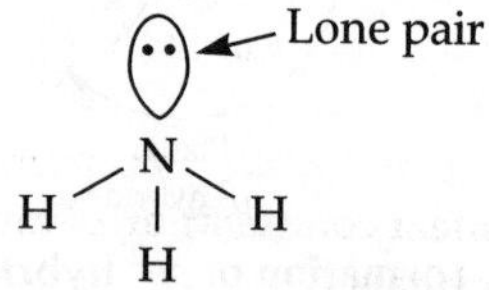

Q. 32. Distinguish between sigma and pi bond.
[NCERT Ex. Q. 4.32, Page 135]

Ans.

Sigma (σ) bond	Pi (π) bond
(i) Overlapping is quite large and hence sigma bond is a strong bond.	Overlapping is to a small extent. Hence, π–bond is a weak bond.
(ii) Electron cloud in this case is symmetrical about the line joining the two nuclei.	Electron cloud of π–bond is unsymmetrical.

Q. 33. Explain the formation of H_2 molecule on the basis of valence bond theory. [NCERT Ex. Q. 4.33, Page 135]

Ans. Consider two hydrogen atoms A and B having one electron in its 1s subshell. These atoms approach each other having nuclei N_A and N_B and electrons present in them are represented by e_A and e_B. When the two atoms are at large distance from each other, there is no interaction between them. As these atoms begin to approach each other, new attractive and repulsive forces begin to operate.

(i) Attractive forces arise between nucleus of A and electron of B and vice-versa, i.e., $N_A - e_B$, $N_B - e_A$ or $N_A - e_B$, $N_B - e_A$.

(ii) Repulsive forces arise between nuclei of two atoms A and B, i.e., $N_A - N_B$.

(iii) Repulsive forces arise between electrons of two atoms A and B, i.e., $e_A - e_B$

Attractive forces tend to bring the two atoms close to each other while repulsive forces tend to push them apart.

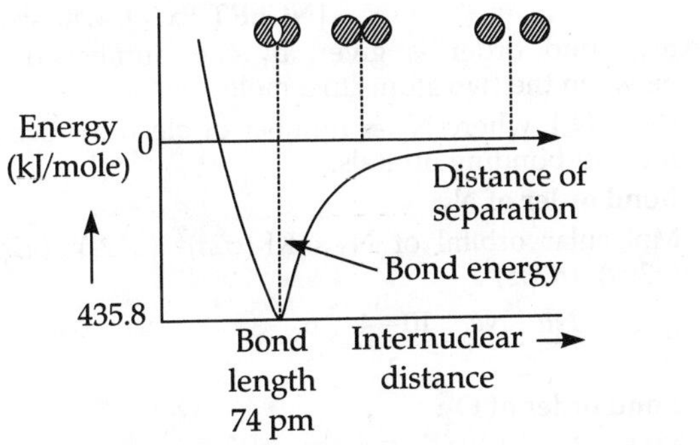

P.E. curve for the formation of H_2 molecule

It has been found that the magnitude of new attractive forces is more than the new repulsive forces. As a result, two atoms approach each other and potential energy decreases. Further, a stage is reached where the net force of attractive balances the force of repulsion and system acquires minimum energy. At this stage, the two hydrogen atoms are said to be bonded together to form a stable molecule having the bond length of 74 pm.

The energy released in the formation of H_2 molecule is called bond enthalpy, which corresponds to the minimum in the curve represented in above figure. 435.8 kJ of energy is required to dissociate one mole of H_2 molecule.

Q. 34. Write the important conditions required for the linear combination of atomic orbitals to form molecular orbitals. [NCERT Ex. Q. 4.34, Page 135]

Ans. The necessary conditions for the linear combination of atomic orbitals to form molecular orbitals are as follows:

(i) The combining atomic orbitals must have almost equal energies.

e.g., 1s – 1s, 2s – 2s, $2p_z - 2p_z$, etc.

(ii) The combining atomic orbitals must have the same symmetry about the molecular axis. e.g., $2p_z$ orbital can combine with $2p_z$ orbital but not with $2p_x$ or $2p_y$ orbitals.

(iii) The combining atomic orbitals must overlap to the maximum extent.

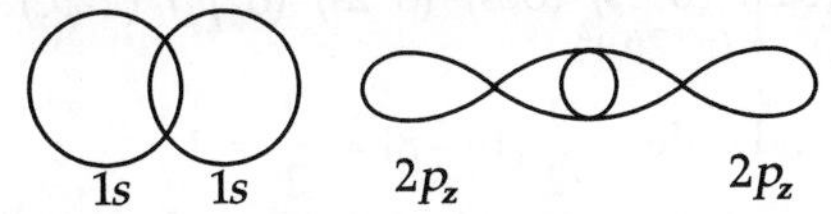

Q. 35. Use molecular orbital theory to explain why Be_2 molecule does not exist? [NCERT Ex. Q. 4.35, Page 135]

Ans. Electronic Configuration :

$$_4Be = 2, 2 = 1s^2, 2s^2$$

$$_4Be = 2, 2 = 1s^2, 2s^2$$

Molecular Orbital Configuration :

$$(\sigma 1s)^2, (\sigma^* 1s)^2, (\sigma 2s)^2, (\sigma^* 2s)^2$$

Molecular Orbital Diagram :

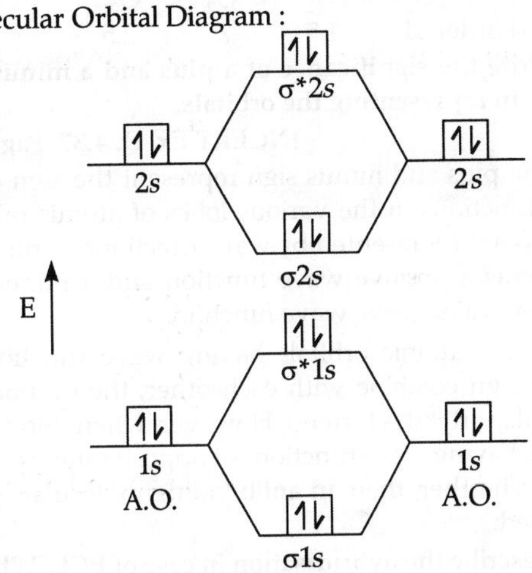

$$\text{Bond order} = \frac{N_b - N_a}{2} = \frac{4-4}{2} = \frac{0}{2} = 0$$

Since, the bond order of Be_2 is zero so Be_2 molecule does not exist. (2)

Q. 36. Compare the relative stability of the following species and indicate their magnetic properties: O_2, O_2^+, O_2^- (Superoxide), O_2^{2-} (peroxide).
[NCERT Ex. Q. 4.36, Page 135]

Ans. Molecular orbitals of O_2, O_2^+, O_2^- and O_2^{2-} are as follows :

$O_2 : (\sigma 1s)^2 (\sigma^* 1s)^2 (\sigma 2s)^2 (\sigma^* 2s)^2 (\sigma 2p_z)^2 \ (\pi 2p_x)^2 = (\pi 2p_y)^2 (\pi^* 2p_x)^1 = (\pi^*{}_2py)^1$

Bond order $= \frac{1}{2}[10-6] = \frac{4}{2} = 2$; It has two unpaired electrons in each of $\pi^*{}_{2px}$ as $\pi^*{}_{2py}$ molecular orbitals. So, it is paramagnetic.

$O_2^+ : (\sigma 1s)^2 (\sigma^* 1s)^2 (\sigma 2s)^2 (\sigma^* 2s)^2 (\sigma 2p_z)^2 (\pi 2p_x)^2 = (\pi 2p_y)^2 (\pi^* 2p_x)^1$

$$\text{Bond order} = \frac{1}{2}[10-5] = \frac{5}{2} = 2.5$$

There is one unpaired electron in π^*2p_x M.O.

$\therefore$ It is also paramagnetic.

But it is less paramagnetic than O_2 and O_2 has 2 unpaired electrons.

O_2^- : $(\sigma 1s)^2 (\sigma^*1s)^2 (\sigma 2s)^2 (\sigma^*2s)^2 (\sigma 2p_z)^2 (\pi 2p_x)^2 = (\pi 2p_y)^2 (\pi^*2p_y)^2 = (\pi^*2p_y)^1$

$$\text{Bond order} = \frac{1}{2}[10-7] = \frac{3}{2} = 1.5$$

There is one unpaired electron present in $(\pi^*2p_y)^1$ M.O.

$\therefore O_2^{2-}$ is also paramagnetic like O_2^+, but less paramagnetic than O_2.

O_2^{2-} : $(\sigma 1s)^2 (\sigma^*1s)^2 (\sigma 2s)^2 (\sigma^*2s)^2 (\sigma 2p_z)^2 (\pi 2p_x)^2 = (\pi 2p_y)^2 (\pi^*2p_x)^2 = (\pi^*2p_y)^2$

$$\text{Bond order} = \frac{1}{2}[10-8] = \frac{2}{2} = 1$$

There is no unpaired electron present in O_2^{2-}.

$\therefore O_2^{2-}$ is diamagnetic.

Thus O_2 is more paramagnetic than O_2^+ or O_2, whereas O_2^{2-} is diamagnetic.

The stability of these species varies directly as bond order.

$\therefore$ Stability increases from O_2^{2-} to O_2^+ as follows:

	O_2^{2-} <	O_2^- <	O_2 <	O_2^+
Bond order	1	1.5	2	2.5

Q. 37. Write the significance of a plus and a minus sign shown in representing the orbitals.

[NCERT Ex. Q. 4.37, Page 135]

Ans. The plus and minus sign represent the sign of the wave functions in the various lobes of atomic orbitals. Orbitals are represented by wave functions. A plus sign represents a positive wave function and a minus sign represents a negative wave function.

When two atomic orbitals having wave functions of similar sign combine with each other, then a bonding molecular orbital is formed. However, when two atomic orbitals having wave functions of opposite sign combine with each other, then an antibonding molecular orbital is formed.

Q. 38. Describe the hybridisation in case of PCl_5. Why are the axial bonds longer as compared to the equatorial bonds? **[NCERT Ex. Q. 4.38, Page 135]**

Ans. $_{15}P = 2, 8, 5 = 1s^2, 2s^2 2p^6, 3s^2 3p^3$

	3s	3p	3d
Ground State (P)	↿⇂	↿ ↿ ↿	(empty)
Excited state (P)	↿	↿ ↿ ↿	↿
PCl_5	↿⇂ (Cl)	↿⇂ ↿⇂ ↿⇂ (Cl Cl Cl)	↿⇂ (Cl)

sp^3d hybridisation

Five orbitals, i.e., one s, three p and one *d*-orbitals are available for hybridisation to form five sp^3d hybrid orbitals in the formation of PCl_5. These five sp^3d hybrid orbitals are directed towards the five corners of trigonal bipyramidal.

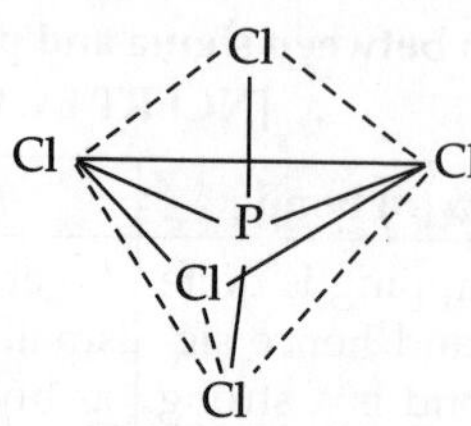

(Trigonal bipyramidal shape of PCl_5)

All the bond angles in this structure are not equivalent. In PCl_5, three P-Cl bonds lie in one plane with bond angle of 120°. These bonds are called equatorial bonds. The remaining two P-Cl bonds, one lying above and other lying below the equatorial plane form an angle of 90° with the plane. These bonds are called axial bonds. Axial bonds are longer as compared to the equatorial bonds due to great repulsion on axial bond pair electrons by equatorial bond pair electrons.

Q. 39. Define hydrogen bond. Is it weaker or stronger than the van der Waals forces?

[NCERT Ex. Q. 4.39, Page 135]

Ans. Hydrogen bond: It is defined as an attractive force which binds hydrogen atom of one molecule with the electronegative atom (F, O or N) of the same or another molecule.

e.g., HF

$$\overset{\delta+}{H}-\overset{\delta-}{F}\cdots\overset{\delta+}{H}-\overset{\delta-}{F}\cdots\overset{\delta+}{H}-\overset{\delta-}{F}$$

↑ Hydrogen bond

Hydrogen bond is stronger than the van der Waals forces.

Q. 40. What is meant by the term bond order? Calculate the bond order of N_2, O_2, O_2^+, and O_2^-.

[NCERT Ex. Q. 4.40, Page 135]

Ans. Bond order is given by the number of bonds between the two atoms in a molecule. = $[N_b - N_a]$, where N_b = number of electrons occupying the anti-bonding orbitals.

Bond order of N_2:

Molecular orbital of N_2 : $KK(\sigma 2s)^2 (\sigma^*2s)^2 (\pi 2px)^2 = (\pi 2py)^2 (\sigma 2pz)^2$

$$B.O = \frac{Nb-Na}{2} = \frac{10-4}{2} = \frac{6}{2} = 3$$

Bond order of O_2:

Molecular orbital of O_2: $KK(\sigma 2s)^2 (\sigma^*2s)^2 (\sigma 2pz)^2 (\pi 2px)^2 = (\pi 2py)^2 (\pi^*2px)^1 = (\pi^*2py)^1$

$$\text{Bond order of } O_2 = \frac{Nb-Na}{2} = \frac{10-6}{2} = \frac{4}{2} = 2$$

Bond order of O_2^+:

M.O. of O_2^+: $KK(\sigma 2s)^2 (\sigma^*2s)^2 (\sigma 2pz)^2 (\pi 2px)^2 = (\pi 2py)^2 (\pi^*2px)^1$

$$\text{Bond order of } O_2^+ = \frac{Nb-Na}{2} = \frac{10-5}{2} = \frac{5}{2} = 2.5$$

Bond order of O_2^- :

Molecular orbital of O_2^- : $KK(\sigma 2s)^2 (\sigma^*2s)^2 (\sigma 2pz)^2 (\pi 2px)^2 = (\pi 2py)^2 (\pi^*2px)^2 = (\pi^*2py)^1$

$$\text{Bond order of } O_2^- = \frac{Nb-Na}{2} = \frac{10-7}{2} = \frac{3}{2} = 1.5$$

□□

CHEMICAL THERMODYNAMICS

CHAPTER 5

Thermodynamic Terms

- **Thermodynamics** is the branch of science that deals with quantitative aspects of interconversion of various forms of energy and the conversion of energy into work and vice versa.
- **System:** Part of universe selected for observations.
- **Surrounding:** Part of universe other than the system.
- **Boundary:** The wall that separates the system from the surroundings.
- **System can be classified as:**

  Open system can exchange matter and energy both with its surroundings.

  Closed system can exchange only energy with its surroundings but not the matter.

  Isolated system can neither exchange matter nor energy with surroundings.
- **State of system:** The conditions of existence of a system when its macroscopic properties have a definite value.
- Properties of a system can be classified into state and path function.
- **State Functions:** The thermodynamic quantities which depend only on initial and final state of the system. e.g., pressure, volume and temperature are the variables which are used to describe the state of the system.

  Path function: Thermodynamic properties which depends upon the path taken by the system during a change in state, e.g., heat and work.

Mnemonics

Concept: State Function

Mnemonics: PVT HUGS

Interpretation: Pressure, Volume, Temp, Enthalpy (H), Internal Energy (U), Gibbs free energy (G) Entropy (S)

- **Isothermal process** is the one which is carried out at a constant temperature.
- **Isobaric process** is the one which is carried out at a constant pressure.
- **Isochoric process** is the one during which the volume remains constant.
- **Adiabatic process** is the one during which no heat is gained or lost by the system to the surroundings.
- A **reversible process** is a process in which the direction of process may be reversed at any stage by a small change in a variable like temperature, pressure, etc. It occurs infinitesimally slowly. All real processes are irreversible in nature.
- A cyclic process is the one that after undergoing a change in state returns back to its initial state.
- An **extensive property** is a property whose value depends on the quantity or size of matter present in the system, e.g., mass, volume, internal energy, enthalpy, heat capacity, etc.
- An **intensive property** is a property which is independent of the mass or quantity or size of matter present in the system e.g., temperature, density, pressure, etc.
- Heat and work are the two common forms of energy which are exchanged between a system and surroundings. Both are path functions and appear only during a change in state.
- **Heat (*q*):** It is an exchange of energy which results in a temperature difference.
- **Work (w):** It is an organised form of energy.
- Heat is positive if it is gained by the system (i.e., heat is transferred from the surroundings to the system) and heat is negative if it is lost by the system (i.e., heat is transferred from system to the surroundings.)
- Work is positive when it is done on the system and negative when done by the system.
- **Internal energy (U):** It is a type of energy associated with the system at particular condition of temperature and pressure.

  Or

  Internal energy is the quantity that represents all the form of the energy of the system, i.e., kinetic and potential energies of the system.
- **Internal energy change (ΔU):** It is a measure of heat change occur during the process at constant temperature and constant volume.

$$\Delta U = U_2 - U_1 = q_v$$

- **Enthalpy (H):** It is the sum of internal energy and *pV* energy of the system at particular conditions of temperature and pressure. It is also called heat content of the system.

$$H = U + pV.$$

- **Enthalpy change (ΔH):** It is the measure of heat change taking place during the process at constant temperature and constant pressure.

$$\Delta H = q_p$$

  ΔH is negative for exothermic reactions and is positive for endothermic reactions.
- **Law of conservation of energy:** It is also called **first law of thermodynamics** and states that energy of universe always remains constant during physical or chemical changes.

Chemical Thermodynamics

Trace the Mind Map: First Level · Second Level · Third Level

Terms:

- Systems and surroundings: A system refers to that part of universe in which observations are made and remaining universe constitutes the surroundings.
- **Types of System:**
  1. **Open System:** There is exchange of energy and matter between system and surroundings.
  2. **Closed System:** There is no exchange of matter but exchange of energy is possible.
  3. **Isolated System:** There is no exchange of energy or matter between the system and surroundings.
  4. **State of system** : It is described by its measurable or macroscopic properties.
  5. **Internal Energy** : It is a state function: It is the sum of chemical, electrical, mechanical or any other type of energy.
  6. **(a) Work:** Adiabatic process is in which there is no transfer of heat between system and surroundings. $\Delta U = U_2 - U_1 = W_{ad}$
     (b) Heat is change in internal energy of a system by transfer of heat from the surroundings to the system or vice-versa without expenditure of work. q is positive: Heat is transferred from surroundings to system. q is negative: Heat is transferred from system to surroundings.
     (c) General Case
     First law of Thermodynamics: $\Delta U = q + w$ the energy of an isolated system is constant.

Applications

Work $= P_{ex}\Delta V = -P_{ex}(V_f - V_i) = \int_{V_i}^{V_f} P_{ex}dV$

Reversible Process: The process which can be reversed at any moment by an infinitesimal change.

Irreversible Process: Processes other than reversible process.

At constant temperature $W_{rev} = 2.303\ nRT \log \frac{V_f}{V_i}$

For adiabatic change, $q = 0$, $\Delta U = W_{ad}$

Enthalpy, H

ΔH is negative: Exothermic reactions.
ΔH is positive: Endothermic reactions.

Heat Capacity

$q = C \times m \times \Delta T = C\Delta T$

Entropy

$\Delta S_{Total} = \Delta S_{systems} + \Delta S_{surroundings}$

$\Delta_S = \frac{q_{rev}}{T}$

A spontaneous process

It is an irreversible process which may be reversed by some external agency.

Lattice Enthalpy

Lattice enthalpy is the enthalpy change when one mole of an ionic compound dissociates into its ions in gaseous state.

$\Delta_r G^\circ = -RT \ln k$

Gibb's Energy

* $\Delta G = \Delta H - T\Delta S$
ΔG is <0, process is spontaneous.
* ΔG is >0, process is non-spontaneous

Enthalpy of Solutions

$\Delta_{sol} H^\circ$ is the enthalpy change when one mole of a substance dissolves in a specified amount of solvent.

Hess's Law of Constant Heat Summation

If a reaction takes place in several steps then its standard reaction enthalpy is the sum of standard enthalpies of international reactions into which the overall reactions may be divided at the same temperature.

$\Delta_r H = \Delta_r H_1 + \Delta_r H_2 + \Delta_r H_3$..........

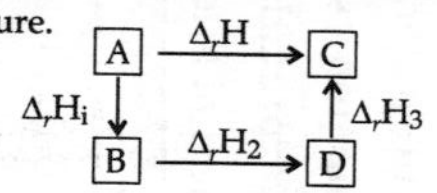

Enthalpy Change, $\Delta_r H$ – Reaction Enthalpy

$\Delta_r H = \sum a_i H_{products} - \sum_i b_i H_{reactants}$

(a) Standard Enthalpy of reactions is the enthalpy change for a reaction when all the participating substances are in their standard states.

(b) Enthalpy changes during phase transformations: Standard enthalpy of fusion / molar enthalpy of fusion, $\Delta_{fus}H^\theta$ is the enthalpy change that accompanies melting of one mole of a solid substance in standard state. Standard enthalpy of vaporization or molar enthalpy of vaporization. $\Delta_{vap}H^\theta$ is the amount of heat required to vaporize one mole of a liquid at constant temperature and under standard pressure.

(c) Standard molar enthalpy of formation $\Delta_f H^\theta$ is the standard enthalpy change for the formation of one mole of a compound from its elements in their most stable state of aggregation.

Measurement of ΔU and ΔH

In calorimetry, the process is carried out in a vessel called calorimeter, immersed in a known volume of a liquid.
(a) ΔU measurements: The energy changes are measured at constant volume. No work is done.
(b) ΔH measurements: In exothermic reaction, heat is evolved, so q_p and $\Delta_r H$ will be negative. In endothermic reaction, heat is absorbed, so q_p and $\Delta_r H$ will be positive.

Extensive property

Property whose value depends in the quantity or size of matter present. e.g., mass, volumes, enthalpy, etc.

Intensive Property

Property which does not depend on the quantity or size of matter present in the system. Temperature density, pressure.

Standard Enthalpy of combustion

$\Delta_c H$ is the enthalpy change per mole of a substance when it undergoes combustion and all reactants and products are in standard state.

Enthalpy of atomization

$\Delta_a H$ is the enthalpy change on breaking one mole of bonds completely to obtain atoms in gas phase.

$\Delta_r H^\circ$

$\sum$bond enthalpies reactants – $\sum$bond enthalpies products

Mnemonics

Concept: First law of Thermodynamics
Mnemonics: I Work Hard
Interpretation: Change in internal energy (U) = Work (w)+Heat (q)

Or

Energy can neither be created nor be destroyed. Mathematically, it can be written as:

$$\Delta U = q + W$$

- **Relation between ΔH and ΔU:**

$$\Delta H = \Delta U + p\Delta V$$
$$\Delta H = \Delta U + \Delta n_g RT$$

- The magnitude of temperature change during heat transfer depends upon the heat capacity of the system according to the relation.

$$q = m \times c \times \Delta t$$

- Specific heat or specific heat capacity is the quantity of heat required to raise the temperature of one unit mass of a substance by one degree celsius (or one kelvin).
- **Limitations of First Law of Thermodynamics:**
  - This law fails to explain the extent and direction of the convertibility of one form of energy into another.
  - This law fails to explain that how much energy would be transferred from one system to another.

Key Terms

- **Free Expansion:** Expansion of a gas in vacuum ($p_{ex} = 0$) is called free expansion.
- **Heat:** The quantity of energy which flows between system and surroundings on account of temperature difference is known as heat.
- **Heat Capacity:** It is defined as the quantity of heat required to raise the temperature of a system by 1°C.
- **Heat Capacity at Constant Volume (C_v):** It is defined as the amount of heat required to raise the temperature of one mole of a gas by one degree at constant volume of the gas.
- **Heat Capacity at Constant Pressure (C_p):** It is defined as the amount of heat required to raise the temperature of one mole of a gas by one degree at constant pressure of the gas.

- Work done $W = F \times dx$
  where F = force
  dx = distance

Work done on the system = Positive

- Work done by the system is considered as negative.

Work done by the system = Negative

- If a system loses energy, work is done by the system.
- If a system gains energy, work is done on the system.
- **Thermodynamic Processes:**
  - Isothermal process: $\Delta T = 0$
  - Adiabatic process: $\Delta q = 0$
  - Isobaric process: $\Delta p = 0$
  - Isochoric process: $\Delta V = 0$
  - Cyclic process : $\Delta U = 0$

Scan to know more about this topic
First Law of Thermodynamics

- Sign Conventions for Heat (Q)
  q = +ve, if heat is absorbed by the system
  q = –ve, if heat is evolved by the system
- Work of expansion/compression: $W = -p_{ext}(V_f - V_i)$
  where, p_{ext} = External pressure
  V_i = Initial volume
  V_f = Final volume
- Work done in isothermal reversible expansion of an ideal gas:

$$W_{rev} = -2.303 nRT \log \frac{V_f}{V_i}$$

Or

$$W_{rev} = -2.303 nRT \log \frac{p_i}{p_f}$$

- Significance of ΔH and ΔU: $\Delta H = q_p$ and $\Delta U = q_v$
- **Relation between ΔH and ΔU:**
  For gaseous reaction, $\Delta H = \Delta U + (n_p - n_r)RT$
  - If $(n_p - n_r) = 0$, then ΔH = ΔU
    e.g., $H_2(g) + I_2(g) \longrightarrow 2HI(g)$
  - If $(n_p - n_r)$ = positive, then ΔH > ΔU
    e.g., $PCl_5(g) \longrightarrow PCl_3(g) + Cl_2(g)$
  - If $(n_p - n_r)$ = negative, then ΔH < ΔU
    e.g., $N_2(g) + 3H_2(g) \longrightarrow 2NH_3(g)$
- $q = C.\Delta T$
  where C = Heat capacity
  ΔT = Change in temperature
  q = Amount of heat

Or

$$q = C_s \times m \times \Delta T$$

where C_s = Specific heat capacity
m = Mass of substance

Or

$$q = C_m \times n \times \Delta T$$

where C_m = Molar heat capacity
n = No. of moles of a substance

- According to first law of thermodynamics,

$$\Delta U = q + W$$

where $\Delta U = (U_2 - U_1)$
= ΔE (change in internal energy)
q = Heat
W = Work done on the system

- When a system undergoes isothermal change, $\Delta U = 0$ i.e., there is no increase or decrease in the internal energy of the system ($\Delta U = 0$) then first law reduces to

$$0 = q + W$$

or $$q = -W$$

- When a system undergoes adiabatic change $q = 0$, i.e., there is no exchange of heat between system and surrounding, the first law reduces to :

$$\Delta U = W_{ad}$$

$\therefore$ The work is done at the expense of internal energy.

- We can measure energy changes associated with chemical or physical processes by an experimental technique called calorimetry.
- In calorimetry, the process is carried out in a vessel called calorimeter.
- $C_p - C_v = R$

Enthalpy Change

- **Enthalpy of Reaction ($\Delta_r H$)**—The enthalpy change accompanying the chemical reaction in which number of moles of reactants consumed and those of products formed are the same as the stoichiometric coefficients.

Scan to know more about this topic

Enthalpy Change of Reaction & Formation

- **Enthalpy of Neutralisation ($\Delta_n H$):** It is the enthalpy change taking place during neutralisation of 1 g equivalent of acid with 1 g equivalent of a base in dilute aqueous solution.
- **Standard Enthalpy of Fusion ($\Delta_{fusion}H^{\ominus}$):** It is the enthalpy change taking place during the fusion of one mole solid at its melting point.
- **Standard Enthalpy of Vaporisation ($\Delta_{vap}H^{\ominus}$):** It is the enthalpy change taking place during the vaporisation of 1 mole of liquid at its boiling point and under standard pressure (1 bar).
- **Standard Enthalpy of Sublimation, ($\Delta_{sub}H^{\ominus}$):** It is the change in the enthalpy when one mole of a solid substance sublimes at a constant temperature and under standard pressure (1 bar).
- **Standard Enthalpy of Formation ($\Delta_f H^{\ominus}$):** It is enthalpy change accompanying the formation of 1 mole of the substance from its constituent elements in their standard state.

$$\Delta_f H^\circ \text{ can be } > 0 \text{ or } < 0.$$

- **Factors affecting Enthalpy of Phase Transformation:** The enthalpy change depends upon the strength of intermolecular forces working on the substances that undergo phase transformation.
- **Hess's law of constant heat summation:** The enthalpy change in a chemical or physical process is same whether the process is carried out in one step or in several steps or if a reaction takes place in several steps then its standard reaction enthalpy is the sum of the standard enthalpies of the intermediate reactions into which the overall reaction may be divided at the same temperature.
- **Applications of Hess's Law:**
  - to determine enthalpies of formation of compounds.
  - to determine enthalpies of extremely slow reactions.
  - to determine enthalpies of transformation of one allotropic form into another.
  - to determine bond energies ($\Delta H_{reaction} = \Sigma$ bond energies of reactants $- \Sigma$ bond energies of products)
  - to determine resonance energy.
- **Standard Enthalpy of Combustion ($\Delta_c H^\circ$):** It is the enthalpy change occurring during the combustion of one mole of the substances in excess of oxygen. $\Delta_c H^\circ$ is always less than zero.
- **Enthalpy of Atomisation ($\Delta_a H^\circ$):** It is the enthalpy change accompanying the dissociation of 1 mole of substance into gaseous atoms.
- **Bond Enthalpy ($\Delta_{bond}H^\circ$):** The average amount of energy required to break one mole of the bond of a particular type in gaseous molecules.
- **Enthalpy of Solution ($\Delta_{sol}H^\circ$):** It is the enthalpy change taking place when 1 mole of the solute is dissolved in specified amount of solvent. The enthalpy of solution at infinite dilution is the enthalpy change observed on dissolving the substance in an infinite amount of solvent when the interactions between the ions (or solute molecules) are negligible.
- **Enthalpy of Hydration ($\Delta_{hyd}H^\circ$):** It is the enthalpy change occurring during the hydration of 1 mole of anhydrous salt by combining with specific number of moles of water.
- **Lattice Enthalpy ($\Delta_{lattice}H^\circ$):** Lattice Enthalpy of an ionic compound is the enthalpy change which occurs when one mole of an ionic compound dissociates into its ions in gaseous state.
- Enthalpy of reaction $\Delta_r H = \sum_i a_i H_{products} - \sum_i b_i H_{reactants}$

  where $\sum_i a_i H_{products}$ = sum of enthalpies of products,

  $\sum_i b_i H_{reactants}$ = sum of enthalpies of reactants
- **Standard enthalpy of reaction ($\Delta_r H^\circ$):** It is the enthalpy change for a reaction when all the participating substances are in their standard states.

Spontaneity

- **Spontaneous process:** A process which has an urge or a natural tendency to occur in a particular direction either of its own or after proper initiation under a given set of conditions.
- **Entropy** is a thermodynamic property which is a measure of disorder or randomness in an isolated system. It is related to heat absorbed at a constant temperature by the system in a reversible process as:

$$\Delta S = \frac{q_{rev}}{T}$$

For a spontaneous change, total entropy change is positive.

Scan to know more about this topic

Second Law of Thermodynamics

- **Second law of Thermodynamics:** The entropy of universe always tends to increase during any spontaneous process.
- A system at higher temperature has greater randomness in it than one at lower temperature.
- $\Delta S_{total} = \Delta S_{system} + \Delta S_{surr} > 0$
- When a system is in equilibrium, the entropy is maximum and the change in entropy, $\Delta S = 0$
- The entropy for a spontaneous process increases till it reaches maximum and at equilibrium the change in entropy is zero. Since entropy is a state property, we can calculate the change in entropy of a reversible process by :

$$\Delta S_{sys} = \frac{q_{sys.rev}}{T}$$

- For reversible and irreversible expansion for an ideal gas, under isothermal conditions, $\Delta U = 0$, but ΔS_{total}, i.e., $\Delta S_{sys} + \Delta S_{surr}$ is not zero for irreversible process. Hence, ΔU does not discriminate between reversible and irreversible process, whereas ΔS does.
- **Third law of Thermodynamics:** At absolute zero, the entropy of any perfectly crystalline substance approaches zero.
- **Gibbs Energy (Extensive property):** It is the maximum amount of energy available to a system, during a process, that can be converted into useful work. It is also called free energy or Gibbs free energy. It is related to changes in enthalpy and entropy of the system during a process as:

$$\Delta G = \Delta H - T\Delta S$$

(Gibbs Helmholtz equation)

Scan to know more about this topic

VSEPR Theory

For a spontaneous change, $\Delta G_{sys} < 0$,
for a non-spontaneous change, $\Delta G_{sys} > 0$, and $\Delta G_{sys} = 0$ shows equilibrium.

- If the system is in thermal equilibrium with the surrounding, then the temperature of the surrounding is same as that of the system. Increase in enthalpy of the surrounding is equal to decrease in the enthalpy of the system.
- For spontaneous process $\Delta S_{total} > U$.
- ΔG (Change in free energy) gives a criteria for spontaneity at constant pressure and temperature.
  (i) If ΔG is negative (< 0), the process is spontaneous.
  (ii) If ΔG is positive (> 0), the process is non-spontaneous.
- $\Delta_r G^{\ominus} = -RT \ln K = -2.303\, RT \log K$
  where R = Gas constant
  T = Temperature (in Kelvin)
  K = Equilibrium constant

Key Terms

- **Calorific Value:** It is the amount of heat produced on complete combustion of one gram of a fuel. Its unit is cal/g.
- **Phase Transition:** The change of matter from one state to another is known as phase transition.

- **Standard Free Energy Change:** It is defined as the free energy change for a process at 298K and 1 atm pressure in which the reactants in their standard state are converted into products in their standard state. It is denoted by $\Delta G°$.

Key Formulae

- $\Delta U = q + W$
- $\Delta H = \Delta U + p\Delta V$
- $\Delta H° = \Sigma\Delta_f H°$ (Products) – $\Sigma\Delta_f H°$ (Reactants)
- $\Delta H°$ = [Sum of bond energies of reactants] – [Sum of bond energies of products]
- $\Delta S = \frac{q_{(rev)}}{T}$
- For process to be spontaneous
  $\Delta S_{system} + \Delta S_{surr} > 0$
- $\Delta G = \Delta H - T\Delta S$
- $\Delta G_{sys} = -T\Delta S_{Total}$
- $\Delta_r G° = \Sigma\Delta_f G°$ (Products) – $\Sigma_f G°$ (Reactants)
- $\Delta G_{T,P} < 0$ refers to spontaneous process.

Key Facts

- The magnitude of the enthalpy change depends on the strength of the intermolecular interactions in the substance undergoing the phase transformations.

Mnemonics

Concept: Heat Capacity
Mnemonics: PVR Cinemas
Interpretation: $C_P - C_V = R$

Concept: Enthalpy of Atomisation
Mnemonics: Be mMy Guest Please
Interpretation: B(a bond) M(1) GP>

Concept: Criteria of Spontaneity
Mnemonics: Good Physicists Have Studied Under Very Ambitious Teachers

Interpretation:
(dH)S,P<0
(dU)S,V<0
(dG)P,T<0
(dA)V,T<0
(dS)H,P>0
(dS)U,V>0

6. Concept: Gibb's Free Energy
Mnemonics: Get High Test Scores
$\Delta G = \Delta H - T\Delta S$

NCERT CORNER

Q. 1. Choose the correct answer. A thermodynamic state function is a quantity:
(i) used to determine heat changes.
(ii) whose value is independent of path.
(iii) used to determine pressure volume work.
(iv) whose value depends on temperature only.
[NCERT Ex. Q. 5.1, Page 165]

Ans. (ii) State function does not depend upon the path followed or is independent of the path followed.

Q. 2. For the process to occur under adiabatic conditions, the correct condition is :
(i) $\Delta T = 0$ (ii) $\Delta p = 0$
(iii) $q = 0$ (iv) W = 0.
[NCERT Ex. Q. 5.2, Page 165]

Ans. (iii) No heat is allowed to enter or leave the system under adiabatic conditions. **(1)**

Q. 3. The enthalpies of all elements in their standard states are :
(i) unity (ii) zero
(iii) < 0 (iv) different for each element
[NCERT Ex. Q. 5.3, Page 165]

Ans. (ii) zero. **(1)**

Q. 4. $\Delta U°$ of combustion of methane is – X kJ mol^{-1}. The value of $\Delta H°$ is :
(i) $= \Delta U°$ (ii) $> \Delta U°$ (iii) $< \Delta U°$ (iv) = 0
[NCERT Ex. Q. 5.4, Page 165]

Ans. (iii)

$$\Delta H° = \Delta U° + \Delta nRT$$
$$CH_4(g) + 2O_2(g) \rightarrow CO_2(g) + 2H_2O(l)$$
$$\Delta n = n_P - n_R = 1 - 3 = -2$$
$$\Delta H = -\Delta U - 2RT$$
$$\Delta H° < \Delta U°$$

Q. 5. The enthalpy of combustion of methane, graphite and dihydrogen at 298 K are – 890.3 kJ mol^{-1}, –393.5 kJ mol^{-1} and –285.8 kJ mol^{-1} respectively. Enthalpy of formation of $CH_{4(g)}$ will be:
(i) – 74.8 kJ mol^{-1} (ii) – 52.27 kJ mol^{-1}
(iii) + 74.8 kJ mol^{-1} (iv) + 52.26 kJ mol^{-1}
[NCERT Ex. Q. 4.5, Page 165]

Ans. (i) –74.8 kJ mol^{-1}

Explanation:

$CH_4(g) + 2O_2(g) \rightarrow CO_2(g) + 2H_{20}$ ΔH = –890.3 kJ/mol

$C(s) + O_2(g) \rightarrow CO_2(g)$

ΔH = – 393.5 kJ/mol

$H_2(g) + 1/2O_2(g) \rightarrow H20(l)$

ΔH = – 285.8 kJ/mol

Therefore, for eqn $C(s) + 2H_2(g) \rightarrow CH_4(g) \Delta H = ?$

– 393.5 + 2(–285.8) – (–890.3)

ΔH = –74.8 kJ/mol

Q. 6. A reaction A + B $\longrightarrow$ C + D + q is found to have a entropy change. The reaction will be:
(i) possible at high temperature.
(ii) possible only at low temperature.
(iii) not possible at any temperature.
(iv) possible at any temperature.
[NCERT Ex. Q. 5.6, Page 165]

Ans. (iv) Since, the reaction is exothermic ($\Delta H < 0$) and has $\Delta S > 0$, therefore, it is feasible at all temperatures because both the factors favour spontaneity.

Q. 7. In a process, 701 J of heat is absorbed by a system and 394 J work is done by the system. What is the change in internal energy for the process?
[NCERT Ex. Q. 5.7, Page 165]

Ans. Given, q = + 701 J (heat is absorbed by system)

W = – 394 J (as work is done by the system)

ΔU = ?

According to first law of thermodynamics,

$$\Delta U = q + W = 701 + (-394)$$
$$= 701 - 394 = 307\text{ J}$$

Q. 8. The reaction of cyanamide $NH_2CN(s)$ with dioxygen was carried out in a bomb calorimeter and ΔU was found to be – 742.7 kJ/mol at 298 K. Calculate enthalpy change for the reaction at 298 K.

$$NH_2CN(s) + \frac{3}{2}O_2(g) \rightarrow N_2(g) + CO_2(g) + H_2O(l)$$

[NCERT Ex. Q. 5.8, Page 165]

Ans. The given reaction is

$$NH_2CN(s) + \frac{3}{2}O_2(g) \rightarrow N_2(g) + CO_2(g) + H_2O(l)$$

$$\Delta U = -742.7\text{ kJ mol}^{-1}$$

Enthalpy change $\Delta H = \Delta U + \Delta n_g RT$

where Δn_g = change in the no. of moles (gaseous)

$$= n_2 - n_1 = 2 - \frac{3}{2} = \frac{1}{2}$$

$$[T = 298\text{ K}, R = 0.0083\text{ kJ mol}^{-1}\text{ K}^{-1}]$$

$$\therefore \quad \Delta H = -742.7 + \frac{1}{2}(0.0083) \times 298$$
$$= (-742.7 + 1.24)\text{ kJ}$$
$$= -743.94\text{ kJ mol}^{-1}$$

$\therefore$ Enthalpy change for the reaction is – 743.9 kJ mol^{-1}.

Q. 9. Calculate the number of kJ of heat necessary to raise the temperature of 60 g of aluminium from 35° to 55°C. Molar heat capacity of Al is 24 J mol^{-1} K^{-1}.
[NCERT Ex. Q. 5.9, Page 165]

Ans. Mass of Al given is 60 g.

$$\Delta T = \text{rise in temperature} = T_f - T_i$$
$$= (273 + 55)\text{ K} - (273 + 35)\text{ K}$$

No. of moles of Aluminium $= \frac{60}{27}$

Molar heat capacity = 24 J mol^{-1} K^{-1}

= Moles × ΔT × Molar heat capacity

Total heat required *i.e.*, $T = \frac{60}{27} \times 20 \times 24$ J

$$= 1066.66\text{ J} \approx 1067\text{ J} = 1.067\text{ kJ}$$

Q. 10. Calculate the enthalpy change on freezing of 1.0 mol of water at 10.0°C to ice at – 10.0°C.

$$\Delta_{fus}H = 6.03 \text{ kJ mol}^{-1} \text{ at } 0°C$$
$$C_p[H_2O(l)] = 75.3 \text{ J mol}^{-1} K^{-1}$$
$$C_p[H_2O(s)] = 36.8 \text{ J mol}^{-1} K^{-1}$$

[NCERT Ex. Q. 5.10, Page 165]

Ans. Enthalpy change for the conversion of 1 mole liquid water at 10°C into 1 mole liquid water at 0°C.

$$\Delta H_1 = C_p[H_2O_{(l)}] \times \Delta T$$
$$= -75.3 \text{ J mol}^{-1} K^{-1} \times 10 \text{ K}$$
$$= -753 \text{ J mol}^{-1} = -0.753 \text{ kJ mol}^{-1}$$

Enthalpy of fusion

$$\Delta H_2 = \Delta H_{freezing} = -\Delta H_{fusion}$$
$$= -6.03 \text{ kJ mol}^{-1}$$

Now, enthalpy change for the conversion of 1 mole of ice at 0°C to 1 mole of ice at 10°C,

$$\Delta H_3 = C_p[H_2O_{(s)}] \times \Delta T$$
$$= -36.8 \text{ J mol}^{-1} K^{-1} \times 10 \text{ K}$$
$$= -368 \text{ J mol}^{-1} = -0.368 \text{ kJ mol}^{-1}$$

∴ According to Hess's law of constant heat summation,

$$\Delta H_{total} = \Delta H_1 + \Delta H_2 + \Delta H_3$$
$$= -(0.753 + 6.03 + 0.368) \text{ kJ mol}^{-1}$$
$$= -7.151 \text{ kJ mol}^{-1}$$

Q. 11. Enthalpy of combustion of carbon to CO_2 is – 393.5 kJ mol^{-1}. Calculate the heat released upon formation of 35.2 g of CO_2 from carbon and O_2 gas ?

[NCERT Ex. Q. 5.11, Page 166]

Ans. $C(s) + O_2(g) \rightarrow CO_2(g);$

1 mole 1 mole 1 mole

$$\Delta H = -393.5 \text{ kJ/mol}^{-1}$$

For the formation of 44 g of CO_2, heat released is = – 393.5 kJ mol^{-1}

For the formation of 35.2 g of CO_2 heat released is

$$= \frac{-393.5}{44} \times 35.2 = -314.8 \text{ kJ mol}^{-1}$$

Q. 12. Enthalpies of formation of CO(g), CO_2(g), N_2O(g) and N_2O_4(g) are –110, –393, 81 and 9.7 kJ mol^{-1} respectively. Find the value of Δ_rH for the reaction:

$N_2O_4(g) + 3CO(g) \rightarrow N_2O(g) + 3CO_2(g)$

[NCERT Ex. Q. 5.12, Page 166]

Ans. $N_2O_4(g) + 3CO(g) \longrightarrow N_2O(g) + 3CO_2(g)\ \Delta_rH = ?$

$$\Delta_rH = \Sigma\Delta_fH_{(product)} - \Sigma\Delta_fH_{(reactants)}$$
$$= [\Delta_fH_{(N_2O)} + 3 \times \Delta_fH_{CO_2}] - [\Delta_fH_{(N_2O_4)} + 3 \times \Delta_{f}{}_{CO}]$$
$$= [81 + 3 \times (-393)] - [9.7 + 3(-110)]$$
$$= -777.7 \text{ kJ/mol}$$

Q. 13. Given $N_2(g) + 3H_2(g) \rightarrow 2NH_3(g); \Delta_rH^{\bullet} = -92.4$ kJ mol^{-1}. What is the Standard enthalpy of formation of NH_3 gas ? **[NCERT Ex. Q. 5.13, Page 166]**

Ans. Given: $N_2(g) + 3H_2(g) \longrightarrow 2NH_3(g);$

$$\Delta_fH° = -92.4 \text{ kJ mol}^{-1}$$

This is heat evolved for 2 moles for NH_3(g)

∴ Heat evolved for 1 mole of NH_3(g)

$$= \frac{-92.4}{2} = -46.2 \text{ kJ}$$

Hence, $\Delta_fH°$ of NH_3 gas = – 46.2 kJ mol^{-1}

Q. 14. Calculate the standard enthalpy of formation of CH_3OH(l) from the following data:

$CH_3OH(l) + 3/2O_2(g) \longrightarrow CO_2(g) + 2H_2O(l); \Delta_rH° = -726$ kJ mol^{-1}

C(graphite) + $O_2(g) \longrightarrow CO_2(g); \Delta_cH° = -393$ kJ mol^{-1}

$H_2(g) + ½O_2(g) \longrightarrow H_2O(l); \Delta_fH° = -286$ kJ mol^{-1}

[NCERT Ex. Q. 5.14, Page 166]

Ans. The required equation is

$$C(s) + 2H_2(g) + \frac{1}{2}O_2(g) \longrightarrow CH_3OH(l);$$
$$\Delta_fH^0 = \pm ?$$

Multiply eq. (iii) by 2 and add to eq. (ii)

$$C(s) + 2H_2(g) + 2O_2(g) \longrightarrow CO_2(g) + 2H_2O(l) \quad ...(iv)$$
$$\Delta_fH^0 = (2 \times -286) + (-393)$$
$$= -572 - 393 = -965 \text{ kJ/mol}$$

Subtract eq. (i) from eq. (iv)

$$C(s) + 2H_2(g) + \frac{1}{2}O_2(g) \longrightarrow CH_3OH(l);$$
$$\Delta H = -965 - (-726) = -239 \text{ kJ/mol}$$
$$\Delta_fH^0 = -239 \text{ kJ/mol}$$

Q. 15. Calculate the enthalpy change for the process.

$CCl_4(g) \longrightarrow C(g) + 4Cl(g)$

and calculate bond enthalpy of C – Cl in CCl_4(g).

$\Delta_{vap}H°(CCl_4) = 30.5$ KJ mol^{-1}

$\Delta_fH°(CCl_4) = -135.5$ KJ mol^{-1}

$\Delta_aH°(C) = 715.0$ KJ mol^{-1}, where $\Delta_aH°$ is enthalpy of atomisation.

$\Delta_aH°(Cl_2) = 242$ KJ mol^{-1} **[NCERT Ex. Q. 5.15, Page 166]**

Ans. **(i)** $CCl_4(l) \longrightarrow CCl_4(g); \Delta H_1 = 30.5$ kJ/mol

(ii) $C_{(s)}(g) + 2Cl_2(g) \longrightarrow CCl_4(l); \Delta H_2 = -135.5$ kJ/mol

(iii) $C(s) \longrightarrow C(g); \Delta H_3 = 715.0$ kJ/mol

(iv) $Cl_2(g) \longrightarrow 2Cl(g); \Delta H_4 = 242$ kJ/mol

Required equation is :

$$CCl_4(g) \longrightarrow C(g) + 4Cl(g), \Delta H = ?$$

Now, carry out the following operations to get the required equation is

Eq(iii) + 2 × Eq(iv) – Eq (i) – Eq (ii)

$$\therefore \Delta H = \Delta H_3 + 2 \times \Delta H_4 - \Delta H_1 - \Delta H_2$$
$$= 715 + (2 \times 242) - 30.5 - (-135.5) \text{ kJ/mol}$$
$$= 1304 \text{ kJ/mol}$$

Since, during this reaction 4C–Cl bonds are broken, bond enthalpy of C—Cl in CCl_4 (average value)

$$= \frac{\Delta H}{4} = \frac{1304}{4} = 326 \text{ kJ/mol.}$$

Q. 16. For an isolated system, ΔU = 0, what will be ΔS?

[NCERT Ex. Q. 5.16, Page 166]

Ans. Since, ΔU = 0 ∴ T = 0

As we know that $\Delta S = \frac{q_{rev}}{T} = \frac{q_{rev}}{0}$

∴ ΔS is more than zero, (ΔS > 0) i.e., positive

Q. 17. For the reaction at 298 K

$$2A + B \rightarrow C$$

ΔH = 400 kJ mol^{-1} and ΔS = 0·2 kJ K^{-1} mol^{-1}

At what temperature, will reaction become spontaneous considering ΔH and ΔS to be constant over the temperature range? **[NCERT Ex. Q. 5.17, Page 166]**

Ans. For the reaction $2A + B \rightarrow C$;

$\Delta H = 400\ kJ\ K^{-1}\ mol^{-1}$

and $\Delta S = 0.2\ kJ\ K^{-1}\ mol^{-1}$

$\Delta G = \Delta H - T\Delta S$

For a spontaneous reaction, ΔG has to be negative value, ΔH is $400\ kJ\ mol^{-1}$ (positive)

$\therefore$ $T\Delta S$ has to be $> \Delta H$

or $T > \frac{\Delta H}{\Delta S} > \frac{400}{0{\cdot}2}$

or $T > 2000\ K$

For the reaction to be spontaneous $T > 2000\ K$.

Q. 18. For the reaction,
$2Cl(g) \longrightarrow Cl_2(g)$, What are the signs of ΔH and ΔS?
[NCERT Ex. Q. 5.18, Page 166]

Ans. $2Cl(g) \longrightarrow Cl_2(g)$

In this reaction, a molecule of chlorine (Cl_2) is formed from its two gaseous atoms and the energy is released with the formation of bond. So, ΔH is negative.

Moreover, in this reaction, randomness decreases with the formation of Cl_2 molecule so entropy also decreases. Thus, ΔS is negative.

Q. 19. For a reaction $2A(g) + B(g) \longrightarrow 2D(g)$.
$\Delta U^0 = -10.5\ kJ$, $\Delta S^0 = -44.1\ JK^{-1}$
Calculate $\Delta G°$ for the reaction and predict whether the reaction may occur spontaneously.
[NCERT Ex. Q. 5.19, Page 166]

Ans. $\Delta H^0 = \Delta U^0 + \Delta n_g RT$

$\Delta U^0 = -10.5\ kJ$

$\Delta n_g = 2 - 3 = -1\ mol$

$T = 298\ K$

(Room temperature 25°C is taken)

$R = 8.314 \times 10^{-3}\ kJ\ K^{-1}\ mol^{-1}$

$\Delta H^0 = -10.5(kJ) + [-1(mol) \times 8.314 \times 10^{-3}\ (kJ\ K^{-1} mol^{-1}) \times 298\ K]$

$= -12.978\ kJ$

According to Gibbs Helmholtz equation:

$\Delta G^0 = \Delta H^0 - T\Delta S^0$

$= -12.978\ (kJ) - 298\ (K) \times -0.0441\ (kJ\ K^{-1})$

$= -12.978 + 13{\cdot}1418 = +0.1638\ kJ$

Since, ΔG^0 is positive, the reaction is non- spontaneous.

Q. 20. The equilibrium constant for a reaction is 10. What will be the value of ΔG^0 ? $R = 8{\cdot}314\ JK^{-1}\ mol^{-1}$, $T = 300\ K$.
[NCERT Ex. Q. 5.20, Page 166]

Ans. The equilibrium constant given for a reaction is 10.

i.e., $K = 10$

$\Delta G° = -2.303\ RT \log K = -2.303 \times 8.314 \times 300 \log 10$

$= -2.303 \times 8.314 \times 300 \times 1$ [as $\log 10 = 1$]

$= -5744{\cdot}142\ J\ mol^{-1} = -5.744\ kJ\ mol^{-1}$

Q. 21. Comment on the thermodynamic stability of NO(g), given :

$$\frac{1}{2}N_2(g) + \frac{1}{2}O_2(g) \longrightarrow NO(g);\ \Delta_r H^0 = 90.0\ kJ\ mol^{-1}$$

$$NO(g) + \frac{1}{2}O_2(g) \longrightarrow NO_2(g);\ \Delta_r H^0 = -74\ kJ\ mol^{-1}$$

[NCERT Ex. Q. 5.21, Page 167]

Ans. As can be seen from the first reaction, formation of NO is endothermic process and will take only when $90\ kJ\ mol^{-1}$ energy is available. However, the second reaction involving the oxidation of NO to NO_2 is an exothermic process and energetically more feasible. Therefore NO(g) is unstable and it would get converted into $NO_{2\ (g)}$ spontaneously.

Q. 22. Calculate the entropy change in surroundings when 1.00 mol of $H_2O(l)$ is formed under standard condition.
$\Delta_f H° = -286\ kJ\ mol^{-1}$ [NCERT Ex. Q. 5.22, Page 167]

Ans. $H_2(g) + \frac{1}{2}O_2(g) \longrightarrow H_2O(l);\ \Delta_f H^\ominus = -286\ kJ\ mol^{-1}$

Since, heat is evolved in the above reaction.

$\therefore$ It is absorbed by the surroundings.

i.e., $q_{surr} = +286\ kJ/mol$

$\Delta S_{surr} = \frac{q_{surr}}{T} = \frac{286000}{298} J$

$\Delta S = 959{\cdot}73\ J\ K^{-1}\ mol^{-1}$

□□

CHAPTER 6

EQUILIBRIUM

Physical and Chemical Equilibrium

- **Equilibrium State:** A state of the system when its observable properties do not change at a given set of conditions. At equilibrium, the forward and backward reactions proceed at same rate.
- The state of equilibrium in which the rate of a forward reaction and rate of backward reaction are equal and there is no net change in composition is known as dynamic equilibrium.
- Equilibrium reached in physical processes is termed as **physical equilibrium**. It may involve an equilibrium between different phases like solid-liquid, liquid-vapour and solid-vapour phases or a dissolution equilibrium of a solid or gaseous solute in a liquid solvent.
- Equilibrium reached in chemical processes is termed as **chemical equilibrium.**
- **Henry's Law:** It states that the mass of a gas dissolved in a given mass of a solvent at any temperature is proportional to the pressure of the gas above the solvent.

$$m \propto P$$

- **Law of Mass Action:** A theoretical concept which states that at constant temperature rate of reaction is directly proportional to the product of molar concentrations of reactants raised to the power equal to stoichiometric coefficient of that species in the balanced chemical equation.
- **Rate constant:** It is the rate of reaction, when concentration of each reacting species is unity.
- The state of chemical equilibrium is characterised by its equilibrium constant K_c or K_p.
- K_c, concentration equilibrium constant is calculated by using equilibrium concentrations of all the reactants and products.
- K_p, pressure equilibrium constant is calculated by using the equilibrium partial pressures of gaseous reactants and products.

Law of Chemical Equilibrium and Equilibrium Constant

- **Equilibrium constant:** It is the ratio of product of the equilibrium concentrations of the products to that of the reactants with each concentration term raised to the power equal to the stoichiometric coefficient of the substance in the balanced chemical equation.
- **Law of Chemical Equilibrium:** At a given temperature, the product of concentrations of the reaction products raised to the respective stoichiometric coefficient in the balanced chemical equation divided by the product of concentrations of the reactants raised to their individual stoichiometric coefficients has a constant value.

For an equilibrium,

$$aA + bB \rightleftharpoons cC + dD$$

Equilibrium constant (K_c) is expressed as:

$$K_c = \frac{[C]^c [D]^d}{[A]^a [B]^b}$$

where [A] and [B] = Equilibrium concentrations of the reactants

[C] and [D] = Equilibrium concentrations of the products

- For solid $\rightleftharpoons$ liquid equilibrium, there is only one temperature (melting point) at 1 atm (1.013 bar) at which the two phases can coexist. If there is no exchange of heat with the surroundings, the mass of the two phases remains constant.
- For liquid $\rightleftharpoons$ vapour equilibrium, the vapour pressure is constant at a given temperature.
- For dissolution of solids in liquids, the solubility is constant at a given temperature.
- For dissolution of gases in liquids, the concentration of a gas in liquid is proportional to the pressure (concentration) of the gas over the liquid.

- **Some Features of Physical Equilibria:**

Process	Conclusion
• Liquid $\rightleftharpoons$ Vapour $H_2O(l) \rightleftharpoons H_2O(g)$	p_{H_2O} constant at given temperature.
• Solid $\rightleftharpoons$ Liquid $H_2O(s) \rightleftharpoons H_2O(l)$	Melting point is fixed at constant pressure
• Solute(s) $\rightleftharpoons$ Solute (solution) Sugar(s) $\rightleftharpoons$ Sugar (solution)	Concentration of solute in solution is constant at a given temperature
• Gas(g) $\rightleftharpoons$ Gas(aq) $CO_2(g) \rightleftharpoons CO_2(aq)$	[gas(aq)]/[gas(g)] is constant at a given temperature

Equilibrium

Factors Affecting Equilibra

- **Le Chatelier's principle:** A change in any of the factors that determine the equilibrium conditions of a system will cause the system to change in such a manner so as to counteract the effect of the change.
- **Effect of Concentration Change:** If concentration of reactants is increased, equilibrium will shift in forward direction and vice-versa.
- **Effect of Pressure Change:** No effect if moles of reactants and products are same. If there is change in number of moles , equilibrium will shift in the direction having smaller number of moles when the pressure is increased and vice-versa.
- **Effect of Inert Gas Addition:** If volume is constant, ie addition does not change partial pressure or molar concentrations, equilibrium is not affected.
- **Effect of Temperature change:** For exothermic, low temperature favours formation of reactants; for endothermic, high temperature favours formation of products.

Acids and Bases

Acids turn blue litmus into red and liberate dihydrogen on reacting with some metals.
Bases turn red litmus into blue, taste bitter and feel soapy. Salts are formed when acids and bases are mixed in right proportion. Lewis Acid accepts an electron pair. Lewis Base donates an electron pair.
Acidic: $[H_3O^+] > [OH^-]$
Neutral $[H_3O^+] = [OH^-]$
Basic $[H_3O^+] < [OH^-]$

Predicting the Extent of a Reaction

- $K_c < 10^{-3}$ reaction proceeds rarely.
- $K_c > 10^3$ reaction proceeds nearly to completion
- K_c ® 10^{-3} to 10^3, reaction is at equilibrium

Predicting the Direction of a Reaction

- If $Q_c < K_c$, net reaction goes from left to right.
- If $Q_c > K_c$, net reaction goes from right to left.
- If $Q_c = K_c$, no net reaction occurs

Calculating Equilibrium Concentrations

Step 1: Write the balanced equation for the reaction.
Step 2: Make a table that lists for each substance involved in reaction; Initial concentration, change in concentration, equilibrium concentration.
Step 3: Substitute the equilibrium concentrations into the equilibrium equation for the reaction and solve.
Step 4: Calculate equilibrium concentrations from the calculated value of concentration of substances.
Step 5: Check results by substituting them into the equilibrium equation.
Buffer Solutions are the solutions which reside change in pH on dilution or addition of acid or alkali.
Solubility Product (K_{sp}):
For a sparingly soluble salt, it is the product of molar concentration of ions raised to power equal to numbers of times each ion.

Relationship Between Equilibrium Constant K, Reaction Quotient Q And Gibbs Energy G

ΔG is negative, reaction is spontaneous and proceeds in forward reaction.
ΔG is positive, reaction is non-spontaneous and proceeds in reserve reaction.
ΔG is 0, reaction has achieved equilibrium.
$K = e^{-\Delta G^\circ/RT}$
Arrhenius Concept of Acids and Bases:
- Arrhenius theory states that acids are substances that dissociates in water give hydrogen ions and bases are substances that produce hydroxyl ions.

Bronsted Lowry Theory states that acid is a substance that is capable of donating hydrogen ion and bases are substances capable of accepting a hydrogen ion.
- Weak acids have very strong conjugate bases.

Types

Homogeneous Equilibria

Reactants and products are in same phase.

Hetrogeneous Equilibria

Reactants and products are present in two or more phases.

Physical

Equilibrium set up in physical processes like evaporation of water, etc.
- Solid $\rightleftharpoons$ Liquid
- Liquid $\rightleftharpoons$ Gas
- Solid $\rightleftharpoons$ Gas

Characteristics:
- Possible only in a closed system at a given temperature.
- Both the reactions occur at same rate.
- All measurable property remains constant.
- When equilibrium is attained one of its parameter remains constant at given temperature.
- Magnitude of such quantities at any stage indicates the extent to which process has proceeded before reaching equilibrium.

Chemical

Speed of forward reaction equals that of backward reaction.
Characteristics:
- Can be achieved from either side.
- Dynamic in nature.
- There is no change in concentration of various species.
- Observable physical properties become constant.
- Equilibrium is attained rapidly by the presence of catalyst.

Under given set of conditions

If a chemical reaction is carried out in a closed container, a constancy in some observable properties like colour, pressure is observed. Such a state is referred as equilibrium state.

Equilibrium In Chemical Processes

Dynamic Equilibrium: Chemical reactions reach a state of dynamic equilibrium in which the rate of forward and reverse reactions are equal and there is no net change in composition.

Equilibrium Law or Law of Chemical Equilibrium

At a given temperature, the product of concentrations of the reaction products raised to the respective stoichiometric coefficient in the balanced chemical equation divided by the product of concentration of the reactions raised to their individual stoichiometric coefficients has a constant value: $aA + bB \rightleftharpoons cC + dD$

$$K_c = \frac{[C]^c [D]^d}{[A]^a [B]^b}$$

Equilibrium Constant

Equilibrium for the reverse reaction is the inverse of the equilibriumconstant for reaction in the forward direction.
Applications of Equilibrium Constants:
- Applicable only when concentrations of the reactants and products have attained constant value at equilibrium state.
- Value of K_c is independent of initial concentrations of the reactants and products.
- Equilibrium constant is temperature dependent.

K_c reverse $= \frac{1}{K_c}$
- Equilibrium constant for a reacting is related to equilibrium constant of corresponding reaction.

PH

pH of a solution is negative logarithm to base 10 of the activity of hydrogen ion

Size increases
HF<<HCl<<HBr<<HI →
Size increases →
Acidic strength increases →

Trace the Mind Map
- First Level
- Second Level
- Third Level

Equilibrium Constant in Gaseous Systems:

Consider a general reaction,

$aA + bB \rightleftharpoons cC + dD$

$$K_p = \frac{[P_C]^c [P_D]^d}{[P_A]^a [P_B]^b}$$

$$= \frac{[C]^c [D]^d (RT)^{(c+d)}}{[A]^a [B]^b (RT)^{(a+b)}}$$

$$= \frac{[C]^c [D]^d}{[A]^a [B]^b}(RT)^{(c+d)-(a+b)}$$

$$= \frac{[C]^c [D]^d}{[A]^a [B]^b}(RT)^{\Delta n_g}$$

$$K_p = K_c (RT)^{\Delta n}$$

where R = Gas constant

T = Absolute temperature

Δn_g = (Number of moles of gaseous products – Number of moles of gaseous reactants) in balanced chemical equation.

= $(c + d) - (a + b)$

Homogeneous Equilibria: In a homogeneous system, all the reactants and products are in the same phase. For example, in the gaseous reaction below, reactants and products are in homogeneous phase.

$$N_2(g) + 3H_2(g) \rightleftharpoons 2NH_3(g)$$

Heterogeneous Equilibria: Equilibrium in a system having more than one phase is called heterogeneous equilibrium. For example, equilibrium between water vapour and liquid water in a closed container.

$$H_2O(l) \rightleftharpoons H_2O(g)$$

Mnemonics

Concept: Homogeneous Equilibria
Mnemonics: RPSP
Interpretation: Reactant and Product in Same Phase
Concept: Hetrogeneous Equilibria
Mnemonics: RPDP
Interpretation: Reactant and Product in Different Phase

Applications of Equilibrium Constant

- To predict the extent of a reaction on the basis of its magnitude.
- To predict the direction of the reaction.
- To calculate equilibrium concentrations.

Predicting the Extent of a Reaction: The magnitude of K_c or K_p is directly proportional to the concentrations of products (as these appear in the numerator of equilibrium constant expression) and inversely proportional to the concentrations of the reactants (these appear in the denominator).

Reaction Quotient (Q): The ratio of the product of molar concentrations of the products to the product of molar concentrations of reactants with each concentration terms raised to the power equal to the stoichiometric coefficient of that species is called reaction quotient.

- At equilibrium, Q = K.
- At concentration other than equilibrium $Q \neq K$.
- If $Q_c > K_c$, the reaction, will proceed in the direction of reactants (backward reaction).
- If $Q_c < K_c$, the reaction will proceed in the direction of the products (forward reaction).
- If $Q_c = K_c$, the reaction mixture is already at equilibrium.

$K = e^{-\Delta G°/RT}$

From this equation, we can predict the spontaneity of the reaction.

- If $\Delta G° < 0$, then $-\Delta G°/RT$ is positive and $e^{-\Delta G°/RT} > 1$, $\therefore K > 1$, the reaction is spontaneous.
- If $\Delta G° > 0$, then $-\Delta G°/RT$ is negative and $e^{-\Delta G°/RT} < 1$, $\therefore K < 1$, the reaction is non-spontaneous.

$\Delta G = \Delta G° + RT \ln Q$

At equilibrium, $\Delta G° = -RT \ln K = -2.303\, RT \log K$.

Le Chatelier's Principle: It states that a change in any of the factors that determine the equilibrium conditions of a system will cause the system to change in such a manner so as to reduce or to counteract the effect of the change.

Factors Affecting Equilibria:

(i) Effect of Concentration Change: When the concentration of any of the reactants or products in a reaction at equilibrium is changed, the composition of the equilibrium mixture changes so as to minimize the effect of concentration changes.

(ii) Effect of Pressure Change: On increasing the pressure, the reaction occurs in that direction in which number of moles of the gas or pressure decreases or the direction in which Δn_g is negative and vice-versa. If the reaction involves solids and/or liquids, *i.e.*, $\Delta n_g = 0$, then there is no effect of pressure change on the system.

(iii) Effect of Temperature Change: The equilibrium constant for an exothermic reaction decreases as the temperature increases. The equilibrium constant for an endothermic reaction increases as the temperature increases.

(iv) Effect of Inert Gas Addition: Addition of inert gas at constant volume does not affect the equilibrium.

(v) Effect of Catalyst: Addition of catalyst does not alter the equilibrium, it just help in attaining the equilibrium faster.

Mnemonics

Concept: Effect of Concentration Change
Mnemonics: Class Rooms gives Ideal Final Result
Interpretation: Concentration of Reactant Increases Forward Reactiona (CRIFR)
Concept: Effect of Pressure Change
Mnemonics: Nuclear Power Plant is Issue For Review
Interpretation: if, Δn_g Pressure Increases Forward Reaction (NPPIFR)
Concept: Effect of Temperature Change
Mnemonics: TIP for Final Exam
Interpretation: Temperature Increases Product Formation for
Exothermic TIPFE

Key Facts

- Chemical equilibria are important in numerous biological and environmental processes.
  For example, equilibria involving O_2 molecules and the protein haemoglobin play an important role in the transport and delivery of O_2 from our lungs to our muscles.
- The normal boiling point is the boiling temperature at 1 atm, whereas the standard boiling point is the boiling temperature at 1 bar.
- Pure water boils as 99.97degree celsius at 1 atm and 99.61 degrees celsius at 1 bar

- **Relation between Equilibrium Constants for a General Reaction and its Multiples:**

Chemical Equation	Equilibrium Constant
• $aA + bB \rightleftharpoons cC + dD$	K
• $cC + dD \rightleftharpoons aA + bB$	$K_c' = (1/K_c)$
• $naA + nbB \rightleftharpoons ncC + ndD$	$K_c'' = (K_c^n)$
• $1/n\ aA + 1/n\ bB \rightleftharpoons 1/n\ cC + 1/n\ dD$	$K_c''' = (K_c^{1/n})$

- 1 pascal (Pa) = 1 Nm^{-2}
  1 bar = 10^5 Pa
- The free energy change at equilibrium state is zero, i.e., $\Delta G = 0$
- The value of the equilibrium constant changes with change to temperature.

$$\log \frac{K_2}{K_1} = \frac{\Delta H}{2.303R}\left[\frac{1}{T_1} - \frac{1}{T_2}\right]$$

Ionic Equilibrium in Solution

- Substances that conduct electricity in aqueous solutions are called electrolytes, e.g., acids, bases and salts are electrolytes and their solution conduct electricity due to the process of ions formed by dissociation of electrolytes in aqueous solution.
- Strong electrolytes completely dissociate in their solutions.
- Weak electrolytes dissociate partially and an equilibrium exists between the ions and the undissociated electrolyte.
- **Acid:** A substance which furnishes H^+ ions in aqueous solution (Arrehenius concept); proton donor (Bronsted concept) and acceptor of electron pair (Lewis concept). Acids turn blue litmus paper into red. Acids liberate dihydrogen on reacting with some metals.
- **Base:** A substance which gives OH^- ions in aqueous solution (Arrehenius concept); acceptor of proton (Bronsted concept) and donor of electron pair (Lewis concept). Bases turn red litmus paper into blue. Bases taste bitter and feel soapy. A common example of a base is washing soda used for washing purposes.
- **Neutralisation:** A combination of H^+ and OH^- ions in solution (Arrhenius concept); transference to proton (Bronsted concept); formation of dative bond (Lewis concept).
- The acid-base pair that differs only by one proton is called a conjugate acid-base pair. If Bronsted acid is a strong acid then its conjugate base is a weak base and vice-versa.

Mnemonics

1. Concept: Lewis concept
Mnemonics: LeeLAA
Interpretation: Lone pair Accepter is Acid
2. Concept: Lewis concept
Mnemonics: BaDaL
Interpretation: Base is Donor of Lone pair
3. Concept: Acids and Bases
Mnemonics: BAAD
Interpretation: Bases accept H^+, acids donate H^+
4. Concept: Bronsted Acid-Base Concept
Mnemonics: Strong Army, Lost to Carelessly Weak Bandits
Interpretation: Strong Acid gives Weak Conjugate Base

- Ionic product of water, K_w, is the product of the concentration of hydronium ions and hydroxyl ions in pure water at a particular temperature.

  $K_w = [H_3O^+][OH]^-$
  $= 1 \times 10^{-14}\ mol^2\ L^{-2}$ at 298 K
- Dissociation refers to the process of separation of ions in water already existing as such in the solid state of the solute, as in sodium chloride. While ionization corresponds to a process in which a neutral molecule splits into charged ions in the solution.
- A bare proton (H^+) is very reactive and can not exist freely in aqueous solutions. So, it bonds to the oxygen atom of a solvent water molecule to give hydronium ion (H_3O^+). It's geometry is trigonal bipyramidal.
- If Bronsted acid is a strong acid then its conjugate base in a weak base and vice-versa.

- The density of pure water is 1000 g/L and its molar mass is 18.0 g/mol.

$$\text{Molarity of pure water} = \frac{\text{Density}}{\text{Molar Mass}} = \frac{1000\ g/L}{18.0\ g/mol} = 55.55\ M$$

- **pH range:**

1 ⟵⟶ 7 ⟵⟶ 14

(Acidic solution) (pH<7) (Neutral solution) (pH = 7) (Basic solution) (pH>7)

- $pH = -\log_{10}[H^+]$
- $[H^+] = 10^{-pH}$
- $K_w = [H_3O^+][OH^-] = 10^{-14}$

  where K_w = Ionic product of water
- $pK_w = pH + pOH = 14$
- Relative order of acidic strength among halogen acids:

  Size increases ⟶

  HF << HCl << HBr << HI

  ⟶ Acid strength increases

  As the size of halogen (X) increases down the group, H – X bond strength decreases and therefore the acid strength increases.
- Relative order of acidic strength among CH_4, NH_3, H_2O and HF (HA) is:

  electronegativity of 'A' increases ⟶

  $CH_4 < NH_3 < H_2O < HF$

  ⟶ Acid strength increases
- **pH of solution:** Potency of H^+ in solution. It is negative logarithm of H_3O^+ ion concentration in solution. $pH = -\log[H_3O^+]$
- **pOH of solution:** It is negative logarithm of OH^- ion concentration of the solution.
- For any solution at 25°C.

$$pK_w = pH + pOH = 14$$
$$pH = -\log[H_3O^+]$$
$$pOH = -\log[OH^-];\ pK_w = -\log K_w$$

- K_w ionic product of water $(H^+)(OH^-) = 1 \times 10^{-14}$ at 0°C.
- Strength of acids or bases is measured in terms of their respective dissociation constants K_a (or pK_a) and K_b or (pK_b).
- Larger the value of K_a or lower value of pK_a corresponds to greater acidic strength of acids. Similarly larger the value of K_b or lower value of pK_b corresponds to more stronger base.
- Dissociation constants of conjugate acid-base pair to each other as:

$$K_a . K_b = K_w$$
$$pK_a + pK_b = pK_w = 14 \text{ (at 298 K)}$$

- For monobasic acid H_A, if C is the molar concentration of H_A and α is the degree of dissociation then

$$(H_3O^+) = C\alpha = \sqrt{K_a \times C}$$

- Similarly for monoacid base

$$[OH^-] = C\alpha = \sqrt{K_b \times C}$$

- We can distinguish acidic, neutral and basic aqueous solutions by the relative values of the H_3O^+ and OH^- concentrations :

Acidic	: $[H_3O^+] > [OH^-]$
Neutral	: $[H_3O^+] = [OH^-]$
Basic	: $[H_3O^+] < [OH^-]$

Scan to know more about this topic

pH of Weak Acids and Bases

- Strength of an acid depends upon (i) strength of H—A bond: weaker the bond, stronger is the acid and (ii) polarity of H—A bond: greater the polarity, stronger is the acid.
- **Ostwald's dilution law:** Relationship between the dissociation constant and the degree of dissociation of a weak electrolyte (acid or base).

  $K = a_2 C$

  or $K = a_2/V$

  where K = Dissociation constant

  a = Degree of dissociation

  C = Concentration of the solution

  V = Volume of the solution
- Dissociation of weak acids and bases is suppressed in the presence of common ion furnished by their salts. This phenomenon is known as **common ion effect.**
- **Hydrolysis:** It is reverse of neutralization. It involves the interactions of ions of electrolyte with H_2O molecules in solution to give acidic or basic solution.
- Salts of strong acids and strong bases do not undergo hydrolysis and their aqueous solutions are neutral.
- Salts of strong acids with weak bases undergo cationic hydrolysis and give acidic solutions.
- Salts of strong bases with weak acids undergo anionic hydrolysis and give basic aqueous solutions.

Buffer Solution

- Buffer solution is the solution which resists change in pH on dilution or with the addition of small amounts of acid or alkali.
- pH of buffer solution is given by Henderson-Hasselbalch equation:

$$pH = pK_a + \log\frac{[\text{Salt}]}{[\text{Acid}]} \text{ (for acidic buffers)}$$

$$pOH = pK_b + \log\frac{[\text{Salt}]}{[\text{Base}]} \text{ (for basic buffers)}$$

- $pH = pK_a$ when [Salt] = [Acid]

- pOH = pK_b when [Salt] = [Base]
- During dissolving of the sparingly soluble salt in water to form a saturated solution, equilibrium is established between undissolved solid and the ions in a saturated solution.

Scan to know more about this topic

Buffer Solutions

$$AB\ (s) \rightleftharpoons A^{n+}\ (aq) + B^{n-}\ (aq)$$

$$K_{sp} = [A^{n+}]\,[B^{n-}] = (S)\,(S) = S^2$$

Solubility Product (K_{sp})

- It is a product of the concentration of ions of electrolyte at the saturation point with each concentration term raised to the power equal to numerical coefficient of that species in the balanced equation. It is the highest value of ionic product for a sparingly soluble salt.
- The solubility of a sparingly soluble salt further decreases due to **Common Ion Effect.**
- Solubility of a salt of a weak acid increases as the pH of the solution decreases as the concentration of H_3O^+ ions increases.
- From the value of K_{sp} (solubility product) and Q (ionic product), we can predict whether the precipitation of salt or dissolution of salt will take place.
  - If Q > K_{sp} , then precipitation will take place.
  - If Q < K_{sp} , then dissolution will take place.
  - If Q = K_{sp} , then reaction is at equilibrium.

Key Terms

- **Equilibrium Mixture:** Equilibrium mixture is the mixture of reactants and products at equilibrium state. The mixture of reactants and products in the equilibrium state is called an equilibrium mixture.
- **Polarity:** Polarity is a separation of electric charge leading to a molecule or its chemical groups having an electric dipole moment, with a negatively charged end and a positively charged end.

Key Facts

- Hydrochloric acid present in the gastric juice is secreted by the lining of our stomach in a significant amount of 1.2 – 1.5 L/day and is essential for digestive process.
- Acetic acid is known to be the main constituent of vinegar.
- Lemon and orange juices contain citric acid and ascorbic acid.
- Tartaric acid is found in tamarind paste.
- As most of the acids taste sour, the term `acid' has been derived from a Latin word "*acidus*" meaning sour.
- When acids and bases are mixed in the right proportion, they react with each other to form salts.
- The electrostatic forces between two charges are inversely proportional to dielectric constant of the medium.
- Water acts as a **universal solvent**. It possesses a **very high dielectric constant** of 80.
- When sodium chloride is dissolved in water, the electrostatic interactions are reduced by a factor of 80 and this facilitates the ions to move freely in the solution.
- The extent to which ionization occurs, depends upon the strength of the bond and the extent of solvation of ions produced.
- **Salt of weak acid and strong base:** CH_3COONa
- **Salt of strong acid and weak base:** NH_4Cl
- **Salt of weak acid and weak base:** CH_3COONH_4
- Many body fluids, e.g., blood or urine have definite pH and any deviation in their pH indicates malfunctioning of the body.
- Buffer solutions of known pH can be prepared from the knowledge of pK_a of the acid or pK_b of the base and by controlling the ratio of the salt and acid or salt and base.
- For a salt to dissolve in a solvent, the strong forces of attraction between its ions (lattice enthalpy) must be overcome by the ion-solvent interactions.
- The amount of solvation enthalpy depends on the nature of solvent. If solvent is non-polar, the solvation enthalpy is small and therefore, not sufficient to overcome lattice enthalpy of the salt.

NCERT CORNER

Q. 1. A liquid is in equilibrium with its vapour in a sealed container at a fixed temperature. The volume of the container is suddenly increased.

(a) What is the initial effect of the change on vapour pressure?

(b) How do rates of evaporation and condensation change initially?

(c) What happens when equilibrium is restored finally and what will be the final vapour pressure?

[NCERT Ex. Q. 6.1, Page 208]

Ans. (a) Initially, the vapour pressure will decrease because the same amount of vapour is now distributed in larger space.

(b) The rate of evaporation remains constant at constant temperature in a closed vessel. However, the rate of condensation will be low initially because there are fewer molecules per unit volume in the vapour phase and hence the number of collisions per unit time with the liquid surface decreases.

(c) When equilibrium is restored, rate of evaporation becomes equal to the rate of condensation. The final vapour pressure will be same as it was originally because vapour pressure of a liquid depends only on temperature and not volume.

Q. 2. What is K_c for the following equilibrium when the equilibrium concentration for each substance is $[SO_2] = 0.60$ M, $[O_2] = 0.82$ M and $[SO_3] = 1.90$ M $2SO_2(g) + O_2(g) \rightleftharpoons SO_3(g)$. [NCERT Ex. Q. 6.2, Page 208]

Ans. $2SO_2(g) + O_2(g) \rightleftharpoons 2SO_3(g)$

$$K_c = \frac{[SO_3]^2}{[SO_2]^2[O_2]} = \frac{(1 \cdot 9)^2}{(0 \cdot 60)^2(0 \cdot 82)}$$

$$= 12.229 \text{ M}$$

Q. 3. At a certain temperature and total pressure of 10^5 Pa, iodine vapour contains 40% by volume of I atoms.

$I_2(g) \rightleftharpoons 2I(g)$.

Calculate K_p for the equilibrium.

[NCERT Ex. Q. 6.3, Page 208]

Ans. $I_2(g) \rightleftharpoons 2I(g)$

Total pressure = 10^5 Pa

Since out of total volume, 40% by volume are I atoms

∴ 60% are I_2 molecules (gaseous)

∴ Partial pressure of $I(g) = \frac{40}{100} \times 10^5$ Pa

Partial pressure of $I_2(g) = \frac{60}{100} \times 10^5$ Pa

$$\therefore \quad K_p = \frac{(p_I)^2}{(p_{I_2})} = \frac{\left(\frac{40}{100} \times 10^5\right)^2}{\frac{60}{100} \times 10^5}$$

$$= 2.67 \times 10^4 \text{ Pa}$$

Q. 4. Write the expression for the equilibrium constant, K_c for each of the following reactions–

(i) $2NOCl(g) \rightleftharpoons 2NO(g) + Cl_2(g)$

(ii) $2Cu(NO_3)_2(s) \rightleftharpoons 2CuO(s) + 4NO_2(g) + O_2(g)$

(iii) $CH_3COOC_2H_5(aq) + H_2O(l) \rightleftharpoons CH_3COOH(aq) + C_2H_5OH(aq)$

(iv) $Fe^{3+}(aq) + 3OH^-(aq) \rightleftharpoons Fe(OH)_3(s)$

(v) $I_2(s) + 5F_2 \rightleftharpoons 2IF_5$

[NCERT Ex. Q. 6.4, Page 208]

Ans. (i) $2NOCl(g) \rightleftharpoons 2NO(g) + Cl_2(g)$

$$K_c = \frac{[NO(g)]^2[Cl_2(g)]}{[NOCl(g)]^2}$$

(ii) $2Cu(NO_3)_2(s) \rightleftharpoons 2CuO(s) + 4NO_2(g) + O_2(g)$

$K_c = [NO_2(g)]^4[O_2(g)] \because [Cu(NO_3)_2(s)] = 1$ & $[CuO(s)] = 1$

(iii) $CH_3COOC_2H_5(aq) + H_2O(l) \rightleftharpoons CH_3COOH(aq) + C_2H_5OH(aq)$

$$K_c = \frac{[CH_3COOH(aq)][C_2H_5OH(aq)]}{[CH_3COOC_2H_5(aq)]} \quad (\because [H_2O(l)] = 1)$$

(iv) $Fe^{3+}(aq) + 3OH^-(aq) \rightleftharpoons Fe(OH)_3(s)$

$$K_c = \frac{1}{[Fe^{3+}(aq)][OH^-(aq)]^3} \quad \because [Fe(OH)_3(s)] = 1$$

(v) $I_2(s) + 5Fe_2 \rightleftharpoons 2IF_5$

$$K_c = \frac{[IF_5]^2}{[F_2]^5} \quad \because [I_2(s) = 1]$$

Q. 5. Find out the value of K_c for each of the following equilibria from the value of K_p

(i) $2\,NOCl\,(g) \rightleftharpoons 2\,NO\,(g) + Cl_2\,(g)$, $K_p = 1.8 \times 10^{-2}$ at 500 K

(ii) $CaCO_3\,(s) \rightleftharpoons CaO\,(s) + CO_2\,(g)$, $K_p = 167$ at 1073 K. [NCERT Ex. Q. 6.5, Page 208]

Ans. (i) $\Delta n_g = 3 - 2 = 1$, $K_p = K_c \times (RT)^{\Delta n}$

or $$K_c = \frac{K_p}{RT} = \frac{1.8 \times 10^{-2}}{0.0831 \times 500}$$

($R = 0.0831$ bar litre $mol^{-1}K^{-1}$)

$$= 4.33 \times 10^{-4}$$

(ii) $\Delta n_g = 1 - 0 = 1$,

$$K_c = \frac{K_p}{RT} = \frac{167}{0.0831 \times 1073}$$

$$= 1.87$$

Q. 6. For the following equilibrium $K_c = 6.3 \times 10^{14}$ at 1000 K

$NO(g) + O_3(g) \rightleftharpoons NO_2(g) + O_2(g)$

Both the forward and reverse reactions in the equilibrium are elementary bimolecular reactions. What is K_c for the reverse reaction? [NCERT Ex. Q. 6.6, Page 209]

Ans. $K_c = 6.3 \times 10^{14}$ at 1000 K for the equilibrium

$NO(g) + O_3(g) \rightleftharpoons NO_2(g) + O_2(g)$

For the reverse reaction,

$$K_c' = \frac{1}{K_c} = \frac{1}{6.3 \times 10^{14}}$$

$$= 1.59 \times 10^{-15}$$

Q. 7. Explain why pure liquids and solids can be ignored while writing the equilibrium constant expression? [NCERT Ex. Q. 6.7, Page 209]

Ans. Concentration of pure solid and liquids remain constant as their molar concentration are constant, i.e., independent of the amount present. Therefore, concentration terms of pure solids and pure liquids can be ignored while writing the equilibrium constant expression.

Q. 8. Reaction between N_2 and O_2 takes place as follows:

$2N_2(g) + O_2(g) \rightleftharpoons 2N_2O(g)$

If a mixture of 0.482 mol N_2 and 0.933 mol of O_2 is placed in a 10 L reaction vessel and allowed to form N_2O at a temperature for which $K_c = 2.0 \times 10^{-37}$, determine the composition of equilibrium mixture. [NCERT Ex. Q. 6.8, Page 209]

Ans. Given,

$K_c = 2.0 \times 10^{-37}$,	$2N_2(g)$ +	$O_2(g) \rightleftharpoons$	$2N_2O(g)$
Initial Conc.	0.482	0.933	0
Equilibrium conc.	(0.482–2x)	(0.933–x)	2x
Active mass	$\left(\frac{0.482-2x}{10}\right)$	$\left(\frac{0.933-x}{10}\right)$	$\left(\frac{2x}{10}\right)$

The value of K_c is negligible, which means negligible amounts of N_2 and O_2 react. So, x is negligible.

Now, $$[N_2]_{eq} = \frac{0.482 - 2x}{10} = \frac{0.482}{10}$$

$$= 0.0482 \text{ mol L}^{-1}$$

Similarly, $$[O_2]_{eq} = \frac{0.933 - x}{10} = \frac{0.933}{10}$$

$$= 0.0933 \text{ mol L}^{-1}$$

Equilibrium constant for the reaction,

$$K_c = \frac{[N_2O]^2}{[N_2]^2[O_2]}$$

$$2.0 \times 10^{-37} = \frac{\left(\frac{2x}{10}\right)^2}{(0.0482)^2(0.0933)}$$

or $$x^2 = 10.837 \times 10^{-40}$$

or $$x = 3.292 \times 10^{-20}$$

$\therefore$ $$[NO_2] = \frac{2x}{10} = \frac{2 \times 3.292 \times 10^{-20}}{10}$$

$$= 6.58 \times 10^{-21} \text{ mol L}^{-1}$$

Q. 9. Nitric oxide reacts with Br_2 and gives nitrosyl bromide as per reaction given below:

$$2NO(g) + Br_2(g) \rightleftharpoons 2NOBr(g)$$

When 0.087 mol of NO and 0.0437 mol of Br_2 are mixed in a closed container at a constant temperature, 0.0518 mol of NOBr is obtained at equilibrium. Calculate equilibrium amount of NO and Br_2.

[NCERT Ex. Q. 6.9, Page 209]

Ans. $2NO(g) + Br_2(g) \rightleftharpoons 2NOBr(g)$

2 mol 1 mol 2 mol

At equilibrium, 0.0518 moles of NOBr are formed, then 0.0518 moles of NO and 0.0518/2 moles of Br_2 would have reacted.

Amount of NO left unreacted

$$= (0.087 - 0.0518)$$
$$= 0.0352 \text{ mol.}$$

Amount of Br_2 left unreacted

$$= (0.0437 - 0.0518/2)$$
$$= 0.0178 \text{ mol.}$$

Q. 10. At 450 K_p, $K_p = 2.0 \times 10^{10}$/bar for the given reaction at equilibrium.

$$2SO_2(g) + O_2(g) \rightleftharpoons 2SO_3(g).$$

What is K_c at this temperature?

[NCERT Ex. Q. 6.9, Page 209]

Ans. $2SO_2(g) + O_2(g) \rightleftharpoons 2SO_3(g)$

For the given reaction

$$\Delta n_g = n_p - n_r = 2 - 3 = -1$$
$$K_p = K_c(RT)^{\Delta n}$$
$$K_p = 2 \times 10^{10} \text{ bar}^{-1}$$
$$K_c = \frac{K_p}{(RT)^{\Delta n}} = \frac{K_p}{(RT)^{-1}}$$
$$= K_p \times (RT)$$
$$= 2 \times 10^{10} \text{ bar}^{-1} (0.0831 \text{ L bar K}^{-1} \text{ mol}^{1}) \times (450 \text{ K})$$
$$= 7.48 \times 10^{11} \text{ L mol}^{-1}$$

Q. 11. A sample of HI (g) is placed in a flask at a pressure of 0.2 atm. At equilibrium, the partial pressure of HI (g) is 0.04 atm. What is K_p for the given equilibrium?

[NCERT Ex. Q. 6.11, Page 209]

$$2HI(g) \rightleftharpoons H_2(g) + I_2(g)$$

Ans.

	2HI (g)	$\rightleftharpoons$ H_2(g) +	I_2(g)
Initial pressure	0.2 atm	0	0
At equilibrium	0.04 atm	$\frac{0.16}{2}$ atm = 0.08 atm	$\frac{0.16}{2}$ atm = 0.08 atm

(Decrease in the pressure of HI = 0.2 – 0.04 = 0.16 atm)

$$K_p = \frac{p_{H_2} \times p_{I_2}}{p_{HI}^2} = \frac{0.08 \text{ atm} \times 0.08 \text{ atm}}{(0.04 \text{ atm})^2} = 4.0$$

Q. 12. A mixture of 1.57 mol of N_2, 1.92 mol of H_2 and 8.13 mol of NH_3 is introduced into a 20 L reaction vessel at 500 K. At this temperature, the equilibrium constant, K_c for the reaction,

$$N_2(g) + 3H_2(g) \rightleftharpoons 2NH_3(g) \text{ is } 1.7 \times 10^2$$

Is the reaction mixture at equilibrium? If not, what is the direction of the net reaction?

[NCERT Ex. Q. 6.12, Page 209]

Ans. The reaction is :

$N_2(g) + 3H_2(g) \rightleftharpoons 2NH_3(g)$

Given concentration of various species are :

$$[N_2] = \frac{1.57}{20} \text{ mol L}^{-1}; [H_2] = \frac{1.92}{20} \text{ mol L}^{-1}$$

$$[NH_3] = \frac{8.13}{20} \text{ mol L}^{-1}$$

$$Q_c = \frac{[NH_3]^2}{[N_2][H_2]^3}$$

$$= \frac{\left(\frac{8.13}{20} \text{ mol L}^{-1}\right)^2}{\left(\frac{1.57}{20} \text{ mol L}^{-1}\right)\left(\frac{1.92}{20} \text{ mol L}^{-1}\right)^3}$$

$$= 2.379 \times 10^3$$

As $Q_c \neq K_c$, the reaction mixture is not in equilibrium.

As $Q_c > K_c$, the net reaction will proceed in the backward direction.

Q. 13. The equilibrium constant expression for a gas reaction is:

$$K_c = \frac{[NH_3]^4[O_2]^5}{[NO]^4[H_2O]^6}$$

Write the balanced chemical equation corresponding of this expression. **[NCERT Ex. Q. 6.13, Page 209]**

Ans. $4NO(g) + 6H_2O(g) \rightleftharpoons 4NH_3(g) + 5O_2(g)$.

Q. 14. One mole of H_2O and one mole of CO are taken in a 10 L vessel and heated to 725 K. At equilibrium 40% of water (by mass) reacts with CO according to the equation

$$H_2O(g) + CO(g) \rightleftharpoons H_2(g) + CO_2(g)$$

Calculate equilibrium constant for the reaction.

[NCERT Ex. Q. 6.14, Page 209]

Ans. At equilibrium, $H_2O = 0.6$ (since 40% reacts)

Also, $[CO] = 0.6$

and, $[H_2] = 0.4$ and $[CO_2] = 0.4$

$$K_c = \frac{[H_2][CO_2]}{[H_2O][CO]}$$

$$= \frac{\frac{0.4}{10} \times \frac{0.4}{10}}{\frac{0.6}{10} \times \frac{0.6}{10}} = \frac{16}{36} = 0.44$$

Q. 15. At 700 K, equilibrium constant for the reaction $H_2(g) + I_2(g) \rightleftharpoons 2\,HI\,(g)$ is 54.8. If 0.5 mol L^{-1} of HI(g) is present at equilibrium at 700 K, what are the concentrations of $H_2(g)$ and $I_2(g)$ assuming that we initially started with HI (g) and allowed it to reach equilibrium at 700 K. [NCERT Ex. Q. 6.15, Page 209]

Ans. $2\,HI\,(g) \rightleftharpoons H_2\,(g) + I_2\,(g), K = \frac{1}{54.8}$

At equilibrium,

$$[HI] = 0.5 \text{ mol } L^{-1},$$

$$[H_2] = [I_2] = x \text{ mol } L^{-1}$$

$$\therefore \quad K_c' = \frac{[H_2][I_2]}{[HI]^2}$$

$$\frac{1}{54.8} = \frac{x \times x}{(0.5)^2}$$

This gives $x = 0.06754 \approx 0.068,$

i.e., $[H_2] = [I_2] = 0.068 \text{ mol } L^{-1}.$

Q. 16. What is the equilibrium concentration of each of the substances in the equilibrium when the initial concentration of ICl was 0.78 M ?

$2ICl\,(g) \rightleftharpoons I_2(g) + Cl_2(g)$; $K_c = 0.14$

[NCERT Ex. Q. 6.16, Page 210]

Ans. Suppose at equilibrium,

$[I_2] = [Cl_2] = x$ mol L^{-1}, then

	$2ICl(g)$	$\rightleftharpoons I_2(g)$	$+ Cl_2(g)$
Initial conc.	0.78 M	0	0
Equilibrium conc.	$(0.78 - 2x)$	x	x

$$K_c = \frac{[I_2] \times [Cl_2]}{[ICl]^2}$$

$$\therefore \quad 0.14 = \frac{x \times x}{(0.78 - 2x)^2}$$

$$x^2 = 0.14\,(0.78 - 2x)^2$$

or $$\frac{x}{0.78 - 2x} = \sqrt{0.14} = 0.374$$

or $$x = 0.292 - 0.748x$$

or $$1.748x = 0.292 \text{ or } x = 0.167$$

Hence, at equilibrium,

$$[I_2] = [Cl_2] = 0.167 \text{ M},$$

$$[ICl] = 0.78 - 2 \times 0.167 \text{ M} = 0.446 \text{ M}$$

Q. 17. K_p = 0.04 atm at 899 K for the equilibrium shown below. What is the equilibrium concentration of C_2H_6 when it is placed in a flask at 4.0 atm pressure and allowed to come to equilibrium ?

$C_2H_6(g) \rightleftharpoons C_2H_4(g) + H_2(g).$

[NCERT Ex. Q. 6.17, Page 210]

Ans. The given reaction is

	$C_2H_6(g) \rightleftharpoons$	$C_2H_4(g)$ +	$H_2(g)$
Initial conc.	4.0 atm	0	0
Equilibrium conc.	$(4 - p)$ atm	p atm	p atm

$$K_p = \frac{p_{C_2H_4} \times p_{H_2}}{p_{C_2H_6}}$$

$$0.04 = \frac{p \times p}{4 - p}$$

$$p^2 + 0.04\,p - 0.16 = 0$$

$$p = \frac{-0.04 \pm \sqrt{(0.04)^2 - 4(-0.16)}}{2}$$

$$= \frac{-0.04 + \sqrt{0.0016 + 0.64}}{2}$$

Consider only (positive) root

$$= \frac{-0.04 + \sqrt{0.6416}}{2}$$

$$= \frac{-0.04 + 0.801}{2} = 0.38 \text{ atm.}$$

$\therefore$ Equilibrium conc. of $C_2H_6(g) = (4.0 - 0.38)$ atm = 3.62 atm.

Q. 18. Ethyl acetate is formed by the reaction between ethanol and acetic acid and the equilibrium is represented as:

$CH_3COOH\,(l) + C_2H_5OH(l) \rightleftharpoons CH_3COOC_2H_5(l) + H_2O\,(l)$

(i) Write the concentration ratio (reaction quotient) Q_c, for this reaction (Note: water is not in excess and is not a solvent in this reaction).

(ii) At 293 K, if one starts with 1.00 ml of acetic acid and 0.18 mol of ethanol, there is 0.171 mol of ethyl acetate in the final equilibrium mixture. Calculate the equilibrium constant.

(iii) Starting with 0.5 mol of ethanol and 1.0 mol of acetic acid and maintaining it at 293 K, 0.214 mol of ethyl acetate is found after sometime. Has equilibrium been reached? [NCERT Ex. Q. 6.18, Page 210]

Ans. The given reaction is

$CH_3COOH(l) + C_2H_5OH(l) \rightleftharpoons CH_3COOC_2H_5(l) + H_2O(l)$

H_2O is not in excess and is not a solvent.

(i) $$Q_c = \frac{[CH_3COOC_2H_5(l)] \times [H_2O(l)]}{[CH_3COOH(l)] \times [C_2H_5OH(l)]}$$

(ii) $[CH_3COOH\,(l)]$ = 1.00 mol

$[C_2H_5OH\,(l)]$ = 0.18 mol

$[CH_3COOC_2H_5\,(l)]$ = 0.171 mol

$CH_3COOH\,(l) + C_2H_5OH\,(l) \rightleftharpoons CH_3COOC_2H_5\,(l) + H_2O\,(l)$

	CH_3COOH	C_2H_5OH	$CH_3COOC_2H_5$	H_2O
Initial conc.	1.0 mol	0.18 mol		
Equilibrium	(1 – 0.171) mol	(0.18 – 0.171) mol	0.171 mol	0.171 mol
Molar conc.	$\frac{0.829}{V}$	$\frac{0.009}{V}$	$\frac{0.171}{V}$	$\frac{0.171}{V}$

$$K_c = \frac{\frac{0.171}{V} \times \frac{0.171}{V}}{\frac{0.829}{V} \times \frac{0.009}{V}} = 3.92$$

(where V = volume of container in L)

$\therefore$ Equilibrium constant = 3.92

(iii) $CH_3COOH + C_2H_5OH \rightleftharpoons CH_3COOC_2H_5 + H_2O$

Initial conc. 1.00 mol 0.50 mol

Equilibrium (1 – 0.214) mol (0.500 – 0.214) mol 0.214 mol 0.214 mol
= 0.786 mol 0.286 mol 0.214 mol 0.214 mol

$$Q_c = \frac{\frac{0.214}{V} \times \frac{0.214}{V}}{\frac{0.786}{V} \times \frac{0.286}{V}} = 0.2037$$

As $Q_c \neq K_c$

∴ Equilibrium is not been attained.

Q. 19. A sample of pure PCl_5 was introduced into an evacuated vessel at 473K. After equilibrium was attained, concentration of PCl_5 was found to be 0.5×10^{-1} mol L^{-1}. If value of K_c is 8.3×10^{-3}, what are the concentrations of PCl_3 and Cl_2 at equilibrium ?

$PCl_5(g) \rightleftharpoons PCl_3(g) + Cl_2(g)$

[NCERT Ex. Q. 6.19, Page 210]

Ans. Let equilibrium conc. $[PCl_3] = [Cl_2] = x$

$$PCl_5(g) \rightleftharpoons PCl_3(g) + Cl_2(g)$$

At equilibrium 0.05 $molL^{-1}$ x x

As PCl_5 dissociates to give PCl_3 and Cl_2.

$$\therefore \quad K_c = \frac{[PCl_3]\times[Cl_2]}{[PCl_5]} = \frac{x \times x}{0.5\times10^{-1}}$$

$$x^2 = 8.3 \times 10^{-3} \times 0.5 \times 10^{-1}$$

or $x^2 = 4 \times 10^{-4}$

$$x = 2 \times 10^{-2} \text{ mol L}^{-1}$$

Hence, the conc. of PCl_3 and Cl_2 at equilibrium $= 0.02$ mol L^{-1}.

Q. 20. One of the reaction that takes place in producing steel from iron ore is the reduction of iron (II) oxide by carbon monoxide to give iron metal and CO_2.

$FeO(s) + CO(g) \rightleftharpoons Fe(s) + CO_2(g)$.

$K_p = 0.265$ atm at 1050 K

What are the equilibrium partial pressures of CO and CO_2 at 1050 K if the initial partial pressures are: $p_{CO} = 1.4$ atm and $p_{CO_2} = 0.80$ atm?

[NCERT Ex. Q. 6.20, Page 210]

Ans. Given, $K_p = 0.265$ atm at 1050 K

$p_{CO} = 1.4$ atm

$p_{CO_2} = 0.80$ atm

For the reaction,

$$FeO(s) + CO(g) \rightleftharpoons Fe(s) + CO_2(g)$$

Initial Pressure 1.4 atm 0.80 atm

$$Q_P = \frac{p_{CO_2}}{p_{CO}} = \frac{0.80}{1.4} = 0.571$$

∵ $Q_p > K_C$, so the reaction will proceed in reverse direction. Due to this reason, pressure of CO_2 will decrease and that of CO will increase to attain equilibrium.

Hence, $p_{CO_2} = (0.80 - p)$

$p_{CO} = (1.4 + p)$

$$\therefore \quad K_p = \frac{p_{CO_2}}{p_{CO}}$$

$$0.265 = \frac{0.80 - p}{1.4 + p}$$

or $1.265\,p = 0.80 - 0.371 = 0.429$

$$\therefore \quad p = \frac{0.429}{1.265} = 0.339 \text{ atm}$$

Hence, at equilibrium,

$p_{CO_2} = 0.80 - p = 0.80 - 0.339 = 0.461$ atm

and $p_{CO} = 1.4 + p = 1.4 + 0.339 = 1.739$ atm

Q. 21. Equilibrium constant, K_c for the reaction, $N_2(g) + 3H_2(g) \rightleftharpoons 2NH_3(g)$ at 500 K is 0.061. At a particular time, the analysis shows that composition of the reaction mixture is 3.0 mol L^{-1} N_2, 2.0 mol L^{-1} H_2 and 0.5 mol L^{-1} NH_3. Is the reaction at equilibrium ? If not, in which direction does the reaction tend to proceed to reach equilibrium ? [NCERT Ex. Q. 6.21, Page 210]

Ans. Given $K_c = 0.061$

For the reaction

$$N_2(g) + 3H_2(g) \rightleftharpoons 2NH_3(g)$$

$$Q_c = \frac{[NH_3]^2}{[N_2][H_2]^3} = \frac{(0.5)^2}{(3.0)(2.0)^3} = 0.0104$$

As $Q_c \neq K_c$, reaction is not in equilibrium.

As $Q_c < K_c$, reaction will proceed in the forward direction.

Q. 22. Bromine monochloride (BrCl) decomposes into bromine and chlorine and reaches the equilibrium

$2BrCl(g) \rightleftharpoons Br_2(g) + Cl_2(g)$

for which $K_c = 32$ at 500 K. If initially pure BrCl is present at a concentration of 3.30×10^{-3} mol L^{-1}, what is its molar concentration in the mixture at equilibrium? [NCERT Ex. Q. 6.22, Page 210]

Ans.

$$2BrCl(g) \rightleftharpoons Br_2(g) + Cl_2(g)$$

Initial Conc. 3.30×10^{-3} 0 0

Equilibrium Conc. $(3.30 \times 10^{-3} - x)$ $x/2$ $x/2$

$$K_c = \frac{(x/2)(x/2)}{(3.30\times10^{-3} - x)^2} \quad ½$$

$$\therefore \quad \frac{x^2}{4(3.30\times10^{-3} - x)} = 32$$

or $$\frac{x}{2(32.30\times10^{-3} - x)} = \sqrt{32} = 5.66$$

$$x = 11.32(3.30 \times 10^{-3} - x)$$

or $12.32\,x = 11.32 \times 3.30 \times 10^{-3}$

or $x = 3.0 \times 10^{-3}$

∴ At equilibrium

$[BrCl] = (3.30 \times 10^{-3} - 3.0 \times 10^{-3})$
$= 0.30 \times 10^{-3}$
$= 3.0 \times 10^{-4}$ mol L^{-1}

Q. 23. At 1127 K and 1 atm pressure, a gaseous mixture of CO and CO_2 in equilibrium with solid carbon has 90.55% CO by mass

$C(s) + CO_2(g) \rightleftharpoons 2CO(g)$

Calculate K_c for this reaction at the above temperature? [NCERT Ex. Q. 6.23, Page 211]

Ans. If total mass of the mixture of CO and CO_2 is 100 g then

Mass of CO = 90.55 g and CO_2 = 9.45 g

No. of moles of CO = 90.55/28 = 3.23

No. of moles of CO_2 = 9.45/44 = 0.22

$$p_{CO} = \frac{3.23}{3.23+0.22} \times 1 \text{ atm} = 0.94 \text{ atm}$$

$$p_{CO_2} = \frac{0.22}{3.23+0.22} \times 1 = 0.06 \text{ atm}$$

$$K_p = \frac{p^2_{CO}}{p_{CO_2}} = \frac{(0.94)^2}{(0.06)} = 14.73$$

$$\Delta n_g = 2 - 1 = 1$$

$$K_p = K_c (RT)^{\Delta n};$$

$$K_c = \frac{K_p}{(RT)^{\Delta n}} = \frac{14.73}{0.0821 \times 1127} = 0.159$$

Q. 24. Calculate (a) $\Delta G^\ominus$ and (b) the equilibrium constant for the formation of NO_2 from NO and O_2 at 298K

$$NO(g) + ½O_2(g) \rightleftharpoons NO_2(g)$$

where, $\Delta_f G^\ominus(NO_2)$ = 52.0 kJ/mol

$\Delta_f G^\ominus(NO)$ = 87.0 kJ/mol

$\Delta_f G^\ominus(O_2)$ = 0 kJ/mol

[NCERT Ex. Q. 6.24, Page 211]

Ans. (a) $NO(g) + \frac{1}{2}O_2(g) \rightleftharpoons NO_2(g)$

$$\because \quad \Delta_r G^\ominus = \sum \Delta_f G^\circ_{(Products)} - \sum \Delta_f G^\circ_{(reactants)}$$

$$\Delta_r G^\ominus = \Delta_\gamma G^\circ_{(NO_2)} - \left[\Delta_f G^\circ_{(NO)} + \frac{1}{2}\Delta_f G^\circ_{(O_2)}\right]$$

$$= 52.0 - \left[87.0 + \frac{1}{2} \times 0\right] \text{kJ mol}^{-1}$$

$$= -35.0 \text{ kJ mol}^{-1}$$

(b) $\because \quad \Delta_r G^\ominus = -2.303 RT \log K_c$

or $\quad \log K_c = \frac{-\Delta_r G^\ominus}{2.303RT}$

$$= \frac{-(-35000 \text{ J mol}^{-1})}{2.303 \times 8.314 \text{ J mol}^{-1} \text{ K}^{-1} \times 298\text{K}}$$

$$= 6.134$$

$\therefore \quad K_c = \text{antilog } 6.134 = 1.361 \times 10^6$

Q. 25. Does the number of moles of reaction products increase, decrease or remain same when each of the following equilibria is subjected to a decrease in pressure by increasing the volume?

(a) $PCl_5(g) \rightleftharpoons PCl(g) + Cl_2(g)$

(b) $CaO(s) + CO_2(g) \rightleftharpoons CaCO_3(s)$

(c) $3Fe(s) + 4H_2O(g) \rightleftharpoons Fe_3O_4(s) + 4H_2(g)$

[NCERT Ex. Q. 6.25, Page 211]

Ans. According to Le-Chatelier's principle, when pressure decreases, equilibrium will shift in that direction where volume increases (i.e., number of moles in gaseous state are more). Hence, the number of moles of reaction products in:

(a) increases [$\because \Delta n_{(g)} = n_p - n_r = 2 - 1 = 1$]

(b) decreases [$\because \Delta n_{(g)} = n_p - n_r = 0 - 1 = -1$]

(c) remains the same [$\because \Delta n_{(g)} = n_p - n_r = 4 - 4 = 0$]

Q. 26. Which of the following reactions will be affected by increase the pressure? Also, mention whether change will cause the reaction to go into forward or backward direction ?

(i) $COCl_2(g) \rightleftharpoons CO(g) + Cl_2(g)$

(ii) $CH_4(g) + 2S_2(g) \rightleftharpoons CS_2(g) + 2H_2S(g)$

(iii) $CO_2(g) + C(s) \rightleftharpoons 2CO(g)$

(iv) $2H_2(g) + CO(g) \rightleftharpoons CH_3OH(g)$

(v) $CaCO_3(s) \rightleftharpoons CaO(s) + CO_2(g)$

(vi) $4NH_3(g) + 5O_2(g) \rightleftharpoons 4NO(g) + 6H_2O(g)$.

[NCERT Ex. Q. 6.26, Page 211]

Ans. (i) $COCl_2(g) \rightleftharpoons CO(g) + Cl_2(g)$

$n_p > n_r$ as $n_p = 2$; $n_r = 1$

$\therefore$ Equilibrium will shift to the backward direction on increasing pressure.

(ii) The reaction proceeds with the same no. of moles on both the sides

i.e., $n_p = n_r = 3$

$\therefore$ This reaction will not be affected by the increase in pressure, i.e., the direction of equilibrium will not be affected by the increase in pressure.

(iii) $CO_2(g) + C(s) \rightleftharpoons 2CO(g)$

Here $n_r = 1; n_p = 2 \therefore n_p > n_r$

$\therefore$ Equilibrium will go to backward direction on increase in pressure.

(iv) $2H_2(g) + CO(g) \rightleftharpoons CH_3OH(g)$

Here, $n_r = 3; n_p = 1 \therefore n_p < n_r$

$\therefore$ Equilibrium will shift to the forward direction on increasing pressure.

(v) $CaCO_3(s) \rightleftharpoons CaO(s) + CO_2(g)$

Here, $n_r = 0; n_p = 1 \therefore n_p > n_r$

$\therefore$ Equilibrium will shift backward direction on increasing pressure.

(vi) $4NH_3(g) + 5O_2(g) \rightleftharpoons 4NO(g) + 6H_2O(g)$

Here, $n_r = 9; n_p = 10 \therefore n_p > n_r$

$\therefore$ Equilibrium shifts in backward direction on increasing the pressure.

Q. 27. The equilibrium constant for the following reaction is 1.6×10^5 at 1024 K.

$$H_2(g) + Br_2(g) \rightleftharpoons 2HBr(g)$$

Find the equilibrium pressure of all gases if 10.0 bar of HBr is introduced into a sealed container at 1024 K ?

[NCERT Ex. Q. 6.27, Page 211]

Ans. $K_p = 1.6 \times 10^5$ $H_2(g) + Br_2(g) \rightleftharpoons 2HBr(g)$

	$H_2(g)$	$Br_2(g)$	$2HBr(g)$
Initial pressure	0	0	10 bar
At equilibrium	$p/2$	$p/2$	$(10 - p)$

$$K_p = \frac{p^2HBr}{pH_2 \times pBr_2}$$

$$1.6 \times 10^5 = \frac{(10-p)^2}{(p/2)(p/2)}$$

Taking square root of both sides

$$4 \times 10^2 = \frac{10-p}{(p/2)}$$

$$200p = 10 - p$$

$$p = \frac{10}{201} \text{ bar}$$

$$p_{H_2} = p/2 = \frac{1}{2}\left(\frac{10}{201}\right) \text{ bar}$$

$$= 2.5 \times 10^{-2} \text{ bar}$$

$$p_{Br_2} = p/2 = 2.5 \times 10^{-2} \text{ bar}$$

$$p_{HBr} = 10 - p = 9.95 \text{ bar}$$

Q. 28. Dihydrogen gas is obtained from natural gas by partial oxidation with steam as per endothermic reaction: $CH_4(g) + H_2O(g) \rightleftharpoons CO(g) + 3H_2(g)$

(i) Write an expression for K_p for the above reaction.

(ii) How will the values of K_p and composition of the equilibrium mixture be affected by

(i) increasing the pressure

(ii) increasing the temperature

(iii) using a catalyst ?

[NCERT Ex. Q. 6.28, Page 211]

Ans. (i) $K_p = \frac{(p_{CO})(p_{H_2})^3}{(p_{CH_4})(p_{H_2O})}$

(ii) (i) By Le Chatelier's principle, equilibrium will shift in the backward direction (as $n_r < n_p$).

(ii) As the given reaction is endothermic, by Le Chatelier's principle, equilibrium will shift in the forward direction.

(iii) Equilibrium composition will not be disturbed but equilibrium will be attained quickly.

Q. 29. Describe the effect of:

(a) addition of H_2

(b) addition of CH_3OH

(c) removal of CO

(d) removal of CH_3OH

on the equilibrium of the reaction

$2H_2(g) + CO(g) \rightleftharpoons CH_3OH(g)$

[NCERT Ex. Q. 6.29, Page 211]

Ans. (a) On addition of H_2, equilibrium will shift in the forward direction.

(b) On addition of CH_3OH, equilibrium will shift in backward direction.

(c) On removal of CO, equilibrium will shift in the backward direction.

(d) On removal of CH_3OH, equilibrium will shift in the forward direction.

Q. 30. At 473K, equilibrium constant K_c for decomposition of phosphorus pentachloride, PCl_5 is 8.3×10^{-3}. If decomposition is depicted as :

$PCl_5(g) \rightleftharpoons PCl_3(g) + Cl_2(g)$, $\Delta_rH^\ominus = 124.0$ kJ mol^{-1}

(a) Write an expression for K_c for the reaction.

(b) What is the value of K_c for the reverse reaction at the same temperature?

(c) What would be the effect on K_c if (i) more PCl_5 is added (ii) pressure is increased (iii) the temperature is increased? [NCERT Ex. Q. 6.30, Page 211]

Ans. (a) For the reaction,

$$PCl_5(g) \rightleftharpoons PCl_3(g) + Cl_2(g)$$

$$K_c = \frac{[PCl_3][Cl_2]}{[PCl_5]}$$

(b) Given, $K_c = 8.3 \times 10^{-3}$

∴ For the reverse reaction,

$$K'_c = \frac{1}{K_c} = \frac{1}{8.3 \times 10^{-3}} = 120.48$$

(c) (i) If more PCl_5 is added, then Q_c becomes less than K_c, so the reaction will proceed in the forward direction.

(ii) If the pressure is increased, the reaction will proceed towards backward direction as it contains less number of reacting gaseous species.

(iii) If the temperature is increased, the reaction will proceed in the forward direction as the reaction is endothermic in nature.

Q. 31. Dihydrogen gas used in Haber's process is produced by reacting methane from natural gas with high temperature steam. The first stage of two stage reaction involves the formation of CO and H_2. In second stage, CO formed in first stage is reacted with more steam in water gas shift reaction.

$CO(g) + H_2O(g) \rightleftharpoons CO_2(g) + H_2(g)$

If a reaction vessel at 400°C is charged with an equimolar mixture of CO and steam such that $P_{CO} = P_{H_2O} = 4.0$ bar, what will be the partial pressure of H_2 at equilibrium? $K_p = 10.1$ at 400°C.

[NCERT Ex. Q. 6.31, Page 212]

Ans. Given, $K_p = 10.1$

For the reaction,

$$CO(g) + H_2O(g) \rightleftharpoons CO_2(g) + H_2(g)$$

	CO(g)	H_2O(g)	CO_2(g)	H_2(g)
Initial Pressure	4.0 bar	4.0 bar	0	0
At Equilibrium	(4.0 – p)	(4.0 – p)	p	p

$$K_p = \frac{(p_{CO_2}).(p_{H_2})}{(p_{CO}).(p_{H_2O})}$$

$$10.1 = \frac{p \times p}{(4-p).(4-p)}$$

or $$10.1 = \frac{p^2}{(4-p)^2}$$

or $$\sqrt{10.1} = \frac{p}{(4-p)}$$

or $$3.17 = \frac{p}{(4-p)}$$

or $$p = 12.71 - 3.17p$$

or $$p + 3.17p = 12.71$$

or $$4.17p = 12.71$$

or $$p = \frac{12.71}{4.17} = 3.04 \text{ bar}$$

Hence, $p_{H_2} = 3.04$ bar $[P_{H_2O} = P_{CO} = 0.96]$

Q. 32. Predict which of the following reaction will have appreciable concentration of reactants and products:

(a) $Cl_2(g) \rightleftharpoons 2Cl(g)$. $K_c = 5 \times 10^{-39}$

(b) $Cl_2(g) + 2NO(g) \rightleftharpoons 2NOCl(g)$, $K_c = 3.7 \times 10^8$

(c) $Cl_2(g) + 2NO_2(g) \rightleftharpoons 2NO_2Cl(g)$, $K_c = 1.8$

[NCERT Ex. Q. 6.32, Page 212]

Ans. **(a)** Since K_c is very small, so, there will be appreciable concentration of reactants only.

(b) Since K_c is very large, so there will be appreciable concentration of products only.

(c) Since $K_c = 1.8$, i.e., neither very small nor very large, so, this reaction will have appreciable concentration of reactants and products.

Q. 33. The value of K_c for the reaction $3O_2(g) \rightleftharpoons 2O_3(g)$ is 2.0×10^{-50} at 25°C. If the equilibrium concentration of O_2 in air at 25°C is 1.6×10^{-2}, what is the concentration of O_3? [NCERT Ex. Q. 6.33, Page 212]

Ans. Given, $K_c = 2.0 \times 10^{-50}$

$[O_2] = 1.6 \times 10^{-2}$

For the reaction,

$3O_2(g) \rightleftharpoons 2O_3(g)$

Equilibrium constant $K_c = \dfrac{[O_3]^2}{[O_2]^3}$

$$2.0 \times 10^{-50} = \frac{[O_3]^2}{\left[1.6 \times 10^{-2}\right]^3}$$

or $[O_3]^2 = 2.0 \times 10^{-50} \times (1.6 \times 10^{-2})^3 = 8.192 \times 10^{-56}$

or $[O_3] = 2.86 \times 10^{-28}$ mol L^{-1}

Q. 34. The reaction, $CO(g) + 3H_2(g) \rightleftharpoons CH_4(g) + H_2O(g)$ is at equilibrium at 1300 K in a 1 L flask. It also contains 0.30 mol of CO, 0.10 mol of H_2 and 0.02 mol of H_2O and an unknown amount of CH_4 in the flask. Determine the concentration of CH_4 in the mixture. The equilibrium constant, K_c for the reaction at the given temperature is 3.90. [NCERT Ex. Q. 6.34, Page 212]

Ans. Given, $K_c = 3.90$

$[CO] = 0.30$

$[H_2] = 0.10$

$[H_2O] = 0.02$

$[CH_4] = ?$

For the reaction

$CO(g) + 3H_2(g) \rightleftharpoons CH_4(g) + H_2O(g)$

Equilibrium constant

$$K_c = \frac{[CH_4][H_2O]}{[CO][H_2]^3}$$

$$3.90 = \frac{[CH_4][0.02]}{[0.30][0.10]^3}$$

$$\therefore \quad [CH_4] = \frac{3.90 \times 0.30 \times (0.10)^3}{0.02} = 0.0585 \text{ M}$$

or $[CH_4]_{eq.} = 5.85 \times 10^{-2}$ M

Q. 35. What is meant by the conjugate acid-base pair? Find the conjugate acid base for the following species: HNO_2, CN^-, $HClO_4$, F^-, OH^-, CO_3^{2-} and S^{2-} [NCERT Ex. Q. 6.35, Page 212]

Ans. Conjugate acid-base pair

The acid base pair that differs only by one proton is called a conjugate acid-base pair.

Species	Conjugate acid	Conjugate base
HNO_2	.....	NO_2^-
CN^-	HCN	.....
$HClO_4$	.....	ClO_4^-
F^-	HF	......
OH^-	H_2O	.....
CO_3^{2-}	HCO_3^-	.....
S^{2-}	HS^-	.....

Q. 36. Which of the following are Lewis acids?

H_2O, BF_3, H^+ and NH_4^+ [NCERT Ex. Q. 6.36, Page 212]

Ans. Lewis acids are electron pair acceptor. So, BF_3, H^+ and NH_4^+ are Lewis acids.

Q. 37. What will be the conjugate bases for the Bronsted acids: HF, H_2SO_4 and HCO_3^-? [NCERT Ex. Q. 6.37, Page 212]

Ans.

Bronsted acid	Conjugate base
HF	F^-
H_2SO_4	HSO_4^-
HCO_3^-	CO_3^{2-}

Q. 38. Write the conjugate acids for the following Bronsted bases : NH_2^-, NH_3 and $HCOO^-$ [NCERT Ex. Q. 6.38, Page 212]

Ans.

Bronsted base	Conjugate acid
NH_2^-	NH_3
NH_3	NH_4^+
$HCOO^-$	HCOOH

Q. 39. The species H_2O, HCO_3, HSO_4^- and NH_3 can act both as Bronsted acid and bases. For each case give the corresponding conjugate acid and base. [NCERT Ex. Q. 6.39, Page 212]

Ans. (i) $H_2O \xrightarrow{-H^+}$ Conjugate base is OH^-

$\downarrow H^+$

Conjugate acid is H_3O^+

(ii) $HCO_3^- \xrightarrow{-H^+}$ Conjugate base is CO_3^{2-}

$\downarrow H^+$

Conjugate acid is H_2CO_3

(iii) $HSO_4^- \xrightarrow{-H^+}$ Conjugate base is SO_4^{2-}

$\downarrow H^+$

Conjugate acid is H_2SO_4

(iv) $NH_3 \xrightarrow{-H^+}$ Conjugate base is NH_2^-

$\downarrow H^+$

Conjugate acid is NH_4^+

Q. 40. Classify the following species into Lewis acids and Lewis bases and show how these act as Lewis acid/base:

(a) OH^- **(b) F^-**

(c) H^+ **(d) BCl_3.**

[NCERT Ex. Q. 6.40, Page 212]

Ans. (a) OH^- Lewis base, as it can donate electron pair because of electron rich.

(b) F^- Lewis base, as it can donate electron pair because of electron rich.

(c) H^+ Lewis acid, as it can accept electron pair because of electron deficiency.

(d) BCl_3 Lewis acid, as it can accept electron pair because of electron deficiency.

Q. 41. The concentration of hydrogen ion in a sample of soft drink is 3.8×10^{-3} M. What is its pH ?

[NCERT Ex. Q. 6.41, Page 212]

Ans.
$$[H^+] = 3.8 \times 10^{-3}\text{ M}$$
$$pH = -\log_{10}[H^+]$$
$$= -\log[3.8 \times 10^{-3}]$$
$$= -[\log 3.8 + \log 10^{-3}]$$
$$= -[0.58 + (-3\log 10)]$$
$$= -[0.58 - 3] = -(-2.42)$$
$$pH = 2.42$$

Q. 42. The pH of a sample of vinegar is 3.76. Calculate the concentration of hydrogen ion in it.

[NCERT Ex. Q. 6.42, Page 212]

Ans. Given, pH = 3.76

$\therefore$ $pH = -\log[H^+]$

$3.76 = -\log[H^+]$

$[H^+] = \text{antilog}(-3.76)$

$= 1.738 \times 10^{-4}$ M

Q. 43. The ionization constant of HF, HCOOH and HCN at 298 K are 6.8×10^{-4}, 1.8×10^{-4} and 4.8×10^{-9} respectively. Calculate the ionization constants of the corresponding conjugate base?

[NCERT Ex. Q. 6.43, Page 212]

Ans. Let K_a = dissociation ionisation constant of a weak acid.

K_b = Ionization constant of its conjugate base

K_w = Ionic product of water

$= 1.0 \times 10^{-14}$ at 298 K

$K_a . K_b = K_w$

HF/F^{-2}

$$K_{HF} \times K_{F^-} = 1.0 \times 10^{-14}$$
$$6.8 \times 10^{-4} \times K_{F^-} = 1.0 \times 10^{-14}$$
$$\therefore \quad K_{F^-} = \frac{1.0 \times 10^{-14}}{6.8 \times 10^{-4}}$$
$$= 1.5 \times 10^{-11}$$

HCOOH/HCOO$^-$

$$K_{HCOOH} \times K_{HCOO^-} = 1.0 \times 10^{-14}$$
$$1.8 \times 10^{-4} \times K_{HCOO^-} = 1.0 \times 10^{-14}$$
$$\therefore \quad K_{HCOO^-} = \frac{1.0 \times 10^{-14}}{1.8 \times 10^{-4}}$$
$$= 5.6 \times 10^{-11}$$

HCN/CN–

$$K_{HCN} \times K_{CN^-} = 1.0 \times 10^{-14}$$
$$4.8 \times 10^{-9} \times K_{CN^-} = 1.0 \times 10^{-14}$$
$$\therefore \quad K_{CN^-} = \frac{1.0 \times 10^{-14}}{4.8 \times 10^{-9}}$$
$$= 2.08 \times 10^{-6}$$

Q. 44. The ionization constant of phenol is 1.0×10^{-10}. What is the concentration of phenolate ion in 0.05 M solution of phenol? What will be its degree of ionization if the solution is also 0.01 M in sodium phenolate?

[NCERT Ex. Q. 6.44, Page 213]

Ans. $K_a = 1.0 \times 10^{-10}$

For the reaction,

$$C_6H_5OH + H_2O \rightleftharpoons C_6H_5O^- + H_3O^+$$

	Phenol	phenolate ion	
Initial Conc.	0.05	0	0
Equilibrium	$(0.05 - x)$	x	x

$$K_a = \frac{[C_6H_5O^-][H_3O^+]}{[C_6H_5OH]}$$
$$1 \times 10^{-10} = \frac{x \times x}{0.05 - x}$$

or
$$1 \times 10^{-10} = \frac{x^2}{0.05} \quad [\because 0.05 - x \simeq 0.05]$$

or
$$x^2 = 5 \times 10^{-12}$$

or
$$x = 2.23 \times 10^{-6}\text{ M}$$

In the presence of 0.01 M C_6H_5ONa, suppose y is the amount of phenol dissociated, then at equilibrium,

$$[C_6H_5OH] = 0.05 - y = 0.05\text{ M}$$
$$[C_6H_5O^-] = 0.01 + y \simeq 0.01\text{M}$$
$$[H_3O^+] = y\text{ M}$$
$$K_a = \frac{[C_6H_5O^-][H_3O^+]}{[C_6H_5OH]}$$
$$1 \times 10^{-10} = \frac{0.01 \times y}{0.05}$$

or
$$y = 5 \times 10^{-10}$$

Degree of ionization

$$\alpha = \frac{y}{c} = \frac{5 \times 10^{-10}}{0.05} = 1 \times 10^{-8} \quad (1)$$

Q. 45. The first ionization constant of H_2S is 9.1×10^{-8}. Calculate the concentration of HS^- ion in its 0.1 M solution. How will this concentration be affected if the solution is 0.1 M in HCl also? If the second dissociation constant of H_2S is 1.2×10^{-13}, calculate the concentration of S^{2-} under both conditions.

[NCERT Ex. Q. 6.45, Page 213]

Ans. Given,
$$K_{a1} = 9.1 \times 10^{-8}$$
$$K_{a2} = 1.2 \times 10^{-13}$$

For the reaction,

$$H_2S \rightleftharpoons HS^- + H^+$$

	H_2S	HS^-	H^+
Initial Conc.	C	0	0
Equilibrium Conc.	$C(1-\alpha)$	$c\alpha$	$c\alpha$

$$\therefore \quad K_a = \frac{[HS^-][H^+]}{[H_2S]} = \frac{C\alpha . C\alpha}{C(1-\alpha)}$$
$$= \frac{C\alpha^2}{(1-\alpha)}$$
$$\simeq C\alpha^2 \; (\because 1 >>> \alpha)$$

and $[HS^-] = C\alpha = \sqrt{K_a C} = \sqrt{9.1 \times 10^{-8} \times 0.1}$

$$= 9.54 \times 10^{-5}\text{ M}$$

In 0.1 M HCl,

$$H_2S \rightleftharpoons HS^- + H^+$$

	H_2S	HS^-	H^+
Initial Conc.	0.1M	0	0
Equilibrium Conc.	$(0.1 - x)$	x	x

$$HCl \rightleftharpoons H^+ + Cl^-$$
$$0.1\ M \quad 0.1M \quad 0.1\ M$$

$$K_{a_1} = \frac{[H^+][HS^-]}{[H_2S]}$$

$$9.1 \times 10^{-8} = \frac{0.1[HS^-]}{0.1}$$

$\therefore$ $[HS^-] = 9.1 \times 10^{-8}$ M

$\therefore$ The concentration of HS^- has decreased in 0.1 M HCl.

Calculation of Concentration of S^{2-} ion –

$$HS^- \rightarrow H^+ + S^{2-}$$

$$H_2S \overset{Ka_1}{\rightleftharpoons} H^+ + HS^-$$

$$HS^- \overset{Ka_2}{\rightleftharpoons} H^+ + S^{2-}$$

$$H_2S \overset{Ka}{\rightleftharpoons} 2H^+ + S^{2-}$$

$\therefore$ Overall ionization constant of H_2S

$$K_a = K_{a_1} \times K_{a_2}$$
$$= 9.1 \times 10^{-8} \times 1.2 \times 10^{-13}$$
$$= 1.092 \times 10^{-20}$$

$$H_2S \rightleftharpoons 2H^+ + S^{2-}$$

	H_2S	$2H^+$	S^{2-}
Initial Conc.	0.1 M	0	0
Equilibrium Conc.	$(0.1 - x)$ ≈ 0.1 M	$2x$	x

In presence of 0.1 M HCl,

$$K_a = \frac{[H^+]^2[S^{2-}]}{[H_2S]}$$

$$1.092 \times 10^{-20} = \frac{[0.1]^2[S^{2-}]}{[0.1]}$$

$\therefore$ $[S^{2-}] = 1.092 \times 10^{-19}$ M

Q. 46. The ionization constant of acetic acid is 1.74 × 10^{-5}. Calculate the degree of dissociation of acetic acid in its 0.05 M solution. Calculate the concentration of acetate in the solution and its pH.

[NCERT Ex. Q. 6.46, Page 213]

Ans. $K_a = 1.74 \times 10^{-5}, \alpha = ?, c = 0.05M$

$[CH_3COO^-] = ?, pH = ?$

$$CH_3COOH + H_2O \rightleftharpoons CH_3COO^- + H_3O^+$$

CH_3COOH	CH_3COO^-	H_3O^+	
1	0	0	[Initial concentration in mol L^{-1}]
$1 - \alpha$	α	α	
$C(1-\alpha)$	$C\alpha$	$C\alpha$	[Final concentration in mol L^{-1}]

[where α = degree of dissociation

C = molar concentration]

$$\therefore \quad K_a = \frac{[CH_3COO^-][H_3O^+]}{[CH_3COO^{-H}]}$$

$$= \frac{C\alpha^2}{1-\alpha}$$

$\alpha << 1$, $\therefore$ α can be ignored from the denominator

$$\therefore \quad K_a = C\alpha^2$$

or $$\alpha = \sqrt{\frac{K_a}{0{\cdot}05}}$$

$$= \sqrt{\frac{1.74 \times 10^{-5}}{0.05}}$$

$$= \sqrt{3.48 \times 10^{-4}}$$

$$= 1.86 \times 10^{-2}$$

$$[CH_3COO^-] = C\alpha = \sqrt{K_aC}$$

$$= \sqrt{1.74 \times 10^{-5} \times 0.05}$$

$$= \sqrt{0.87 \times 10^{-16}}$$

$$[CH_3COO^-] = 0.933 \times 10^{-3}$$
$$= 9.33 \times 10^{-4}\ M$$

$$pH = -\log [H^+]$$
$$= -\log 9.33 \times 10^{-4}$$
$$= -(-4) - \log 9.3$$
$$= 4 - 0.97$$
$$= 3.03$$

Q. 47. It has been found that the pH of a 0.01 M solution of an organic acid is 4.15. Calculate the concentration of anion, the ionization constant of the acid and its pK_a ?

[NCERT Ex. Q. 6.47, Page 213]

Ans. $HA \rightleftharpoons H^+ + A^-$

$$pH = -\log [H^+]$$
$$[H^+] = \text{antilog} - 4.15$$
$$= \overline{5}{\cdot}85$$
$$= 7.08 \times 10^{-5}\ M$$
$$[A^-] = [H^+] = 7.08 \times 10^{-5}\ M$$

$$K_a = \frac{[H^+][A^-]}{[HA]}$$

$$= \frac{(7.08 \times 10^{-5})(7.08 \times 10^{-5})}{10^{-2}}$$

$$= 5.01 \times 10^{-7}$$

$$pK_a = -\log K_a$$
$$= -\log (5.01 \times 10^{-7})$$
$$= 7 - 0.699 = 6.301.$$

Q. 48. Assuming complete dissociation, calculate pH for the following solutions :

(a) 0.003 M HCl **(b) 0.005 M NaOH**

(c) 0.002 M HBr **(d) 0.002 M KOH**

[NCERT Ex. Q. 6.48, Page 213]

Ans. (a) $HCl(aq) \rightarrow H^+(aq) + Cl^-(aq)$

$[HCl] = 0.003$ M

As HCl is completely dissociated into H^+ ions

$\therefore \quad [H^+] = [HCl] = 0.003$ M

$pH = -\log [H^+] = -\log 3 \times 10^{-3}$

$= -(-3) \log 3 = 3 - \log 3$

$= 3 - 0.477 = 2.523$

(b) $NaOH(aq) \rightarrow Na^+(aq) + OH^-(aq)$

$[NaOH] = 0.005 = 5 \times 10^{-3}$ M

$[OH^-] = [NaOH] = 5 \times 10^{-3}$ M

$$[H^+] = \frac{K_w}{[OH^-]} = \frac{1.0 \times 10^{-14}}{5.0 \times 10^{-3}}$$

$[H^+] = 2.0 \times 10^{-12}$

$\therefore \quad pH = -\log 2 \times 10^{-12} = -(-12) - \log 2$

$= 12 - 0.30 = 11.70$

(c) $HBr \rightarrow H^+ + Br^-$

$[HBr] = 0.002$ M

As HBr is completely dissociated

$[H^+] = [HBr] = 0.002$ M

$= 2.0 \times 10^{-3}$ M

$pH = -\log [H^+]$

$= -\log 2 \times 10^{-3} = -(-3) - \log 2$

$= 3 - \log 2 = 3 - 0.3 = 2.70$

(d) $KOH \rightarrow K^+ + OH^-$, completely dissociated,

0.002 M   0.002 M

$[OH^-] = 0.002$ M

$$[H^+] = \frac{K_w}{[OH^-]} = \frac{1.0 \times 10^{-14}}{5.0 \times 10^{-3}}$$

$= 5 \times 10^{-12}$ M

$pH = -\log (H^+) = -(-12) - \log 5$

$= 12 - 0.70 = 11.30$

Q. 49. Calculate the pH of the following solutions:

(a) 2 g of TlOH dissolved in water to give 2 litre of solution.

(b) 0.3 g of $Ca(OH)_2$ dissolved in water to give 500 ml of solution.

(c) 0.3 g of NaOH dissolved in water to give 200 ml of solution.

(d) 1 ml of 13.6 M HCl is diluted with water to give 1 litre of solution. [NCERT Ex. Q. 6.49, Page 213]

Ans. (a) Given,

Mass of TlOH = 2 g

Volume of solution = 2 litre

Molecular mass of TlOH = 204 + 16 + 1 = 221 g mol^{-1}

$\therefore$ Concentration of TlOH in mol/L, i.e., molarity

$$= \frac{\text{Mass of TlOH (g)}}{\text{Molar mass of TlOH} \times \text{Volume of Solution (L)}}$$

$$= \frac{2}{221 \times 2}$$

$= 0.00452 = 4.52 \times 10^{-3}$ M

$\because \quad pOH = -\log[OH^-]$

$= -\log[4.52 \times 10^{-3}]$

$= -\log 4.52 + 3 \log 10$

$= -0.6551 + 3 = 2.3449 \approx 2.34$

$\because \quad pH + pOH = 14$

or $\quad pH = 14 - pOH = 14 - 2.34 = 11.66$

(b) Given,

Mass of $Ca(OH)_2$ = 0.3 g

Volume of Solution = 500 mL = 0.5 L

Molar mass of $Ca(OH)_2 = 40 + [(16+1) \times 2]$

$= 74$ g mol^{-1}

Concentration of $Ca(OH)_2$ in mol/L, i.e., molarity

$$= \frac{\text{Mass of } Ca(OH)_2 \text{ in g}}{\text{Molar mass of } Ca(OH)_2 \times \text{Volume of Solution(L)}}$$

$$= \frac{0.3}{74 \times 0.5}$$

$= 0.0081 = 8.1 \times 10^{-3}$

1 mole of $Ca(OH)_2$ given 2 moles of OH^-. So,

$[OH^-] = 2 \times 8.1 \times 10^{-3} = 16.2 \times 10^{-3}$

$= 1.62 \times 10^{-2}$

Now, $pOH = -\log[OH^-]$

$= -\log[1.62 \times 10^{-2}]$

$= -\log 1.62 + 2 \log 10$

$= -0.2095 + 2 = 1.7905 \approx 1.79$

$pH + pOH = 14$

or $\quad pH = 14 - pOH = 14 - 1.79 = 12.21$

(c) Given,

Mass of NaOH = 0.3 g

Volume of Solution = 200 ml = 0.2 L

Molar mass of NaOH = 23 + 16 + 1

= 40 g mol^{-1}

$\therefore$ Concentration of NaOH in mol/L, i.e., molarity

$$= \frac{\text{Mass of NaOH in g}}{\text{Molar mass of NaOH} \times \text{Volume of Solution (L)}}$$

$$= \frac{0.3}{40 \times 0.2} = 0.0375$$

$= 3.75 \times 10^{-2}$

Now, $\quad pOH = -\log[OH^-]$

$= -\log[3.75 \times 10^{-2}]$

$= -\log 3.75 + 2 \log 10$

$= -0.5740 + 2 = 1.426 \approx 1.43$

$\because \quad pH + pOH = 14$

or $\quad pH = 14 - pOH = 14 - 1.43 = 12.57$

(d) Given,

Volume of HCl(V_1) = 1 mL

Molarity of HCl (M_1) = 13.6 M

Volume of Solution (V_2) = 1 litre = 1000 mL

In case of dilution,

$M_1V_1 = M_2V_2$

$13.6 \times 1 = M_2 \times 1000$

$$M_2 = \frac{13.6 \times 1}{1000} = 0.0136$$

$= 1.36 \times 10^{-2}$ M

$\because$ $pH = -\log[H^+]$

$= -\log[1.36 \times 10^{-2}]$

$= -\log 1.36 + 2 \log 10$

$= -0.1335 + 2 = 1.8665 \approx 1.87$

Q. 50. The degree of ionization of 0.1 M bromoacetic acid solution is 0.132. Calculate the pH of the solution and the pK_a of bromoacetic acid.

[NCERT Ex. Q. 6.50, Page 213]

Ans. $BrCH_2COOH \rightleftharpoons BrCH_2COO^- + H^+$

Initial conc.	C	0	0
Equilibrium conc.	$C(1-\alpha)$	$C\alpha$	$C\alpha$

$$K_a = \frac{C\alpha^2}{(1-\alpha)} \simeq C\alpha^2$$

$= 0.1 \times (0.132)^2$

$= 1.74 \times 10^{-3}$

$pK_a = -\log K_a$

$= -\log(1.74 \times 10^{-3})$

$= 3 - 0.2405 = 2.76$

$(H^+) = C\alpha = 0.1 \times 0.132$

$= 1.32 \times 10^{-2}$ M

$pH = -\log[H^+] - \log(1.32 \times 10^{-2})$

$= 2 - 0.1206 = 1.8794 \approx 1.88$ (2)

Q. 51. The pH of 0.005 M codeine ($C_{18}H_{21}NO_3$) solution is 9.95. Calculate is ionization constant and pK_b.

[NCERT Ex. Q. 6.51, Page 213]

Ans. Codeine is a base.

$$B + H_2O \rightleftharpoons BH^+ + OH^-$$

$pH = 9.95$

$\therefore$ $pOH = 14 - 9.95 = 4.05$

or $-\log[OH^-] = 4.05$

$OH^- = \text{antilog}(-4.05)$

$= \bar{5}.95 = 8.91 \times 10^{-5}$

$$K_b = \frac{(BH^+)(OH^-)}{(B)}$$

$$= \frac{(OH^-)^2}{(B)} = \frac{(8.91 \times 10^{-5})^2}{5 \times 10^{-3}}$$

$= 1.588 \times 10^{-6}$

$pK_b = -\log(1.588 \times 10^{-6})$

$= 6 - 0.2 = 5.8$

Q. 52. What is the pH of 0.001 M aniline solution ? The ionization constant of aniline is 4.27×10^{-10}. Calculate the degree of ionization of aniline in the solution. Also calculate the ionization constant of the conjugate acid of aniline ? **[NCERT Ex. Q. 6.52, Page 213]**

Ans. $C_6H_5NH_2 + H_2O \rightleftharpoons C_6H_5NH_3^{\oplus} + OH^{\ominus}$

Initial Conc.	C	0	0
Equilibrium Conc.	$C(1-\alpha)$	$C\alpha$	$C\alpha$

Ionization constant of base

$$K_b = \frac{C\alpha \cdot C\alpha}{C(1-\alpha)}$$

$$= \frac{C^2\alpha^2}{C(1-\alpha)} = \frac{C\alpha^2}{(1-\alpha)}$$

For weak base $1 - \alpha \simeq 1$

So, $K_b = C\alpha^2$

or Degree of ionization,

$$\alpha = \sqrt{\frac{K_b}{C}}$$

$$= \sqrt{\frac{4.27 \times 10^{-10}}{0.001}}$$

$= 6.53 \times 10^{-4}$

Then, $[OH^-] = C\alpha = 0.001 \times 6.534 \times 10^{-4}$

$= 0.065 \times 10^{-5}$

$pOH = -\log(0.065 \times 10^{-5}) = 6.187$

$pH = 14 - 6.187 = 7.813$

Ionization constant (K_a) of conjugate acid of aniline

$$K_a = \frac{K_w}{K_b}$$

$$= \frac{10^{-14}}{4.27 \times 10^{-10}}$$

$= 2.34 \times 10^{-5}$

Q. 53. Calculate the degree of ionization of 0.05 M acetic acid if its pK_a value is 4.74. How is the degree of dissociation affected when its solution also contains (a) 0.01 M in HCl (b) 0.1 M in HCl?

[NCERT Ex. Q. 6.53, Page 213]

Ans. Given,

Concentration of acetic acid (C) = 0.05 M

$pK_a = 4.74$

$\because$ $pK_a = -\log K_a$

$4.74 = -\log K_a$

or $\log K_a = -4.74 = \bar{5}.26$

$K_a = \text{antilog } \bar{5}.26$

$= 1.82 \times 10^{-5}$

Degree of ionization

$$\alpha = \sqrt{\frac{K_a}{C}}$$

$$= \sqrt{\frac{1.82 \times 10^{-5}}{0.05}}$$

$$= \sqrt{3.64 \times 10^{-4}}$$

$= 1.908 \times 10^{-2}$

(a) When solution contains 0.01 M HCl

$$CH_3COOH \rightleftharpoons CH_3COO^- + H^+$$

Initial Conc.	0.05M	**0**	**0**
Equilibrium conc.	$0.05 - C\alpha \simeq 0.05$	$C\alpha$	$(C\alpha + 0.01) \simeq 0.01$

$\because$ CH_3COOH is a weak acid and HCl is a strong acid, so we can assume that, $C\alpha + 0.01 \simeq 0.01$

$$K_a = \frac{[CH_3COO^-][H^+]}{[CH_3COOH]}$$

$$1.82 \times 10^{-5} = \frac{C\alpha \times 0.01}{0.05}$$

or $$C\alpha = \frac{1.82 \times 10^{-5} \times 0.05}{0.01}$$

or $$C\alpha = 9.1 \times 10^{-5}$$

or $$\alpha = \frac{9.1 \times 10^{-5}}{C} = \frac{9.1 \times 10^{-5}}{0.05}$$

$$= 1.82 \times 10^{-3}$$

(b) When solution contains 0.1 M HCl

Similarly, for the reaction

$$CH_3COOH \rightleftharpoons CH_3COO^- + H^+$$

	CH_3COOH	CH_3COO^-	H^+
Initial Conc.	0.05 M	0	0
Equilibrium conc.	$(0.05 - C\alpha) \approx 0.05$	$C\alpha$	$(C\alpha + 0.1) \approx 0.1$

$$K_a = \frac{[CH_3COO^-][H^+]}{[CH_3COOH]}$$

$$1.82 \times 10^{-5} = \frac{C\alpha \times 0.1}{0.05}$$

or $$C\alpha = \frac{1.82 \times 10^{-5} \times 0.05}{0.1}$$

$$= 0.91 \times 10^{-5}$$

or $$\alpha = \frac{0.91 \times 10^{-5}}{C} = \frac{0.91 \times 10^{-5}}{0.05}$$

$$= 1.82 \times 10^{-4}$$

Q. 54. The ionization constant of dimethylamine is 5.4 × 10^{-4}. Calculate its degree of ionization in its 0.02 M solution. What percentage of dimethylamine is ionized if the solution is also 0.1 M in NaOH? [NCERT Ex. Q. 6.54, Page 213]

Ans. Given,

$$K_b = 5.4 \times 10^{-4}$$
$$C = 0.02\ M$$

Degree of ionization $$\alpha = \sqrt{\frac{K_b}{C}}$$

$$= \sqrt{\frac{5.4 \times 10^{-4}}{0.02}}$$

$$= 1.64 \times 10^{-1} = 0.164$$

In the presence of 0.1 M NaOH,

$$(CH_3)_2NH + H_2O \rightleftharpoons (CH_3)_2\overset{+}{N}H_2 + OH^-$$

	$(CH_3)_2NH$	$(CH_3)_2\overset{+}{N}H_2$	OH^-
Initial con.	0.02 M	0	0
Equilibrium conc.	$(0.02 - C\alpha) \approx 0.02$	$C\alpha$	$C\alpha + 0.1 \approx 0.1$

$$K_b = \frac{[(CH_3)_2\overset{+}{N}H_2][OH^-]}{[(CH_3)_2NH]}$$

$$5.4 \times 10^{-4} = \frac{C\alpha \times 0.1}{0.02}$$

$$C\alpha = \frac{5.4 \times 10^{-4} \times 0.02}{0.1}$$

$$= 108 \times 10^{-6}$$

$$\alpha = \frac{108 \times 10^{-6}}{C}$$

$$= \frac{108 \times 10^{-6}}{0.02}$$

$$= 54 \times 10^{-4}$$

$$= 5.4 \times 10^{-3}$$

Percentage of ionization $= 5.4 \times 10^{-3} \times 100$
$= 0.54\%$

Q. 55. Calculate the hydrogen ion concentration in the following biological fluids whose pH are given below:
(a) Human muscle-fluid, 6.83
(b) Human stomach fluid, 1.2
(c) Human blood, 7.38
(d) Human saliva, 6.4. [NCERT Ex. Q. 6.54, Page 213]

Ans. (a) pH of human muscle fluid = 6.83

$$pH = -\log [H^+]$$
$$6.83 = -\log [H^+]$$
$$\log [H^+] = -6.83$$
$$[H^+] = \text{antilog} (-6.83)$$
$$\therefore [H^+] = \text{antilog} (-6.4)$$
$$\therefore [H^+] = \text{antilog } \bar{7}.17$$
$$= 1.48 \times 10^{-7}\ M$$

(b) pH of human stomach-fluid = 1.2

$$-\log [H^+] = 1.2$$
$$[H^+] = \text{antilog} (-1.2)$$
$$\therefore [H^+] = \text{antilog } \bar{2}.8$$
$$= 6.3 \times 10^{-2}$$
$$= 0.063\ M$$

(c) pH of human blood = 7.38

$$-\log [H^+] = 7.38$$
or $$[H^+] = \text{antilog} (-7.38)$$
$$\therefore [H^+] = \text{antilog } \bar{8}.62$$
$$= 4.17 \times 10^{-8}\ M$$

(d) pH of human saliva = 6.4

$$-\log [H^+] = 6.4$$
$$\therefore [H^+] = \text{antilog} (-6.4)$$
$$[H^+] = \text{antilog } \bar{7}.6$$
$$= 3.98 \times 10^{-7}\ M$$

Q. 56. The pH of milk, black coffee, tomato juice, lemon juice and egg white are 6.8, 5.0, 4.2, 2.2 and 7.8 respectively. Calculate corresponding hydrogen ion concentration in each. [NCERT Ex. Q. 6.56, Page 213]

Ans. For milk –

$$pH = 6.8$$
$$\because pH = -\log[H^+]$$
$$6.8 = -\log [H^+]$$
or $$\log [H^+] = -6.8 = \bar{7}.20$$
$$[H^+] = \text{antilog } \bar{7}.20$$
$$= 1.585 \times 10^{-7}\ M$$

For black coffee –

$$pH = 5.0$$
$\because$ $pH = -\log [H^+]$
$$5.0 = -\log [H^+]$$
or $\log [H^+] = -5.0$
$$[H^+] = 10^{-5} M$$

For tomato juice –

$$pH = 4.2$$
$\because$ $pH = -\log [H^+]$
$$4.2 = -\log [H^+]$$
or $\log [H^+] = -4.2 = \bar{5}.80$
$$[H^+] = \text{antilog } \bar{5}.80$$
$$= 6.310 \times 10^{-5} M$$

For lemon juice –

$$pH = 2.2$$
$\because$ $pH = -\log [H^+]$
$$2.2 = -\log [H^+]$$
or $\log [H^+] = -2.2 = \bar{3}.80$
$$[H^+] = \text{antilog } \bar{3}.80$$
$$= 6.310 \times 10^{-3} M$$

For egg white –

$$pH = 7.8$$
$\because$ $pH = -\log [H^+]$
$$7.8 = -\log [H^+]$$
or $\log [H^+] = -7.8 = \bar{8}.20$
$$[H^+] = \text{antilog } \bar{8}.20$$
$$= 1.585 \times 10^{-8} M$$

Q. 57. If 0.561 g of KOH is dissolved in water to give 200 mL of solution at 298 K, Calculate the concentrations of potassium, hydrogen and hydroxyl ions. What is its pH? [NCERT Ex. Q. 6.57, Page 213]

Ans. Given, Mass of KOH = 0.561 g

Volume of solution = 200 mL = 0.2 L

Molar mass of KOH = 39.1 + 16 + 1 = 56.1

Molarity of KOH

$$= \frac{\text{Mass of KOH (in g)}}{\text{Molar mass of KOH} \times \text{Volume of solution (in L)}}$$

$$= \frac{0.561}{56.1 \times 0.2}$$

$$= 0.05 M$$

$$\underset{0.05 M}{KOH} \rightleftharpoons \underset{0.05M}{K^+} + \underset{0.05M}{OH^-}$$

$$[K^+] = 0.05 M$$
$$[OH^-] = 0.05 M$$
$$[H^+][OH^-] = K_w$$
$\because$ $[H^+] = \dfrac{K_w}{[OH^-]}$

$$= \frac{1.0 \times 10^{-14}}{0.05} \quad [\because K_w = 1.0 \times 10^{-14}]$$
$$= 20 \times 10^{-14} M$$
$$= 2.0 \times 10^{-13} M$$

Now, $pH = -\log [H^+]$
$$= -\log [2.0 \times 10^{-13}]$$
$$= -\log 2 + 13 \log 10$$
$$= -0.3010 + 13$$
$$= 12.699$$
$$\simeq 12.7$$

Q. 58. The solubility of $Sr(OH)_2$ at 298 K is 19.23 g/L of solution. Calculate the concentrations of strontium and hydroxyl ions and the pH of the solution. [NCERT Ex. Q. 6.58, Page 213]

Ans. The solubility of $Sr(OH)_2$ at 298 K
$$= 19.23 \text{ g L}^{-1}$$

Molecular mass of $Sr(OH)_2$ = 121.6

Molar concentration of $Sr(OH)_2$

$$= \frac{w}{M} = \frac{19.23}{121.6} = 0.1581 \text{ mol L}^{-1}$$

$\therefore$ $\underset{0.1581 M}{Sr(OH)_2} \rightleftharpoons \underset{0.1581 M}{Sr^{2+}} + \underset{2 \times 0.1581 M}{2OH^-}$

$\therefore$ $[Sr^{2+}] = [Sr(OH)_2]_{diss.}$
$$= 0.1581 \text{ mol L}^{-1}$$
$$[OH^-] = 2 \times 0.1581$$
$$= 0.3162 \text{ mol L}^{-1}$$

$\therefore$ $[H^+] = \dfrac{K_w}{[OH^-]} = \dfrac{1.0 \times 10^{-14}}{0.3162}$
$$= 3.1625 \times 10^{-14} M$$

$\therefore$ $pH = -\log [H^+]$
$$= -\log 3.1625 \times 10^{-14}$$
$$= -(-14) - \log 3.1625$$
$$= 14 - \log 3.1625 = 13.50$$

Q. 59. The ionization constant of propanoic acid is 1.32 × 10^{-5}. Calculate the degree of ionization of acid in its 0.05 M solution and also its pH. What will be its degree of ionization if the solution is 0.01 M in HCl also? [NCERT Ex. Q. 6.59, Page 214]

Ans. Given $K_a = 1.32 \times 10^{-5}$
$$C = 0.05$$

	$CH_3CH_2COOH + H_2O \rightleftharpoons$	$CH_3CH_2COO^-$	$+ H_3O^+$
Initial Conc.	0.05	0	0
Equilibrium Conc.	$(0.05 - C\alpha)$	$C\alpha$	$C\alpha$

From Ostwald dilution law,

Degree of ionization,

$$\alpha = \sqrt{\frac{K_a}{C}}$$

$$= \sqrt{\frac{1.32 \times 10^{-5}}{0.05}}$$

$= 0.016248$
$= 1.6248 \times 10^{-2}$
$= 1.62 \times 10^{-2}$

$[H_3O^+] = C\alpha = 0.05 \times 1.62 \times 10^{-2}$
$= 0.081 \times 10^{-2}$
$= 8.1 \times 10^{-4}$

Now, $pH = -\log [H_3O^+]$
$= -\log [8.1 \times 10^{-4}]$
$= -\log 8.1 + 4 \log 10$
$= -0.9084 + 4$
$= 3.0916 \approx 3.09$

When the solution contains 0.01 M HCl then $[H_3O^+] = C\alpha + 0.01 \approx 0.01$

$$K_a = \frac{[CH_3CH_2COO^-][H_3O^+]}{[CH_3CH_2COOH]}$$

$$1.32 \times 10^{-5} = \frac{C\alpha \times 0.01}{(0.05 - C\alpha)}$$

or $1.32 \times 10^{-5} = \frac{C\alpha \times 0.01}{0.05}$ [as $(0.05 - C\alpha) \approx 0.05$]

or $C\alpha = 6.60 \times 10^{-5}$

Degree of ionization $\alpha = \frac{6.60 \times 10^{-5}}{C}$

$= \frac{6.60 \times 10^{-5}}{0.05}$

$= 1.32 \times 10^{-3}$

Q. 60. The pH of 0.1 M solution of cyanic acid (HCNO) is 2.34. Calculate the ionisation constant of the acid and its degree of ionization in the solution.
[NCERT Ex. Q. 6.60, Page 214]

Ans. $HCNO \rightleftharpoons H^+ + CNO^-$

$pH = -\log [H^+]$
$= 2.34$

or $\log [H^+] = -2.34 = \bar{3}.66$

or $[H^+] = \text{Antilog } \bar{3}.66$
$= 4.57 \times 10^{-3}$ M

$[CNO^-] = [H^+] = 4.57 \times 10^{-3}$ M

$$K_a = \frac{(4.57 \times 10^{-3})(4.57 \times 10^{-3})}{0.1}$$

$= 2.09 \times 10^{-4}$

$\alpha = \sqrt{K_a/C}$

$= \sqrt{2.09 \times 10^{-4}/0.1}$

$= 0.0457$

Q. 61. The ionization constant of nitrous acid is 4.5×10^{-4}. Calculate the pH of 0.04 M sodium nitrite solution and also its degree of hydrolysis.
[NCERT Ex. Q. 6.61, Page 214]

Ans. Sodium nitrite is a salt of weak acid and strong base. Hence,

$K_h = K_w/K_a$

$= 10^{-14}/(4.5 \times 10^{-4})$
$= 2.22 \times 10^{-11}$

$h = \sqrt{K_h/C}$

$= \sqrt{2.22 \times 10^{-11}/0.04}$

$= \sqrt{5.5 \times 10^{-10}}$

$= 2.36 \times 10^{-5}$

	$NO_2^- + H_2O \rightleftharpoons$	HNO_2 +	OH^-
Initial conc.,	C	0	0
After hydrolysis	$C - a$	a	a

$[OH^-] = a = 0.04 \times 2.36 \times 10^{-5}$
$= 9.44 \times 10^{-7}$

$pOH = -\log (9.44 \times 10^{-7})$
$= 7 - 0.9750 = 6.03$

$pH = 14 - pOH$
$= 14 - 6.03 = 7.97$

Q. 62. A 0.02 M solution of pyridinium hydrochloride has pH = 3.44. Calculate the ionization constant of pyridine. **[NCERT Ex. Q. 6.62, Page 214]**

Ans. Pyridinium hydrochloride is the salt of a weak base pyridine and a strong acid HCl.
Hence,

$$pH = -\frac{1}{2}[\log K_w - \log K_b + \log c]$$

$$\therefore \quad 3.44 = -\frac{1}{2}[-14 - \log K_b + \log 2.0 \times 10^{-2}]$$

$6.88 = 14 + \log K_b + 1.70$

or $\log K_b = -8.82 = \bar{9}.18$

$K_b = \text{antilog } \bar{9}.18 = 1.5 \times 10^{-9}$

Q. 63. Predict if the solutions of the following salts are neutral, acidic or basic:
NaCl, KBr, NaCN, NH_4NO_3, $NaNO_2$ and KF
[NCERT Ex. Q. 6.63, Page 214]

Ans. **NaCl:** Its solution is neutral as it is the salt of a strong acid HCl and a strong base NaOH.

KBr: Its solution is neutral as it is the salt of strong acid HBr and a strong base KOH.

NaCN: Its solution is basic as it is the salt of a strong base NaOH and a weak acid HCN.

NH_4NO_3: Its solution is acidic as it is the salt of a strong acid HNO_3 and a weak base NH_4OH.

$NaNO_2$: Its solution is basic as it is the salt of a strong base NaOH and a weak acid HNO_2.

KF: Its solution is basic as it is the salt of a weak acid HF and a strong base KOH.

Q. 64. The ionisation constant of chloroacetic acid is 1.35×10^{-3}. What will be the pH of 0.1 M acid and its 0.1 M sodium salt solution ? **[NCERT Ex. Q. 6.64, Page 214]**

Ans. The given reaction is

$CH_2ClCOOH \rightleftharpoons CH_2ClCOO^- + H^+$

$[H^+] = \sqrt{K_a/C} = \sqrt{1.35 \times 10^{-3}/0.1}$
$= 0.116$

$\therefore$ $$pH = -\log [H^+] = -\log 1.16 \times 10^{-1} = 2 - 0.06 = 1.94$$

Sodium salt of chloroacetic acid is salt of strong base NaOH and weak acid chloroacetic acid ($ClCH_2COOH$)

Hence, $$pH = -\frac{1}{2}[\log K_w + \log K_a - \log c]$$

$$pH = -\frac{1}{2}[\log K_w + \log K_a - \log c]$$

$$pH = \frac{1}{2}[-\log K_w - \log K_a + \log c]$$

$$= [+14 - \log 1.35 \times 10^{-3} + \log 10^{-1}]/2$$

$$= \frac{14 + 2.87 - 1}{2} = 7.94$$

Hence, $pH = 7.94.$

Q. 65. Ionic product of water at 310 K is 2.7×10^{-14}. What is the pH of neutral water at this temperature ?
[NCERT Ex. Q. 6.65, Page 214]

Ans. $$K_w = [H_3O^+][OH^-]$$

For pure water

$$[H_3O^+] = [OH^-]$$

$$K_w = [H_3O^+]^2$$

$$[H_3O^+] = \sqrt{K_w} = \sqrt{2.7 \times 10^{-14}}$$

$$= 1.643 \times 10^{-7} \text{ mol L}^{-1}$$

$$pH = -\log (H_3O^+)$$

$$= -\log (1.643 \times 10^{-7})$$

$$= 7 - \log 1.643$$

$$= 7 - 0.2156 = 6.78.$$

Q. 66. Calculate the pH of the resultant mixtures:

(a) 10 mL of 0.2 M $Ca(OH)_2$ + 25 mL of 0.1 M HCl

(b) 10 mL of 0.01 M H_2SO_4 + 10 mL of 0.01 M $Ca(OH)_2$

(c) 10 mL of 0.1 M H_2SO_4 + 10 mL of 0.1 M KOH

[NCERT Ex. Q. 6.66, Page 214]

Ans. (a) Base, $Ca(OH)_2$ = Acid, HCl

$$M_1V_1 = M_2V_2$$

Given, $$M_1 = [OH^-] = 2 \times 0.2 = 0.4 \text{ M}$$

$$V_1 = 10 \text{ mL}, M_2 = 0.1 \text{ M},$$

$$V_2 = 25 \text{ mL}$$

$$M_1V_1 = M_2V_2$$

$$0.4 \times 10 = 0.1 \times 25$$

$M_1V_1 > M_2V_2$ hence, solution is basic.

$$[OH^-] = \frac{M_1V_1 - M_2V_2}{V_1 + V_2} = \frac{4 - 2.5}{10 + 25} = 0.043\text{M}$$

$$pOH = -\log [4.3 \times 10^{-2}]$$

$$= 2 - 0.6335 = 1.3665$$

$$pH = 14 - pOH = 14 - 1.3665$$

$$= 12.6335 = 12.63$$

(b) Similarly, base, $Ca(OH)_2$ = Acid, H_2SO_4

$$M_1V_1 = M_2V_2$$

$$(2 \times 0.01) \times 10 = (2 \times 0.01) \times 10$$

Because $M_1V_1 = M_2V_2$, hence solution is neutral.

$\therefore$ $pH = 7$

(c) Acid, H_2SO_4 = Base, KOH

$$M_1V_1 = M_2V_2$$

$$(2 \times 0.1)10 = 0.1 \times 10$$

Because $M_1V_1 > M_2V_2$, hence solution is acidic.

$$[H^+] = \frac{M_1V_1 - M_2V_2}{V_1 + V_2}$$

$$= \frac{(0.2 \times 10) - (0.1 \times 10)}{10 + 10} = \frac{2 - 1}{20} = 0.05\text{ M}$$

$$pH = -\log [0.05] = -\log [5.0 \times 10^{-2}]$$

$$pH = 2 - 0.6990 = 1.301 = 1.30$$

$$pH = 1.30$$

Q. 67. Determine the solubilities of silver chromate, barium chromate, ferric hydroxide, lead chloride and mercurous iodide at 298 K from their solubility product constants given below :
[$K_{sp}(Ag_2CrO_4) = 1.1 \times 10^{-12}$, $K_{sp}(BaCrO_4) = 1.2 \times 10^{-10}$, $K_{sp}[Fe(OH)_3] = 1.0 \times 10^{-38}$, $K_{sp}(PbCl_2) = 1.6 \times 10^{-5}$ $K_{sp}(Hg_2I_2) = 4.5 \times 10^{-29}$]
Determine also the molarities of individual ions.
[NCERT Ex. Q. 6.67, Page 214]

Ans. For silver chromate:

$$Ag_2CrO_4 \rightleftharpoons 2Ag^+ + CrO_4^{2-}; K_{sp} = 1.1 \times 10^{-12}$$

$$\quad S \qquad 2S \qquad S$$

$$K_{sp} = [Ag^+]^2.[CrO_4^{2-}]$$

$$K_{sp} = [2S]^2.[S] = 4S^3$$

$$S^3 = \frac{K_{sp}}{4}$$

or $$S^3 = \frac{1.1 \times 10^{-12}}{4} = 0.275 \times 10^{-12}$$

$$3 \log S = \log 2.75 \times 10^{-13}$$

$$3 \log S = -13 + 0.4393 = -12.5607$$

$$\log S = \frac{-12.5607}{3} = -4.1869 = -5.8131$$

$$S = \text{antilog } \bar{5}.8131 = 6.503 \times 10^{-5}\text{M}$$

$$[Ag^+] = 2S = 2 \times 6.503 \times 10^{-5}$$

$$= 13.006 \times 10^{-5} = 1.3 \times 10^{-4}\text{ M}$$

$$\left[CrO_4^{2-}\right] = S = 6.503 \times 10^{-5}\text{M}$$

For barium chromate

$$BaCrO_4 \rightleftharpoons Ba^{2+} + CrO_4^{2-}; K_{sp} = 1.2 \times 10^{-10}$$

$$S \qquad S \qquad S$$

(Solubility of $BaCrO_4$ is S mol L^{-1})

$$K_{sp} = 1.2 \times 10^{-10} = \left[Ba^{2+}\right].\left[CrO_4^{2-}\right] = S^2$$

$$S = \sqrt{1.2 \times 10^{-10}} = 1.1 \times 10^{-5}\text{M}$$

$$[Ba^{2+}] = \left[CrO_4^{2-}\right] = 1.1 \times 10^{-5}\text{ M}$$

For ferric hydroxide-

$$Fe(OH)_3 \rightleftharpoons Fe^{3+} + 3OH^-; K_{sp} = 10 \times 10^{-38}$$

$$S \qquad 2S \qquad S$$

(Solubility of $Fe(OH)_3$ is S mol L^{-1})

$$K_{sp} = [Fe^{3+}][OH^-]^3$$

$$K_{sp} = S.(3S)^3 = 27S^4 \text{ or } S^4 = \frac{K_{sp}}{27}$$

$$S^4 = \frac{1.0 \times 10^{-38}}{27} = 0.037 \times 10^{-38}$$

$$4 \log S = \log 3.7 \times 10^{-40}$$

$$4 \log S = -40 + 0.5682 = -39.4318$$

$$\log S = \frac{-39.4318}{4} = -9.8579 = \overline{10}.1421$$

$$S = \text{antilog } \overline{10}.1421 = 1.387 \times 10^{-10}$$

$$S = 1.39 \times 10^{-10}$$

$$[Fe^{3+}] = 1.39 \times 10^{-10} M$$

$$[OH^-] = 3S = 3 \times 1.39 \times 10^{-10}$$

$$= 4.17 \times 10^{-10} M$$

For lead chloride

$$PbCl_2 \rightleftharpoons Pb^{2+} + 2Cl^-; K_{sp} = 1.6 \times 10^{-5}$$

S 2S S

(Solubility of $PbCl_2$ is S mol L^{-1})

$$K_{sp} = [Pb^{2+}][Cl^-]^2$$

$$K_{sp} = S \cdot (2S)^2 = 4S^3$$

$$S^3 = \frac{K_{sp}}{4} = \frac{1.6 \times 10^{-5}}{4} = 0.4 \times 10^{-5}$$

$$3 \log S = \log 0.4 \times 10^{-5} = \log 4.0 \times 10^{-5}$$

$$3 \log S = -6 + 0.6021 = -5.3979$$

$$\log S = \frac{-5.3979}{3} = -1.7993 = -2.2007$$

$$S = \text{antilog } \bar{2}.2007 = 1.585 \times 10^{-2}$$

$$\approx 1.59 \times 10^{-2} M$$

Solubility of

$$PbCl_2 = 1.59 \times 10^{-2} M$$

$$[Pb^{2+}] = 1.59 \times 10^{-2} M$$

$$[Cl^-] = 2 \times 1.59 \times 10^{-2} M = 3.18 \times 10^{-2} M$$

For mercurous iodide:

$$Hg_2I_2 \rightleftharpoons Hg_2^{2+} + 2I^-; K_{sp} = 4.5 \times 10^{-29}$$

S S 2S

(Solubility of Hg_2I_2 is S mol L^{-1})

$$K_{sp} = [Hg_2^{2+}][I^-]^2$$

$$K_{sp} = S.(2S)^2 = 4S^3$$

$$S^3 = \frac{K_{sp}}{4} = \frac{4.5 \times 10^{-29}}{4} = 1.125 \times 10^{-29}$$

$$3 \log S = \log(1.125 \times 10^{-29})$$

$$3 \log S = -29 + 0.0512 = -28.9488$$

$$\log S = \frac{-28.9488}{3} = -9.6496$$

$$\log S = 9.6496 = \overline{10}.3504$$

$$\log S = \text{anti log } \overline{10}.3504 = 2.241 \times 10^{-10} M$$

$$\text{Solubility of } Hg_2I_2 = 2.241 \times 10^{-10} M$$

$$[Hg_2^{2+}] = 2.241 \times 10^{-10} M$$

$$[I^-] = 2 \times 2.241 \times 10^{-10} M = 4.482 \times 10^{-10} M$$

Q. 68. The solubility product constant of Ag_2CrO_4 and AgBr are 1.1×10^{-12} and 5.0×10^{-13} respectively. Calculate the ratio of the molarities of their saturated solutions. [NCERT Ex. Q. 6.68, Page 214]

Ans. K_{sp} of $Ag_2CrO_4 = 1.1 \times 10^{-12}$

K_{sp} of AgBr $= 5 \times 10^{-13}$

Let x be the solubility of Ag_2CrO_4

$$Ag_2CrO_4(s) \rightleftharpoons 2Ag^+(aq) + CrO_4^{2-}(q)$$

2x x

$$K_{sp} = [Ag^+]^2[CrO_4^{2-}]$$

$$K_{sp} = (2x)^2(x) = 4x^3$$

$$x^3 = \frac{K_{sp}}{4} = \frac{1.1 \times 10^{-12}}{4}$$

$$x = 6.5 \times 10^{-5} M$$

Let solubility of AgBr is y

$$AgBr(s) \rightleftharpoons Ag^+(aq) + Br^-(aq)$$

y y

$$K_{sp} = y^2$$

$$5 \times 10^{-13} = y^2; y = 7.07 \times 10^{-7} M$$

Ratio of molarities of their saturated solutions

$$= \frac{6.5 \times 10^{-5}}{7.07 \times 10^{-7}} = 91.9$$

Q. 69. Equal volumes of 0.002 M solutions of sodium iodate and cupric chlorate are mixed together. Will it lead to precipitation of copper iodate. For cupric iodate, $K_{sp} = (7.4 \times 10^{-8})$ [NCERT Ex. Q. 6.69, Page 214]

Ans. K_{sp} of $Cu(IO_3)_2 = 7.4 \times 10^{-8}$

When equal volumes of sodium iodate and copper chlorate are mixed, the molar concentrations of both the solutions would be reduced to half, i.e., 0.001 M.

$$NaIO_3 \longrightarrow Na^+ + IO_3^-$$

0.001 M 0.001 M

$$Cu(ClO_3)_2 \longrightarrow Cu^{2+} + 2ClO_3^-$$

0.001 M 0.001 M

After mixing $[IO_3^-] = [NaIO_3] = 0.001$ M

$$[Cu^{2+}] = [Cu(IO_3)_2]$$

$$= 0.001 M$$

$$Cu(IO_3)_2(s) \rightleftharpoons Cu^{2+}(aq) + 2IO_3^-(aq)$$

$$\text{Ionic Product} = [Cu^{2+}][IO_3^-]^2$$

$$= (0.001)(0.001)^2$$

$$= 1 \times 10^{-9}$$

Since ionic product is less than K_{sp}, therefore no precipitation occurs.

Q. 70. The ionisation constant of benzoic acid is 6.46×10^{-5} and K_{sp} for silver benzoate is 2.5×10^{-13}. How many times is silver benzoate more soluble in a buffer of pH 3.19 compared to its solubility in pure water? [NCERT Ex. Q. 6.70, Page 214]

Ans. $C_6H_5COOAg(s) \rightleftharpoons C_6H_5COO^- + Ag^+; K_1 = K_{sp}$

$$C_6H_5COO^- + H^+ \rightleftharpoons C_6H_5COOH; K_2 = \frac{1}{K_a}$$

$$\mathbf{C_6H_5COOAg(s) + H^+} \rightleftharpoons C_6H_5COOH + Ag^+; K_3 = \frac{K_{sp}}{K_a}$$

$$K_3 = \frac{[C_6H_5COOH][Ag^+]}{[H^+]} = \frac{S \cdot S}{[H^+]} = \frac{S^2}{[H^+]} = \frac{K_{sp}}{[K_a]}$$

where, S is the solubility of C_6H_5COOAg.

In a buffer of pH = 3.19

$$\log[H^+] = -3.19 = \bar{4}.81$$

$$[H^+] = \text{antilog } \bar{4}.81 = 6.46 \times 10^{-4}$$

$$\frac{S^2}{[H^+]} = \frac{K_{sp}}{K_a} \text{ or } S^2 = \frac{K_{sp} \times [H^+]}{K_a}$$

$$S = \sqrt{\frac{2.5 \times 10^{-13} \times 6.46 \times 10^{-4}}{6.46 \times 10^{-5}}}$$

$$S = \sqrt{2.5 \times 10^{-13} \times 10}$$

$$S = 1.6 \times 10^{-6} \text{ M (in buffer)}$$

In aqueous solution, solubility of C_6H_5COOAg :

$$K_{sp} = [C_6H_5COO^-][Ag^+] = S \cdot S = S^2$$

$$S = \sqrt{K_{sp}} = \sqrt{2.5 \times 10^{-13}} = 5 \times 10^{-7} \text{ M}$$

$$\frac{S(C_6H_5COOAg) \text{ in buffer}}{S(C_6H_5COOAg) \text{ in aqueous solution}} = \frac{1.6 \times 10^{-6}}{5.0 \times 10^{-7}} = 3.2$$

Therefore, C_6H_5COOAg is 3.2 times more soluble in buffer than in pure water.

Q. 71. What is the maximum concentration of equimolar solutions of ferrous sulphate and sodium sulphide so that when mixed in equal volumes, there is no precipitation of iron sulphide ? (For iron sulphide $K_{sp} = 6.3 \times 10^{-18}$).

[NCERT Ex. Q. 6.71, Page 214]

Ans. Given, $K_{sp} = 6.3 \times 10^{-18}$

Suppose, the concentration of each of $FeSO_4$ and Na_2S is x mol L^{-1}. Then after mixing equal volumes:

$$[FeSO_4] = \frac{x}{2} \text{ M}$$

$$[Na_2S] = \frac{x}{2} \text{ M or } [Fe^{2+}] = \frac{x}{2} \text{ M}$$

$$[S^{2-}] = \frac{x}{2} \text{ M}$$

$$FeS \rightleftharpoons Fe^{2+} S^{2-}$$

$$K_{sp} = [Fe^{2+}][S^{2-}]$$

$$6.3 \times 10^{-18} = \frac{x}{2} \times \frac{x}{2}$$

or $x^2 = 6.3 \times 10^{-18} \times 4$

$$= 25.2 \times 10^{-18}$$

$\therefore$ $x = 5.02 \times 10^{-9}$ mol L^{-1}

Hence, maximum concentration of $FeSO_4$ and Na_2S which will not precipitate FeS = 5.02×10^{-9} mol L^{-1}.

Q. 72. What is the minimum volume of water required to dissolve 1g of calcium sulphate at 298 K ? (For calcium sulphate, K_{sp} is 9.1×10^{-6}).

[NCERT Ex. Q. 6.72, Page 214]

Ans. $CaSO_4(s) \rightleftharpoons Ca^{2+}(aq) + SO_4^{2-}(aq)$

If S is the solubility of $CaSO_4$ in mol L^{-1}, then

$$K_{sp} = [Ca^{2+}][SO_4^{2-}]$$

$$= S \times S = S^2$$

$$K_{sp} \text{ for } CaSO_4 = 9.1 \times 10^{-6}$$

$\therefore$ $S^2 = 9.1 \times 10^{-6}$

or $S = \sqrt{9.1 \times 10^{-6}}$

$$= 3.02 \times 10^{-3} \text{ mol } L^{-1}$$

Now, molecular mass of $CaSO_4$

$$= 40 + 32 + 4 \times 16$$

$$= 136 \text{ g}$$

$$S = \frac{n}{V} = \frac{w}{M.V}$$

$$\frac{w}{V} = SM$$

$\therefore$ $= 3.02 \times 10^{-3} \times 136$ gL^{-1}

$$= 0.411 \text{ g}L^{-1}$$

Thus for dissolving 0.411 g water required = 1 L.

$\therefore$ For dissolving 1 gm $CaSO_4$

$$\text{water required} = \frac{1}{0.411} = 2.43 \text{ L}$$

Q. 73. The concentration of sulphide ion in 0.1 M HCl solution saturated with hydrogen sulphide is 1.0×10^{-19} M. If 10 mL of this is added to 5 mL of 0.04 M solution of the following : $FeSO_4$, $MnCl_2$, $ZnCl_2$ and $CdCl_2$, in which of these solutions precipitation will take place? (Given, K_{sp} of FeS = 6.3×10^{-18}, K_{sp} of MnS = 2.5×10^{-13} K_{sp} of ZnS = 1.6×10^{-24}, K_{sp} of CdS = 8.0×10^{-27})

[NCERT Ex. Q. 6.73, Page 214]

Ans. $[S^{2-}] = 1 \times 10^{-19}$ M

10 mL of S^{2-} is mixed with 5 mL of 0.04 M solution of different solutes so that final volume of solution is 15 mL.

$$[S^{2-}]_{mix} = \frac{1.0 \times 10^{-19} \times 10}{15} = 6.67 \times 10^{-20} \text{ M}$$

$$[M^{2+}] = \frac{5 \times 0.04}{15} = 1.33 \times 10^{-2} \text{ M}$$

where, $[M^{2+}] = Fe^{2+}, Mn^{2+}, Zn^{2+}, \text{or } Cd^{2+}$

$$[M^{2+}][S^{2-}] = 1.33 \times 10^{-2} \times 6.67 \times 10^{-20}$$

Ionic product of $[M^{2+}][S^{2-}] = 8.87 \times 10^{-22}$

IP of $[M^{2+}][S^{2-}] > K_{sp}$ of ZnS and CdS

So, these ($CdCl_2$ and $ZnCl_2$) are precipitated as CdS and ZnS.

CHAPTER 7

REDOX REACTIONS

Classical Idea of Redox Reactions-Oxidation and Reduction Reaction

- **Oxidation:** It is defined as the addition of oxygen/ electronegative element to a substance or removal of hydrogen/electropositive element from a substance.

eg., $CH_4(g) + 2O_2(g) \longrightarrow CO_2(g) + 2H_2O(l)$
(Addition of oxygen)

$Mg(s) + F_2(g) \longrightarrow MgF_2(s)$
(Addition of electronegative element)

$2H_2S(g) + O_2(g) \longrightarrow 2S(s) + 2H_2O(l)$
(Removal of hydrogen)

$2K_4[Fe(CN)_6](aq) + H_2O_2(aq) \longrightarrow 2K_3[Fe(CN)_6](aq) + 2KOH(aq)$
(Removal of electropositive element)

- **Reduction:** It is defined as the removal of oxygen/ electronegative element from a substance or addition of hydrogen/electropositive element to a substance.

e.g.,

$2HgO(s) \xrightarrow{\Delta} 2Hg(l) + O_2(g)$
(Removal of oxygen)

$2FeCl_3(aq) + H_2(g) \longrightarrow 2FeCl_2(aq) + 2HCl(aq)$
(Removal of electronegative element)

$CH_2 = CH_2(g) + H_2(g) \longrightarrow CH_3 - CH_3(g)$
(Addition of hydrogen)

$2HgCl_2(aq) + SnCl_2(aq) \longrightarrow Hg_2Cl_2(s) + SnCl_4(aq)$
(Addition of electropositive element)

- **Redox Reaction:** The reaction which involves oxidation and reduction reactions simultaneously is called redox reaction.

e.g., $2\,Na(s) + Cl_2(g) \longrightarrow 2NaCl(s)$

Redox Reaction in Terms of Electron Transfer Reaction

- Consider a redox reaction,

loss of $2e^-$

$2Na(s) + Cl_2(g) \longrightarrow 2Na^+Cl^-(s)$

gain of $2e^-$

(Oxidation half reaction)

$2Na(s) \longrightarrow 2Na^+ + 2e^-$

$Cl_2(g) + 2e^- \longrightarrow 2Cl^-(g)$

(Reduction half reaction)

According to electronic concept, the half reaction that involves loss of electron is called oxidation half reaction and the half reaction that involves gain of electron is called reduction half reaction.

- **Oxidising Agent:** The species which can oxidise other substance and itself reduces is called oxidising agent. It is an acceptor of electrons.
- **Reducing Agent:** The species which can reduce other substance and itself oxidises is called reducing agent. It is a donor of electrons.

Oxidation Number

- **Oxidation Number:** Oxidation number denotes the oxidation state of an element in a compound ascertained according to a set of rules formulated on the basis that electron pair in a covalent bond belongs entirely to a more electronegative element.
- According to oxidation number concept,
  - Oxidation is defined as an increase in the oxidation number of the element in the given substance.
  - Reduction is defined as a decrease in the oxidation number of the element in the given substance.
  - Oxidising agent is a reagent which can increase the oxidation number of an element in a given substance.
  - Reducing agent is a reagent which can decrease the oxidation number of an element in a given substance.
  - Redox reactions are those reactions which involve change in oxidation number of the interacting species.
- An element, in the free or the uncombined state, bears an oxidation number of zero.

e.g., Each atom in H_2, O_2, O_3, P_4, Na, Mg, etc., has the oxidation number zero.

- For ions composed of only one atom, the oxidation number is equal to the charge on the ion.

e.g.,

Ion	Oxidation Number
Na^+	+1
Mg^{2+}	+2
Fe^{3+}	+3
Cl^-	– 1
O^{2-}	– 2

Scan to know more about this topic

REDOX REACTIONS OXIDATION NUMBERS

- The oxidation number of oxygen in most compounds is –2.
- **Exception:**

(i) In case of peroxides and superoxides, the oxidation numbers of oxygen are –1 and –1/2 respectively.

e.g., Peroxides = H_2O_2, Na_2O_2
(Oxidation number of O = –1)
Superoxides = KO_2, RbO_2
(Oxidation number of O = –1/2)

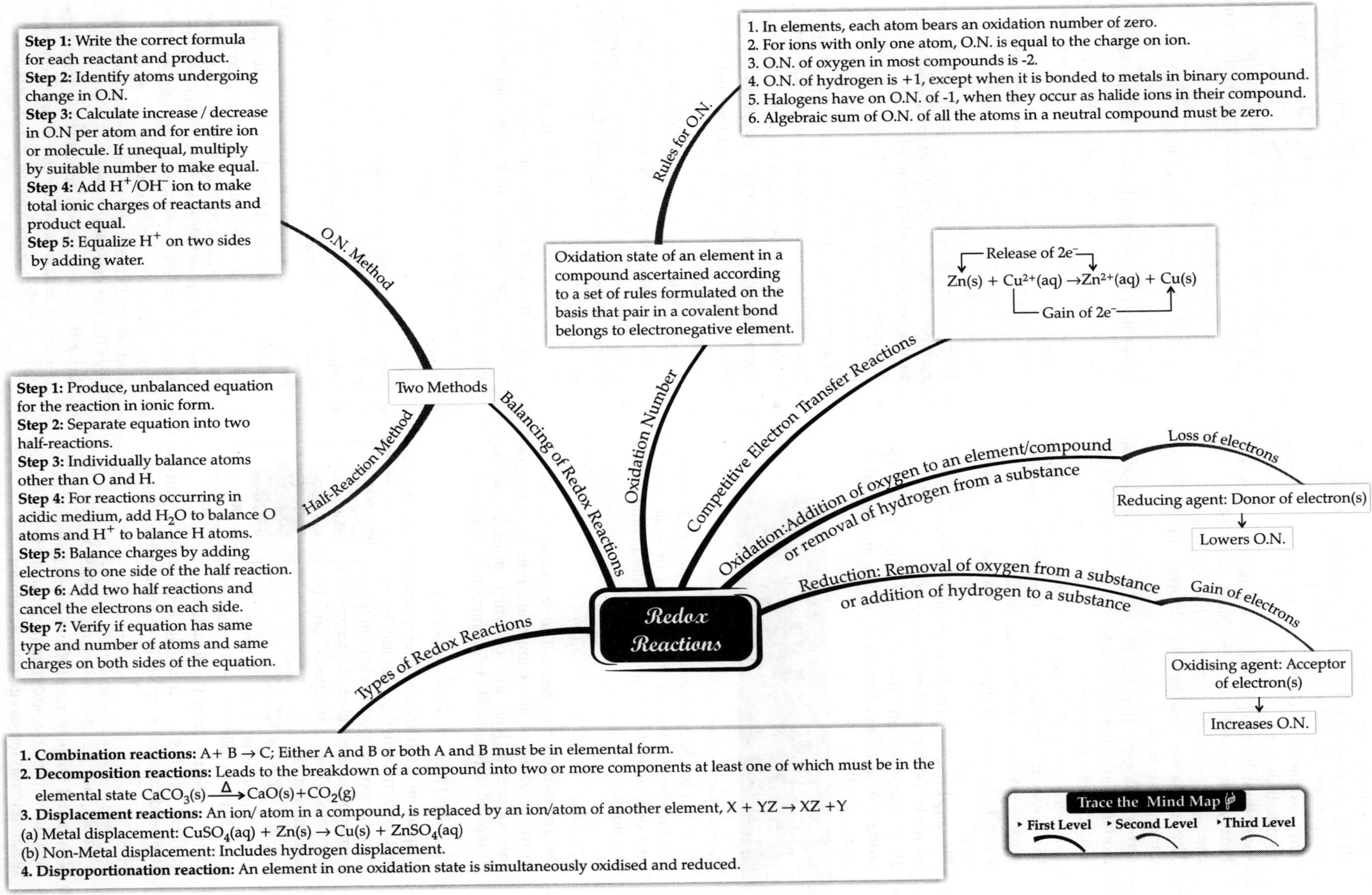
Redox Reactions
Rules for O.N.
1. In elements, each atom bears an oxidation number of zero.
2. For ions with only one atom, O.N. is equal to the charge on ion.
3. O.N. of oxygen in most compounds is -2.
4. O.N. of hydrogen is +1, except when it is bonded to metals in binary compound.
5. Halogens have on O.N. of -1, when they occur as halide ions in their compound.
6. Algebraic sum of O.N. of all the atoms in a neutral compound must be zero.
Oxidation Number
Oxidation state of an element in a compound ascertained according to a set of rules formulated on the basis that pair in a covalent bond belongs to electronegative element.
Competitive Electron Transfer Reactions
Release of $2e^-$
$Zn(s) + Cu^{2+}(aq) \rightarrow Zn^{2+}(aq) + Cu(s)$
Gain of $2e^-$
Oxidation:Addition of oxygen to an element/compound or removal of hydrogen from a substance
Loss of electrons
Reducing agent: Donor of electron(s)
Lowers O.N.
Reduction: Removal of oxygen from a substance or addition of hydrogen to a substance
Gain of electrons
Oxidising agent: Acceptor of electron(s)
Increases O.N.
Balancing of Redox Reactions
Two Methods
O.N. Method
Step 1: Write the correct formula for each reactant and product.
Step 2: Identify atoms undergoing change in O.N.
Step 3: Calculate increase / decrease in O.N per atom and for entire ion or molecule. If unequal, multiply by suitable number to make equal.
Step 4: Add H^+/OH^- ion to make total ionic charges of reactants and product equal.
Step 5: Equalize H^+ on two sides by adding water.
Half-Reaction Method
Step 1: Produce, unbalanced equation for the reaction in ionic form.
Step 2: Separate equation into two half-reactions.
Step 3: Individually balance atoms other than O and H.
Step 4: For reactions occurring in acidic medium, add H_2O to balance O atoms and H^+ to balance H atoms.
Step 5: Balance charges by adding electrons to one side of the half reaction.
Step 6: Add two half reactions and cancel the electrons on each side.
Step 7: Verify if equation has same type and number of atoms and same charges on both sides of the equation.
Types of Redox Reactions
1. Combination reactions: $A + B \rightarrow C$; Either A and B or both A and B must be in elemental form.
2. Decomposition reactions: Leads to the breakdown of a compound into two or more components at least one of which must be in the elemental state $CaCO_3(s) \xrightarrow{\Delta} CaO(s) + CO_2(g)$
3. Displacement reactions: An ion/ atom in a compound, is replaced by an ion/atom of another element, $X + YZ \rightarrow XZ + Y$
(a) Metal displacement: $CuSO_4(aq) + Zn(s) \rightarrow Cu(s) + ZnSO_4(aq)$
(b) Non-Metal displacement: Includes hydrogen displacement.
4. Disproportionation reaction: An element in one oxidation state is simultaneously oxidised and reduced.
Trace the Mind Map
First Level
Second Level
Third Level

(ii) When oxygen is bonded to fluorine, then in such compounds, e.g., oxygen difluoride (OF_2) and dioxygen difluoride (O_2F_2), the oxidation numbers of oxygen are +2 and +1 respectively.

- The oxidation number of hydrogen in most compounds is +1.
- **Exception:** When hydrogen is bonded to metals in binary compounds. e.g., LiH, NaH and CaH_2, in such cases, the oxidation number of hydrogen is –1.
- The oxidation number of fluorine in all of its compounds is –1.

  Other halogens like Cl, Br and I also possess an oxidation number of –1, when they occur as halide ions in their compounds.

  However, when Cl, Br or I is combined with oxygen like oxoacids and oxoanions, then these halogens possess positive oxidation numbers.

  e.g., Cl_2O_7, in this compound, oxidation number of Cl is +7.
- The algebraic sum of the oxidation number of all the atoms in a compound must be zero.
- In polyatomic ion, the algebraic sum of all the oxidation numbers of atoms of the ion must equal the charge on the ion.

Redox Reactions and Electrode Processes

- **Redox reactions are of various types:**

1. **Combination Reactions:** The reactions which involve combination of two or more atoms or molecules to give only a single compound are called combination reactions.

$$\text{e.g., } \overset{0}{C}(s) + \overset{0}{O_2}(g) \xrightarrow{\Delta} \overset{+4\ -2}{CO_2}(g)$$

2. **Decomposition Reactions:** The reactions which lead to the breakdown of a compound into two or more components at least one of which must be in the elemental state are called decomposition reactions.

$$\text{e.g., } 2\overset{+1}{Na}\overset{-1}{H}(s) \xrightarrow{\Delta} 2\overset{0}{Na}(s) + \overset{0}{H_2}(g)$$

3. **Displacement Reactions:** The reactions which involve replacement of an atom (or ion) by an atom (or ion) of another element from a compound are called displacement reactions. These reactions can be represented as:

   e.g., $X + YZ \longrightarrow XZ + Y$

   These reactions can further be classified into following categories:

Scan to know more about this topic

Redox Reactions

(i) Metal Displacement Reactions: In these reactions, a metal in a compound can be displaced by another metal in the uncombined state. e.g.,

$$\overset{+2}{Cu}\overset{+6}{S}\overset{-2}{O_4}(aq) + \overset{0}{Zn}(s) \longrightarrow \overset{0}{Cu}(s) + \overset{+2}{Zn}\overset{+6}{S}\overset{-2}{O_4}(aq)$$

(ii) Non-metal Displacement Reactions: These reactions include hydrogen displacement and a rarely occurring reaction involving oxygen displacement.

e.g.,

$$2\overset{0}{Na}(s)+2\overset{+1}{H_2}\overset{-2}{O}(l)\longrightarrow 2\overset{+1}{Na}\overset{-1}{OH}(aq)+\overset{0}{H_2}(g)$$

$$\overset{0}{Mg}(s) + 2\overset{+1}{H_2}\overset{-2}{O}(l) \xrightarrow{\Delta} \overset{+2}{Mg}\overset{-1}{(OH)_2}(s)+\overset{0}{H_2}(g)$$

4. **Disproportionation Reactions :** These reactions are a special type of redox reactions. In these reactions, an element in one oxidation state is simultaneously oxidized and reduced.

$$\text{e.g., } 2\overset{+1}{H_2}\overset{-1}{O_2}(aq) \longrightarrow 2\overset{+1}{H_2}\overset{-2}{O}(l) + \overset{0}{O_2}(g)$$

$$\overset{0}{P_4}(s)+3OH^-(aq)+3H_2O(l)\longrightarrow \overset{-3}{P}H_3(g) + 3H_2\overset{+1}{P}O_2^-(g)$$

- **Balancing of Redox Reactions:** Following methods are used to balance chemical equations for redox processes:

1. **Oxidation Number Method:** It involves following steps:
   - Write the correct chemical formula for each reactant and product.
   - Identify atoms which undergo change in oxidation number in the reaction by assigning oxidation number to all elements in the reaction.
   - Calculate the increase or decrease in the oxidation number per atom and for the entire molecule/ion in which it occurs. If these are not equal, then multiply by suitable number so that these become equal.
   - Ascertain the involvement of ions if the reaction is occurring in water, add H^+ or OH^- to the expression on the appropriate side so that the total ionic charges of reactants and products are equal.

     If the reaction is carried out in acidic solution, use H^+ ions in the equation; if in basic solution, use OH^- ions.
   - Make the numbers of H–atoms in the expression on the two sides equal by adding H_2O molecules to the reactants or products.

     Now, check the number of O–atoms. If there are the same number of oxygen atoms in the reactants and products, then the equation represents the balanced redox reaction.
2. **Half Reaction Method:** It involves following steps:
   - Produce unbalanced equation for the reaction in ionic form.
   - Separate the equation into half reactions, i.e., oxidation and reduction half reactions.
   - Balance the atoms other than O and H in each half reaction individually.
   - For reactions occurring in acidic medium, add H_2O to balance O atoms and H^+ to balance H atoms.
   - Add electrons to one side of the half reaction to balance the charges. If required, make the number of electrons equal in the two half reactions by multiplying one or both half reactions by appropriate number.
   - Now, add two half reactions to achieve overall reaction and cancel the electrons on each side. This gives the net ionic equation.
   - Verify that the equation contains the same type and number of atoms and the same charges on both sides of the equation.

Note: For the reaction in a basic medium, first balance the atoms as is done in acidic medium. Then for each H^+ ions, add an equal number of OH^- ions to both sides of the equation. Where H^+ and OH^- appear on the same side of the equation, combine these to give H_2O.

- **Electrode Processes:**
- The redox reactions in which the oxidation and reduction half reactions take place in the same container, are called the **direct redox reactions.**

  e.g.,When Zn strip is placed in $CuSO_4$ solution, Zn is oxidized to Zn^{2+} and $CuSO_4$ is reduced to metallic copper. Such type of cell is called electrolytic cell and the phenomenon is known as electrolysis.
- The redox reactions in which the oxidation and reduction half reactions take place in the separate containers, are called **indirect redox reactions**. Such type of cell is called **electrochemical cell.**

  For e.g., $CuSO_4$ solution is placed in a beaker with a copper strip or rod and $ZnSO_4$ solution is placed in separate beaker with a zinc strip or rod. In this experiment, two redox couples are represented as: Zn/Zn^{2+} and Cu^{2+}/Cu

  The solutions of two beakers are connected by a salt bridge (a U-tube containing a solution of KCl or NH_4NO_3). The Zn and Cu rods are connected by a metallic wire with a provision for an ammeter and switch. This set-up is known as Daniel cell. The two half reactions taking place are:

$$Zn \longrightarrow Zn^{2+} + 2e^- \text{ (Oxidation) at anode}$$
$$Cu^{2+} + 2e^- \longrightarrow Cu \text{(Reduction) at cathode}$$

Overall reaction, $Zn + Cu^{2+} \longrightarrow Zn^{2+} + Cu$

- **Redox Couple:** It is defined as having together the oxidized and reduced forms of a substance taking part in an oxidation or reduction half reaction.
- **Electrode:** It is an electrical conductor used to make contact with a non-metallic part of a circuit.
- **Electrode Potential:** The potential associated with each electrode is called electrode potential.
- **Salt Bridge:** It is an inverted U-tube that contains an electrolyte and connects the two half cells in a galvanic cell.
- **Functions of Salt bridge in an Electrochemical cell :**
- It completes the cell circuit by connecting the solutions of two half cells, without allowing them to mix with each other.
- It maintains the electrical neutrality of the solutions in the two half cells due to the flow of ions.
- **Representation of an Electrochemical Cell**

Flow of electrons →

Flow of current ←

$Zn(s) \mid Zn^{2+}(aq) \parallel Cu^{2+}(aq) \mid Cu(s)$

Left electrode (Anode) Oxidation (Negative)	Salt bridge	Right electrode (Cathode) Reduction (Positive)

- A metal having more negative value of $E^{\ominus}$ (Standard electrode potential) can displace the metal having less negative value of $E^{\ominus}$ from their salt solution.

  e.g., Zn can displace Cu from $CuSO_4$ solution ($Zn^{2+}/Zn = -0.76V$, $Cu^{2+}/Cu = 0.34V$)

  So, Zn is more reactive than Cu.
- The feasibility of a reaction is decided by its electromotive force (emf) or cell potential.

  i.e., $E^\circ_{cell} = E^\circ_{cathode} - E^\circ_{anode}$
- A positive value of E°_{cell} suggests that the cell reaction is feasible.
- A negative or zero value of E°_{cell} suggests that the cell reaction does not feasible.
- **Standard Electrode Potential:** The potential of an electrode in which the concentration of each species taking part in the electrode reaction is unity (if any gas is involved in the electrode reaction, its pressure is taken as 1 atmosphere) and the temperature is maintained at 298 K is called the standard electrode potential.
- The standard electrode potential ($E^{\ominus}$) value for each electrode process is a measure of the relative tendency of the active species in the process to remain in the oxidized/reduced form.
- A negative $E^{\ominus}$ means that the redox couple is a **stronger** reducing agent than the H^+/H_2 couple.
- A positive $E^{\ominus}$ means that the redox couple is a **weaker** reducing agent than the H^+/H_2 couple.
- **Electrochemical Series:** The series in which different electrodes are arranged in decreasing order of their standard reduction potentials ($E^{\ominus}$) is called electrochemical series.

Key Terms

- **Oxidation number:** It is defined as the charge that an atom of an element has on its ion or appear to have when present in the combined state with other atoms.
- **Electrochemical Cell:** It is a device which is used to convert chemical energy into electrical energy.

Key Facts

- Electron releasing tendency among Zn, Ag and Cu is in the order: Zn > Cu > Ag.
- A term that is often used inter changeably with the oxidation number is the **oxidation state.**

  e.g., In CO_2, the oxidation state of carbon is +4, that is also its oxidation number.
- The oxidation number or state of a metal in a compound is sometimes presented according to the notation given by German chemist, Alfred Stock. It is popularly known as **Stock notation.**

  According to this notation, the oxidation number is expressed by putting a Roman numeral representing the oxidation number in parenthesis after the symbol of the metal in the molecular formula.

e.g., Stannous chloride is written as $Sn(II)Cl_2$, Stannic chloride in written as $Sn(IV)Cl_4$, etc.

- All combustion reactions, which make use of elemental dioxygen, as well as other reactions involving elements other than dioxygen, are redox reaction.
- All decomposition reactions are not redox reactions. For example, decomposition of calcium carbonate is not a redox reaction.

$$\overset{+2\ +4-2}{CaCO_3(s)} \xrightarrow{\Delta} \overset{+2\ -2}{CaO(s)} + \overset{+4-2}{CO_2(g)}$$

- All alkali metals and some alkaline earth metals (Ca, Sr and Ba) which are very good reducing agents, will displace hydrogen from cold water.

e.g., $Ca(s) + 2H_2O(l) \longrightarrow Ca(OH)_2(aq) + H_2(g)$

- Less active metals such as magnesium and iron react with steam to produce dihydrogen gas.

$$\underset{\text{steam}}{2Fe(s) + 3H_2O(g)} \xrightarrow{\Delta} Fe_2O_3(s) + 2H_2(g)$$

- Many metals, including those which do not react with cold water, are capable of displacing hydrogen from acids.

$Zn(s) + 2HCl(aq) \longrightarrow ZnCl_2(aq) + H_2(g)$

This reaction is used to prepare dihydrogen gas in the laboratory.

- Very less active metals, which may occur in the native state such as silver (Ag) and gold (Au) do not react even with hydrochloric acid.
- Fluorine is so reactive that it can replace chloride, bromide and iodide ions in solution. Infact, fluorine is so reactive that it attacks water and displaces the oxygen of water.

$$2H_2O(l) + 2F_2(g) \longrightarrow 4HF(aq) + O_2(g)$$

- Phosphorus, sulphur and chlorine undergo disproportionation in the alkaline medium as shown below :

$$P_4(s) + 3OH^-(aq) + 3H_2O(l) \longrightarrow PH_3(g) + 3H_2PO_2^-(aq) \quad ...(1)$$

$$S_8(s) + 12OH^-(aq) \longrightarrow 4S^{2-}(aq) + 2S_2O_3^{2-}(aq) + 6H_2O(l) \quad ...(2)$$

$$Cl_2(g) + 2OH^-(aq) \longrightarrow ClO^-(aq) + Cl^-(aq) + H_2O(l) \quad ...(3)$$

The third reaction describes the formation of household bleaching agents. The hypochlorite ion (ClO^-) formed in the reaction oxidises the colour bearing stains of the substances to colourless compounds.

- The reaction that takes place in the case of fluorine is as follows:

$$2F_2(g) + 2OH^-(aq) \longrightarrow 2F^-(aq) + OF_2(g) + H_2O(l)$$

- In acid-base systems, titration is used to find the strength of one solution against the other using a pH sensitive indicator.
- Highly reactive metals (i.e. having negative value of $E^\ominus$) displace hydrogen from acids. For e.g., Metals like Mg, Al, Zn, Fe etc. can replace hydrogen from HCl or H_2SO_4.

However, metals with positive values of $E^\ominus$ are not capable to replace hydrogen from mineral acids.

Mnemonics

Concept: Redox reaction
Mnemonics: OiL RiG
Interpretation: Oxidation Is Losing (electrons), Reduction Is Gaining (electrons)

Concept: An Oil Rig Cat
Mnemonics: At the ANode, Oxidation Involves Loss of electrons.
Interpretation: Reduction Involves Gaining electrons at the Cathode

Concept: Electrons flow From Anode To Cathode
Mnemonics: Fat Cat
Interpretation: LOAN: Left side, Oxidation, Anode, Negative

Concept: soak a jerk
Mnemonics: SOAC a GERC
Interpretation: Strongest Oxidizing Agent at the Cathode Gains Electrons and is Reduced at the Cathode.

Concept: Activity Series of Metals
Mnemonics: Please Stop Calling Me A Cute Zebra I Like Her Call Smart Goat. Kangaroos Naturally Muck About in Zoos For Purple Hippos Chasing Aardvarks.
Interpretation: Calcium > Magnesium > Aluminium > (Carbon)* > Zinc > Iron > Lead > Hydrogen > Copper > Silver
> Gold), OR (K > Na > Mg > Al > Zn > Cr > Fe > Pd > H > Cu > Au)

Concept: For Galvanic Cell
Mnemonics: LOAN
Interpretation: Loss of e–Oxidation Anode Negative

Concept: Electrolytic Cell
Mnemonics: LOAP
Interpretation: Loss of e–Oxidation Anode Positive

NCERT CORNER

Q. 1. Assign oxidation number to the underlined elements in each of the following species :

(a) $NaH_2\underline{P}O_4$ **(b)** $NaH\underline{S}O_4$
(c) $H_4\underline{P}_2O_7$ **(d)** $K_2\underline{Mn}O_4$
(e) $Ca\underline{O}_2$ **(f)** $Na\underline{B}H_4$
(g) $H_2\underline{S}_2O_7$ **(h)** $KAl(\underline{S}O_4)_2.12H_2O$.

[NCERT Ex. Q. 7.1, Page 252]

Ans. (a) Let the oxidation no. of P in NaH_2PO_4 be x.

$$+1 + 2(+1) + 1(x) + 4(-2) = 0$$
$$+1 + 2 + x - 8 = 0$$
$$x = +5$$

Oxidation number of P in $NaH_2PO_4 = +5$.

(b) Let the oxidation no. of S in $NaHSO_4$ be x.

$$+1 + 1 + x + 4(-2) = 0$$
$$+2 + x - 8 = 0$$
$$x = +6$$

Oxidation number of S in $NaHSO_4 = +6$.

(c) Let the oxidation number of P in $H_4P_2O_7$ be x.

$$4(+1) + 2(x) + 7(-2) = 0$$
$$+4 + 2x - 14 = 0$$
$$2x = 10$$
$$x = +5$$

Oxidation number of P in $H_4P_2O_7 = +5$.

(d) Let the oxidation no. of Mn in K_2MnO_4 be x.

$$2(+1) + x + 4(-2) = 0$$
$$+2 + x - 8 = 0$$
$$x = +6$$

Oxidation number of Mn in $K_2MnO_4 = +6$.

(e) Let the oxidation number of oxygen in CaO_2 be x.

$$+2 + 2x = 0$$
$[\because$ oxidation no. of Ca $= +2]$
$$2x = -2$$
$$x = -1$$

Oxidation number of O in $CaO_2 = -1$.

(f) Let the oxidation no. of B in $NaBH_4$ be x.

$$+1 + x + 4(-1) = 0$$
$[\because$ oxidation no. of H $= -1]$
$$x - 3 = 0$$
$$x = +3$$

Oxidation number of B in $NaBH_4 = +3$.

(g) Let the oxidation no. of S in $H_2S_2O_7$ be x.

$$2(+1) + 2(x) + 7(-2) = 0$$
$$+2 + 2x - 14 = 0$$
$$2x = 12$$
$$x = +6$$

Oxidation number of S in $H_2S_2O_7 = +6$.

(h) Let the oxidation no. of S in

$$KAl(SO_4)_2.12H_2O = x$$
$$+1 + 3 + 2(x) + 8(-2) + 24(+1) + 12(-2) = 0$$
$$+4 + 2x - 16 = 0$$
[Oxidation number of K = 1, Oxidation number of Al = 3]
$$2x = 12$$
$$x = +6$$

$\therefore$ Oxidation number of S in $KAl(SO_4)_2.\,12H_2O = +6$.

Q. 2. What are the oxidation number of the underlined elements in each of the following and how do you rationalise your results ?

(a) $K\underline{I}_3$ **(b)** $H_2\underline{S}_4O_6$
(c) $\underline{Fe}_3O_4$ **(d)** $\underline{C}H_3\underline{C}H_2OH$
(e) $\underline{C}H_3\underline{C}OOH$

[NCERT Ex. Q. 7.2, Page 252]

Ans. (a) Let the oxidation number of I is x:

$$1 + 3x = 0$$
$$x = -\frac{1}{3}$$

Hence, the average oxidation number of I is $-\frac{1}{3}$. But we know, oxidation number can't be fractional. The structure of KI_3, $K^+ (I^0\text{------}I^0 \leftarrow I^-)^-$

In this structure, a coordination bond is formed between I_2 molecule and I^- ion. hence, oxidation of I_3 is –1.

(b) Oxidation no. of S in $H_2S_4O_6$

By conventional method, Oxidation no. (average) of S in $H_2S_4O_6 = +\frac{5}{3}$. But oxidation number cannot be fraction.

Structure of $H_2S_4O_6$ is

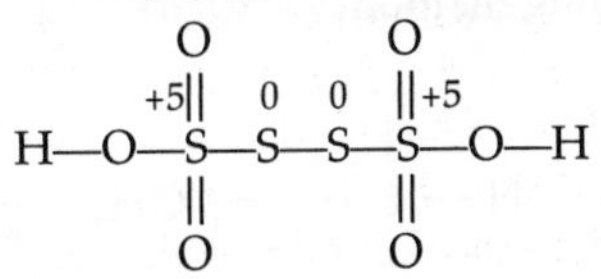

The oxidation no. of each of S-atoms linked to each other in the middle is zero whereas the oxidation no. of the two S atoms is + 5 each.

(c) Oxidation no. of Fe in Fe_3O_4

By conventional method:

$$3x + 4(-2) = 0$$

or
$$x = +\frac{8}{3}$$

The value of $\frac{8}{3}$ for oxidation no. of Fe as obtained by conventional method is in fact the average of the actual oxidation no. of all the atoms in the formula, e.g., $\frac{(1\times2+2\times3)}{3} = +\frac{8}{3}$. But oxidation no. cannot be fraction.

Fe_3O_4 is known to be a mixture of FeO and Fe_2O_3 having composition FeO. Fe_2O_3. The oxidation no. of Fe in FeO is + 2, whereas it is + 3 in Fe_2O_3. [By stoichiometry].

(d) $\underline{C}H_3\underline{C}H_2OH$

Oxidation no. of underlined carbon atoms can be calculated as follows:

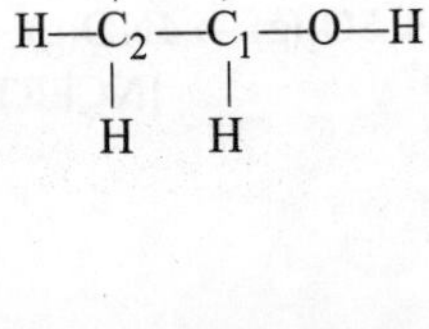

C_2 is attached to three H atoms (less electronegative than C) and one —CH_2OH (more electronegative than C)

Oxidation no. of C_2 is

$$3(+1) + x + 1(-1) = 0$$
$$+3 + x - 1 = 0$$
$$x = -2$$

[For each covalent bond between two dissimilar atoms, assign an oxidation no. of +1 to the less electronegative atom and – 1 to the more electronegative element.]

C_1 is attached to one OH [O. No. = – 1] one —CH_3 group [O. No. + 1], two H atoms [O. No. = + 1]

∴ O. No. of C_1 is

$$+1 + 2(+1) + x - 1 = 0$$
$$+1 + 2 + x - 1 = 0$$
$$x = -2.$$

(e) $\underline{CH_3C}OOH$

By conventional method

$$CH_3COOH = \overset{x}{C_2}\overset{+1}{H_4}\overset{-2}{O_2}$$

or
$$2(x) + 4(1) + 2(-2) = 0$$
$$2(x) + 4 - 4 = 0$$
$$2x = 0$$
$$x = 0$$

By chemical bonding method,

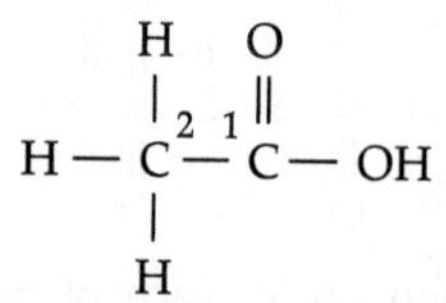

C_2 is attached to three H-atoms (less electronegative than carbon) and one -COOH group (more electronegative than carbon).

∴ Oxidation No. of $C_2 = 3(+1) + x + 1(-1) = 0$

$$3 + x - 1 = 0$$
$$x + 2 = 0$$
$$x = -2$$

However C_1 is attached to one oxygen atom by a double bond, one OH group (O.N. = –1) and one CH_3 group (O. N. = +1)

∴Oxidation No. of $C_1 = 1 + x + 1(-2) + 1(-1) = 0$

$$1 + x - 2 - 1 = 0$$
$$1 + x - 3 = 0$$
$$x - 2 = 0$$
$$x = +2$$

Q. 3. Justify that the following reactions are redox reactions:

(a) $CuO(s) + H_2(g) \rightarrow Cu(s) + H_2O(g)$

(b) $Fe_2O_3(s) + 3CO(g) \rightarrow 2Fe(s) + 3CO_2(g)$

(c) $4BCl_3(g) + 3LiAlH_4(s) \rightarrow 2B_2H_6(g) + 3\,LiCl(s) + 3AlCl_3(s)$

(d) $2K(s) + F_2(g) \rightarrow 2K^+F^-(s)$

(e) $4NH_3(g) + 5O_2(g) \rightarrow 4NO(g) + 6H_2O(g)$

[NCERT Ex. Q. 7.3, Page 252]

Ans. (a) Assign oxidation numbers of each atom in the given reaction:

$$\overset{+2}{Cu}\overset{-2}{O}(s) + \overset{0}{H_2}(g) \rightarrow \overset{0}{Cu}(s) + \overset{+1}{H_2}\overset{-2}{O}(g)$$

Since, the oxidation number of Cu decreases from + 2 to 0, so, it undergoes reduction and the oxidation number of hydrogen increases from 0 to +1, so, it undergoes oxidation. Hence, this reaction is a redox reaction.

(b) $$\overset{+3}{Fe_2}\overset{-2}{O_3}(g) + 3\overset{+2}{C}\overset{-2}{O}(g) \rightarrow 2\overset{0}{Fe}(s) + 3\overset{+4}{C}\overset{-2}{O_3}(g)$$

Since, the oxidation number of Fe decreases from +3 to 0, it undergoes reduction and the oxidation number of carbon increases from + 2 to + 4, so, it undergoes oxidation. Hence, this reaction is a redox reaction.

(c) $$4\overset{+3}{B}\overset{-1}{Cl_3}(g) + 3\,\overset{+1}{Li}\overset{+3}{Al}\overset{-1}{H_4}(s) \rightarrow 2\overset{-3}{B_2}\overset{+1}{H_6}(g) + 3\overset{+1}{Li}\overset{-1}{Cl}(s) + 3\overset{+3}{Al}\overset{-1}{Cl_3}(s)$$

Since, the oxidation number of B decreases from +3 to –3, so, it undergoes reduction i.e., BCl_3 is reduced to B_2H_6. The oxidation number of H increases from –1 to + 1, so, it undergoes oxidation, i.e., $LiAlH_4$ is oxidised. Hence, this reaction is a redox reaction.

(d) $$2\overset{0}{K}(s) + \overset{0}{F_2}(g) \rightarrow 2\overset{+1}{K^+}\overset{-1}{F^-}(s)$$

Since, the oxidation number of K increases from 0 to + 1, so, it undergoes oxidation and the oxidation number of F decreases from 0 to –1, so, it undergoes reduction. Hence, this reaction is a redox reaction.

(e) $$4\overset{-3}{N}\overset{+1}{H_3}(g) + 5\overset{0}{O_2}(g) \rightarrow 4\overset{+2}{N}\overset{-2}{O}(g) + 6\overset{+1}{H_2}\overset{-2}{O}(g)$$

Since, the oxidation number of N increases from – 3 to +2, so, it undergoes oxidation and the oxidation number of O decreases from 0 to –2, so, it undergoes reduction. Hence, this reaction is a redox reaction.

Q. 4. Fluorine reacts with ice and results in the change:

$$H_2O(s) + F_2(g) \rightarrow HF(g) + HOF(g)$$

Justify that this reaction is a redox reaction.

[NCERT Ex. Q. 7.4, Page 252]

Ans. Assign oxidation numbers of each atom in the given reaction.

$$\overset{+1}{H_2}\overset{-2}{O}(s) + \overset{0}{F_2}(g) \rightarrow \overset{+1}{H}\overset{-1}{F}(g) + \overset{+1}{H}\overset{-2}{O}\overset{+1}{F}(g)$$

In this reaction, F_2 is reduced to HF and oxidised to HOF, so, it is a redox reaction. However, HOF is a highly unstable molecule and so it decomposes to form HF and O_2.

$$2\,\overset{+1}{H}\overset{-2}{O}\overset{+1}{F} \rightarrow 2\overset{+1}{H}\overset{-1}{F} + \overset{0}{O_2}$$

In above reaction, F of HOF is reduced while O of HOF is oxidised. So, it is a redox reaction.

Q. 5. Calculate the oxidation number of sulphur, chromium and nitrogen in H_2SO_5, $Cr_2O_7^{2-}$ and NO_3^-. Suggest structure of these compounds. Count for the fallacy. **[NCERT Ex. Q. 7.5, Page 252]**

Ans. H_2SO_5:

Let oxidation number of S is x

∴
$$2(1) + x + 5(-2) = 0$$
$$2 + x - 10 = 0$$
$$x - 8 = 0$$
$$x = +8$$

But oxidation number of 'S' cannot be more than 6 because S has only 6 valence electrons. This fallacy is removed by calculating oxidation number of S by chemical bonding method.

Structure of H_2SO_5 is :

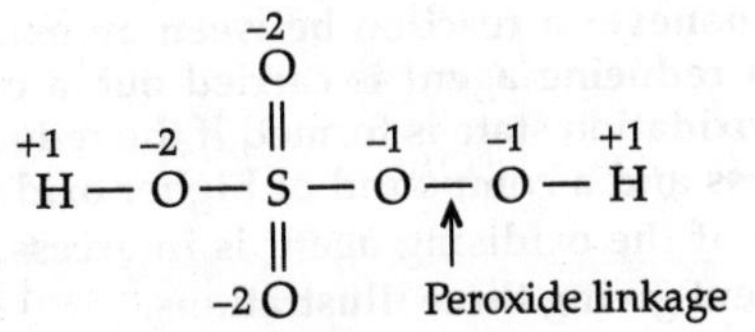

Chemical bonding method:

$$2(+1) + 3(-2) + x + 2(-1) = 0$$
(for H) (for 3 'O) (S) (For O – O)

or
$$2 - 6 + x - 2 = 0$$
$$2 + x - 8 = 0$$
$$x - 6 = 0$$
$$x = +6$$

$Cr_2O_7^{2-}$:

Let, oxidation number of Cr = x

$$2(x) + 7(-2) = -2$$
$$2x - 14 = -2$$
$$2x = -2 + 14 = +12$$
$$x = \frac{+12}{2} = +6$$

Structure of $Cr_2O_7^{2-}$ ion is :

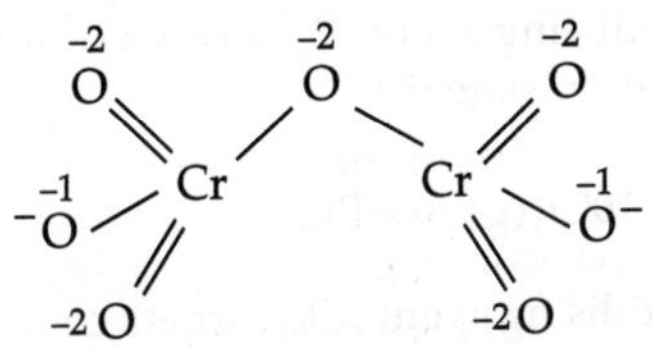

Chemical bonding method

$$4(-2) + 2(-1) + 1(-2) + 2x = 0$$
(for 4 'O') (for 2 'O') (for 1 'O') (Cr)

$$-8 - 2 - 2 + 2x = 0$$
$$-12 + 2x = 0$$
$$2x = +12$$
$$x = \frac{+12}{2} = +6$$

∵ Oxidation number of Cr in $Cr_2O_7^{2-}$ is found to be same, i.e., +6 calculated by conventional method or by chemical bonding method. So, there is no fallacy.

NO_3^-:

Let, oxidation number of N = x

$$x + 3(-2) = -1$$
$$x - 6 = -1$$
$$x = -1 + 6 = +5$$

Structure of NO_3^- ion is:

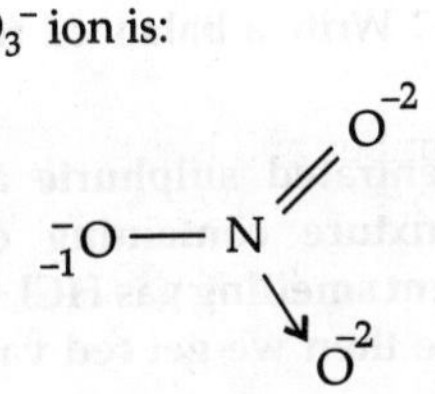

Chemical Bonding Method :

$$1(-1) + x + 1(-2) + 1(-2) = 0$$
(for O^-) (for N) (for = O) (for → O)

$$-1 + x - 2 - 2 = 0$$
$$x - 5 = 0$$
$$x = +5$$

Since, the oxidation of N in NO_3^- is found to be same, i.e., +5 by conventional method or by chemical bonding method. So, there is no fallacy.

Q. 6. Write formulas for the following compounds :

(a) Mercury (II) chloride **(b) Nickel (II) sulphate**

(b) Tin (IV) oxide **(d) Thallium (I) sulphate**

(e) Iron (III) sulphate **(f) Chromium (III) oxide**

[NCERT Ex. Q. 7.6, Page 252]

Ans.

	Compound	**Formula**
(a)	Mercury (II) chloride	$HgCl_2$
(b)	Nickel (II) sulphate	$NiSO_4$
(c)	Tin (IV) oxide	SnO_2
(d)	Thallium (I) sulphate	Tl_2SO_4
(e)	Iron (III) sulphate	$Fe_2(SO_4)_3$
(f)	Chromium (III) oxide	Cr_2O_3

Q. 7. Suggest a list of the substances where carbon can exhibit oxidation states from –4 to +4 and nitrogen from –3 to +5. **[NCERT Ex. Q. 7.7, Page 252]**

Ans. List of Substances of Carbon :

Compound	**Oxidation State of C**
CH_4	– 4
C_2H_6	–3
CH_3Cl	–2
C_2H_2	–1
CH_2Cl_2	0
C_6Cl_6	+1
$CHCl_3$	+2
$(COOH)_2$	+3
CCl_4	+4

List of Substances of Nitrogen :

Compound	**Oxidation State of N**
NH_3	–3
N_2H_4	–2
N_2H_2	–1
N_2 0	
N_2O	+1
NO +2	
N_2O_3	+3
N_2O_4	+4
N_2O_5	+5

Q. 8. While sulphur dioxide and hydrogen peroxide can act as oxidizing as well as reducing agents in their reactions, ozone, and nitric acid act only as oxidants. Why? **[NCERT Ex. Q. 7.8, Page 252]**

Ans. SO_2:

Let oxidation number of S is x:

$$\therefore \quad x + 2(-2) = 0$$
$$x - 4 = 0$$
$$x = +4$$

Sulphur can have minimum oxidation number –2 and maximum oxidation number +6. Hence, in SO_2, S can either decrease or increase its oxidation number. So, SO_2 can act both as oxidizing as well as reducing agent.

H_2O_2:

Let, oxidation number O = x

$$\therefore \quad 2(1) + 2(x) = 0$$
$$2 + 2x = 0$$
$$2x = -2$$
$$x = \frac{-2}{2} = -1$$

Since, oxygen can have minimum oxidation number – 2 and maximum oxidation number 0. So, in H_2O_2, 'O' can either decrease or increase its oxidation number. Hence, H_2O_2 can act both as oxidizing as well as reducing agent.

O_3: Oxidation number of O in O_3 is zero. It cannot increase is oxidation number. However, it can decrease its oxidation number from 0 to –1 or –2. So, ozone (O_3) can act only as an oxidizing agent.

HNO_3 : Let, oxidation number of N = x

$$\therefore \quad 1 + x + 3(-2) = 0$$
$$1 + x - 6 = 0$$
$$x - 5 = 0$$
$$x = +5$$

It is maximum value of oxidation number of nitrogen. So, it can only decrease its oxidation number. Hence, HNO_3 can act only as an oxidizing agent.

Q. 9. Consider the reactions:

(a) $6CO_2(g) + 6H_2O(l) \rightarrow C_6H_{12}O_6(aq) + 6O_2(g)$

(b) $O_3(g) + H_2O_2(l) \rightarrow H_2O(l) + 2O_2(g)$

Why it is more appropriate to write these reactions as:

(a) $6CO_2(g) + 12H_2O(l) \rightarrow C_6H_{12}O_6(aq) + 6H_2O(l) + 6O_2(g)$

(b) $O_3(g) + H_2O_2(l) \rightarrow H_2O(l) + O_2(g) + O_2(g)$

Also suggest a technique to investigate the path of the above (a) and (b) redox reactions.

[NCERT Ex. Q. 7.9, Page 252]

Ans. (a) This reaction can be explained by using mechanism of photosynthesis. It involves following steps:

Step-I: Decomposition of water

$$12H_2O(l) \rightarrow 12H_2(g) + 6O_2(g)$$

Step-II: Reduction of CO_2

$$6CO_2(g) + 12H_2(g) \rightarrow C_6H_{12}O_6(s) + 6H_2O(l)$$

Overall reaction:

$$6CO_2(g) + 12H_2O(l) \rightarrow C_6H_{12}O_6(s) + 6H_2O(l) + 6O_2(g)$$

Actually in the process of photosynthesis, $12H_2O$ are used up in first step and $6H_2O$ are formed per molecule of glucose in second step.

(b) This reaction can be explained by using mechanism of reaction of ozone with H_2O_2. It involves following steps:

Step-I: $O_3(g) \rightarrow O_2(g) + O(g)$

Step-II: $H_2O_2(l) + O(g) \rightarrow H_2O(l) + O_2(g)$

Overall reaction:

$H_2O_2(l) + O_3(g) \rightarrow H_2O(l) + O_2(g) + O_2(g)$

In this reaction, O_2 is written by two times as it is released in two different steps.

Q. 10. The compound AgF_2 is unstable compound. However, if formed, the compound acts as a very strong oxidising agent, why? [NCERT Ex. Q. 7.10, Page 253]

Ans. The oxidation number of Ag in AgF_2 is +2. It is highly unstable so it readily accepts an electron to attain +1 oxidation state which is more stable.

$$Ag^{2+} + e^- \rightarrow Ag^+$$

It is due to the fact that AgF_2 acts as a strong oxidising agent.

Q. 11. Whenever a reaction between an oxidizing agent and an reducing agent is carried out, a compound of lower oxidation state is formed if the reducing agent is in excess and a compound of higher oxidation state is formed if the oxidising agent is in excess. Justify this statement giving three illustrations.

[NCERT Ex. Q. 7.11, Page 253]

Ans. (a) C = Reducing agent

O_2 = Oxidising agent

(i) $\underset{\text{(excess)}}{2\overset{0}{C}(s)} + O_2(g) \rightarrow 2\overset{+2}{C}O(g)$

(ii) $\overset{0}{C}(s) + \underset{\text{(excess)}}{O_2(g)} \rightarrow \overset{+4}{C}O_2(g)$

So, when carbon (reducing agent) is taken in excess, a compound, i.e., CO of lower oxidation state is obtained, if O_2 (oxidising agent) is taken in excess, a compound (CO_2) of higher oxidation state is formed.

(b) P_4 = Reducing agent

Cl_2 = Oxidising agent

(i) $\underset{\text{(excess)}}{\overset{0}{P_4}(s)} + 6Cl_2(g) \rightarrow 4\overset{+3}{P}Cl_3$

Excess of reducing agent (P_4) forms a compound having lower oxidation state.

(ii) $\overset{0}{P_4}(s) + \underset{\text{(excess)}}{10Cl_2(g)} \rightarrow 4\overset{+5}{P}Cl_5$

Excess of oxidising agent (Cl_2) forms a compound having higher oxidation state.

(c) Na = Reducing agent

O_2 = Oxidising agent

(i) $\underset{\text{(excess)}}{4\overset{0}{N}a(s)} + O_2(g) \rightarrow 2Na_2\overset{-2}{O}(s)$

Excess of reducing agent (Na) forms a compound of lower oxidation state.

(ii) $2\overset{0}{N}a(s) + \underset{\text{(excess)}}{2O_2(g)} \rightarrow Na_2\overset{-2}{O_2}(s)$

Excess of oxidising agent (O_2) forms a compound of higher oxidation state.

Q. 12. How do you count for the following observations?

(a) Though alkaline potassium permanganate and acidic potassium permanganate both are used as oxidants, yet in the manufacture of benzoic acid from toluene we use alcoholic potassium permanganate as an oxidant. Why? Write a balanced redox equation for the reaction.

(b) When concentrated sulphuric acid is added to an inorganic mixture containing chloride, we get colourless pungent smelling gas HCl, but if the mixture contains bromide then we get red vapour of bromine. Why?

[NCERT Ex. Q. 7.12, Page 253]

Ans. (a) In the manufacturing of benzoic acid from toluene, alcoholic $KMnO_4$ is preferred to acidic or alkaline $KMnO_4$ because in the presence of alcohol, both the reactants toluene and $KMnO_4$ are mixed very well and form a homogeneous solution. In homogeneous medium, rate of reaction is higher than in heterogeneous medium. Furthermore, in neutral medium, OH^- ions are produced in the reaction itself.

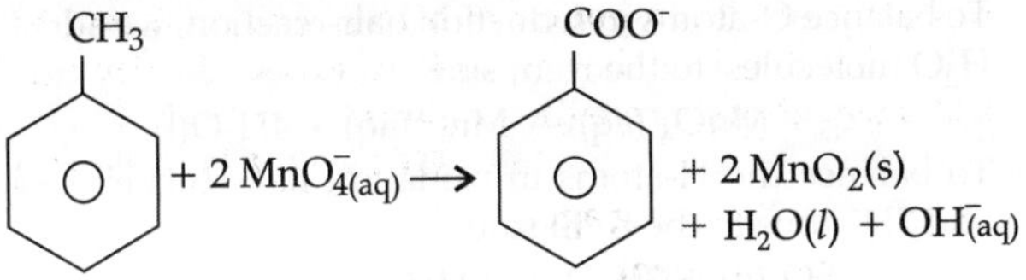

Toluene Benzoate ion

(b) When conc. H_2SO_4 is added to an inorganic mixture containing chloride, we get colourless pungent smelling gas HCl because HCl is a weak reducing agent. It cannot reduce H_2SO_4 to SO_2.

$$\underset{\text{(from inorganic mixture)}}{2NaCl} + 2H_2SO_4 \rightarrow 2NaHSO_4 + 2HCl$$

If the mixture contains bromide then we get red vapours of bromine because HBr is a strong reducing agent, it reduces H_2SO_4 to SO_2 and is itself oxidised to Br_2.

$$\underset{\text{(From inorganic mixture)}}{2NaBr} + 2H_2SO_4 \rightarrow 2NaHSO_4 + 2HBr$$

$$2HBr + H_2SO_4 \rightarrow \underset{\text{Red vapours}}{Br_2 \uparrow} + SO_2 \uparrow + 2H_2O \quad (1\tfrac{1}{2})$$

Q. 13. Identify the substance oxidised, reduced, oxidising agent and reducing agent for each of the following reactions:

(a) $2AgBr(s) + C_6H_6O_2(aq) \rightarrow 2Ag(s) + 2HBr(aq) + C_6H_4O_2(aq)$

(b) $HCHO(l) + 2[Ag(NH_3)_2]^+(aq) + 3OH^-(aq) \rightarrow 2Ag(s) + HCOO^-(aq) + 4NH_3(aq) + 2H_2O(l)$

(c) $HCHO(l) + 2Cu^{2+}(aq) + 5OH^-(aq) \rightarrow Cu_2O(s) + HCOO^-(aq) + 3H_2O(l)$

(d) $N_2H_4(l) + 2H_2O_2(l) \rightarrow N_2(g) + 4H_2O(l)$

(e) $Pb(s) + PbO_2(s) + 2H_2SO_4(aq) \rightarrow 2PbSO_4(s) + 2H_2O(l)$

[NCERT Ex. Q. 7.13, Page 253]

Ans.

Substance Oxidised (Reducing Agent)	Substance Reduced (Oxidising agent)
(a) $C_6H_6O_2(aq)$	$AgBr(s)$
(b) $HCHO(l)$	$[Ag(NH_3)_2]^+(aq)$
(c) $HCHO(l)$	$Cu^{2+}(aq)$
(d) $N_2H_4(l)$	$H_2O_2(l)$
(e) $Pb(s)$	$PbO_2(s)$

Q. 14. Consider the reactions:

$2S_2O_3^{2-}(aq) + I_2(s) \rightarrow S_4O_6^{2-}(aq) + 2I^-(aq)$

$S_2O_3^{2-}(aq) + 2Br_2(l) + 5H_2O(l) \rightarrow 2SO_4^{2-}(aq) + 4Br^-(aq) + 10H^+(aq)$

Why does the same reductant, thiosulphate react differently with iodine and bromine?

[NCERT Ex. Q. 7.14, Page 253]

Ans. Assign oxidation number to each atom in given reactions:

$$2\overset{+2}{S_2}\overset{-2}{O_3^{2-}}(aq) + \overset{0}{I_2}(s) \rightarrow \overset{+2.5}{S_4}\overset{-2}{O_6^{2-}}(aq) + 2\overset{-1}{I^-}(aq)$$

$$2\overset{+2}{S_2}\overset{-2}{O_3^{2-}}(aq) + 2\overset{0}{Br_2}(s) + 5\overset{+1}{H_2}\overset{-2}{O}(l) \rightarrow 2\overset{+6}{S}\overset{-2}{O_4^{2-}}(aq) + 4\overset{-1}{Br^-}(aq) + 10\overset{+1}{H^+}(aq)$$

In above reactions, thiosulphate acts as reductant and bromine (Br_2) and iodine (I_2) act as oxidising agent. Bromine is strong oxidising agent than iodine. Br_2 oxidises S of $S_2O_3^{2-}$ to higher oxidation state + 6 in SO_4^{2-}. Whereas, I_2 oxidises S of $S_2O_3^{2-}$ to a lower oxidation state 2.5 in $S_4O_6^{2-}$. That's why the same reductant, thiosulphate reacts differently with iodine and bromine.

Q. 15. Justify giving reactions that among halogens, fluorine is the best oxidant and among hydrohalic compounds, hydroiodic acid is the best reductant.

[NCERT Ex. Q. 7.15, Page 253]

Ans. The oxidising power of halogens decreases in the order:

$$\underset{\text{Strong Oxidant}}{F_2} > Cl_2 > Br_2 > \underset{\text{Weak Oxidant}}{I_2}$$

This is evident from the following reactions:

(a) F_2 oxidises Cl^- to Cl_2, Br^- to Br_2 and I^- to I_2.

$$F_2(g) + 2Cl^-(aq) \rightarrow 2F^-(aq) + Cl_2(g)$$
$$F_2(g) + 2Br^-(aq) \rightarrow 2F^-(aq) + Br_2(g)$$
$$F_2(g) + 2I^-(aq) \rightarrow 2F^-(aq) + I_2(g)$$

(b) Cl_2 oxidises only Br^- to Br_2 and I^- to I_2 but not F^- to F_2.

$$Cl_2(g) + 2Br^-(aq) \rightarrow 2Cl^-(aq) + Br_2(g)$$
$$Cl_2(g) + 2I^-(aq) \rightarrow 2Cl^-(aq) + I_2(g)$$

(c) Br_2 oxidises only I^- to I_2.

$$Br_2(g) + 2I^-(aq) \rightarrow 2Br^-(aq) + I_2(g)$$

(d) I_2 cannot oxidise any halide ion.

Hence, F_2 is the best oxidant.

The reducing power of hydrohalic acids decreases in the order:

$$\underset{\text{Strong reductant}}{HI} > HBr > HCl > \underset{\text{Weak reductant}}{HF}$$

This is evident from the following reactions:

HF does not reduce very strong oxidising agent such as H_2SO_4 while HI reduces strong oxidising agent and is itself oxidised to I_2.

$$2HF + H_2SO_4 \rightarrow \text{No reaction}$$

(HCl also does not react with H_2SO_4)

$$2HI + H_2SO_4 \rightarrow SO_2 + 2H_2O + I_2$$

(HBr also reacts with H_2SO_4)

Hence, HI is the best reductant.

Q. 16. Why does the following reaction occur?

$XeO_6^{4-}(aq) + 2F^-(aq) + 6H^+(aq) \rightarrow XeO_3(g) + F_2(g) + 3H_2O(l)$

What conclusion about the compound Na_4XeO_6 (of which XeO_6^{4-} is a part) can be drawn from the reaction.

[NCERT Ex. Q. 7.16, Page 253]

Ans. $XeO_6^{4-}(aq) + 2F^-(aq) + 6H^+(aq) \longrightarrow XeO_3(g) + F_2(g) + 3H_2O(l)$

It is a redox reaction in which xenon (oxidation number 8) from XeO_6^{4-} is reduced to XeO_3 [Oxidation number of Xe = 6]

and F^- is oxidised to F_2 [oxidation number increases from 1 in F^- to 0 in F_2.

Sodium xenate (Na_4XeO_6) is an ionic compound in which oxidation number of sodium does not undergo a change and it is xenon whose oxidation no. changes from + 8 to + 6. It is a powerful oxidising agent which oxidises even F^- to F_2.

Q. 17. Consider the reactions:

(a) $H_3PO_2(aq) + 4\,AgNO_3(aq) + 2\,H_2O(l) \rightarrow H_3PO_4(aq) + 4\,Ag(s) + 4HNO_3(aq)$

(b) $H_3PO_2(aq) + 2CuSO_4(aq) + 2\,H_2O(l) \rightarrow H_3PO_4(aq) + 2Cu(s) + H_2SO_4(aq)$

(c) $C_6H_5CHO(l) + 2[Ag(NH_3)_2]^+(aq) + 3OH^-(aq) \rightarrow C_6H_5COO^-(aq) + 2Ag(s) + 4NH_3(aq) + 2\,H_2O(l)$

(d) $C_6H_5CHO(l) + 2Cu^{2+}(aq) + 5OH^-(aq) \rightarrow$ No change observed.

What inference do you draw about the behaviour of Ag^+ and Cu^{2+} from these reactions?

[NCERT Ex. Q. 7.17, Page 253]

Ans. (a) $H_3PO_2(aq) + 4AgNO_3(aq) + 2H_2O(l) \rightarrow H_3PO_4(aq) + 4Ag(s) + 4HNO_3(aq)$

In this reaction, Ag^+ ions have been reduced to Ag(s). It oxidises H_3PO_2 to H_3PO_4.

(b) $H_3PO_2(aq) + 2CuSO_4(aq) + 2H_2O(l) \rightarrow H_3PO_4(aq) + 2Cu(s) + H_2SO_4(aq)$

In this reaction, Cu^{++} ions are reduced to Cu(s). Thus, it acts as an oxidising agent and oxidises H_3PO_2 to H_3PO_4.

(c) $C_6H_5CHO(l) + 2[Ag(NH_3)_2]^+(aq) + 3OH^-(aq) \rightarrow C_6H_5COO^-(aq) + 2Ag(s) + 4NH_3(aq) + 2H_2O(l)$

In this reaction, Ag^+ present in the complex $[Ag(NH_3)_2]^+$ is reduced to Ag(s). It oxidises C_6H_5CHO to $C_6H_5COO^-$.

(d) $C_6H_5CHO(l) + 2Cu^{2+}(aq) + 5OH^-(aq) \rightarrow$ No change observed.

Cu^{2+} ions cannot oxidise C_6H_5CHO to C_6H_5COOH.

This indicates that Ag^+ is a stronger oxidising agent than Cu^{2+}.

Q. 18. Balance the following redox reactions by ion – electron method:

(a) $MnO_4^-(aq) + I^-(aq) \rightarrow MnO_2(s) + I_2(s)$ (in basic medium)

(b) $MnO_4^-(aq) + SO_2(g) \rightarrow Mn^{2+}(aq) + HSO_4^-(aq)$ (in acidic solution)

(c) $H_2O_2(aq) + Fe^{2+}(aq) \rightarrow Fe^{3+}(aq) + H_2O(l)$ (in acidic solution)

(d) $Cr_2O_7^{2-} + SO_2(g) \rightarrow Cr^{3+}(aq) + SO_4^{2-}(aq)$ (in acidic solution) **[NCERT Ex. Q. 7.18, Page 254]**

Ans. (a) Try yourself and refer Q. 3. of SATQ-II of topic-2.

(b) Step-1 : First we write the skeletal ionic equation,

$$\overset{+7\ -2}{MnO_4^-}(aq) + \overset{+4\ -2}{SO_2}(g) \rightarrow \overset{+2\ +2}{Mn}(aq) + \overset{+1\ +6\ -1}{HSO_4^-}(aq)$$

Step-2 : The two half reactions are:

Oxidation half-reaction:

$$\overset{+4}{S}O_2(g) \rightarrow H\overset{+6}{S}O_4^-(aq)$$

Reduction half-reaction

$$\overset{+7}{Mn}O_4^-(aq) \rightarrow \overset{+2}{Mn}^{2+}(aq)$$

Step-3: To balance O-atoms in oxidation half reaction, add two H_2O molecules to the left side.

$$SO_2(g) + 2H_2O(l) \rightarrow HSO_4^-(aq)$$

To balance O-atoms in reduction half-reaction, we add 4 H_2O molecules to the right side.

$$MnO_4^-(aq) \rightarrow Mn^{2+}(aq) + 4H_2O(l)$$

To balance the H-atoms in oxidation half-reaction, we add $3H^+$ ions to the right side

$$SO_2(g) + 2H_2O(l) \rightarrow HSO_4^-(aq) + 3H^+(aq)$$

To balance the H-atoms in reduction half-reaction, we add $8H^+$ ions to the left side.

$$MnO_4^-(aq) + 8H^+(aq) \rightarrow Mn^{2+}(aq) + 4H_2O(l)$$

Step-4: Balance the charges of two half reactions:

$$\overset{+4}{S}O_2(g) + 2H_2O(l) \rightarrow H\overset{+6}{S}O_4^-(aq) + 3H^+(aq) + 2e^- \quad [\times 5]$$

$$\overset{+7}{Mn}O_4^-(aq) + 8H^+(aq) + 5e^- \rightarrow Mn^{2+}(aq) + 4H_2O(l) \quad [\times 2]$$

Now, to equalize the number of electrons, we multiply the oxidation half reaction by 5 and reduction half reaction by 2, then we get,

$$5SO_2(g) + 10H_2O(l) \rightarrow 5HSO_4^-(aq) + 15H^+(aq) + 10e^-$$

$$2MnO_4^-(aq) + 16H^+(aq) + 10e^- \rightarrow 2Mn^{2+}(aq) + 8H_2O(l)$$

Step-5 : Add two half reactions to obtain the net reaction after cancelling the electrons and other species on both sides. The net equation is:

$$5SO_2(g) + 2MnO_4^-(aq) + H^+(aq) + 2H_2O(l) \rightarrow 5HSO_4^-(aq) + 2Mn^{2+}(aq)$$

A final verification shows that the equation is balanced in respect of the number of atoms and charges on both sides.

(c) Try yourself as method given in Q. 18(b) part.

(d) Try yourself as method given in Q. 18(b) part.

Q. 19. Balance the following equations in basic medium by ion-electron method and oxidation number methods and identify the oxidising agent and the reducing agent.

(a) $P_4(s) + OH^-(aq) \rightarrow PH_3(g) + HPO_2^-(aq)$

(b) $N_2H_4(l) + ClO_3^-(aq) \rightarrow NO(g) + Cl^-(aq)$

(c) $Cl_2O_7(g) + H_2O_2(aq) \rightarrow ClO_2^-(aq) + O_2(g) + H^+$

[NCERT Ex. Q. 7.19, Page 254]

Ans. (a) $P_4(s) + OH^-(aq) \rightarrow PH_3(g) + H_2PO_2^-(aq)$

Ion electron method

Reduction half Reaction

$$\overset{0}{P_4}(s) \longrightarrow \overset{-3}{P}H_3(g) \quad ...(i)$$

Balance P atoms $P_4(s) \longrightarrow 4PH_3(g)$ ...(ii)

Balance oxidation number by adding electrons,

$$P_4(s) + 12e^- \longrightarrow 4PH_3(g) \quad ...(iii)$$

Balance charge by adding OH^- ions.

$$P_4(s) + 12e^- \longrightarrow 4PH_3(g) + 12OH^-(aq) \quad ...(iv)$$

Balance 'O' atoms by adding H_2O

$$12H_2O + P_4(s) + 12e^- \longrightarrow 4PH_3(g) + 12OH^-(aq) \quad ...(v)$$

Oxidation half reaction

$$P_4(s) \longrightarrow H_2PO_2^-(aq) \quad ...(vi)$$

Balance P atoms,

$$\overset{0}{P_4}(s) \longrightarrow 4H_2\overset{+1}{P}O_2^-(aq) \quad ...(vii)$$

Balance oxidation number by adding electrons,

$$P_4(s) \longrightarrow 4H_2PO_2^-(aq) + 4e^- \quad ...(viii)$$

Balance charge by adding OH^- ions

$$P_4(s) + 8OH^-(aq) \longrightarrow 4H_2PO_2^-(aq) + 4e^- \quad ...(ix)$$

Oxygen and hydrogen are balanced automatically.

Multiply above equation by 3 to equalise number of electrons gain and lose and add it to equation (v), we get,

$$4P_4(s) + 12OH^-(aq) + 12H_2O(l) \longrightarrow 4PH_3(g) + 12H_2PO_2^-(aq)$$

or $P_4(s) + 3OH^-(aq) + 3H_2O(l) \longrightarrow PH_3(g) + 3H_2PO_2^-(aq)$

Oxidation number method

$$\overset{0}{P_4}(s) + OH^-(aq) \longrightarrow \overset{-3+1}{PH_3}(g) + \overset{+1\,+1\,-2}{H_2PO_2}(aq)$$

O.N. decreases by 3 per P atom (3 electron gain)

O.N. increases by 1 per P atom (1 electron loss)

In a balanced chemical reaction, loss of electrons = gain of electrons so multiply $H_2PO_2^-$ by 3 and we get

$$P_4(s) + OH^-(aq) \longrightarrow PH_3(g) + 3H_2PO_2^-$$

Multiply OH^- by 3 to balance the charge

$$P_4(s) + 3OH^-(aq) \longrightarrow PH_3(g) + 3H_2PO_2^-(aq)$$

Balance H by adding $3H_2O$ to left side

$$P_4(s) + 3H_2O(l) + 3OH^-(aq) \longrightarrow PH_3(g) + 3H_2PO_2^-(aq)$$

In this equation, P_4 acts both as an oxidising agent as well as a reducing agent. **(5)**

(b) $N_2H_4(l) + ClO_3^-(aq) \longrightarrow NO(g) + Cl^-(g)$

Ion electron method

Oxidation half reaction,

$$\overset{-2}{N_2H_4}(l) \longrightarrow \overset{+2}{NO}(g)$$

Balance N atoms,

$$N_2H_4(l) \longrightarrow 2NO(g)$$

Balance O.N. by adding electrons,

$$N_2H_4(l) \longrightarrow 2NO(g) + 8e^-$$

Balance charge by adding OH– ions,

$$N_2H_4(l) + 8OH^-(aq) \longrightarrow 2NO(g) + 8e^-$$

Balance O-atoms By adding H_2O

$$N_2H_4(l) + 8OH^-(aq) \longrightarrow 2NO(g) + 6H_2O + 8e^- \quad ...(i)$$

Reduction half reaction

$$\overset{+5}{ClO_3^-}(aq) \longrightarrow \overset{-1}{Cl^-}(aq)$$

Balance O.N. by adding electrons,

$$ClO_3^-(aq) + 6e^- \longrightarrow Cl^-$$

Balance charge by adding OH^- ions,

$$ClO_3^-(aq) + 6e^- \longrightarrow Cl^-(aq) + 6OH^-(aq)$$

Balance O-atoms by adding H_2O

$$ClO_3^-(aq) + 3H_2O(l) + 6e^- \longrightarrow Cl^-(aq) + 6OH^-(aq) \quad ...(ii)$$

To equalise electrons lost or gained multiply equation (i) by 3 and (ii) by 4 respectively and add to get

$$3N_2H_4(l) + 4ClO^-_3(l) \longrightarrow 6NO(g) + 4Cl^-(aq) + 6H_2O(l)$$

This equation is the balanced redox reaction.

Oxidation number method

$$\overset{-2}{N_2H_4}(l) + \overset{+5}{ClO_3^-}(aq) \longrightarrow \overset{+2}{NO}(g) + \overset{-1}{Cl^-}(aq)$$

O.N. increases by 4 per P atom

O.N. decreases by 6 per Cl atom

Multiply NO by 2 because in N_2H_4 there are 2N atoms.

$$N_2H_4(l) + ClO_3^-(aq) \longrightarrow 2NO(g) + Cl^-(aq)$$

Total increase in oxidation number of N = 2 × 4 = 8 ($8e^-$ lost)

Total decrease in oxidation number of Cl = 1 × 6 = 6 ($6e^-$ gain)

Therefore, to balance increase or decrease in oxidation number, multiply N_2H_4 by 3, 2NO by 3 and ClO_3^-, Cl^- by 4.

$$3N_2H_4(l) + 4ClO_3^-(aq) \longrightarrow 6NO(g) + 4Cl^-(aq)$$

Balance O and H atoms by adding $6H_2O$ to right side

$$3N_2H_4(l) + 4ClO_3^-(aq) \longrightarrow 6NO(g) + 4Cl^-(aq) + 6H_2O(l)$$

In this reaction, N_2H_4 acts as a reducing agent and ClO_3^- acts as an oxidising agent.

(c) $Cl_2O_7(g) + H_2O_2(aq) \longrightarrow ClO_2^-(g) + O_2(g) + H^+$

Ion electron method

Reduction half reaction,

Multiply ClO_2^- by 2 because in Cl_2O_7 there are 2 Cl atoms.

$$\overset{+7}{Cl_2O_7}(g) \longrightarrow \overset{+3}{2ClO_2^-}(ag)$$

Balance oxidation number by adding electrons,

$$Cl_2O_7(g) + 8e^- \longrightarrow 2ClO_2^-(aq)$$

Balance charge by adding OH^- ions,

$$Cl_2O_7(g) + 8e^- \longrightarrow 2ClO_2^-(aq) + 6OH^-$$

Balance O-atoms by adding H_2O to left side,

$$Cl_2O_7(g) + 3H_2O(l) + 8e^- \longrightarrow 2ClO_2^-(aq) + 6OH^- \quad ...(i)$$

Oxidation half reaction,

$$\overset{-1}{H_2O_2}(aq) \longrightarrow \overset{0}{O_2}(g)$$

Balance oxidation number by adding electrons,

$$H_2O_2(aq) \longrightarrow O_2(g) + 2e^-$$

Balance charge by adding OH^- ions,

$$H_2O_2(aq) + 2OH^-(aq) \longrightarrow O_2(g) + 2e^-$$

Balance H atoms by adding H_2O to right side

$$H_2O_2(aq) + 2OH^-(aq) \longrightarrow O_2(g) + 2H_2O(l) + 2e^- \quad ...(ii)$$

Multiply equation (ii) by 4 to equalise electrons gained and lost

$$4H_2O_2(aq) + 8OH^-(aq) \longrightarrow 4O_2(g) + 8H_2O + 8e^- \quad ...(iii)$$

Add equation (i) and (iii), we get

$$Cl_2O_7(g) + 4H_2O_2(aq) + 2OH^-(aq) \longrightarrow 2ClO_2^-(aq) + 5H_2O(l) + 4O_2(g)$$

Oxidation number method

$$\overset{+7\ -2}{Cl_2O_7}(g) + \overset{+1\ -1}{H_2O_2^{-1}}(aq) \longrightarrow \overset{+3\ -2}{ClO_2}(g) + \overset{0}{O_2}(g)$$

O.N. increases by 1 per O atom

O.N. decreases by 4 per Cl atom

Multiply ClO_2 by 2 because in Cl_2O_7, two Cl atoms are present.

$$Cl_2O_7(g) + H_2O_2(aq) \longrightarrow 2ClO_2^-(g) + O_2(g)$$

Total decrease in oxidation number of

$$Cl = 2 \times 4 = 8 \ (8\bar{e} \text{ gain})$$

Total increase in oxidation number of

$$O = 1 \times 2 = 2 \ (2\bar{e} \text{ lost})$$

So, to balance increase or decrease in oxidation number, multiply H_2O and O_2 by 4

$$Cl_2O_7(g) + 4H_2O_2(aq) \rightarrow 2ClO_2^-(aq) + 4O_2(g)$$

Balance charge by adding $2OH^-$ to left side of the reaction,

$$Cl_2O_7(g) + 4H_2O_2(aq) + 2OH^-(aq) \rightarrow 2ClO_2^-(aq) + 4O_2(g)$$

Balance H and O by adding 5 H_2O molecules to right side

$$Cl_2O_7(g) + 4H_2O_2(aq) + 2OH^-(aq) \rightarrow 2ClO_2^-(g) + 4O_2(g) + 5H_2O(l)$$

In this reaction, Cl_2O_7 acts as oxidising agent and H_2O_2 acts as reducing agent. (5)

Q. 20. What sorts of information can you draw from the following reaction?

$(CN)_2(g) + 2OH^-(aq) \rightarrow CN^-(aq) + CNO^-(aq) + H_2O(l)$

[NCERT Ex. Q. 7.20, Page 254]

Ans. Assign oxidation number to carbon atoms in the given reaction:

$$(\overset{+3}{C}N)_2(g) + 2OH^-(aq) \longrightarrow \overset{+2}{C}N^-(aq) + \overset{+4}{C}NO^-(aq) + H_2O(l)$$

O.N. decreases

O.N. increases

The following informations can be drawn from the above reaction:

(i) Decomposition of cyanogen in the cyanide ion (CN^-) and cyanate ion (CNO^-) occurs in basic medium.

(ii) Cyanogen $(CN)_2$ acts as both reducing agent as well as oxidising agent.

(iii) The reaction is an example of disproportionation reaction (a special type of redox reaction).

(iv) Cyanogen $(CN)_2$ is called pseudohalogen while CN^-, CNO^- ions are called pseudohalide ions.

Q. 21. The Mn^{3+} ion is unstable in solution and undergoes disproportionation to give Mn^{2+}, MnO_2 and H^+ ion. Write a balanced ionic equation for the reaction.

[NCERT Ex. Q. 7.21, Page 254]

Ans. The skeletal ionic equation is,

$$Mn^{3+}(aq) \longrightarrow Mn^{2+}(aq) + MnO_2(s) + H^+(aq)$$

Reduction half reaction

$$Mn^{3+}(aq) + e^- \longrightarrow Mn^{2+}$$

Oxidation half reaction

$$Mn^{3+}(aq) \longrightarrow \overset{+4}{Mn}O_2 + e^-$$

Balance charge by adding $4H^+$ to right side and then balance O atoms by adding $2H_2O$ to left side in oxidation half reaction

$$Mn^{3+}(aq) + 2H_2O(l) \longrightarrow MnO_2(s) + e^- + 4H^+(aq)$$

By adding both equations, we get

$$2Mn^{3+}(aq) + 2H_2O(l) \longrightarrow Mn^{2+} + MnO_2(s) + 4H^+(aq)$$

This represents the balanced redox reaction (disproportionation reaction).

Q. 22. Consider the elements:

Cs, Ne, I and F

(a) Identify the element that exhibits only negative oxidation state.

(b) Identify the element that exhibits only positive oxidation state.

(c) Identify the element that exhibits only positive and negative oxidation states.

(d) Identify the element which exhibits neither the negative nor does the positive oxidation state.

[NCERT Ex. Q. 7.22, Page 254]

Ans. (a) F exhibits only negative oxidation state as it is most electronegative element.

(b) Cs exhibits only positive oxidation state as it is most electropositive element.

(c) I exhibits both positive and negative oxidation states due to presence of vacant *d*-orbital.

(d) Ne exhibits neither the negative nor the positive oxidation state as it is an inert gas.

Q. 23. Chlorine is used to purify drinking water. Excess of chlorine is removed by treating with sulphur dioxide. Present a balanced equation for this redox change taking place in water.

[NCERT Ex. Q. 7.23, Page 254]

Ans.

$$\overset{0}{Cl_2}(aq) + \overset{+4}{S}O_2(aq) + H_2O(l) \longrightarrow \overset{-1}{Cl^-}(aq) + \overset{+6}{S}O_4^{2-}(aq)$$

O.N. decreases by 1 per Cl atom

O.N. increases by 2 per S atom

Multiply Cl^- by 2 because in Cl_2 there are two chlorine atoms.

$$Cl_2(aq) + SO_2(aq) + H_2O(l) \longrightarrow 2Cl^-(aq) + SO_4^{2-}(aq)$$

Balance first charge by adding $4H^+$ to right side and then multiply H_2O by 2.

$$Cl_2(aq) + SO_2(aq) + 2H_2O(l) \longrightarrow 2Cl^-(aq) + SO_4^{2-} + 4H^+$$

This represents the balanced redox reaction.

Q. 24 Refer to the periodic table given in you book and now answer the following questions:

(a) Select the possible non metals that can show disproportionation reaction.

(b) Select three metals that can show disproportionation reaction.

[NCERT Ex. Q. 24, Page 254]

Ans. (a) Phosphorus, sulphur and chlorine can show disproportionation reactions in the alkaline medium.

$$\overset{0}{P_4}(s) + 3OH^-(aq) + 3H_2O(l) \rightarrow \overset{-3}{P}H_3(g) + 3H_2\overset{+1}{P}O_2^-(aq)$$

$$\overset{0}{S_8}(s) + 12OH^-(aq) \rightarrow 4\overset{-2}{S^{2-}}(aq) + 2\overset{+2}{S_2}O_3^{2-}(aq) + 6H_2O(l)$$

$$\overset{0}{Cl_2}(g) + 2OH^-(aq) \rightarrow \overset{+1}{Cl}O^-(aq) + \overset{-1}{Cl^-}(aq) + H_2O(l)$$

(b) Copper, manganese and gallium can show disproportionation reactions.

$$2\overset{+1}{Cu^+}(aq) \rightarrow \overset{+2}{Cu^{2+}}(aq) + \overset{0}{Cu}(s)$$

$$2\overset{+3}{Mn^{3+}}(aq) + 2H_2O(l) \rightarrow \overset{+4}{Mn}O_2(s) + \overset{+2}{Mn^{2+}}(aq) + 4H^+$$

$$3\overset{+1}{Ga^+}(aq) \rightarrow \overset{+3}{Ga^{3+}}(aq) + 2\overset{0}{Ga}(s)$$

Q. 25. In Ostwald's process for the manufacture of nitric acid, the first step involves the oxidation of ammonia gas by oxygen gas to give nitric oxide gas and steam. What is the maximum weight of nitric oxide that can be obtained starting only with 10.00 g of ammonia and 20.00 g of oxygen? [NCERT Ex. Q. 7.25, Page 254]

Ans.

$$\underset{\substack{4 \times 17 \\ = 68\text{ g}}}{4NH_3(g)} + \underset{\substack{5 \times 32 \\ = 160\text{ g}}}{5O_2(g)} \xrightarrow[\text{Pt}]{1100\text{K}} \underset{\substack{4 \times 30 \\ = 120\text{ g}}}{4NO(g)} + 6H_2O(g)$$

68 g NH_3 reacts with = 160 g O_2

1 g NH_3 reacts with = $\frac{160 \times 1}{68}$ g O_2

$\therefore$ 10 g NH_3 reacts with = $\frac{160 \times 10}{68}$ = 23.5 g O_2

But available amount of O_2 is 20.0 g which is less than the amount which is required to react with 10 g NH_3. So, O_2 is the limiting reagent and it limits the amount of NO produced. From the above balanced equation,

$\because$ 160 g of O_2 produces 120 g NO

1 g of O_2 produces $\frac{120 \times 1}{160}$ g NO

$\therefore$ 20 g of O_2 will produce $\frac{120 \times 1 \times 20}{160}$ = 15g NO

Q. 26. Using the standard electrode potentials given below predict if the reaction between the following is feasible:

(a) Fe^{3+}(aq) and I^-(aq) (b) Ag^+(aq) and Cu(s)

(c) Fe^{3+}(aq) and Cu(s) (d) Ag(s) and Fe^{3+}(aq).

(e) Br_2(aq) and Fe^{2+}(aq).

Given, $E^\circ_{I_2/I^-} = +0.54V$

$E^\circ_{Fe^{3+}/Fe^{2+}} = +0.77V$

$E^\circ_{Cu^{2+}/Cu} = +0.34V$

$E^\circ_{Ag^+/Ag} = +0.80V$

$E^\circ_{Br_2/Br^-} = +1.09V$

[NCERT Ex. Q. 7.26, Page 254]

Ans. (a) Fe^{3+}(aq) and I^-(aq)

Possible reaction between Fe^{3+}(aq) and I^-(aq) is given as below.

$$2Fe^{3+}(aq) + 2I^-(aq) \rightarrow 2Fe^{2+}(aq) + I_2(s)$$

Oxidation half reaction $2I^-(aq) \rightarrow I_2(s) + 2e^-$; $E^\circ = -0.54$ V

Reduction half reaction

$2Fe^{3+}(aq) + 2e^- \rightarrow 2Fe^{2+}(aq)$; $E^\circ = +0.77$ V

Overall reaction:

$2Fe^{3+}(aq) + 2I^-(aq) \rightarrow 2Fe^{2+}(aq) + I_2(s)$; $E^\circ = +0.23$ V

Positive emf indicates that the reaction is feasible.

(b) The possible reaction between Ag^+(aq) and Cu(s) is given as below :

$$2Ag^+(aq) + Cu(s) \rightarrow Cu^{2+}(aq) + 2Ag(aq)$$

Separate the equation into two half reactions and write electrode potential for each half reaction.

Oxidation half reaction:

$Cu(s) \rightarrow Cu^{2+}(aq) + 2e^-$; $E^\circ = -0.34$ V

Reduction half reaction:

$2Ag^+(aq) + 2e^- \rightarrow 2Ag(s)$:$E^\circ = +0.80$ V

Overall reaction,

$Cu(s) + 2Ag^+(aq) \rightarrow Cu^{2+}(aq) + 2Ag$; $E^\circ = +0.46$ V

Positive emf indicates that the reaction is feasible.

(c) Possible reaction between Fe^{3+}(aq) and Cu(s) is given as below :

$$Fe^{3+}(aq) + Cu(s) \rightarrow Fe^{2+}(aq) + Cu^{2+}(aq)$$

Oxidation half reaction:

$Cu(s) \rightarrow Cu^{2+}(aq) + 2e^-$; $E^\circ = -0.34$ V

Reduction half reaction:

$Fe^{3+}(aq) + e^- \rightarrow Fe^{2+}(aq) \times 2$; $E^\circ = +0.77$ V

Overall reaction;

$Cu(s) + 2Fe^{3+}(aq) \rightarrow Cu^{2+}(aq) + 2Fe^{2+}(aq)$; $E^\circ = +0.43$ V

Positive emf indicates that the reaction is feasible.

(d) Possible reaction between Fe^{3+}(aq) and Ag(s) is given as below :

$$Ag(s) + Fe^{3+}(aq) \rightarrow Ag^+(aq) + Fe^+(aq)$$

Oxidation half reaction;

$Ag(s) \rightarrow Ag^+(aq) + e^-$; $E^\circ = -0.80$ V

Reduction half reaction ;

$Fe^{3+}(aq) + e^- \rightarrow Fe^{2+}(aq)$; $E^\circ = 0.77$ V

Overall reaction:

$Ag(s) + Fe^{3+}(aq) \rightarrow Ag^+(aq) + Fe^{2+}(aq)$; $E^\circ = -0.03$ V

Negative emf indicates that the reaction is not feasible.

(e) Possible reaction between Br_2(aq) and Fe^{2+}(aq) is given below:

$Br_2(aq) + 2Fe^{2+}(aq) \rightarrow 2Br^- + 2Fe^{3+}(aq)$

Oxidation half reaction

$Fe^{2+}(aq) \rightarrow Fe^{3+}(aq) + e^-] \times 2$; $E^\circ = -0.77$ V

Reduction half reaction;

$Br_2(aq) + 2e^- \rightarrow 2Br^-(aq)$; $E° = +1.09$ V

Overall reaction;

$2Fe^{2+}(aq) + Br_2(aq) \rightarrow 2Fe^{3+}(aq) + 2Br^-(aq)$;

$E° = +0.32$ V

Positive emf indicates that the reaction is feasible.

Q. 27. Predict the products of electrolysis in each of following:

(i) An aqueous solution of $AgNO_3$ with silver electrodes

(ii) An aqueous solution $AgNO_3$ with platinum electrodes

(iii) A dilute solution of H_2SO_4 with platinum electrodes

(iv) An aqueous solution of $CuCl_2$ with platinum electrodes. [NCERT Ex. Q. 7.27, Page 255]

Ans. (i) Electrolysis of aqueous solution of $AgNO_3$ with silver electrodes is given as below.

At cathode: $Ag^+ + e^- \rightarrow Ag$

At anode: $Ag \rightarrow Ag^+ + e^-$

(ii) Electrolysis of aqueous solution of $AgNO_3$ using platinum electrodes is given as below.

At cathode: $Ag^+ + e^- \rightarrow Ag$; since reduction potential of Ag is higher than water.

At anode: $OH^- \rightarrow OH + e^-$,

$4OH^- \rightarrow 2H_2O + O_2$ since reduction potential of water is less than nitrate ion. Thus, oxygen gas will be liberated.

(iii)Electrolysis of dil. H_2SO_4 with platinum electrodes is given as below.

$$H_2SO_4 \rightarrow 2H^+(aq) + SO_4^{-2}(aq)$$

$$H_2O \rightarrow H^+ + OH^-$$

At cathode: $2H^+ + 2e^- \rightarrow H_2$, hydrogen gas will be liberated.

At anode: $OH^- \rightarrow OH + e^-$,

$$4OH \rightarrow 2H_2O + O_2$$

since reduction potential of water is less than sulphate ion. Thus, oxygen gas will be liberated.

(iv) Electrolysis of $CuCl_2$ (aq) with platinum electrodes is given below.

$$CuCl_2 \rightarrow Cu^2 + 2Cl^-$$

$$H_2O \rightarrow H^+ + OH^-$$

At cathode: $Cu^{2+} + 2e^- \rightarrow Cu$, copper will be liberated as copper has higher reduction potential than water.

At anode: $2Cl^- \rightarrow Cl_2 + 2e^-$, chlorine will be discharged due to over-voltage.

Q. 28. Arrange the following metals in the order in which they displace each other from the solution of their salts. Al, Cu, Fe, Mg and Zn. [NCERT Ex. Q. 7.28, Page 255]

Ans. This is based upon the relative positions of these metals in the activity series. The metal placed lower in the series can displace the metals occupying a higher position present as its salt. on this basis, the correct order is:

Mg > Al > Zn > Fe > Cu > Ag.

Q. 29. Given the standard electrode potentials,
$K^+/K = -2.93V$, $Ag^+/Ag = 0.80V$,
$Hg^{2+}/Hg = 0.79V$
$Mg^{2+}/Mg = -2.37V$, $Cr^{3+}/Cr = -0.74V$
arrange these metals in their increasing order of reducing power. [NCERT Ex. Q. 7.29, Page 255]

Ans. Lower the reduction potential, more easily the metal is oxidised and so greater is the reducing power. Hence, increasing order of reducing power will be Ag < Hg < Cr < Mg < K.

Q. 30. Depict the galvanic cell in which the reaction $Zn(s) + 2Ag^+(aq) \rightarrow Zn^{2+}(aq) + 2Ag(s)$ takes place. Further show:

(i) which of the electrode is negatively charged,

(ii) the carriers of the current in the cell, and

(iii) individual reaction at each electrode.

[NCERT Ex. Q. 7.30, Page 255]

Ans. For the reaction,

$$Zn(s) + 2Ag^+(aq) \rightarrow Zn^{2+}(aq) + 2Ag(s)$$

Cell representation is:

$$\underset{\text{Anode}}{Zn|Zn^{2+}(aq)} \ \underset{\text{Salt bridge}}{||} \ \underset{\text{Cathode}}{Ag^+(aq)|Ag}$$

(i) Zinc acts as anode as oxidation occurs at the zinc electrode so it is negatively charged.

(ii) Since electrons flow from zinc electrode (anode) to silver electrode (cathode), so current will flow from silver electrode (cathode) towards zinc electrode (anode) through wires fitted externally.

(iii) At anode:

Oxidation half reaction:

$Zn \rightarrow Zn^{2+} + 2e^-$(Loss of electrons)

Reduction half reaction :

$Ag^+ + e^- \rightarrow Ag$(Gain of electron)

ORGANIC CHEMISTRY-SOME BASIC PRINCIPLES AND TECHNIQUES

CHAPTER 8

Introduction

- The hydrides of carbon (hydrocarbons) and their derivatives are called organic compounds. The branch of chemistry which deals with these compounds is called organic chemistry.
- Berzilius (1808) defined organic chemistry as the chemistry of substances found in living matter and gave the vital force theory. Urea is the first organic compound synthesised in laboratory by F. Wohler in 1828.
- **Properties:** Organic compounds may be gases, liquids or solids. Being covalent in nature, these have low boiling point and melting point and soluble in organic solvents. These are generally volatile and inflammable. They do not conduct electricity because of the absence of free ions. They possess distinct colour and odour.
- **Reasons for large number of organic compounds:**

(i) Catenation: It is the tendency of self-combination or self linkage of atoms of an element to form a ring or chain, and carbon shows maximum catenation property. A carbon atom can combine with other carbon atoms by single, double or triple bonds. Thus, it forms more compounds than the others.

(ii) Tetravalency: Carbon being tetravalent is capable of bonding with four other C atoms or some other monovalent atoms.

Bond angles in sp^3 hybridised C is 109°28′, in sp^2 hybridised C is 120° and in sp hybridised C is 180°.

The C–C, C = C and C ≡ C bond lengths are 1.54 Å, 1.34 Å and 1.20 Å respectively (the shorter the bond, greater is its strength). Also, greater the bond strength, greater is the bond energy.

(iii) Small size: Furthermore, these compounds are exceptionally stable because of the small size of carbon. Carbon forms straight, branched and ring structured compounds.

- The three dimensional structure of organic molecule can be represented on paper by using wedge-and-dash representation. In these formulas, the solid wedge (◢) is used to show a bond coming out of the paper towards the observer and dashed wedge (||||||||) is used to show a bond going away from the observer.

Classification of Organic Compound

- Organic compounds are broadly classified as follows:

Organic compounds
- Acyclic or open chain compounds
- Cyclic or closed chain or ring compounds
  - Alicylic
    - Homocyclic or carbocyclic
    - Heterocyclic or non-aromatic
  - Aromatic
    - Benzenoid
    - Heterocyclic aromatic
    - Non-benzenoid

- **Functional Group:** The atom or group of atoms e.g., –COOH, – CHO, which is responsible for the chemical properties of the molecule, is called functional group. Double and triple bonds are also functional groups.

  R – ← functional group
- **Homologous series**: Homologous series is defined as a family or group of structurally similar organic compounds all members of which contain the same functional group, show a gradation in physical and similarity in chemical properties and any two adjacent members of which differ by $-CH_2$ group. The individual members of this group are called homologous and the phenomenon is called homology.

Nomenclature of Organic Compounds

- **Common name (Common system)**: Before the IUPAC system of nomenclature, organic compounds were named after the sources of origin, for example, urea was so named because it was obtained from the urine of mammals.

Scan to know more about this topic

IUPAC Nomencalture

IUPAC (International Union of Pure and Applied Chemistry) System:

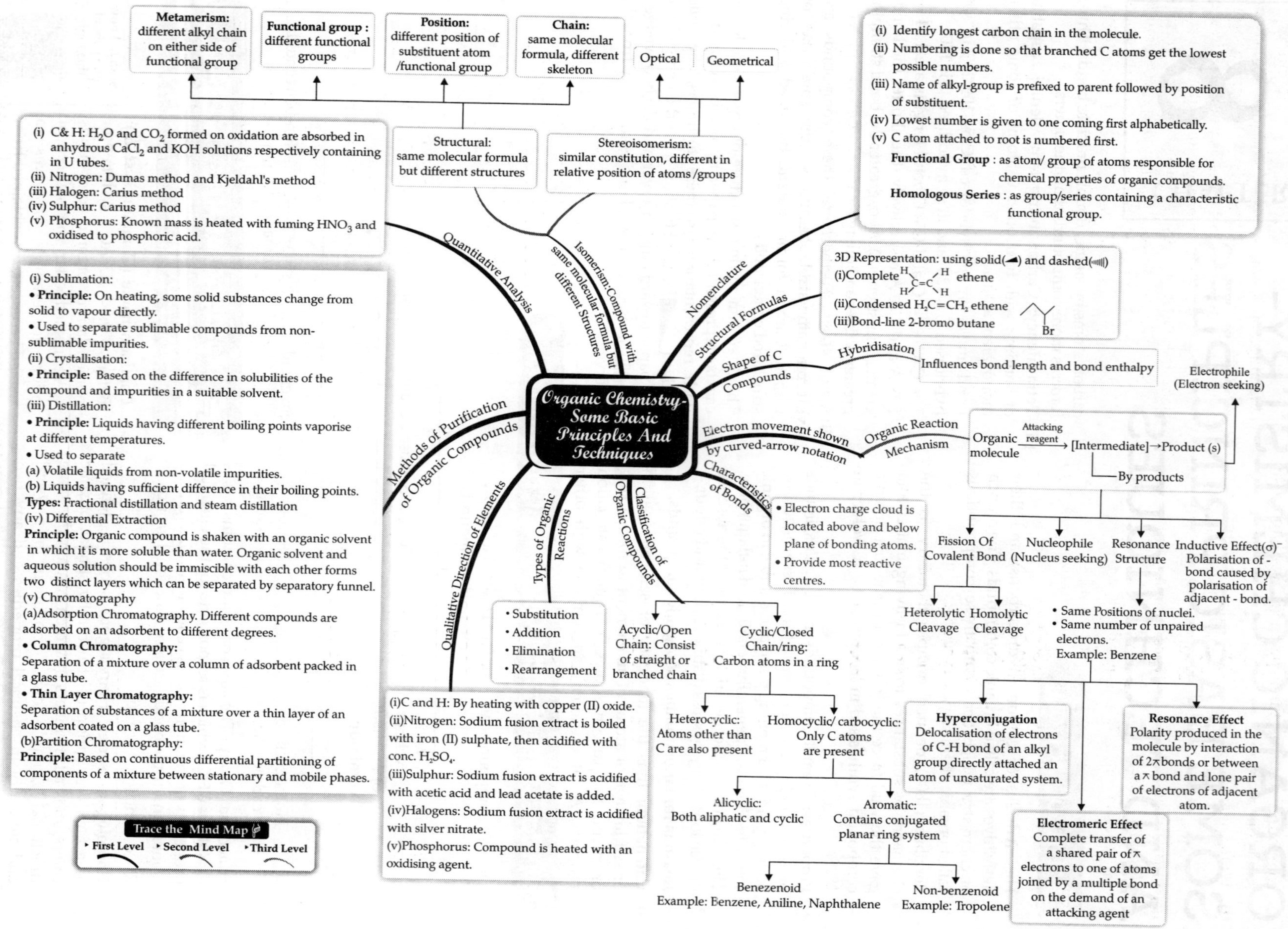
Organic Chemistry- Some Basic Principles And Techniques
Nomenclature
(i) Identify longest carbon chain in the molecule.
(ii) Numbering is done so that branched C atoms get the lowest possible numbers.
(iii) Name of alkyl-group is prefixed to parent followed by position of substituent.
(iv) Lowest number is given to one coming first alphabetically.
(v) C atom attached to root is numbered first.
Functional Group : as atom/ group of atoms responsible for chemical properties of organic compounds.
Homologous Series : as group/series containing a characteristic functional group.
Structural Formulas
3D Representation: using solid and dashed
(i)Complete ethene
(ii)Condensed $H_2C=CH_2$ ethene
(iii)Bond-line 2-bromo butane
Br
Shape of C Compounds
Hybridisation
Influences bond length and bond enthalpy
Electron movement shown by curved-arrow notation
Organic Reaction Mechanism
Organic molecule
Attacking reagent
[Intermediate]→Product (s)
By products
Electrophile (Electron seeking)
Fission Of Covalent Bond
Heterolytic Cleavage
Homolytic Cleavage
Nucleophile (Nucleus seeking)
Resonance Structure
• Same Positions of nuclei.
• Same number of unpaired electrons.
Example: Benzene
Inductive Effect(σ)
Polarisation of σ-bond caused by polarisation of adjacent σ-bond.
Hyperconjugation
Delocalisation of electrons of C-H bond of an alkyl group directly attached an atom of unsaturated system.
Electromeric Effect
Complete transfer of a shared pair of π electrons to one of atoms joined by a multiple bond on the demand of an attacking agent
Resonance Effect
Polarity produced in the molecule by interaction of 2π bonds or between a π bond and lone pair of electrons of adjacent atom.
Characteristics of Bonds
• Electron charge cloud is located above and below plane of bonding atoms.
• Provide most reactive centres.
Classification of Organic Compounds
Acyclic/Open Chain: Consist of straight or branched chain
Cyclic/Closed Chain/ring: Carbon atoms in a ring
Heterocyclic: Atoms other than C are also present
Homocyclic/ carbocyclic: Only C atoms are present
Alicyclic: Both aliphatic and cyclic
Aromatic: Contains conjugated planar ring system
Benezenoid
Example: Benzene, Aniline, Naphthalene
Non-benzenoid
Example: Tropolene
Types of Organic Reactions
• Substitution
• Addition
• Elimination
• Rearrangement
Qualitative Direction of Elements
(i)C and H: By heating with copper (II) oxide.
(ii)Nitrogen: Sodium fusion extract is boiled with iron (II) sulphate, then acidified with conc. H_2SO_4.
(iii)Sulphur: Sodium fusion extract is acidified with acetic acid and lead acetate is added.
(iv)Halogens: Sodium fusion extract is acidified with silver nitrate.
(v)Phosphorus: Compound is heated with an oxidising agent.
Methods of Purification of Organic Compounds
(i) Sublimation:
• Principle: On heating, some solid substances change from solid to vapour directly.
• Used to separate sublimable compounds from non-sublimable impurities.
(ii) Crystallisation:
• Principle: Based on the difference in solubilities of the compound and impurities in a suitable solvent.
(iii) Distillation:
• Principle: Liquids having different boiling points vaporise at different temperatures.
• Used to separate
(a) Volatile liquids from non-volatile impurities.
(b) Liquids having sufficient difference in their boiling points.
Types: Fractional distillation and steam distillation
(iv) Differential Extraction
Principle: Organic compound is shaken with an organic solvent in which it is more soluble than water. Organic solvent and aqueous solution should be immiscible with each other forms two distinct layers which can be separated by separatory funnel.
(v) Chromatography
(a)Adsorption Chromatography. Different compounds are adsorbed on an adsorbent to different degrees.
• Column Chromatography:
Separation of a mixture over a column of adsorbent packed in a glass tube.
• Thin Layer Chromatography:
Separation of substances of a mixture over a thin layer of an adsorbent coated on a glass tube.
(b)Partition Chromatography:
Principle: Based on continuous differential partitioning of components of a mixture between stationary and mobile phases.
Quantitative Analysis
(i) C& H: H_2O and CO_2 formed on oxidation are absorbed in anhydrous $CaCl_2$ and KOH solutions respectively containing in U tubes.
(ii) Nitrogen: Dumas method and Kjeldahl's method
(iii) Halogen: Carius method
(iv) Sulphur: Carius method
(v) Phosphorus: Known mass is heated with fuming HNO_3 and oxidised to phosphoric acid.
Isomerism:Compound with same molecular formula but different Structures
Structural: same molecular formula but different structures
Metamerism: different alkyl chain on either side of functional group
Functional group : different functional groups
Position: different position of substituent atom /functional group
Chain: same molecular formula, different skeleton
Stereoisomerism: similar constitution, different in relative position of atoms /groups
Optical
Geometrical
Trace the Mind Map
First Level
Second Level
Third Level

According to IUPAC system, the name of an organic compound contains three parts: (i) word root, (ii) suffix, (iii) prefix.

(i) Word root: Word root represents the number of carbon atoms present in the principal chain, which is the longest possible chain of carbon atoms.

(ii) Suffix: Suffix is of two types, primary suffix and secondary suffix.

(a) Primary Suffix: It indicates the type of bond in the carbon chain.

(b) Secondary Suffix: Secondary suffix is used to represent the functional group.

(iii) Prefix: Prefix is a part of IUPAC name which appears before the word root. Prefix is of two types:

(a) Primary prefix: For example, primary prefix cyclo is used to differentiate cyclic compounds.

(b) Secondary prefix: Some functional groups are considered as substituent and denoted by secondary prefixes. For example :

Substituted Group	Secondary prefix
— F	Fluoro
— Cl	Chloro
— Br	Bromo
— NO_2	Nitro
— NO	Nitroso
— CH_3	Methyl
— OCH_3	Methoxy

Naming of Compounds Containing Functional Groups : (i) The longest chain of carbon atoms containing the functional group is numbered in such a manner that the functional group is attached at the carbon atoms possessing lowest possible number in the chain. In case of polyfunctional compounds, one of the functional group is selected as principal functional group and the compound is named on that basis. The choice of principal functional group is made on the basis of order of preference.

The order of decreasing priority for the functional group is :

–COOH, –SO_3H, –COOR (R=alkyl group), COCl, –$CONH_2$, –CN, –HC=O, >C=O, –OH, -NH_2, >C=C<, –C≡C–.

(ii) The number of carbon atoms in parent chain is enoted by proper root word.

(iii) Name the groups attached to the parent chain and prefix with the number of carbon atoms to which they are attached in the parent chain.

(iv) If the compound contains two or more functional groups, numerical prefixes like di, tri, tetra are used and the terminal e from the primary suffix is retained while writing the IUPAC name.

Some functional Groups and Classes of Qrganic Compounds

Class of compounds	Functional group structure	IUPAC group prefix	IUPAC group suffix	Example
Alkanes	>C—C<		-ane	Butane, $CH_3(CH_2)_2CH_3$
Alkenes	>C=C<		-ene	But-1-ene, $CH_2=CHCH_2CH_3$
Alkynes	-C≡C-		-yne	But-1-yne, $CH≡CCH_2CH_3$
Arenes	—			Benzene
Halides	-X (X=F, Cl, Br, I)	halo-		1-Bromobutane, $CH_3(CH_2)_2CH_2Br$
Alcohols	-OH	hydroxy-	-ol	Butan-2-ol, $CH_3CH_2CHOHCH_3$
Aldehydes	-CHO	Formyl, or oxo	-al	Butanal, $CH_3(CH_2)_2CHO$
Ketones	>C=O	oxo-	-one	Butan-2-one, $CH_3CH_2COCH_3$
Nitriles	-C≡N	cyano	nitrile	Pentanenitrile, $CH_3CH_2CH_2CH_2CN$
Ethers	-R-O-R-	alkoxy-		Ethoxyethane, $CH_3CH_2OCH_2CH_3$
Carboxylic acids	-COOH	carboxy	-oic acid	Butanoic acid, $CH_3(CH_2)_2CH_2H$
Carboxylate ions	-COO^-		-oate	Sodium butanoate, $CH_3(CH_2)2CO_2^-Na^+$
Esters	-COOR	alkoxycarbonyl	-oate	Methyl propanoate, $CH_3CH_2COOCH_3$
Acyl halides	-COX (X=F, Cl, Br, I)	halocarbonyl	-oyl halide	Butanoyl chloride, $CH_3(CH_2)_2COCl$

Amines	$-NH_2$, $>NH$, $>N-$	amino-	-amine	Butan-2-amine, $CH_3CHNH_2CH_2CH_3$
Amides	$-CONH_2$, $-CONHR$, $-CONR_2$	-carbamoly	-amide	Butanamide, $CH_3(CH_2)2CONH_2$
Nitro compounds	$-NO_2$	nitro		1-Nitrobutane, $CH_3(CH_2)_3NO_2$
Sulphonic acids	$-SO_3H$	sulpho	sulphonic acid	Methylsulphonic acid CH_3SO_3H

Mnemonics

1. Concept: Functional group preference order
Mnemonics: ASEHA NAKAA Delhi Training Camp
Interpretation: Carboxylic Acid > Sulphonic Acid > Ester > Acid Halides > Acid Amides >Nitrile > Aldehyde > Ketone > Alcohol > Amines = > =

2. Concept: No Preference Functional Group
Mnemonics: NAHE
Interpretation: Nitro, Alkyl / Aryl, Halo, Ethers

3. Concept: Carbon Chain
Mnemonics: Monkey Eat Peeled Bananas
Interpretation: Meth, Eth, Prop, But

4. Concept: To Learn Order of Bond Enthalpy
Mnemonics: To Do Sum
Interpretation: C-C Triple bond > Double bond > Single bond To Learn Bond Length
See Duet Trial -C-C Single bond>Double bond > Triple bond

Isomerism: Two or more compounds having the same molecular formula but different physical and chemical properties are called isomers and this phenomenon is called isomerism. It is of two types-

(1) Structural Isomerism: Structural isomerism is shown by compounds having the same molecular formula but different structural formulae differing in the arrangement of atoms. Structural Isomerism is of four types:

(i) Chain isomerism: When two or more compounds have similar molecular formula but different carbon skeletons, these are referred to as chain isomers and the phenomenon is termed as chain isomerism. For example, C_5H_{12} represents three compounds-

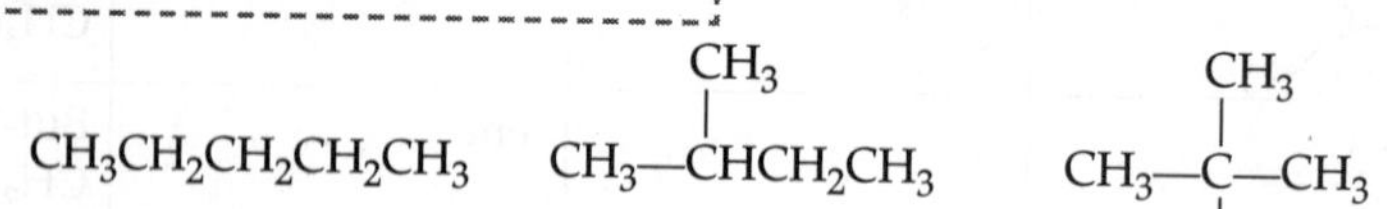

Pentane; Isopentane (2-Methylbutane); Neopentane (2, 2-Dimethyl propane)

(ii) Position Isomerism: When two or more compounds differ in the position of substituent atom or functional group on the carbon skeleton, they are called position isomers and this phenomenon is termed as position isomerism. For example, the molecular formula C_3H_8O represents two alcohols:

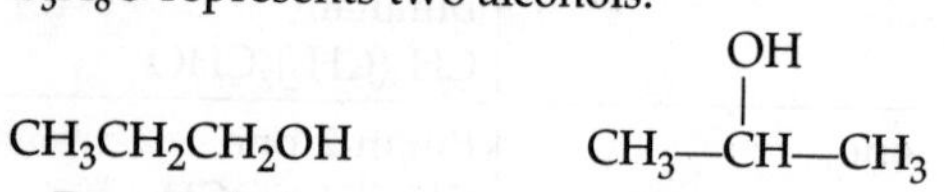

Propan-1-ol; Propan-2-ol

(iii) Functional Isomerism: Two or more compounds having the same molecular formula but different functional groups are called functional isomers and this phenomenon is termed as functional group isomerism. For example, the molecular formula C_3H_6O represents an aldehyde and a ketone :

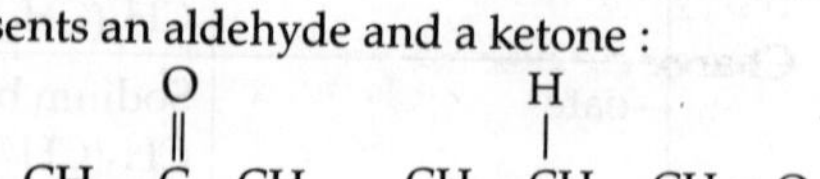

Propanone; Propanal

(iv) Metamerism: It arises due to different alkyl chains on either side of the functional group in the molecule. For example, $C_4H_{10}O$ represents methoxypropane ($CH_3OC_3H_7$) and ethoxyethane ($C_2H_5OC_2H_5$).

(2) Stereoisomerism: The compounds that have the same constitution and sequence of covalent bonds but differ in relative positions of their atoms or groups in space are called stereoisomers. This phenomenon is called as stereoisomerism.

(i) Geometrical or *Cis-trans* Isomerism: Isomerism in which the compounds possessing same molecular formula differ in their properties due to the difference in their geometry, due to difference in the direction of attachment of same atoms or groups in their molecule. For example,

cis; *trans*

(ii) Optical Isomerism: Optical isomers are two compounds which contain the same number and kinds of atoms, and bonds (i.e., the connectivity between atoms is the same), and different spatial arrangements of the atoms, but which have non-super imposable mirror images. Each non-super imposable mirror image structure is called an enantiomer. Molecules or ions that exist as optical isomers are called chiral.

Fundamental Concepts in Organic Reaction Mechanism

- The general reaction is depicted as follows:

$$\text{Organic molecule (Substrate)} \xrightarrow{\text{Attacking Reagent}} [\text{Intermediate}] \longrightarrow \text{Products(s)}$$

[Intermediate] → By products

- The sequential account of each step, describing details of electron movement, energetics during bond cleavage and bond formation, and the rates of transformation of reactants into products (kinetics) is referred to as **reaction mechanism.**
- Organic reactions involve breaking and making of covalent bonds. A covalent bond can undergo fission in two ways:

(i) By Homolytic Cleavage or Homolysis

(ii) By Heterolytic Cleavage or Heterolysis

- **Homolytic Cleavage**: In this process, each of the atoms acquires one of the bonding electrons.

  $$A\text{-}B \text{ or } A:B \longrightarrow \dot{A} + \dot{B}$$

  The products are called free radicals. They are electrically neutral and have one unpaired electron associated with them. Homolytic fission is the most common mode of fission in vapour phase. Alkyl radicals are classified as primary, secondary, or tertiary. Alkyl radical stability increases as we proceed from primary to tertiary:

CH_3	< CH_2CH_3	< $CH(CH_3)_2$	< $C(CH_3)_3$
Methyl free radical	Ethyl free radical	Isopropyl free radical	Tert-butyl free radical

- **Heterolytic Cleavage**: In this process, one of atoms acquires both of the bonding (shared pair of electrons) electrons when the bond is broken. If one is more electronegative than other which thereby acquires both the bonding electrons and become negatively charged. The products of heterolytic fission are carbonium ions and carbanions.
- **Carbonium Ions (carbocations):** A species having a carbon atom possessing sextet of electrons and a positive charge is called a carbocation.

$$-\overset{|}{\underset{|}{C}}:Z \longrightarrow -\overset{|}{\underset{|}{C}}^{+} + :Z$$

where Z is more electronegative than carbon. The carbocation is sp^2-hybridised having trigonal planar geometry. Tertiary carbonium ion is more stable than a secondary, which in turn is more stable than a primary because of inductive effect (+I) associated with alkyl group.

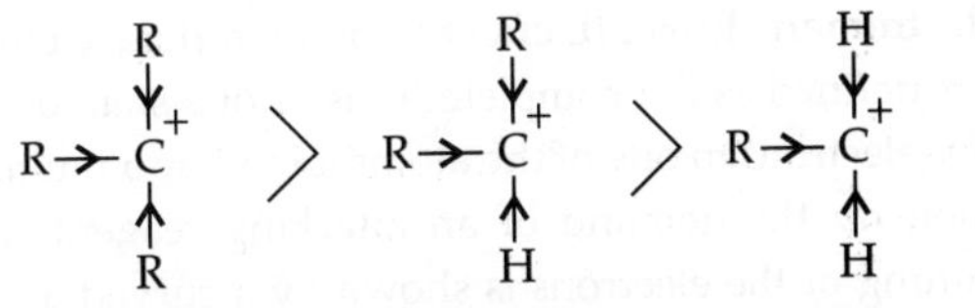

3° TERTIARY 2° SECONDARY 1° PRIMARY

- **Carbanion**: Organic ion which contains a negatively charged carbon atom is called carbanion.

$$-\overset{|}{\underset{|}{C}}:Z \longrightarrow -\overset{|}{\underset{|}{C}}\vdots^{-} + Z^{+}$$

where Z is less electronegative than carbon. The carbanions are sp^3-hybridised species carrying negative charge and have pyramidal shape. Primary carbanion is more stable than a secondary, which in turn is more stable than a tertiary because of inductive effect (+I) associated with alkyl group.

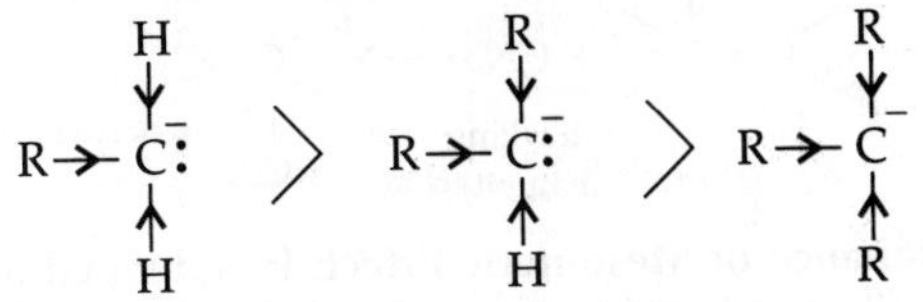

Primary > Secondary > Tertiary

- **Electrophile:** A reagent that takes away an electron pair from reactive site, i.e., electron seeking, e.g., H^+, CH_3^+, NH_4^+, $AlCl_3$, SO_3, BF_3, etc.

  Nucleophile: A reagent that brings an electron pair to the reactive site, i.e., nucleus seeking, e.g., OH^- CN^-, H_2O, R_3N, R_2NH, etc.
- **Electron Displacement Effects in Covalent Bonds:** Electronic displacements in covalent bonds occur due to the presence of an atom or group of different electronegativity or under the influence of some outside attacking group. These lead to a number of effects which are as follows:

(i) Inductive effect

(ii) Electromeric effect

(iii) Resonance or Mesomeric effect

(iv) Hyperconjugation.

- **Inductive effect**: Electron displacement along the carbon chain in an organic molecule due to the presence of a polar covalent bond at one end of the chain. Due to different electronegativity, electrons are displaced towards the more electronegative atom. The more electronegative atom acquires a small negative charge (δ^-). The less electronegative atom acquires a small positive charge (δ^+).
- Atoms or groups which lose electrons towards a carbon atom are said to have a +I effect. Those atoms or groups which draw electrons away from a carbon atom are said to have a -I effect. Some common atoms or groups which cause +I or -I effects are shown below:

(i) The – I effect (electron attracting) shows the trend: $NO_2 > F > COOH > Cl > Br > I > OH > C_6H_5$.

(ii) The +I effect (electron releasing) shows the trend: $(CH_3)_3C— > (CH_3)_2CH— > CH_3CH_2— > CH_3$.

- **Electromeric Effect (E effect)**: It is a temporary effect. It is defined as the complete transfer of a shared pair of π-electrons to one of the atoms joined by a multiple bond on the demand of an attacking reagent. The shifting of the electrons is shown by a curved arrow (↷). There are two distinct types of electromeric effect:

(i) Positive Electromeric Effect (+E effect): In this effect, the π-electrons of the multiple bond are transferred to that atom to which the reagent gets attached. For example,

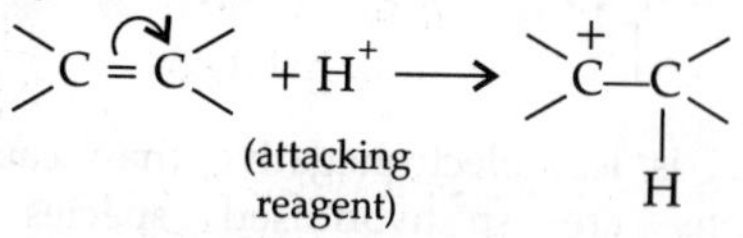

(ii) Negative Electromeric Effect (–E effect): In this effect, the π - electrons of the multiple bond are transferred to that atom to which the attacking reagent does not get attached. For example,

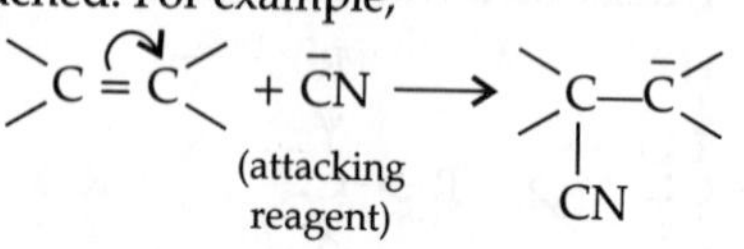

- **Resonance or Mesomeric Effect**: It is defined as the polarity produced in the molecule by the interaction of two π-bonds or between a π-bond and a lone pair of electrons present on an adjacent atom. There are two types of resonance or mesomeric effects designated as R or M effect.

Positive Resonance Effect (+R effect): Those atoms which lose electrons towards a carbon atom are said to have a +M effect or +R effect. For example: —Cl, —Br, —I, —NH_2, —NR_2, —OH, —OCH_3.

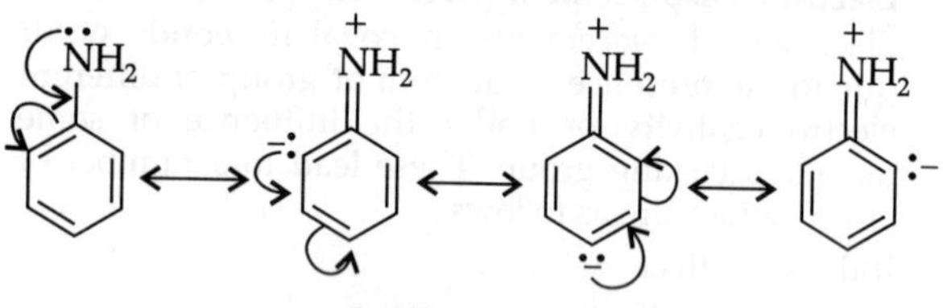

+R effect in aniline

Negative Resonance Effect (-R effect): Those atoms or groups which draw electrons away from a carbon atom are said to have a -M effect or -R effect. For example: –COOH, -CHO, -CN.

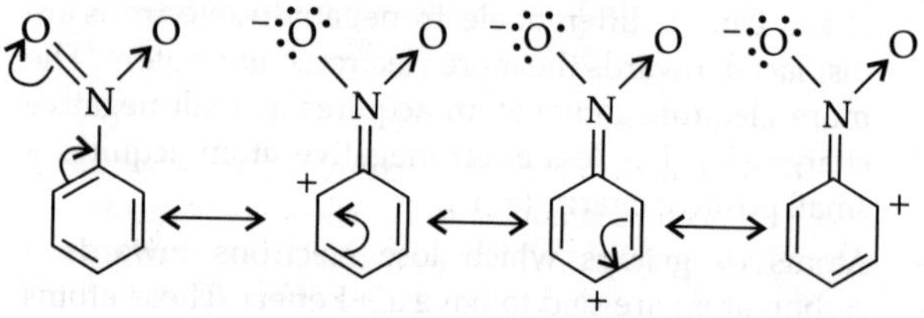

–R effect in nitrobenzene

- **Hyperconjugation:** Orbital interactions between the π systems and the adjacent sigma bonds of the substituent group (s) in organic compounds.

It involves delocalisation of σ electrons of C—H bond of an alkyl group directly attached to an atom of unsaturated system or to an atom with an unshared *p* orbital. The σ electrons of C—H bond of the alkyl group enter into partial conjugation with the attached unsaturated system or with the unshared *p* orbital. Hyperconjugation is a permanent effect which is also called "No bond resonance".

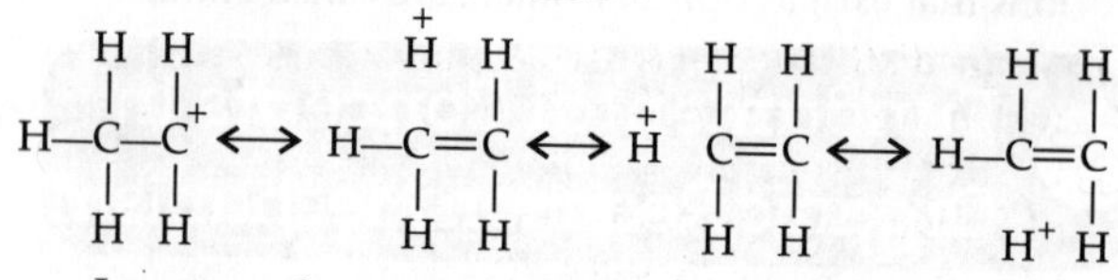

In general, greater the number of alkyl groups attached to a positively charged carbon atom, the greater is the hyperconjugation.

$$CH_3-\overset{+}{C}(CH_3)_2 > (CH_3)_2\overset{+}{C}H > CH_3\overset{+}{C}H_2 > \overset{+}{C}H_3$$

- **Types of Organic Reactions and Mechanisms:**

(i) Substitution reactions: Reactions involving replacement of an atom or group in a molecule by different atoms or groups, *e.g.*, chlorination of methane.

(ii) Addition reactions: Reactions when two molecules form a single product, *e.g.*, reaction of but-1-ene with HBr to give 2-bromobutane.

(iii) Elimination reactions: Reactions in which two atoms or groups in a molecule are eliminated to give the product, *e.g.*, formation of alkene from alkyl bromide.

(iv) Rearrangement reaction: Reactions involving migration of atoms to other position within the molecule.

Methods of Purification of organic compound

- Purification of organic compounds can be done by sublimation, crystallisation, distillation, differential extraction and chromatography.

(i) Sublimation: This technique is used only for those solids which changes from solid to vapour state directly without passing through liquid state.

(ii) Crystallisation: This is used for purification of solid organic compounds. This is based on the difference in the solubilities of compound and the impurities in a suitable solvent.

(iii) Distillation: It can be used (i) to separate volatile liquids from non-volatile impurities (ii) to separate the liquids having sufficient difference in their boiling points (>25 K). Liquids having different boiling points vaporise at different temperatures. The vapours are cooled and the liquids so formed are collected separately.

There are various distillation techniques. These are:

(a) Fractional distillation: It is used for separating liquids if the difference in boiling points is not much. In this technique, vapours of a liquid mixture are passed through a fractionating column before condensation. A fractionating column provides many surfaces for heat exchange between the ascending vapours and the descending condensed liquid. This technique is used to separate different fractions of crude oil in petroleum industry.

(b) Distillation under reduced pressure: It is carried out to purify those liquids that have high boiling points and those which decompose at or below their boiling points.

(c) Steam distillation: It is used to purify those substances which are steam volatile and immiscible with water. In steam distillation, the liquids boils when the sum of vapour pressures due to the organic compound (P_1) and that due to water (P_2) becomes equal to the atmospheric pressure (P), *i.e.*, $P = P_1 + P_2$.

(iv) Differential extraction: Here, extraction of compound takes place based on difference in solubility. An organic compound present in aqueous medium is separated by shaking it with an organic solvent in which it is more soluble than in water. Organic solvent and water being immiscible are separated by using separating funnel. Removal of organic compound by distillation or evaporation yields pure compound.

(v) Chromatography: It is based on the general principle of distributing the components of a mixture of organic compounds between two phases-a stationary phase and mobile phase. The stationary phase can be solid or liquid supported on a solid, while the mobile phase is a liquid or a gas. When the stationary phase is a solid, the basis of separation is adsorption; when it is a liquid, the basis of separation is partition.

Based on the principle involved, chromatography is classified into two categories:

(i) Adsorption Chromatography is based on the fact that different compounds are adsorbed on an adsorbent to different degrees. Commonly used adsorbents are silica gel and alumina. When a mobile phase is allowed to move over a stationary phase (adsorbent), the components of the mixture move by varying distances over the stationary phase. It is of two types:

(a) Column chromatography involves separation of a mixture over a column of adsorbent (stationary phase) packed in a glass tube. The column is fitted with a stopcock at its lower end. The mixture adsorbed on adsorbent is placed on the top of the adsorbent column packed in a glass tube. An appropriate eluant which is a liquid or a mixture of liquids is allowed to flow down the column slowly. Depending upon the degree to which the compounds are adsorbed, complete separation takes place. The most readily adsorbed substances are retained near the top and others come down to various distances in the column.

(b) Thin layer chromatography (TLC) is a type of adsorption chromatography, which involves separation of substances of a mixture over a thin layer of an adsorbent coated on glass plate. The plate is known as thin layer chromatography plate or chromaplate. The relative adsorption of each component of the mixture is expressed in terms of its retardation factor i.e.,

$$R_f \text{ value} = \frac{\text{Distance moved by the substance from base line } (x)}{\text{Distance moved by the solvent from base line } (y)}$$

(ii) Partition chromatography is based on continuous differential partitioning of components of a mixture between stationary and mobile phases. e.g., Paper chromatography. Chromatography paper contains water trapped in it, which acts as the stationary phase.

Qualitative Analysis of Organic Compounds

- Almost all the organic compounds contain carbon and hydrogen (CCl_4 is exception as it does not contain hydrogen). They may contain oxygen, nitrogen, sulphur, halogens and phosphorus.

Scan to know more about this topic

Steam Distillation

Detection of Carbon and Hydrogen: Carbon and hydrogen are detected as carbon dioxide and water respectively by heating with cupric oxide. Carbon dioxide is detected as it turns lime water milky, however, water is detected as it turns anhydrous copper sulphate to blue.

$$C + 2CuO \xrightarrow{\Delta} 2Cu + CO_2$$
$$2H + CuO \xrightarrow{\Delta} Cu + H_2O$$
$$CO_2 + Ca(OH)_2 \rightarrow CaCO_3\downarrow + H_2O$$
$$\underset{\text{White}}{5H_2O + CuSO_4} \rightarrow \underset{\text{Blue}}{CuSO_4.5H_2O}$$

Lassaigne's test: Nitrogen, sulphur, halogens and phosphorus present in organic compound are detected by 'Lassaigne's test. In this test, organic compound is fused with sodium metal so that elements present in organic compound are converted from covalent form into the ionic form.

$$Na + C + N \xrightarrow{\Delta} NaCN$$
$$2Na + S \xrightarrow{\Delta} Na_2S$$
$$Na + X \xrightarrow{\Delta} NaX\ (X = Cl, Br \text{ or } I)$$

These fused mass are extracted by boiling with water to form sodium fusion extract.

Test for Nitrogen—The sodium fusion extract is boiled with iron (II) sulphate and then acidified with concentrated sulphuric acid. The formation of Prussian blue colour confirms the presence of nitrogen.

$$6CN^- + Fe^{2+} \rightarrow [Fe(CN)_6]^{4-}$$
$$3[Fe(CN)_6]^{4-} + 4Fe^{3+} \xrightarrow{xH_2O} Fe_4[Fe(CN)_6]_3.xH_2O$$

Prussian blue
(Ferric ferrocyanide)

Test for Sulphur:

(a) The sodium fusion extract is acidified with acetic acid and lead acetate is added to it. A black precipitate of lead sulphide indicates the presence of sulphur.

$$S^{2-} + Pb^{2+} \longrightarrow \underset{\text{Black}}{PbS}$$

(b) Add 2-3 drops of freshly prepared sodium nitroprusside solution to sodium metal extract. Appearance of violet colour confirms the presence of sulphur.

$$[Fe(CN)_5NO]^{2-} + S^{2-} \rightarrow [Fe(CN)_5NOS]^{4-}$$

Sulpho nitroprusside ion
(violet colour)

If both sulphur and nitrogen are present, sodium thiocyanate is produced in sodium metal extract which gives red colour with Fe^{3+} ions while testing for nitrogen.

$$Na + C + N + S \longrightarrow NaSCN$$

$$Fe^{3+} + SCN^- \longrightarrow [Fe(SCN)]^{2+}$$

Blood red

Test for Halogens—For this, sodium fusion extract is acidified with nitric acid and then treated with silver nitrate:

(i) A white precipitate, soluble in ammonium hydroxide shows the presence of chlorine.

(ii) A yellowish precipitate, sparingly soluble in ammonium hydroxide shows the presence of bromine.

(iii) A yellow precipitate, insoluble in ammonium hydroxide shows the presence of iodine.

$$X^- + Ag^+ \rightarrow AgX \ (X = -Cl, -Br, -I)$$

Test for Phosphorus—The compound is heated with an oxidising agent (e.g., sodium peroxide), that oxidises phosphorus to phosphate. This solution on boiling with nitric acid followed by treatment with ammonium molybdate produces canary yellow precipitate confirming phosphorus:

$$Na_3PO_4 + 3HNO_3 \rightarrow H_3PO_4 + 3NaNO_3$$

$$H_3PO_4 + 12(NH_4)_2MoO_4 + 21HNO_3$$

Ammonium molybdate

$$\rightarrow (NH_4)_3PO_4.12MoO_3 + 21NH_4NO_3 + 12\,H_2O$$

Ammonium phosphomolybdate (Canary yellow precipitate)

Quantitative Analysis

- Quantitative analysis of organic compound gives the percentage composition of elements in an organic compound.
- **Estimation of Carbon and Hydrogen** : A known mass of an organic compound is burnt in the presence of excess of oxygen and copper(II) oxide. Carbon and hydrogen in the compound are oxidised to carbon dioxide and water respectively.

$$C_xH_y + (x + y/4)\,O_2 \longrightarrow xCO_2 + (y/2)H_2O$$

The mass of water produced is determined by passing the mixture through a weighed U-tube containing anhydrous calcium chloride. Carbon dioxide is absorbed in another U-tube containing concentrated solution of potassium hydroxide. These tubes are connected in series.

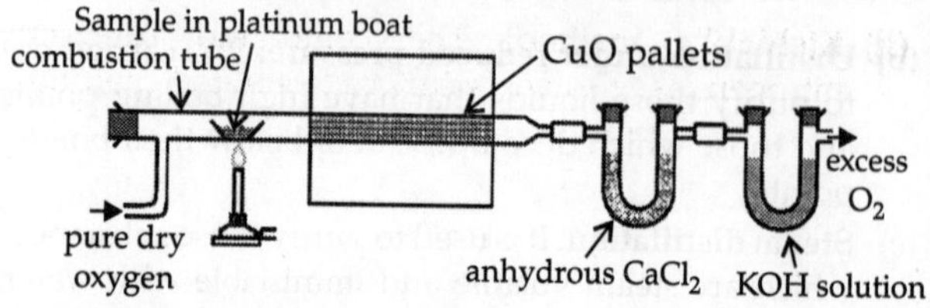

Estimasion of carbon and hydrogen

Fig. 8.1

The increase in masses of calcium chloride and potassium hydroxide gives the amounts of water and carbon dioxide from which the percentages of carbon and hydrogen are calculated. Let the mass of organic compound be *m* g, mass of water and carbon dioxide produced be m_1 and m_2 g respectively.

$$\text{Percentage of carbon} = \frac{12 \times m_2 \times 100}{44 \times m}$$

$$\text{Percentage of hydrogen} = \frac{2 \times m_1 \times 100}{18 \times m}$$

- **Estimation of Nitrogen:**

(i) Dumas method: The nitrogen containing organic compound, when heated with copper oxide in an atmosphere of carbon dioxide, yields free nitrogen in addition to carbon dioxide and water.

$$C_xH_yN_z + (2x + y/2)CuO \longrightarrow xCO_2 + y/2H_2O + z/2N_2 + (2x + y/2)Cu$$

Traces of nitrogen oxides formed, if any, are reduced to nitrogen by passing the gaseous mixture over a heated copper gauze. The mixture of gases so produced is collected over an aqueous solution of potassium hydroxide which absorbs carbon dioxide. Nitrogen is collected in the upper part of the graduated tube.

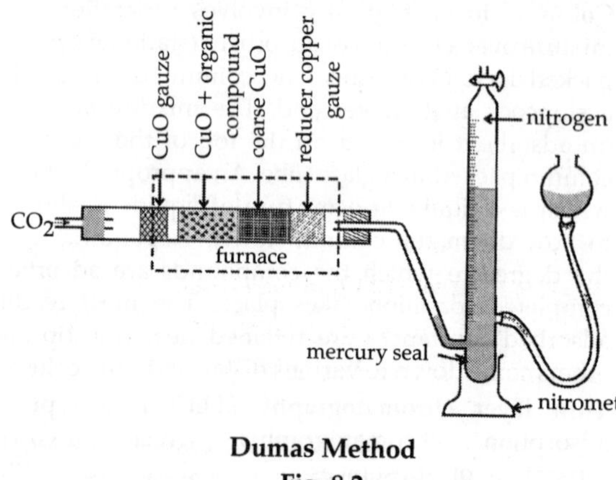

Dumas Method

Fig. 8.2

Let the mass of organic compound = *m* g

Volume of nitrogen collected = V_1 mL

Room temperature = T_1K

$$\text{Volume of nitrogen at STP} = \frac{p_1 \times V_1 \times 273}{760 \times T_1}$$

Percentage of nitrogen

$$= \frac{28 \times \text{volume of } N_2 \text{ at STP} \times 100}{22400 \times \text{Mass of organic compound}}$$

(ii) Kjeldahl's method: The compound containing nitrogen is heated with concentrated sulphuric acid. Nitrogen in the compound gets converted to ammonium sulphate.

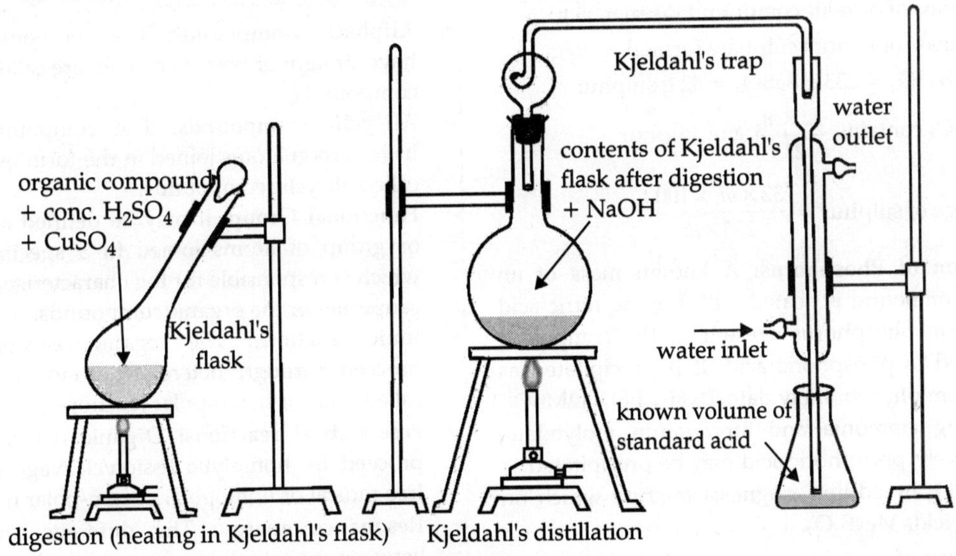

Fig. 8.3 : Kjeladane's Method

The resulting acid mixture is then heated with excess of sodium hydroxide. The liberated ammonia gas is absorbed in an excess of standard solution of sulphuric acid. The amount of ammonia produced is determined by estimating the amount of sulphuric acid consumed in the reaction.

$$\text{Organic compound} + H_2SO_4 \longrightarrow (NH_4)_2SO_4 \xrightarrow{2NaOH} Na_2SO_4 + 2NH_3 + 2H_2O$$

$$2NH_3 + H_2SO_4 \longrightarrow (NH_4)_2SO_4$$

Let the mass of organic compound taken = m g

Volume of H_2SO_4 of molarity, M, taken = V mL

Volume of NaOH of molarity, M, used for titration of excess of H_2SO_4 = V_1 mL

V_1 mL of NaOH of molarity M = $V_1/2$ mL of H_2SO_4 of molarity M

Volume of H_2SO_4 of molarity M unused

= $(V - V_1/2)$ mL

$(V - V_1/2)$ mL of H_2SO_4 of molarity M

= $2(V - V_1/2)$ mL of NH_3 solution of molarity M.

1000 mL of 1 M NH_3 solution contains 17g NH_3 or 14 g of N

2 $(V - V_1/2)$ mL of NH_3 solution of molarity M contains:

$$\frac{14 \times M \times 2(V - V_1/2 g_N)}{1000}$$

$$\text{Percentage of N} = \frac{1.4 \times M \times 2(V - V_1/2)}{m}$$

► **Estimation of Halogens:**

Carius method: A known mass of an organic compound is heated with fuming nitric acid in the presence of silver nitrate contained in a hard glass tube known as Carius tube, in a furnace.

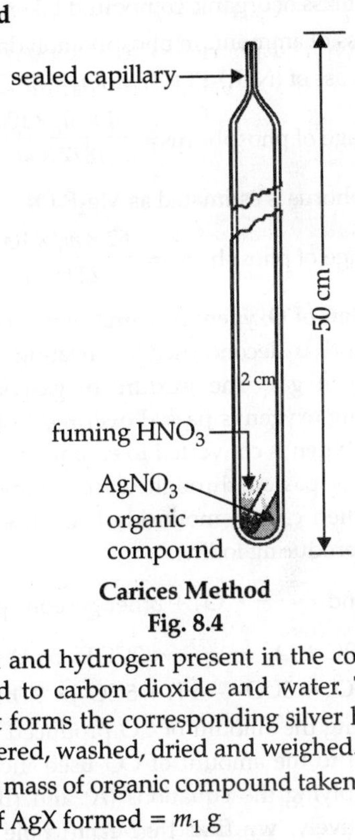

Carices Method

Fig. 8.4

Carbon and hydrogen present in the compound are oxidised to carbon dioxide and water. The halogen present forms the corresponding silver halide (AgX). It is filtered, washed, dried and weighed.

Let the mass of organic compound taken = m g

Mass of AgX formed = m_1 g

1 mol of AgX contains 1 mol of X

Mass of halogen in m_1g of AgX

$$= \frac{\text{Atomic mass of X} \times m_1 g}{\text{Molecular mass of AgX}}$$

$$\text{Percentage of halogen} = \frac{\text{Atomic mass of X} \times m_1 \times 100}{\text{molecular mass of AgX} \times m}$$

► **Estimation of Sulphur:** A known mass of an organic compound is heated in a Carius tube with sodium peroxide or fuming nitric acid. Sulphur present in the compound is oxidised to sulphuric acid. It is precipitated as barium sulphate by adding excess of barium chloride solution in water. The precipitate is filtered, washed, dried and weighed.

Let the mass of organic compound taken = m g

and the mass of barium sulphate formed = m_1 g

1 mol of $BaSO_4$ = 233 g $BaSO_4$ = 32 g sulphur

m_1 g $BaSO_4$ contains $\frac{32 \times m_1}{233}$ g of sulphur

$$\text{Percentage of sulphur} = \frac{32 \times m_1 \times 100}{233 \times m}$$

- **Estimation of Phosphorus:** A known mass of an organic compound is heated with fuming nitric acid whereupon phosphorus present in the compound is oxidised to phosphoric acid. It is precipitated as ammonium phosphomoly date, $(NH_4)_3PO_4.12MoO_3$, by adding ammonia and ammonium molybdate. Alternatively, phosphoric acid may be precipitated as $MgNH_4PO_4$ by adding magnesia mixture which on ignition yields $Mg_2P_2O_7$.

Let the mass of organic compound taken = m g

and mass of ammonium phosphomolydate = m_1g

Molar mass of $(NH_4)_3PO_4.12MoO_3$ = 1877 g

$$\text{Percentage of phosphorus} = \frac{31 \times m_1 \times 100}{1877 \times m}\%$$

If phosphorus is estimated as $Mg_2P_2O_7$,

$$\text{Percentage of phosphorus} = \frac{62 \times m_1 \times 100}{222 \times m}\%$$

- **Estimation of Oxygen:** A definite mass of an organic compound is decomposed by heating in a stream of nitrogen gas. The mixture of gaseous products containing oxygen is passed over red-hot coke when all the oxygen is converted to carbon monoxide. This mixture is passed through warm iodine pentoxide (I_2O_5) when carbon monoxide is oxidised to carbon dioxide producing iodine.

$$\text{Compound} \xrightarrow{\text{Heat}} O_2 + \text{other gaseous products}$$

$$2C + O_2 \xrightarrow{1373\,K} 2CO] \times 5\ (A)$$

$$I_2O_5 + 5CO \longrightarrow I_2 + 5CO_2] \times 2\ (B)$$

On making the amount of CO produced in equation (A) equal to the amount of CO used inequation (B) by multiplying the equations (A) and (B) by 5 and 2 respectively; we find that each mole of oxygen liberated from the compound will produce two moles of carbondioxide.

Thus, 88 g carbon dioxide is obtained if 32 g oxygen is liberated.

Let the mass of organic compound taken be m g

Mass of carbon dioxide produced be m_1 g

$\therefore$ m_1 g carbon dioxide is obtained from $\frac{32m_1}{88}$ gO_2

$$\therefore \text{Percentage of oxygen} = \frac{32 \times m_1 \times 100}{88 \times m}\%$$

Key Terms

- **Aliphatic Compounds:** The compounds which have straight or branched chain are called aliphatic compounds.
- **Alicyclic Compounds:** The compounds which have carbon atoms joined in the form of a ring are called alicyclic compounds.
- **Functional Group:** It may be defined as an atom or group of atoms joined in a specific manner which is responsible for the characteristic chemical properties of the organic compounds.
- **Ionic reactions:** The organic reactions which proceed through heterolytic bond cleavage are called ionic or heteropolar reactions.
- **Free radical reactions:** Organic reactions which proceed by homolytic fission/cleavage are called free radical or homopolar or non-polar reactions.
- **Resonance energy:** The difference in energy between the actual structure and the lowest energy resonance structure is called resonance energy.
- Adsorption Chromatography: It is a chromatographic technique which is based on the fact that different compounds are adsorbed on an adsorbent at different degrees.
- Mixed melting point: The melting point of two thoroughly mixed substances is called mixed melting point. This can also be used for ascertaining the purity of a compound.

Key Facts

- Buckminsterfullerene is a common name given to the newly discovered C_{60} cluster (a form of carbon) noting its structural similarity to the geodesic domes popularised by the famous architect R. Buckminster Fuller.
- Acetic acid is the first organic compound synthesised in the laboratory from its elements.
- Heterolytic and homolytic bond fission results in the formation of short-lived fragments called reaction intermediates.
- During a polar organic reaction, nucleophile attacks an electrophilic centre of the substrate which is that specific atom or part of the elecrophile that is electron deficient.
- The energy of actual structure of the molecule (the resonance hybrid) is lower than that of any of the canonical structures.
- The resonance structures have **(i)** the same positions of nuclei and **(ii)** the same number of unpaired electrons.
- **Criteria of purity of organic compounds:** The purity of an organic compound can be ascertained by determining its some physical constants like mailing point, boiling point, specific gravity, refractive index and viscosity.

Mnemonics

1. Concept: 3-D Representation
Mnemonics: So towards Do away
Interpretation: Solid → Towards observer ( )
Dashed → Away from observer (IIIII)

2. Concept: Structural Isomerism
Mnemonics: Poor Farmer Managing Crops (PFMC)
Interpretation:
(a) Position
(b) Functional Group
(c) Metamerism
(d) Chair

7. Concept: Optical Isomerism
Mnemonics: GO
Interpretation:
(a) Geometrical
(b) Optical

Concept: Types of Organic Reaction
Mnemonics: EARS
Interpretation:
(a) Elimination
(b) Addition
(c) Rearrangement
(d) Substitution

Concept: Method of Purification of Organic Compound
Mnemonics: Some CD of DC
Interpretation: Sublimation, Crystallisation, Distillation, Differential Extraction, Chromatography

NCERT CORNER

Q. 1. What are hybridisation states of each carbon atom in the following compounds? $CH_2=C=O$, $CH_3CH=CH_2$, $(CH_3)_2CO$, $CH_2=CHCN$, C_6H_6
[NCERT Ex. Q. 8.1, Page 292]

Ans.

(i) $\overset{sp^2}{CH_2}=\overset{sp}{C}=O$ (ii) $\overset{sp^3}{CH_3}-\overset{sp^2}{CH}=\overset{sp^2}{CH_2}$ (iii) $\overset{sp^3}{CH_3}-\underset{sp^2}{\overset{O\,\|}{C}}-\overset{sp^3}{CH_3}$

(iv) $\overset{sp^2}{CH_2}=\overset{sp^2}{CH}-\overset{sp}{C}\equiv N$ (v) 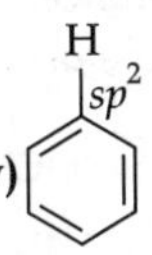 Each carbon is sp^2-hybrized in benzene.

Q. 2. Indicate the σ and π bonds in the following molecules:
C_6H_6, C_6H_{12}, CH_2Cl_2, $CH_2=C=CH_2$, CH_3NO_2, $HCONHCH_3$
[NCERT Ex. Q. 8.2, Page 292]

Ans. (i)

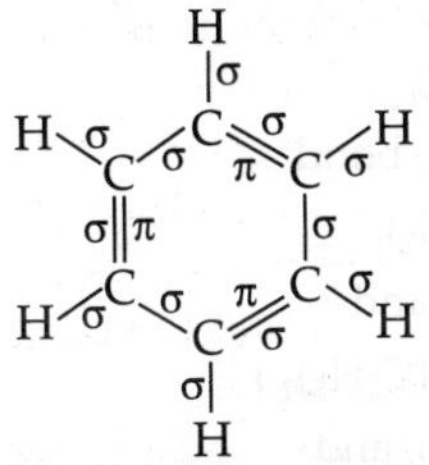

There are six C – C sigma bonds, six C–H sigma bonds, and three C=C π resonating bonds in the given compound.

(ii)

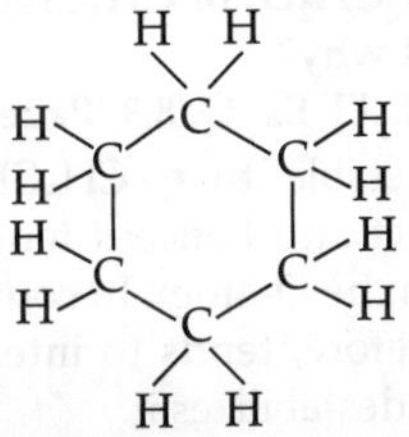

There are 12σ bonds in the given compound.

(iii)

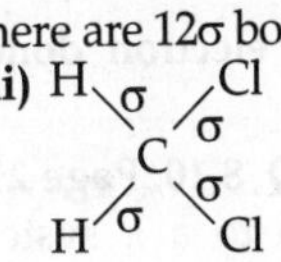

There are 4σ bonds, in the given compound.

(iv)

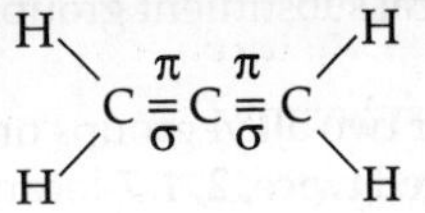

There are 6σ bonds and 2π bonds in the given compound.

(v)

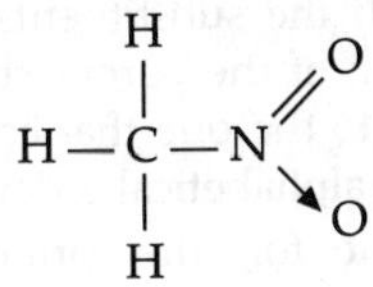

There are 5 σ bonds and 1π bond in the given compound.

(vi)

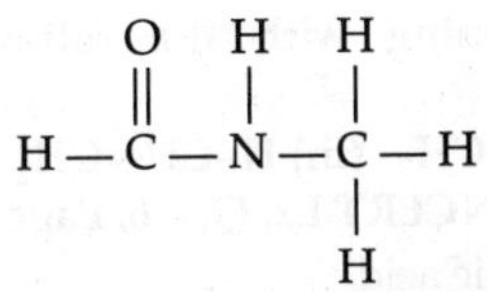

There are 8 σ bonds and 1π bond in the given compound.

Q. 3. Write bond line formulas for: Isopropyl alcohol, 2,3-Dimethylbutanal, Heptan-4- one.
[NCERT Ex. Q. 8.3, Page 292]

Ans.

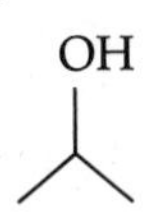
Isopropyl alcohol

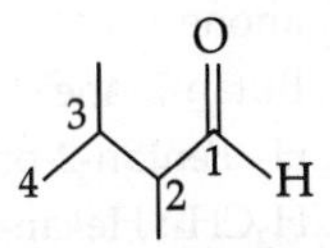
2,3-Dimethylbutanal

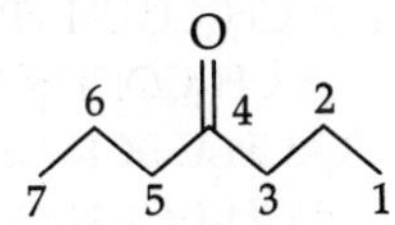
Heptan-4-one

(3)

Q. 4. Give the IUPAC names of the following compounds:

(i) 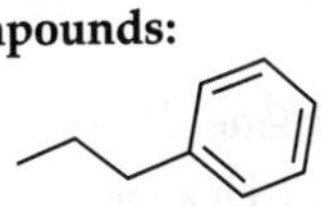 (ii) 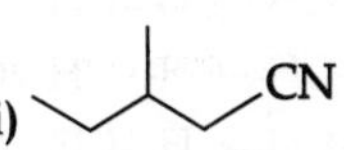

(iii) 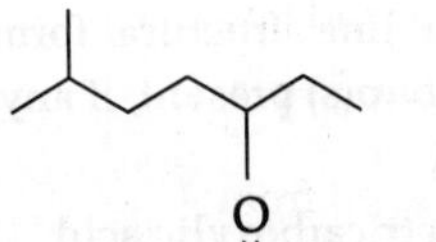 (iv) 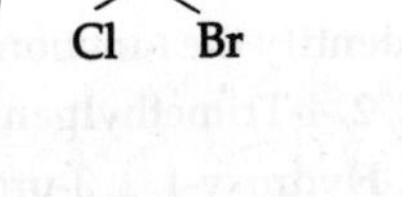

(v) 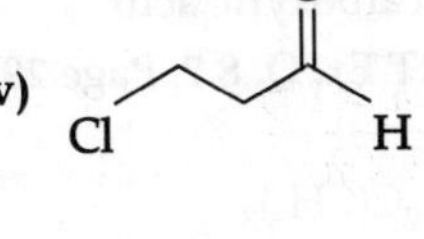 (vi) Cl_2CHCH_2OH

[NCERT Ex. Q. 8.4, Page 292]

Ans. **(i)** 1-phenyl propane

(ii) 3–methylpentane nitrile

(iii) 2, 5-Dimethylheptane

(iv) 3-Bromo- 3-chloroheptane

(v) 3-Chloropropanal

(vi) 2, 2-dichloroethanol

Q. 5. Which of the following represents the correct IUPAC name for the compounds concerned ?

(i) 2,2-Dimethylpentane

or

2-Dimethylpentane

(ii) 2,4,7- Trimethyloctane

or

2,5,7-Trimethyloctane

(iii) 2-Chloro-4-methylpentane or 4-Chloro-2-methylpentane

(iv) But-3-yn-1-ol or But-4-ol-1-yne.

[NCERT Ex. Q. 8.5, Page 292]

Ans. **(i)** 2,2-Dimethylpentane. The prefix di in the IUPAC name indicates that two identical substituent groups are present in the parent chain.

(ii) 2, 4, 7-Trimethyloctane. For two alkyl groups on the same carbon its locant is repeated twice, 2, 4, 7-locant set is lower than 2, 5, 7.

(iii) 2-Chloro-4-methylpentane. If the substituents are present in the equivalent position of the parent chain, then the lower number is given to the one that comes first in the name according to the alphabetical order.

(iv) But-3-yn-1-ol. Lower locant for the principal functional group, i.e., alcohol.

Q. 6. Draw formulas for the first five members of each homologous series beginning with the following compounds.

(i) H–COOH (ii) CH_3COCH_3 (iii) H–CH=CH_2

[NCERT Ex. Q. 8.6, Page 292]

Ans. **(i)** H–COOH: Methanoic acid

CH_3–COOH: Ethanoic acid

CH_3–CH_2–COOH: Propanoic acid

CH_3–CH_2–CH_2–COOH: Butanoic acid

CH_3–CH_2–CH_2–CH_2–COOH: Pentanoic acid

(ii) CH_3COCH_3: Propanone

$CH_3COCH_2CH_3$: Butan-2-one

$CH_3COCH_2CH_2CH_3$: Pentan-2-one

$CH_3COCH_2CH_2CH_2CH_3$: Hexan-2-one

$CH_3COCH_2CH_2CH_2CH_2CH_3$: Heptan-2-one

(iii) H–CH=CH_2: Ethene

CH_3–CH=CH_2: Propene

CH_3–CH_2–CH=CH_2: 1-Butene

CH_3–CH_2–CH_2–CH=CH_2: 1-Pentene

CH_3–CH_2–CH_2–CH_2–CH=CH_2: 1-Hexene

Q. 7. Give condensed and bond line structural formulas and identify the functional group(s) present, if any, for:

(i) 2, 2, 4-Trimethylpentane

(ii) 2-Hydroxy-1, 2, 3-propanetricarboxylic acid

(iii) Hexanedial **[NCERT Ex. Q. 8.7, Page 292]**

Ans. **(i)** 2, 2 ,4-Trimethylpentane

Condensed formula-$(CH_3)_2CHCH_2C(CH_3)_3$

Bond line formula:

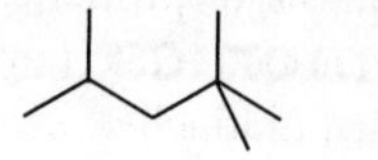

No functional group.

(ii) 2–hydroxy–1, 2, 3–propanetricarboxylic acid

Condensed Formula–(COOH) $CH_2C(OH)$ (COOH) $CH_2(COOH)$

Bond line formula:

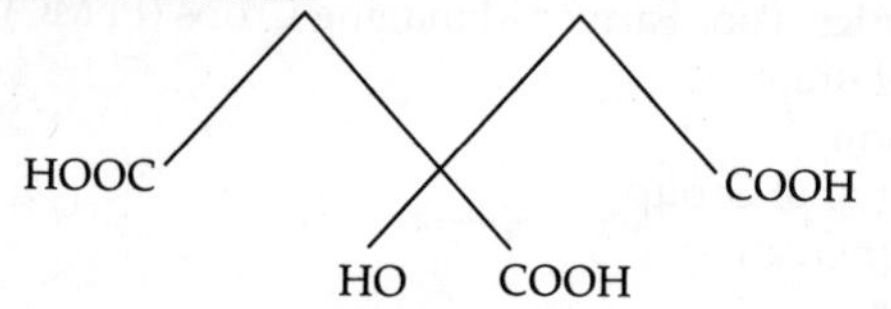

Functional groups present in the given compound are –COOH and – OH.

(iii) Hexanedial

Condensed Formula-(CHO)$(CH_2)_4$(CHO)

Bond line formula:

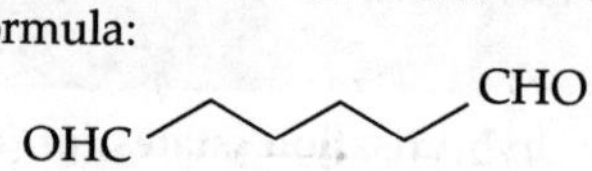

Functional group present in the given compound is -CHO.

Q. 8. Identify the functional groups in the following compounds:

(i)

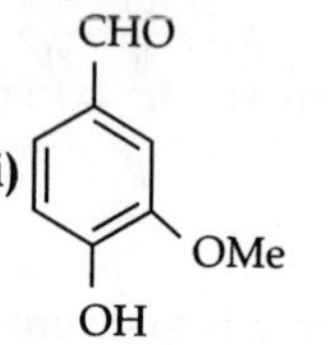

(ii)

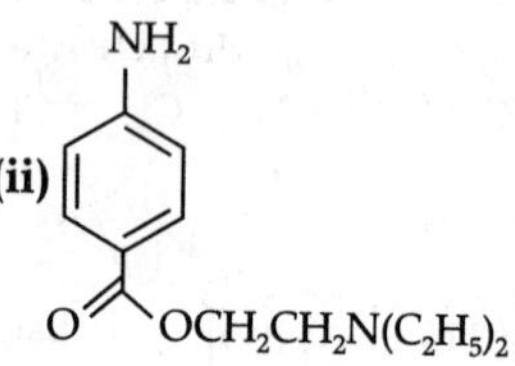

(iii)

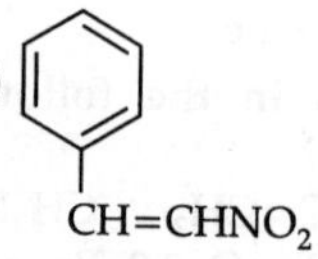

[NCERT Ex. Q. 8.8, Page 292]

Ans. **(i)** Aldehyde (–CHO),

Hydroxyl (–OH),

Methoxy (–OMe),

and C=C double bond

(ii) Amino (–NH_2),

Ketone (C = O), and

Diethylamine ($N(C_2H_5)_2$)

(iii) Nitro (–NO_2), and

C=C double bond

Q. 9. Which of the two: $O_2NCH_2CH_2O^-$ or $CH_3CH_2O^-$ is expected to be more stable and why?

[NCERT Ex. Q. 8.9, Page 292]

Ans. $O_2NCH_2CH_2O^-$ is more stable than $CH_3CH_2O^-$ because NO_2 group has -I-effect and hence it tends to disperse the negative charge on the O-atom. In contrast, CH_3CH_2 has +I-effect. It, therefore, tends to intensify the negative charge and hence destabilizes it.

Q. 10. Explain why alkyl groups act as electron donors when attached to a π system.

[NCERT Ex. Q. 8.10, Page 292]

Ans. When an alkyl group is attached to a π system, it acts as an electron-donor group by the process of hyperconjugation. To understand this concept better, let us take the example of propene. In hyperconjugation, the sigma electrons of the C-H bond of an alkyl group are delocalised which is attached to an unsaturated system. This results in delocalization due to partial overlap of a sp^3-s sigma bond orbital with an empty p-orbital of the pi bond of adjacent carbon atom. This kind of overlap leads to delocalization of the pi electrons, making it more stable.

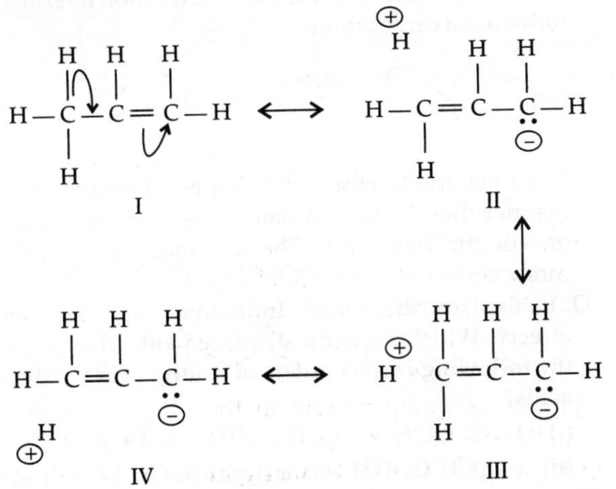

Q. 11. Draw the resonance structures for the following compounds. Show the electron shift using curved-arrow notation.

(i) C_6H_5OH **(ii) $C_6H_5NO_2$**
(iii) $CH_3CH=CHCHO$ **(iv) C_6H_5–CHO**
(v) $C_6H_5\overset{+}{C}H_2$ **(vi) $CH_3CH=CH-\overset{+}{C}H_2$**

[NCERT Ex. Q. 8.11, Page 292]

Ans.

(i)

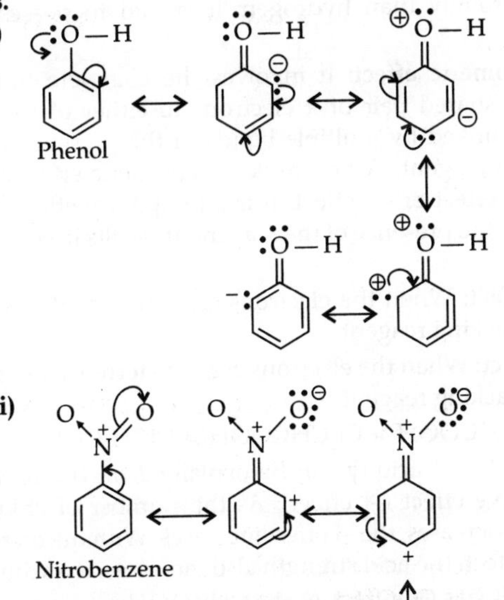

(ii)

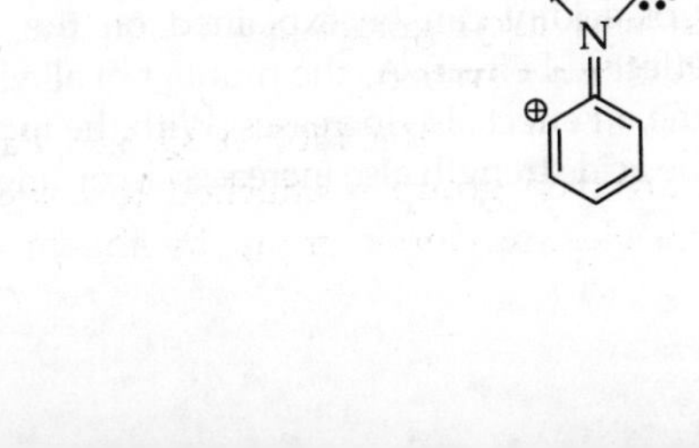

(iii)

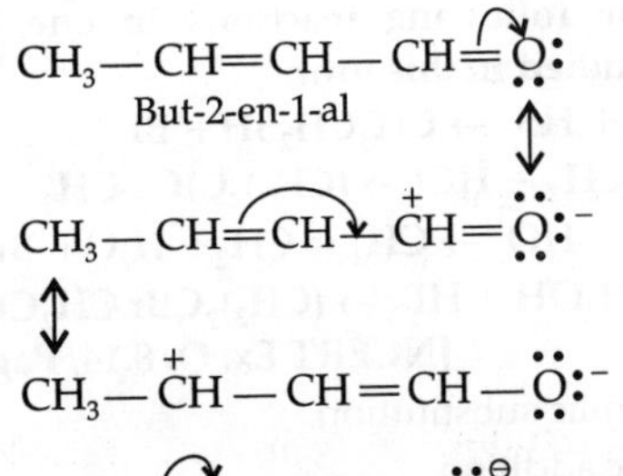

(iv)

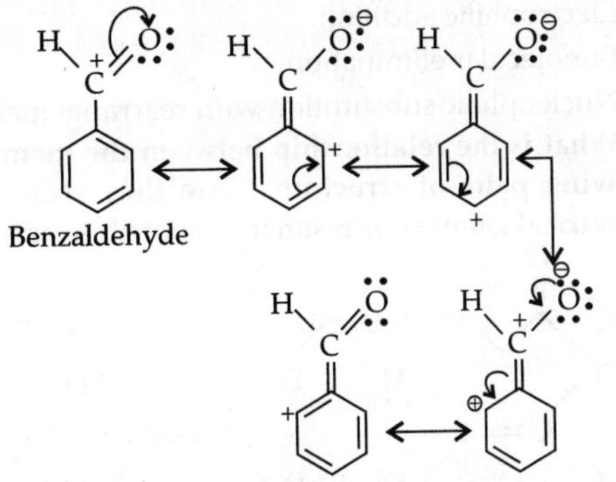

(v)

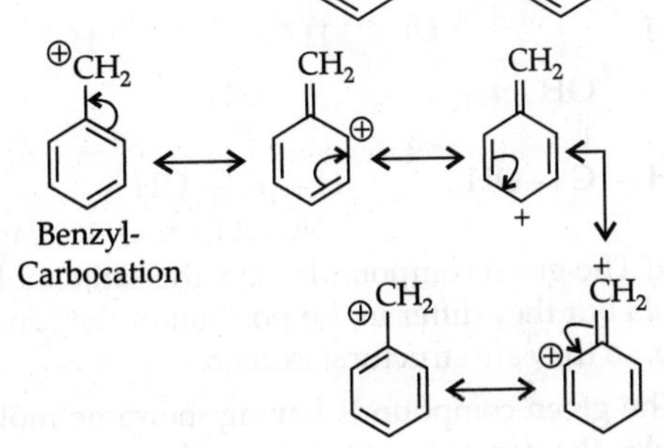

(vi) $CH_3-CH=CH-\overset{+}{C}H_2 \longrightarrow CH_3-\overset{\oplus}{C}H-CH=CH_2$

But-2-en-1-yl carbocation

Q. 12. What are electrophiles and nucleophiles? Explain with examples. **[NCERT Ex. Q. 8.12, Page 292]**

Ans. Electrophiles: A reagent that takes away an electron pair from the reactive site is called electrophile (E^+) *i.e.*, electron seeking.

e.g., H^+, Cl^+, Br^+, NO_2^+, R_3C^+, RN_2^+, $AlCl_3$, BF_3. etc.

Nucleophiles: A reagent that brings an electron pair to the reactive site is called a nucleophile (Nu:) i.e., nucleus seeking.

e.g., Cl^-, Br^-, CN^-, OH^-, RCR_2^-, NH_3, RNH_2, H_2O, ROH, etc.

Q. 13. Identify the reagents shown in bold in the following equations as nucleophiles or electrophiles:

(i) $CH_3COOH + HO^- \rightarrow CH_3COO^- + H_2O$

(ii) $CH_3COCH_3 + \bar{C}N \rightarrow (CH_3)_2C(CN)(OH)$

(iii) $C_6H_6 + CH_3CO^+ \rightarrow C_6H_5COCH_3$

[NCERT Ex. Q. 8.13, Page 292]

Ans. (i) HO^- acts as a nucleophile as it is an electron-rich species, i.e., it is a nucleus seeking species.

(ii) CN^- acts as a nucleophile as it is an electron-rich species, i.e., it is a nucleus seeking species.

(iii) $CH_3\overset{+}{C}N$ acts as an electrophile as it is an electron-deficient species.

Q. 14. Classify the following reactions in one of the reaction type studied in this unit.

(i) $CH_3CH_2Br + HS^- \rightarrow CH_3CH_2SH + Br^-$

(ii) $(CH_3)_2C = CH_2 + HCl \rightarrow (CH_3)_2ClC - CH_3$

(iii) $CH_3CH_2Br + HO^- \rightarrow CH_2 = CH_2 + H_2O + Br^-$

(iv) $(CH_3)_3C\text{-}CH_2OH + HBr \rightarrow (CH_3)_2CBr\,CH_2CH_2CH_3 + H_2O$ **[NCERT Ex. Q. 8.14, Page 293]**

Ans. (i) Nucleophilic substitution.

(ii) Electrophilic addition.

(iii) Bimolecular elimination.

(iv) Nucleophilic substitution with rearrangement.

Q. 15. What is the relationship between the members of following pairs of structures? Are they structural or geometrical isomers or resonance contributors?

(i) 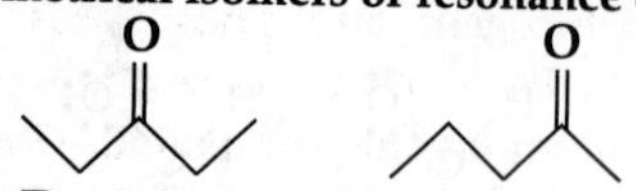

(ii) 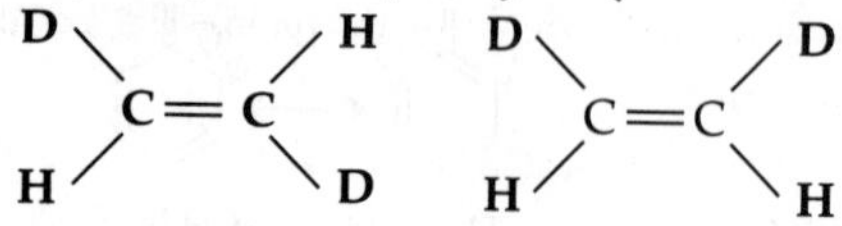

(iii) 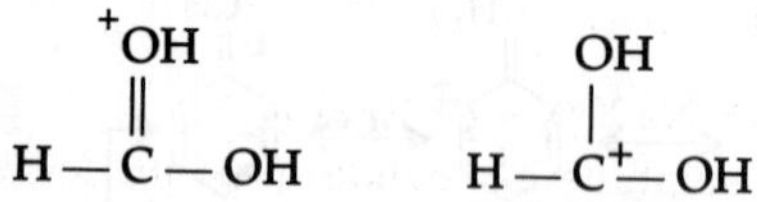

[NCERT Ex. Q. 15, Page 293]

Ans. (i) The given compounds have the same molecular formula but they differ in the position of the functional group, so they are structural isomers.

(ii) The given compounds having the same molecular formula, the same constitution, and the sequence of covalent bonds, but with different relative position of their atoms in space, so they are called geometrical isomers.

(iii) The given compounds are resonance contributors or canonical structures because they differ in the position of electrons but not atoms. **(1)**

Q. 16. For the following bond cleavages, use curved-arrows to show the electron flow and classify each as homolysis or heterolysis. Identify reactive intermediate produced as free radical, carbocation and carbanion.

(i) $CH_3O - OCH_3 \rightarrow CH_3\dot{O} + \dot{O}CH_3$

(ii) 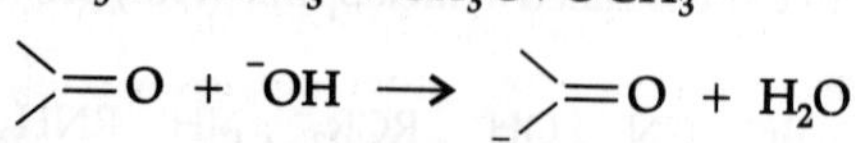

(iii) 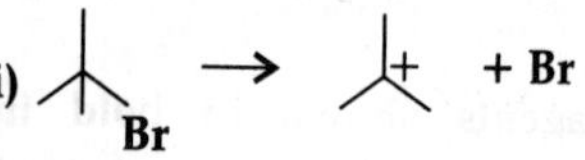

(iv) 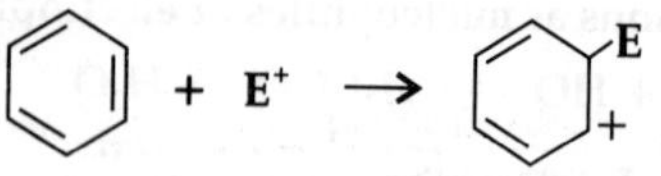

[NCERT Ex. Q. 8.16, Page 293]

Ans. (i) 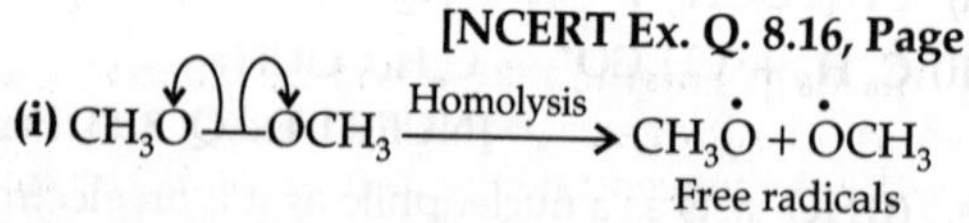

It is an example of homolytic cleavage as one of the shared pair in a covalent bond goes with the bonded atom. The reaction intermediate formed is a free radical.

(ii) 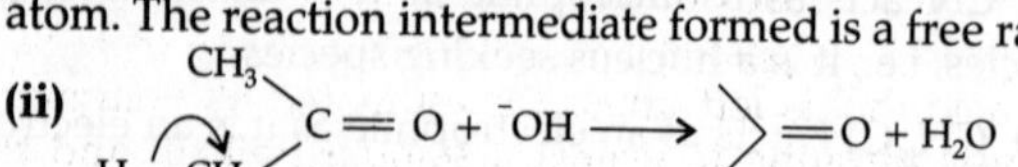

It is an example of heterolytic cleavage as the bond breaks in such a manner that the shared pair of electrons remains with the carbon of propanone. The reaction intermediate formed is carbanion.

(iii) 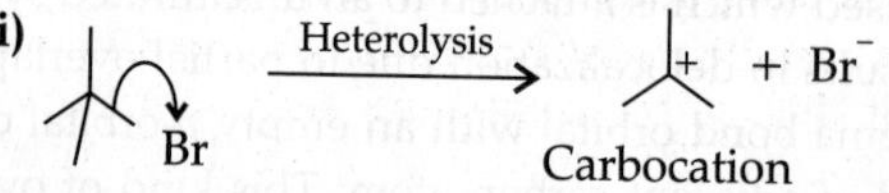

It is an example of heterolytic cleavage as the bond breaks in such a manner that the shared pair of electrons remains with the bromine ion. The reaction intermediate formed is a carbocation.

(iv) 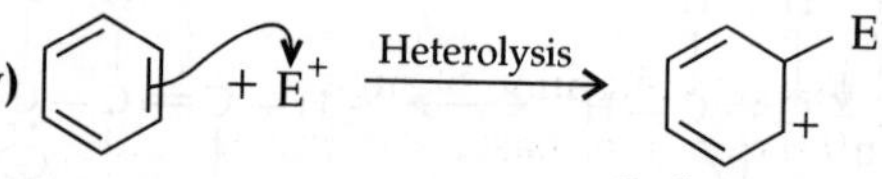

It is a heterolytic cleavage as the bond breaks in such a manner that the shared pair of electrons remains with one of the fragments. The intermediate formed is a carbocation.

Q. 17. Explain the terms Inductive and Electromeric effects. Which electron displacement effect explains the following correct orders of acidity of the carboxylic acids?

(i) $Cl_3CCOOH > Cl_2CHCOOH > ClCH_2COOH$

(ii) $CH_3CH_2COOH > (CH_3)_2CHCOOH > (CH_3)_3CCOOH$

[NCERT Ex. Q. 8.17, Page 293]

Ans. Inductive effect: The permanent displacement of sigma (σ) electrons along a saturated chain, whenever an electron withdrawing or electron donating group is present is called inductive effect.

Inductive effect could be +I effect or –I effect. When an atom or group attracts electrons towards itself more strongly than hydrogen, it is said to possess –I effect. When an atom or group attracts electrons towards itself less strongly than hydrogen, it is said to possess +I effect.

Electromeric effect: It involves the complete transfer of the shared pair of π electrons to either of the two atoms linked by multiple bonds in the presence of an attacking agent. For example, electromeric effect could be +E effect or –E effect. It is a temporary effect, exist only in the presence of the reagent. It results in complete charge.

+E effect: When the electrons are transferred towards the attacking reagent.

–E effect: When the electrons are transferred away from the attacking reagent.

(i) $Cl_3CCOOH > Cl_2CHCOOH > ClCH_2COOH$

The order of acidity can be explained on the basis of inductive effect (–I effect). As the number of chlorine atoms increases, the –I effect increases. With the increase in –I effect, the acid strength also increases accordingly.

(ii) $CH_3CH_2COOH > (CH_3)_2CHCOOH > (CH_3)_3CCOOH$

The order of acidity can be explained on the basis of inductive effect (+I effect). As the number of alkyl groups increases, the +I effect also increases. With the increase in +I effect, the acid strength also increases accordingly.

Q. 18. Give a brief description of the principles of the following techniques taking an example in each case.
(i) Crystallisation (ii) Distillation
(iii) Chromatography [NCERT Ex. Q. 8.18, Page 293]

Ans. (i) Crystallisation: It is based on the difference in the solubilities of the compound and the impurities in a given solvent. The impure compound gets dissolved in the solvent in which it is sparingly soluble at room temperature, but appreciably soluble at higher temperature. The solution is concentrated to obtain a nearly saturated solution. On cooling the solution, the pure compound crystallises out and is removed by filtration.

For example: crystallisation of sugar.

(ii) Distillation: It is based on the fact that liquids having different boiling points vapourise at different temperatures. The vapours are then cooled and the liquids so formed are collected separately. This method is used to separate volatile liquids from non-volatile impurities or a mixture of those liquids that have a sufficient difference in their boiling points.

For example : a mixture of chloroform (b.p = 334 K) and aniline (b.p = 457 K) can be separated by the method of distillation.

(iii) Chromatography: Chromatography is based on the principle of selective distribution of the components of a mixture between two phases, a stationary phase and a moving phase. The stationary phase can be a solid or liquid, while the mobile phase is a liquid or a gas. When the stationary phase is solid the basis is adsorption and when it is a liquid the basis is partition.

For example : Chromatography is generally used for the separation of coloured substances such as plant pigments or dye stuffs.

Q. 19. Describe the method, which can be used to separate two compounds with different solubilities in a solvent S. [NCERT Ex. Q. 8.19, Page 293]

Ans. Fractional crystallisation is used for this purpose. A hot saturated solution of these two compounds is allowed to cool. The less soluble compound crystallises out while the more soluble remains in the solution. The crystals are separated from the mother liquor and the mother liquor is again concentrated and the hot solution is again allowed cool when the crystals of the second compound are obtained. These are again filtered and dried.

Q. 20. What is the difference between distillation, distillation under reduced pressure and steam distillation? [NCERT Ex. Q. 8.20, Page 293]

Ans. Distillation: It is used for the purification of compounds that are associated with non-volatile impurities or those liquids, which do not decompose on boiling.

Mixture of petrol and kerosene is separated by this method.

Distillation under reduced pressure: This method is used to purify a liquid that tends to decompose on boiling. Under the conditions of reduced pressure, the liquid will boil at a low temperature than its boiling point and will, therefore, not decompose.

Glycerol is purified by this method. It boils with decomposition at a temperature of 593 K. At a reduced pressure, it boils at 453 K without decomposition.

Steam distillation: It is used to purify an organic compound, which is steam volatile and immiscible in water. On passing steam, the compound gets heated up and the steam gets condensed to water. After sometime, the mixture of water and liquid starts to boil and passes through the condenser. This condensed mixture of water and liquid is then separated by using a separating funnel.

A mixture of water and aniline is separated by steam distillation.

Q. 21. Discuss the chemistry of Lassaigne's test. [NCERT Ex. Q. 8.21, Page 294]

Ans. This test is employed to detect the presence of nitrogen, sulphur, halogens and phosphorus in an organic compound. These elements are present in the covalent form in an organic compound. These are converted into the ionic form by fusing the compound with sodium metal.

$$Na + C + N \xrightarrow{\Delta} NaCN$$

$$2Na + S \xrightarrow{\Delta} Na_2S$$

$$Na + X \xrightarrow{\Delta} NaX \ (X = Cl, Br \text{ or } I)$$

The cyanide, sulphide, and halide of sodium formed are extracted from the fused mass by boiling it in distilled water. The extract so obtained is called Lassaigne's or sodium fusion extract. This Lassaigne's or sodium fusion extract is then tested for the presence of nitrogen, sulphur, halogens, and phosphorus.

Q. 22. Differentiate between the principle of estimation of nitrogen in an organic compound by (i) Dumas method and (ii) Kjeldahl's method. [NCERT Ex. Q. 8.22, Page 294]

Ans. (i) Dumas method: In Dumas method, a known quantity of nitrogen containing organic compound is heated strongly with excess of copper oxide in an atmosphere of carbon dioxide to produce free nitrogen in addition to carbon dioxide and water.

The traces of nitrogen oxides can also be produced in the reaction, which can be reduced to dinitrogen by passing the gaseous mixture over a heated copper gauge. The dinitrogen produced is collected over an aqueous solution of potassium hydroxide. The volume of nitrogen produced is then measured at room temperature and atmospheric pressure.

$$C_xH_yN_z + \left(2x + \frac{y}{2}\right) CuO$$

$$\downarrow$$

$$\left(2x + \frac{y}{2}\right) Cu + xCO_2 + \frac{y}{2} H_2O + \frac{z}{2} N_2$$

(ii) Kjeldahl's method: In Kjeldahl's method, a known quantity of nitrogen containing organic compound is heated with concentrated sulphuric acid. The nitrogen present in the compound is quantitatively converted into ammonium sulphate. It is then distilled with excess of sodium hydroxide. The ammonia evolved during this process is passed into a known volume of H_2SO_4. The acid that is left unused is estimated by volumetric analysis (titrating it against a standard alkali) and the amount of ammonia produced can be determined. The difference between the initial amount of acid taken and that left after the reaction gives the amount of acid reacted with ammonia.

$$\text{Organic compound} + H_2SO_4 \longrightarrow (NH_4)_2SO_4$$

$$Na_2SO_4 + 2NH_3 + 2H_2O \xleftarrow{2NaOH} (NH_4)_2SO_4$$

$$2NH_3 + H_2SO_4 \longrightarrow (NH_4)_2SO_4$$

Q. 23. Discuss the principle of estimation of halogens, sulphur and phosphorus present in an organic compound. [NCERT Ex. Q. 8.23, Page 294]

Ans. Estimation of halogens: Halogens are estimated by the Carius method. In this method, a known quantity of organic compound is heated with fuming nitric acid in the presence of silver nitrate, present in a hard glass tube called the Carius tube, taken in a furnace. Carbon and hydrogen that are present in the compound are oxidised to form CO_2 and H_2O respectively and the halogen present in the compound is converted in the form of AgX. This AgX is then filtered, washed, dried, and weighed.

Let the mass of organic compound be m g.

Mass of AgX formed = m_1 g

1 mol of AgX contains 1 mol of X.

Therefore,

Mass of halogen in m_1 g of AgX

$$= \frac{\text{Atomic mass of } X \times m_1 g}{\text{molecular mass of } Agx}$$

Percentage of halogen

$$= \frac{\text{Atomic mass of } X \times m_1 g \times 100}{\text{molecular mass of } Agx \times m}$$

Estimation of Sulphur: In this method, a known quantity of organic compound is heated with either fuming nitric acid or sodium peroxide in a hard glass tube called the Carius tube. Sulphur, present in the compound, is oxidised to form sulphuric acid. On addition of excess of barium chloride to it, the precipitation of barium sulphate takes place. This precipitate is then filtered, washed, dried, and weighed.

Let the mass of organic compound be m g.

Mass of $BaSO_4$ formed = m_1 g

1 mol of $BaSO_4$ = 233 g $BaSO_4$ = 32 g of Sulphur

Therefore, m_1 g of $BaSO_4$ contains $\frac{32 \times m_1}{233}$ g of sulphur

$$\text{Percentage of sulphur} = \frac{32 \times m_1 \times 100}{233 \times m}$$

Estimation of phosphorus: In this method, a known quantity of organic compound is heated with fuming nitric acid. Phosphorus, present in the compound is oxidised to form phosphoric acid. By adding ammonia and ammonium molybdate to the solution, phosphorus can be precipitated as ammonium phosphomolybdate.

Phosphorus can also be estimated by precipitating it as $MgNH_4PO_4$ by adding magnesia mixture, which on ignition yields $Mg_2P_2O_7$.

Let the mass of organic compound be m g.

Mass of ammonium phosphomolybdate formed = m_1 g

Molar mass of ammonium phosphomolybdate = 1877 g

$$\text{Percentage of phosphorus} = \frac{31 \times m_1 \times 100}{1877 \times m}\ \%$$

If phosphorus is estimated as $Mg_2P_2O_7$,

$$\text{Percentage of phosphorus} = \frac{62 \times m_1 \times 100}{222 \times m}\ \%$$

Q. 24. Explain the principle of paper chromatography. [NCERT Ex. Q. 8.28, Page 294]

Ans. In paper chromatography, chromatography paper is used. This paper contains water trapped in it, which acts as the stationary phase. On the base of this chromatography paper, the solution of the mixture is spotted. The paper strip is then suspended in a suitable solvent, which acts as the mobile phase. This solvent rises up the chromatography paper by capillary action and in the procedure, it flows over the spot. The components are selectively retained on the paper (according to their differing partition in these two phases). The spots of different components travel with the mobile phase to different heights. The paper so obtained is known as a chromatogram.

Q. 25. Why is nitric acid added to sodium extract before adding silver nitrate for testing halogens? [NCERT Ex. Q. 8.25, Page 294]

Ans. While testing the Lassaigne's extract for the presence of halogens, it is first boiled with dilute nitric acid. This is done to decompose NaCN to HCN and Na_2S to H_2S and to expel these gases. That is, if any nitrogen and sulphur are present in the form of NaCN and Na_2S, then they are removed. These ions would otherwise interfere with silver nitrate test for halogens.

$$NaCN + HNO_3 \rightarrow NaNO_3 + HCN$$

$$Na_2S + 2HNO_3 \rightarrow 2NaNO_3 + H_2S$$

Q. 26. Explain the reason for the fusion of an organic compound with metallic sodium for testing nitrogen, sulphur and halogens. [NCERT Ex. Q. 8.26, Page 294]

Ans. Nitrogen, sulphur, and halogens are covalently bonded in organic compounds. For their detection, they have to be first converted to ionic form. This is done by fusing the organic compound with sodium metal. This is called "Lassaigne's test".

$$Na + C + N \xrightarrow{\Delta} NaCN$$

$$2Na + S \xrightarrow{\Delta} Na_2S$$

$$Na + X \xrightarrow{\Delta} NaX\ (X = Cl, Br \text{ or } I)$$

Carbon, nitrogen, sulphur, and halogens come from organic compounds.

Q. 27. Name a suitable technique of separation of the components form a mixture of calcium sulphate and camphor ? [NCERT Ex. Q. 8.27, Page 294]

Ans. Sublimation.

Q. 28. Explain, why an organic liquid vaporises at a temperature below its boiling point in its steam distillation? [NCERT Ex. Q. 8.28, Page 294]

Ans. In steam distillation, the organic liquid starts to boil when the sum of vapour pressure due to the organic liquid (p_1) and the vapour pressure due to water (p_2) becomes equal to atmospheric pressure (p), that is,

$p = p_1 + p_2$

Since $p_1 < p_2$, organic liquid will vaporise at a lower temperature than its boiling point.

Q. 29. Will CCl_4 gives white precipitate of AgCl on heating it with silver nitrate? Give reason for your answer. [NCERT Ex. Q. 8.29, Page 294]

Ans. CCl_4 will not give the white precipitate of AgCl on heating it with silver nitrate. This is because the chlorine atoms are covalently bonded to carbon in CCl_4. To obtain the precipitate, it should be present in ionic form and for this, it is necessary to prepare the Lassaigne's extract of CCl_4. On heating with silver nitrate the chlorine bonded with carbon remains in molecular state and does not dissociate into chloride ions.

Q. 30. Why is a solution of potassium hydroxide used to absorb carbon dioxide evolved during the estimation of carbon present in an organic compound? [NCERT Ex. Q. 8.30, Page 294]

Ans. Carbon dioxide is acidic in nature and potassium hydroxide is a strong base. Hence, carbon dioxide reacts with potassium hydroxide to form potassium carbonate and water as follows:

$2KOH + CO_2 \rightarrow K_2CO_3 + H_2O$

Thus, the mass of the U-tube containing KOH increases. This increase in the mass of U- tube gives the mass of CO_2 produced. From its mass, the percentage of carbon in the organic compound can be estimated.

Q. 31. Why is it necessary to use acetic acid and not sulphuric acid for acidification of sodium extract for testing sulphur by lead acetate test? [NCERT Ex. Q. 8.31, Page 294]

Ans. Although the addition of sulphuric acid will precipitate lead sulphate which interferes with the test of sulphur, the addition of acetic acid will ensure a complete precipitation of sulphur in the form of lead sulphate due to common ion effect. Hence, it is necessary to use acetic acid for acidification of sodium extract for testing sulphur by lead acetate test.

Q. 32. An organic compound contains 69% carbon and 4.8% hydrogen, the remainder being oxygen. Calculate the masses of carbon dioxide and water produced when 0.20 g of this substance is subjected to complete combustion. [NCERT Ex. Q. 8.32, Page 294]

Ans. Percentage of carbon in organic compound = 69 %

That is, 100 g of organic compound contains 69 g of carbon.

0.2 g of organic compound will contain = $\frac{69 \times 0.2}{100}$ = 0.138 g of C

Molecular mass of carbon dioxide, CO_2 = 44 g

That is, 12 g of carbon is contained in 44 g of CO_2.

Therefore, 0.138 g of carbon will be contained in $\frac{44 \times 0.138}{12}$ = 0.506 g of CO_2

Thus, 0.506 g of CO_2 will be produced on complete combustion of 0.2 g of organic compound.

Percentage of hydrogen in organic compound is 4.8.

i.e., 100 g of organic compound contains 4.8 g of hydrogen.

Therefore, 0.2 g of organic compound will contain $\frac{4.8 \times 0.2}{100}$ = 0.0096 g of H

It is known that molecular mass of water (H_2O) is 18 g.

Thus, 2 g of hydrogen is present in 18 g of water.

0.0096 g of hydrogen will be contained in $\frac{18 \times 0.0096}{2}$ = 0.0864 g of water

Thus, 0.0864 g of water will be produced on complete combustion of 0.2 g of the organic compound.

Q. 33. A sample of 0.50 g of an organic compound was treated according to Kjeldahl's method. The ammonia evolved was absorbed in 50 ml of 0.5 M H_2SO_4. The residual acid required 60 mL of 0.5 M solution of NaOH for neutralisation. Find the percentage composition of nitrogen in the compound. [NCERT Ex. Q. 8.33, Page 294]

Ans. Given that, total mass of organic compound = 0.50 g

60 mL of 0.5 M solution of NaOH was required by residual acid for neutralisation.

60 mL of 0.5 M NaOH solution= $\frac{60}{2}$ ml of 0.5 M

H_2SO_4 = 30 mL of 0.5 M H_2SO_4

Acid consumed in absorption of evolved ammonia is (50–30) mL = 20 mL

Again, 20 mL of 0.5 M H_2SO_4 = 40 mL of 0.5 M NH_3

Also, since 1000 mL of 1 M NH_3 contains 14 g of nitrogen,

40 mL of 0.5 M NH_3 will contain = $\frac{14 \times 40}{1000} \times 0.5$

= 0.28 g of N

Therefore, percentage of nitrogen in 0.50 g of organic compound = $\frac{0.28}{0.50} \times 100$ = 56 %

Q. 34. 0.3780 g of an organic chloro compound gave 0.5740 g of silver chloride in Carius estimation. Calculate the percentage of chlorine present in the compound. [NCERT Ex. Q. 8.34, Page 294]

Ans. Given that,

Mass of organic compound is 0.3780 g,

Molecular mass of AgCl = 108 + 35.5 = 143.5 g mol^{-1}

Mass of AgCl formed = 0.5740 g

1 mol of AgCl contains 1 mol of Cl.

Thus, mass of chlorine in 0.5740 g of AgCl

$$\frac{35.5 \times 0.5740}{143.5} = \mathbf{0.142g}$$

Percentage of chlorine = $\frac{0.142}{0.3780} \times 100$ = 37.57%

Hence, the percentage of chlorine present in the given organic chloro compound is 37.57%.

Q. 35. In the estimation of sulphur by Carius method, 0.468 g of an organic sulphur compound afforded 0.668 g of barium sulphate. Find out the percentage of sulphur in the given compound.

[NCERT Ex. Q. 8.35, Page 294]

Ans. Given, total mass of organic compound = 0.468 g

Mass of barium sulphate formed = 0.668 g

1 mol of $BaSO_4$ = 233 g of $BaSO_4$ = 32 g of sulphur

Thus, 0.668 g of $BaSO_4$ contains $\frac{32 \times 0.668}{233}$ g of sulphur = 0.0917 g of sulphur

Therefore, percentage of sulphur = $\frac{0.0917}{0.468} \times 100$

= 19.59 %

Hence, the percentage of sulphur in the given compound is 19.59 %.

Q. 36. In the organic compound $CH_2 = CH - CH_2 - CH_2 - C \equiv CH$, the pair of hybridised orbitals involved in the formation of $C_2 - C_3$ is:

(A) $sp - sp^2$
(B) $sp - sp^3$
(C) $sp^2 - sp^3$
(D) $sp^3 - sp^3$

[NCERT Ex. Q. 8.36, Page 294]

Ans. Option (C) is correct.

Explanation:

$$\overset{1}{C}H_2 = \underset{sp^2}{\overset{2}{C}}H - \underset{sp^3}{\overset{3}{C}}H_2 - \overset{4}{C}H_2 - \overset{5}{C} \equiv \overset{6}{C}H$$

Q. 37. If the lassaigne's test for nitrogen in an organic compound, the Prussian blue colour is obtained due to the formation of:

(A) $Na_4[Fe(CN)_6]$
(B) $Fe_4[Fe(CN)_6]_3$
(C) $Fe_2[Fe(CN)_6]$
(D) $Fe_3[Fe(CN)_6]_4$

[NCERT Ex. Q. 8.37, Page 294]

Ans. Option (B) is correct.

Q. 38. Which of the following carbocation is most stable ?

(A) $(CH_3)_3C.\overset{+}{C}H_2$
(B) $(CH_3)_3\overset{+}{C}$
(C) $CH_3CH_2\overset{+}{C}H_2$
(D) $CH_3\overset{+}{C}HCH_2CH_3$

[NCERT Ex. Q. 8.38, Page 294]

Ans. Option (A) is correct.

Explanation: Tertiary carbocation is most stable.

Q. 39. The best and latest technique for isolation, purification and separation of organic compounds is:

(A) Crystallisation
(B) Distillation
(C) Sublimation
(D) Chromatography

[NCERT Ex. Q. 8.39, Page 294]

Ans. Option (D) is correct.

Q. 40. The reaction:

CH_3CH_2I + KOH (aq) → CH_3CH_2OH + KI is classified as:

(A) electrophilic substitution
(B) nucleophilic substitution
(C) elimination
(D) addition

[NCERT Ex. Q. 8.40, Page 294]

Ans. Option (B) is correct.

CHAPTER 9

HYDROCARBONS

Classification of Hydrocarbons

- Hydrocarbons are carbon and hydrogen compounds derived mainly from coal and petroleum. They are classified into three categories:

1. **Saturated hydrocarbon** – C – C single bonds; eg. $CH_3 - CH_3$ ethane
2. **Unsaturated hydrocarbon** – C = C, and C ≡ C or both e.g $CH_2 = CH_2$, ethene, or CH ≡ CH, ethyne.
3. **Aromatic hydrocarbon**-One aromatic ring atleast; e.g C_6H_6, benzene.

Alkanes

- Alkanes are the simplest organic compounds made of carbon and hydrogen only. They have the general formula C_nH_{2n+2} (where n = 1, 2, 3, etc.) Alkanes contain strong C—C and C—H bonds. Therefore, this class of hydrocarbons is relatively chemically inert. Hence, they are sometimes referred to as paraffins (Latin: parum affinis = little affinity).
- Methane (CH_4) is the first member of this family. In methane, carbon forms single bonds with four hydrogen atoms. All H—C—H bond angles are of 109.5°. Methane has a tetrahedral structure. C—C and C—H bonds are formed by head-on overlapping of sp^3 hybrid orbitals of carbon and 1s orbitals of hydrogen atoms.

Scan to know more about this topic

Alkanes

- Alkanes exhibit chain isomerism, position isomerism and conformational isomerism.
- Based upon the number of carbon atoms attached to a carbon atom, the carbon atom is termed as primary (1°), secondary (2°), tertiary (3°) or quaternary (4°).
- Groups or substituents derived from alkanes by removal of one hydrogen atom is known as alkyl groups. Their general formula is C_nH_{2n+1}.
- **Steps to write correct structure from the given IUPAC name:**

(i) Write the longest chain of carbon atoms corresponding to the parent alkane.

(ii) Give number to carbon atoms.

(iii) The substituents are attached to the correct carbon atoms after their numbering.

(iv) Satisfy the valency of each carbon atom by putting the correct number of hydrogen atoms.

- **Preparation of Alkanes:**

(i) Alkanes can be prepared by hydrogenation of unsaturated hydrocarbons in the presence of catalyst (Ni, Pd or Pt).

$$\underset{\text{Ethene}}{CH_2 = CH_2} + H_2 \xrightarrow{\text{Ni/Pd/Pt}} \underset{\text{Ethane}}{CH_3—CH_3}$$

$$\underset{\text{Ethyne}}{HC \equiv CH} + 2H_2 \xrightarrow{\text{Ni/Pd/Pt}} \underset{\text{Ethane}}{H_3C—CH_3}$$

(ii) By reduction of alkyl halides: Alkanes can be prepared by the reduction of alkyl halides (except fluorides) with zinc and dilute hydrochloric acid.

$$\underset{\text{Chloromethane}}{CH_3—Cl} + H_2 \xrightarrow{\text{Zn, H}^+} \underset{\text{Methane}}{CH_4} + HCl$$

(iii) Wurtz Reaction: This reaction is used to increase the length of the carbon chain.

$$CH_3Br + 2Na + BrCH_3 \xrightarrow{\text{dry ether}} CH_3—CH_3 + 2NaBr$$

Note: From wurtz reaction only these alkane can be formed which have even number of C atom.

(iv) Decarboxylation: Sodium salts of carboxylic acids on heating with soda lime (mixture of sodium hydroxide and calcium oxide) give alkanes containing one carbon atom less than the carboxylic acid.

Scan to know more about this topic

Methods of preparation of alkanes

$$\underset{\text{Sodium ethanoate}}{CH_3COO^-Na^+} + NaOH \xrightarrow[\Delta]{\text{CaO}} \underset{\text{Methane}}{CH_4} + Na_2CO_3$$

(v) Kolbe's Electrolytic Method:

$$\underset{\text{Sodium acetate}}{2CH_3COO^- Na^+} + 2H_2O \xrightarrow{\text{Electrolysis}} \underset{\text{Ethane}}{CH_3—CH_3} + 2CO_2 + H_2 + 2NaOH$$

- **Physical properties:** Alkanes are almost non-polar molecule. They possess weak van der Waals forces. Due to the weak forces, the first four members, C_1 to C_4 are gases, C_5 to C_{17} are liquids and those containing 18 carbon atoms or more are solids at 298 K. They are colourless and odourless. With the increase of branching, the boiling points of alkanes decrease as on increasing the branching, the molecule attains the shapes of a sphere, decreasing surface area, thereby decreasing van der Waals forces. Alkanes with even number of carbon atoms have higher melting points as compared to next higher or lower alkanes with odd number of carbon atoms.

Hydrocarbons

Compounds of Carbon and Hydrogen

Aromatic Hydrocarbon

- Types: Benzenoids – contain benzene ring, Non-benzenoids – does not contain benzene ring.
- Isomerism: Ortho (o-), Meta (m-), Para (p-)
- Structure:

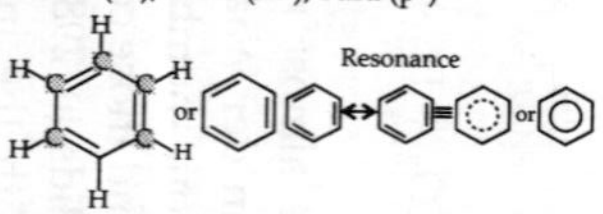

- Aromaticity: Planarity, complete delocalisation of the π–electros in the ring, presence of (4n + 2) π electrons in the ring where n is an integer (n = 0,1,2,......) (Huckel rule)

Preparation:

- Cyclic polymerisation of ethyne

$C_6H_5COONa + NaOH \xrightarrow[\Delta]{CaO} C_6H_6 + Na_2CO_3$

$C_6H_5OH + Zn \xrightarrow{\Delta} C_6H_6 + ZnO$

Mechanism of Electrophilic substitution reactions

(i) Generation of Electrophile
(ii) Formation of carbocation intermediate
(iii) Removal of proton

Physical Properties:

- Non-polar, usually colourless liquids or solids with characteristic aroma.
- Immiscible with water but miscible with organic solvents.
- Burns with sooty flame.

Chemical Properties:

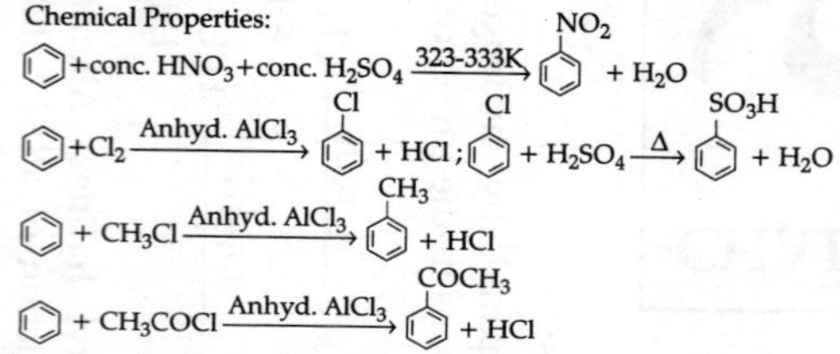

Classification

- **Saturated:** Contain C-C and C-H single bonds. (alkanes)
- **Unsaturated:** Contain C-C multiple bonds (alkenes, alkynes)
- **Aromatic**: Contain cyclic compounds

Alkynes (C_nH_{2n-2})

- IUPAC name: replacing 'ane' by the suffix 'yne'.
- Shows position and chain isomerism

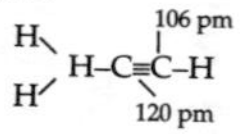

Preparation:

$CaCO_3 \xrightarrow{\Delta} CaO + CO_2$

$CaO + 3C \longrightarrow CaC_2 + CO$

$CaC_2 + 2H_2O \longrightarrow Ca(OH)_2 + C_2H_2$

$CH_2Br-CH_2Br + KOH \xrightarrow[-KBr, -H_2O]{alcohol} H_2C=CHBr \xrightarrow[-NaBr, -NH_3]{NaNH_2} CH\equiv CH$

Physical Properties:

- First three members are gases, next eight are liquids and higher ones are solids.
- Colourless, ethyne has characteristic odour and other are odourless.
- Lighter than water, immiscible with water but soluble in organic solvents.
- M.p, b.p. and density increase with increase in molar mass.

Chemical Properties:

$HC\equiv CH + Na \longrightarrow HC\equiv CNa + 1/2H_2$

$HC\equiv CH + H_2 \xrightarrow{Pt/Pd/Ni} [H_2C=CH_2] \xrightarrow{H_2} CH_3-CH_3$

$CH_3-C\equiv CH + Br_2 \longrightarrow [CH_3CBr=CHBr] \xrightarrow{Br_2} CH_3-CBr_2-CHBr_2$

$HC\equiv C-H + HBr \longrightarrow [CH_2C=CH-Br] \longrightarrow CHBr_2-CH_3$

$HC\equiv CH + H_2O \xrightarrow[333\,K]{Hg^{2+}/H^+} [CH_2=C(OH)-H] \xrightarrow{Isomersation} CH_3-C(=O)-H$

Polymerisation

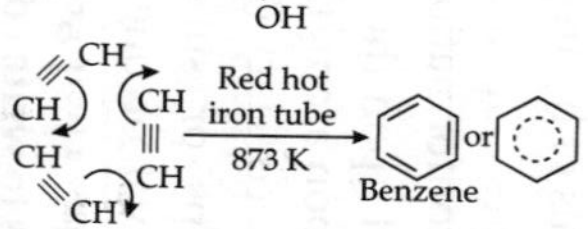

Alkenes (C_nH_{2n})

- Shows structural and geometrical isomerism
- Preparation:

$RC\equiv CR' + H_2 \xrightarrow{Pd/C}$ R(H)C=C(H)R' *cis*-Alkene

$RC\equiv CR' + H_2 \xrightarrow{Na/Liquid\ NH_3}$ R(H)C=C(R')H *trans*-Alkene

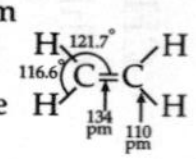

$H_3C-CH_2X \xrightarrow[\Delta]{Alc.KOH} H_2C=CH_2$

$CH_2Br-CH_2Br + Zn \longrightarrow CH_2=CH_2 + ZnBr_2$

$H_3CCH_2OH \xrightarrow[\Delta]{conc.H_2SO_4} CH_2=CH_2 + H_2O$

- Physical Properties :
  - Ethene is a colourless gas with faint sweet smell.
  - All other are colourless and odourless, insoluble in water but fairly soluble in non-polar solvents.
  - Increase in b.p. with increase in molecular size.
- Chemical Properties:

$CH_2=CH_2 + Br_2 \xrightarrow{CCl_4} BrCH_2-CH_2Br$

$CH_2=CH_2 + HBr \longrightarrow CH_3CH_2Br$

$CH_3-CH=CH_2 + HBr \xrightarrow[rule]{Markovnikov}$ $CH_3-CH(Br)-CH_3$; $CH_3-CH_2-CH_2-Br$

$H_3C-C(CH_3)=CH_2 + H_2O \xrightarrow{H^+} (CH_3)_2C(OH)-CH_3$

$CH_3-CH=CH-CH_3 \xrightarrow{KMnO_4/H^+} 2CH_3COOH$

$n(CH_2=CH_2) \xrightarrow[Catalyst]{HighTemp/Pressure} -(CH_2-CH_2)-_n$

$n(CH_3-CH=CH_2) \xrightarrow[Catalyst]{HighTemp/Pressure} -(CH_3-CH_2-CH_2)-_n$

Alkane (C_nH_{2n+2})

- H-C-H bond angles – 190.5°, C-C and C-H bond lengths are 154 pm and 112 pm respectively.
- Shows structural and chain isomerism.

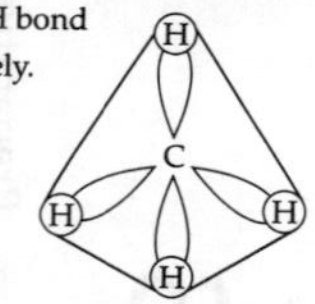

Preparation :

$CH_2=CH_2 + H_2 \xrightarrow{pt/pd} CH_3-CH_3$

$CH_3Cl + H_2 \xrightarrow{Zn,H^+} CH_4 + HCl$

Wurtz reaction :

$CH_3Br + 2Na + BrCH_3 \xrightarrow{Dryether} CH_3-CH_3 + 2NaBr$

$CH_3COO^-Na^+ + NaOH \xrightarrow[\Delta]{CaO} CH_4 + Na_2CO_3$

$2CH_3COONa + 2H_2O \longrightarrow C_2H_6 + 2CO_2 + H_2 + 2NaOH$

- Physical Properties:

Non-polar, weak van der Waals forces, colourless, odourless.

B.P. increases with increases in molecular size.

Chemical Properties:

$CH_4 \xrightarrow[hv/-HCl]{+Cl_2} CH_3Cl \xrightarrow[hv/-HCl]{+Cl_2} CH_2Cl_2 \xrightarrow[hv/-HCl]{+Cl_2} CHCl_3 \xrightarrow[hv/-HCl]{+Cl_2}$

$C_nH_{2n+2} + \left(\frac{3n+1}{2}\right)O_2 \longrightarrow nCO_2 + (n+1)H_2O$

$2CH_4 + O_2 \xrightarrow{Cu/523K/100atm} 2CH_3OH$

$CH_4 + O_2 \xrightarrow[\Delta]{Mn_2O_3} HCHO + H_2O$

$CH_4(CH_2)CH_3 \xrightarrow{Anhyd.AlCl_3/HCl} CH_3-CH(CH_3)-(CH_2)_2-CH_3 + CH_3-CH_2-CH(CH_3)-CH_2-CH_3$

$CH_4 + H_2O \xrightarrow[\Delta]{Ni} CO + 3H_2$

$C_6H_{14} \xrightarrow{733\,K}$ $C_6H_{12} + H_2$; $C_4H_8 + C_2H_6$; $C_3H_6 + C_2H_4 + CH_4$

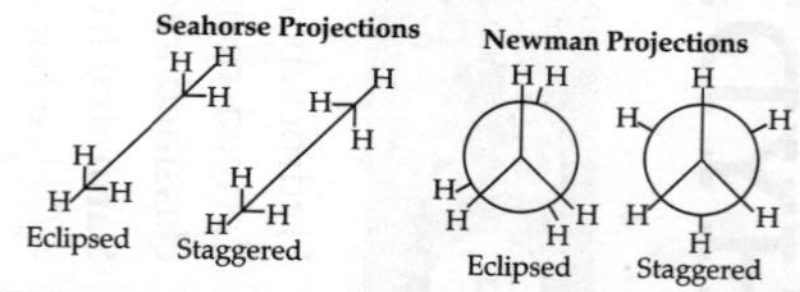

Trace the Mind Map
- First Level
- Second Level
- Third Level

Chemical Properties:

(i) Substitution Reactions: One or more atom of alkanes is replaced by halogens, nitro group and sulphonic acid group, e.g., halogenation.

$$CH_4 + Cl_2 \xrightarrow{hv} \underset{\text{Chloromethane}}{CH_3Cl} + HCl$$

$$CH_3Cl + Cl_2 \xrightarrow{hv} \underset{\text{Dichloromethane}}{CH_2Cl_2} + HCl$$

$$CH_2Cl_2 + Cl_2 \xrightarrow{hv} \underset{\text{Trichloromethane (chloroform)}}{CHCl_3} + HCl$$

$$CHCl_3 + Cl_2 \xrightarrow{hv} \underset{\text{Tetrachloromethane}}{CCl_4} + HCl$$

Mechanism:

(i) Initiation: Homolysis of chlorine molecule in the presence of light or heat.

$$Cl_2 \xrightarrow{hv} 2Cl^{\bullet}$$

(ii) Propagation: Chlorine free radical attacks the methane molecule and takes the reaction in the forward direction by breaking the C–H bond to generate methyl free radical with the formation of H–Cl.

$$Cl^{\bullet} + CH_4 \longrightarrow HCl + CH_3^{\bullet}$$

The methyl radical obtained attacks the second molecule of chlorine to form CH_3–Cl with the liberation of another chlorine free radical by homolysis of chlorine molecule.

$$CH_3^{\bullet} + Cl_2 \longrightarrow CH_3Cl + Cl^{\bullet}$$

(iii) Termination:

$$Cl^{\bullet} + Cl^{\bullet} \longrightarrow Cl_2$$

$$CH_3^{\bullet} + CH_3^{\bullet} \longrightarrow CH_3-CH_3$$

$$Cl^{\bullet} + CH_3^{\bullet} \longrightarrow CH_3Cl$$

(ii) Combustion: Due to the evolution of a large amount of heat during combustion, alkanes are used as fuels.

$$C_nH_{2n+2} + \left(\frac{3n+1}{2}\right)O_2 \rightarrow nCO_2 + (n+1)H_2O$$

e.g., $C_4H_{10}(g) + \frac{13}{2}O_2(g) \rightarrow 4CO_2(g) + 5H_2O(l)$;

$\Delta H° = -2875.84$ kJ mol^{-1}

(iii) Controlled Oxidation:

(i) $2CH_4 + O_2 \xrightarrow{Cu/523K/100\ atm} \underset{\text{Methanol}}{2CH_3OH}$

(ii) $CH_4 + O_2 \xrightarrow[\Delta]{Mo_2O_3} \underset{\text{Methanal}}{HCHO} + H_2O$

(iii) $2CH_3CH_3 + 3O_2 \xrightarrow{(CH_3COO)_2Mn} \underset{\text{Ethanoic acid}}{2CH_3COOH} + 2H_2O$

(iv) $\underset{\substack{\text{2-Methylpropane} \\ (3°\text{-alkane})}}{(CH_3)_3CH} \xrightarrow[{[O]}]{KMnO_4} \underset{\text{2-Methylpropan-2-ol}}{(CH_3)_3COH}$

(iv) Isomerisation: *n*-Alkanes on heating in the presence of anhydrous aluminium chloride and hydrogen chloride gas isomerise to branched chain alkanes.

$$\underset{n\text{-hexane}}{CH_3(CH_2)_4CH_3} \xrightarrow{\text{Anhyd. } AlCl_3/HCl} \underset{\text{2-methylpentane}}{CH_3CH(CH_3)-(CH_2)_2-CH_3} + \underset{\text{3-methylpentane}}{CH_3CH_2-CH(CH_3)-CH_2-CH_3}$$

(v) Aromatization or Reforming: Dehydrogenation and cyclization to benzene and its homologues.

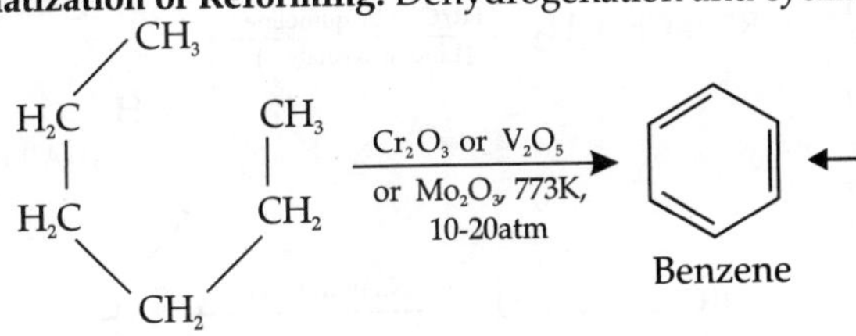

n–Hexane

(vi) Reaction with steam: (Industrial preparation of dihydrogen gas)

$$CH_4 + H_2O \xrightarrow[\Delta]{Ni(1273\ K)} CO + 3H_2$$

(vii) Pyrolysis: Decomposition of higher alkanes to lower alkanes by the application of heat is called pyrolysis or cracking.

$$C_6H_{14} \xrightarrow{773\ K} C_6H_{12} + H_2$$
$$\phantom{C_6H_{14}} \longrightarrow C_4H_8 + C_2H_6$$
$$\phantom{C_6H_{14}} \longrightarrow C_3H_6 + C_2H_4 + CH_4$$

Conformations of Alkanes: Alkanes have C—C sigma (σ) bonds and rotation about C—C single bond is allowed. This rotation results in different spatial arrangements of atoms in space which can change into one another, such spatial arrangements are called conformations or conformers or rotamers. Alkanes can have infinite number of conformations. Ethane shows eclipsed, staggered and skew conformations. Eclipsed form is least stable but staggered form is most stable due to greater distance between the bond pairs or lesser torsional strain. The energy difference between the two extreme forms is of the order of 12.5 kJ mol^{-1}.

(i) Sawhorse projections: In this projection, the molecule is viewed along the molecular axis.

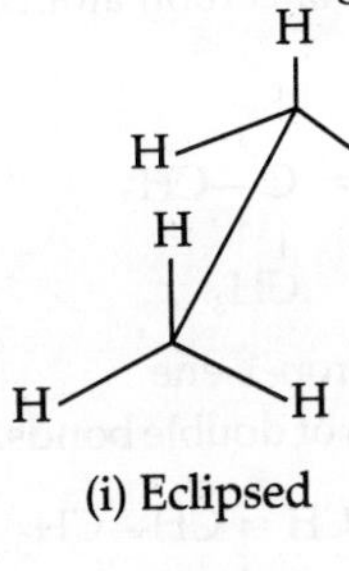

(i) Eclipsed

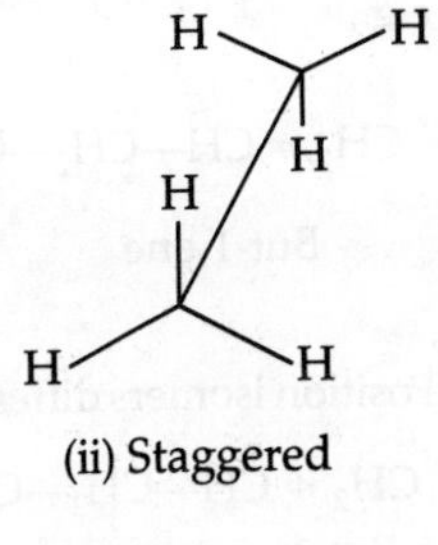

(ii) Staggered

(ii) Newman projections: In this projection, the molecule is viewed at the C–C bond head on.

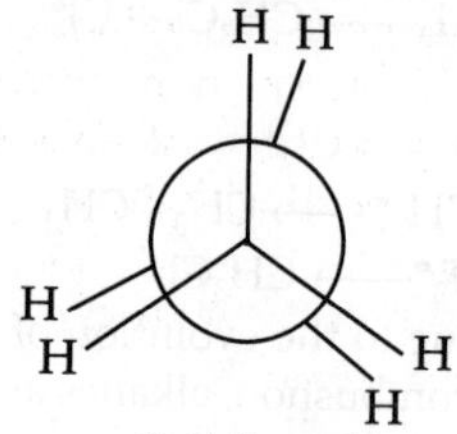

(i) Eclipsed

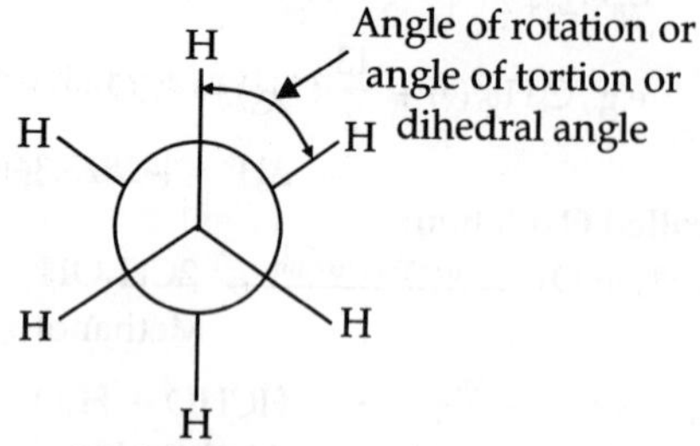

(ii) Staggered

Newman's Projections of ethane

Alkenes

- These are unsaturated non-cyclic hydrocarbons containing at least one double bond and have sp^2 -hybridisation with 120° bond angle. Alkenes are also called olefins [oil forming] which indicates their high reactive nature. Alkenes have general formula C_nH_{2n}, where n = 2,3,4 ...

  Example- C_2H_4 (ethene), C_3H_6 (propene), etc.

- **Structure of Double Bond:** Carbon-carbon double bond in alkenes consists of one strong sigma (σ) bond (bond enthalpy about 397 kJ mol^{-1}) due to head-on overlapping of sp^2 hybridised orbitals and one weak pi (π) bond (bond enthalpy about 284 kJ mol^{-1}) obtained by lateral or sideways overlapping of the two $2p$ orbitals of the two carbon atoms. The double bond is shorter in bond length (134 pm) than the C–C single bond (154 pm).

- **Nomenclature:**

(i) The longest chain of carbon atoms containing the double bond is selected.

(ii) Numbering of the chain is done from the end which is nearer to the double bond.

(iii) The suffix 'ene' replaces 'ane' of alkanes.

- **Isomerism:** Alkenes show chain, position and geometrical isomerism.

  Chain isomers have different chains of carbon atoms, e.g.,

$CH_2 = CH—CH_2—CH_3$ and $CH_2 = C(CH_3)—CH_3$

But-1-ene 2-Methyprop-1-ene

Position isomers differ in the position of double bonds.

$CH_2 = CH—CH_2—CH_3$ and $CH_3—CH = CH—CH_3$

But-1-ene But-2-ene

The stereoisomerism is exhibited by alkenes due to difference in the spatial arrangement of groups around double bonded carbon atoms. The simplest alkene that can exhibit geometrical isomerism is but-2-ene. Cis form of alkene is more polar than the trans form.

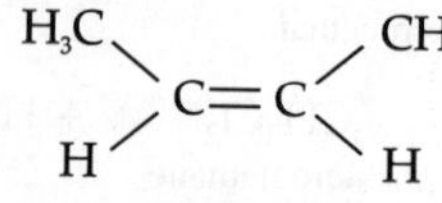

cis-But-2-ene

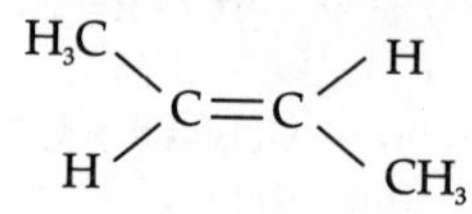

trans-But-2-ene

The boiling point of *cis*-form is more than the *trans*-form due to high polarity of *cis*-form. However, melting point of trans-form is more than that the *cis*-form.

Mnemonics

Concept: To Learn Bond Length

Mnemonics: See Duet Trial

Interpretation:-C-C Single bond>Double bond > Triple bond

- **Preparation of Alkenes:**

Scan to know more about this topic

Alkynes

(i) From alkynes: Alkynes on partial reduction with calculated amount of dihydrogen in the presence of palladised charcoal partially deactivated with poisons like sulphur compounds or quinoline give alkenes. Partially deactivated palladised charcoal is known as Lindlar's catalyst.

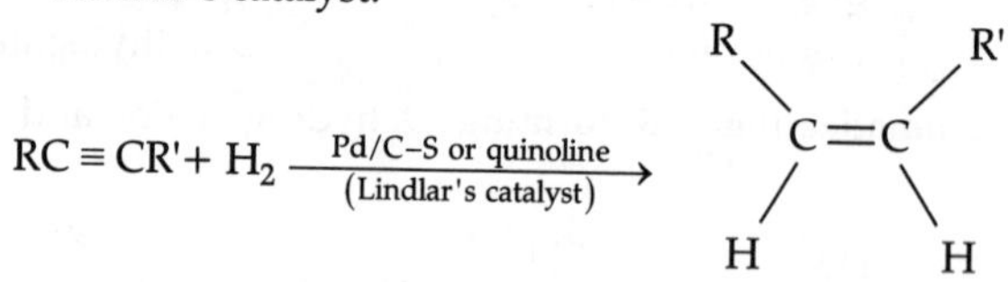

cis-Alkene

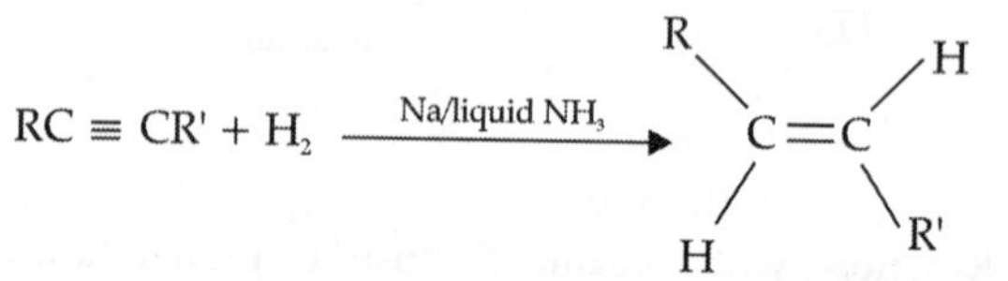

trans-Alkene

(ii) From alkyl halides: Alkyl halides (R-X) on heating with alcoholic potash (potassium hydroxide dissolved in alcohol) eliminate one molecule of halogen acid to form alkenes. This reaction is known as dehydrohalogenation, i.e., removal of halogen acid. This is example of β-elimination reaction, since hydrogen atom is eliminated from the β carbon atom.

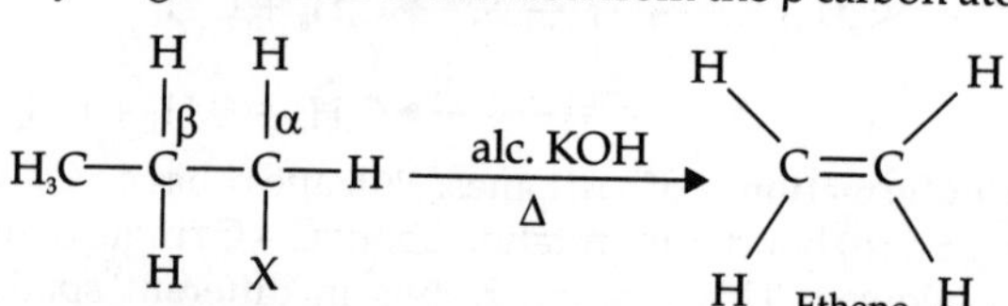

(X = Cl, Br, I)

The rate of the reaction:

For halogens: Iodine > Bromine > Chlorine

For alkyl group: Tertiary > Secondary > Primary

(iii) From vicinal dihalides: Dihalides in which two halogen atoms are attached to two adjacent carbon atoms are known as vicinal dihalides. Vicinal dihalides on treatment with zinc metal lose a molecule of ZnX_2 to form an alkene. The reaction is known as dehalogenation.

$$CH_3CHBr—CH_2Br + Zn \rightarrow CH_3CH = CH_2 + ZnBr_2$$

(iv) From Alcohols: Alcohols on heating with concentrated sulphuric acid form alkenes with the elimination of one water molecule. This reaction is known as acidic dehydration of alcohols.

$$H-\overset{H}{\underset{H}{\overset{|\beta}{\underset{|}{C}}}}-\overset{H}{\underset{OH}{\overset{|\alpha}{\underset{|}{C}}}}-H \xrightarrow[\Delta]{\text{conc. } H_2SO_4} \underset{\text{Ethene}}{CH_2 = CH_2} + H_2O$$

Ethanol

▶ **Physical Properties:** Alkenes as a class resembles alkanes in physical properties, except in types of isomerism and difference in polar nature. Ethene is a colourless gas with a faint sweet smell. All other alkenes are colourless and odourless, insoluble in water but fairly soluble in nonpolar solvents like benzene, petroleum, ether. Alkenes show a regular increase in boiling point with increase in size.

▶ **Chemical Properties:** Alkenes undergo electrophilic addition reaction because of loosely held π-electrons.

(i) Addition of dihydrogen:

$$\underset{\text{Ethene}}{H_2C = CH_2} \xrightarrow[\text{Ni/Pt/Pd}]{H_2} \underset{\text{Ethane}}{H_3C—CH_3}$$

(ii) Addition of halogen: This reaction is used for the test of unsaturation.

$$H_2C = CH_2 + \underset{\text{(Reddish orange)}}{Br—Br} \xrightarrow{CCl_4} \underset{\text{(Colourless)}}{\underset{Br\qquad Br}{CH_2—CH_2}}$$

(iii) Addition of hydrogen halides: The order of reactivity of the hydrogen halide is HI > HBr > HCl.

(a) $CH_2 = CH_2 + HBr \rightarrow CH_3—CH_2—Br$
(symmetrical alkene)

(b) However, addition of hydrogen halide to an unsymmetrical alkene takes place according to Markovnikov's rule. This rule states that, "the negative part of the addendum (adding molecule) gets attached to that carbon atom which possesses lesser number of hydrogen atoms". e.g.,

$$\underset{\text{Propene}}{H_3C—CH{=}CH_2} + H—Br \longrightarrow \underset{\substack{\text{2-Bromopropane} \\ \text{(major product)}}}{H_3C—\underset{Br}{\underset{|}{CH}}—CH_3} + \underset{\substack{\text{1-Bromopropane} \\ \text{(minor product)}}}{CH_3—CH_2—CH_2—Br}$$

Mechanism:

Hydrogen bromide provides an electrophile, H^+, which attacks the double bond to form carbocation as:

$$H_3\overset{3}{C}—\overset{2}{C}H = \overset{1}{C}H_2 + H-Br \xrightarrow{H^+}$$

(a) $H_3C—CH_2—\overset{+}{C}H_2 + Br^-$ — less stable primary carbocation

(b) $H_3C—\overset{+}{C}H—CH_3 + Br^-$ — more stable secondary carbocation

(i) The secondary carbocation is more stable than the primary carbocation, therefore, the former predominates because it is formed at a faster rate.

(ii) The secondary carbocation is attacked by Br^- ion to form the product as:

$$Br^- + H_3C—\overset{+}{C}H—CH_3 \longrightarrow \underset{\text{2-Bromopropane}}{H_3C—\overset{Br}{\overset{|}{C}H}—CH_3}$$

Peroxide effect or Kharash effect or Anti-Markovnikov addition: In the presence of peroxide, addition of HBr to unsymmetrical alkene takes place contrary to Markovnikov rule. This reaction is known as peroxide or Kharash effect or anti-Markovnikov addition. e.g.,

$$H_3C—CH{=}CH_2 + HBr \xrightarrow{(C_6H_5CO)_2O_2} \underset{\text{1-Bromopropane}}{CH_3—CH_2—CH_2Br}$$

This reaction proceeds by free radical mechanism. Peroxide effect is observed only in case of HBr and not in case of H—Cl and H—I.

(i) $$\underset{\text{Benzoylperoxide}}{C_6H_5—\overset{O}{\overset{\|}{C}}—O—O—\overset{O}{\overset{\|}{C}}—C_6H_5} \xrightarrow{\text{Homolysis}} 2C_6H_5—\overset{O}{\overset{\|}{C}}—\dot{O} \longrightarrow 2\dot{C}_6H_5 + CO_2$$

(ii) $$\dot{C}_6H_5 + H—Br \xrightarrow{\text{Homolysis}} C_6H_6 + \dot{Br}$$

$$CH_3—CH = CH_2 + \dot{Br} \xrightarrow{\text{Homolysis}}$$

(iii) (a) $CH_3—\underset{Br}{\underset{|}{CH}}—\dot{C}H_2$ — less stable primary free radical

(b) $CH_3—\dot{C}H—CH_2—Br$ — more stable secondary free radical

(iv) $CH_3—\dot{C}H—CH_2Br + H—Br \xrightarrow{\text{Homolysis}} CH_3—CH_2—CH_2Br + \dot{B}r$ (major product)

(v) $CH_3—CH(Br)—\dot{C}H_2 + H—Br \xrightarrow{\text{Homolysis}} CH_3—CH(Br)—CH_3 + \dot{B}r$ (minor product)

(iv) Addition of sulphuric acid:

$$CH_2 = CH_2 + H—O—SO_2—O—H \longrightarrow CH_3—CH_2—OSO_2—OH\ (C_2H_5HSO_4)$$

Ethyl hydrogen sulphate

(v) Addition of water: In presence of few drops of concentrated sulphuric acid alkenes react with water to form alcohols, in accordance with the Markovnikov rule.

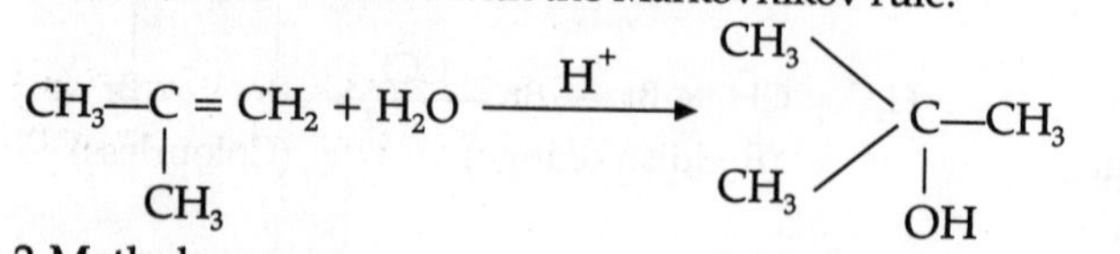

2-Methylpropene → 2-Methylpropan-2-ol

(vi) Oxidation:

(a) Oxidation with cold dilute, aqueous solution of potassium permanganate (Baeyer's reagent). This reaction is used as a test for unsaturation as it decolourises $KMnO_4$ solution.

$$\underset{\text{Ethene}}{CH_2 = CH_2} + H_2O + [O] \xrightarrow[273\ K]{\text{dil. } KMnO_4} \underset{\text{Ethane-1, 2-diol (Glycol)}}{CH_2(OH)—CH_2(OH)}$$

(b) Oxidation with acidic potassium permanganate or acidic potassium dichromate to ketones and/or acids.

$$\underset{\text{2-Methylpropene}}{(CH_3)_2C = CH_2} \xrightarrow{KMnO_4/H^+} \underset{\text{Propan-2-one}}{(CH_3)_2C = O} + CO_2 + H_2O$$

$$\underset{\text{But-2-ene}}{CH_3—CH = CH—CH_3} \xrightarrow{KMnO_4/H^+} \underset{\text{Ethanoic acid}}{2CH_3COOH}$$

(vii) Ozonolysis:

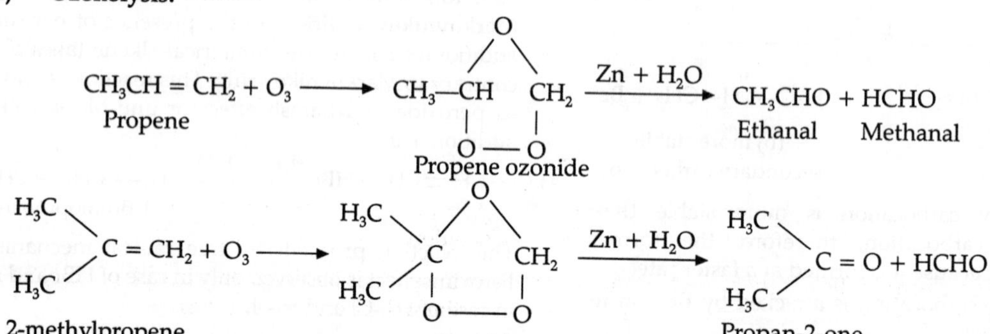

Propene → Propene ozonide → Ethanal + Methanal

2-methylpropene → Ozonide → Propan-2-one

(viii) Polymerisation: Polythene is obtained by the combination of large number of ethene molecules at high temperature, high pressure and in the presence of a catalyst. The large molecules thus obtained are called polymers. This reaction is known as polymerisation. The simple compounds from which polymers are made are called monomers.

$$n(CH_2CH = CH_2) \xrightarrow[\text{Catalyst}]{\text{High Temp. (Pressure)}} \underset{\text{Polythene}}{—(CH_2—CH_2—)_n—}$$

Alkynes

- Alkynes are unsaturated hydrocarbons that contain at least one carbon-carbon triple bond. General formula of alkyne is C_nH_{2n-2} e.g., C_2H_2 (ethyne), C_2H_4 (propyne). The first and the most important member of this series of hydrocarbons is ethyne, C_2H_2 and hence they are also called the acetylene.

- **Structure:** In ethyne, the carbon atoms are *sp* hybridised. Carbon-carbon sigma (σ) bond is obtained by the head on overlapping of the two *sp* hybridised orbitals of the two carbon atoms. The remaining *sp* hybridised orbital of each carbon atom undergoes overlapping along the internuclear axis with 1*s* orbital of each of the two hydrogen atoms forming two C–H sigma bonds. H–C–C bond angle is of 180°. Ethyne H—C ≡ C—H is a linear molecule.

- **Preparation of alkynes:**

(i) From calcium carbide: Ethyne is prepared by treating calcium carbide with water. Calcium carbide is prepared as follows:

$$\underset{\text{Limestone}}{CaCO_3} \xrightarrow{\Delta} \underset{\text{Quicklime}}{CaO} + CO_2$$

$$CaO + 3C \longrightarrow \underset{\text{Calcium carbide}}{CaC_2} + CO$$

$$CaC_2 + 2H_2O \longrightarrow Ca(OH)_2 + \underset{\text{Acetylene}}{C_2H_2}$$

(ii) From vicinal dihalides: When vicinal dihalides react with alcoholic potassium hydroxide then they undergo dehydrohalogenation. One molecule of hydrogen halide is eliminated to form alkenyl halide which on treatment with sodamide gives alkyne.

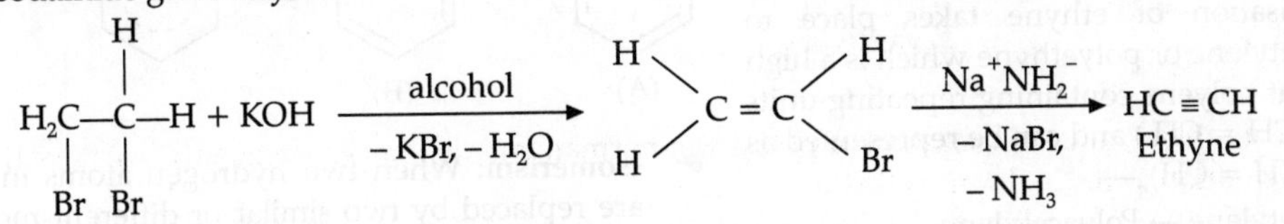

- **Physical Properties:** Physical properties of alkynes follow the same trend of alkenes and alkanes. First three members are gases, the next eight are liquids and higher ones are solids. All alkynes are colourless. Ethyene has characteristic odour. Other members are odourless. They are weakly polar in nature. Alkynes are insoluble in water but soluble in organic solvents like ethers, carbon tetrachloride and benzene. Melting point, boiling point and density increase with increase in molar mass.
- **Chemical Properties:** Alkynes show electrophilic as well as nucleophilic addition reactions.

(i) Acidic character of alkyne:

$$HC \equiv CH + Na \rightarrow \underset{\text{Monosodium ethynide}}{HC \equiv C^-Na^+} + \tfrac{1}{2}H_2$$

$$HC \equiv C^-Na^+ + Na \rightarrow \underset{\text{Disodium ethynide}}{Na^+C^- \equiv C^-Na^+} + \tfrac{1}{2}H_2$$

$$CH_3—C \equiv C—H + Na^+NH_2^- \rightarrow \underset{\text{Sodium propynide}}{CH_3C \equiv C^-Na^+} + NH_3$$

This reaction can be used for the distinction among alkynes, alkenes and alkanes and even for distinguishing terminal alkynes from non-terminal alkynes as only terminal alkynes undergo this reaction.

(ii) Addition reactions:

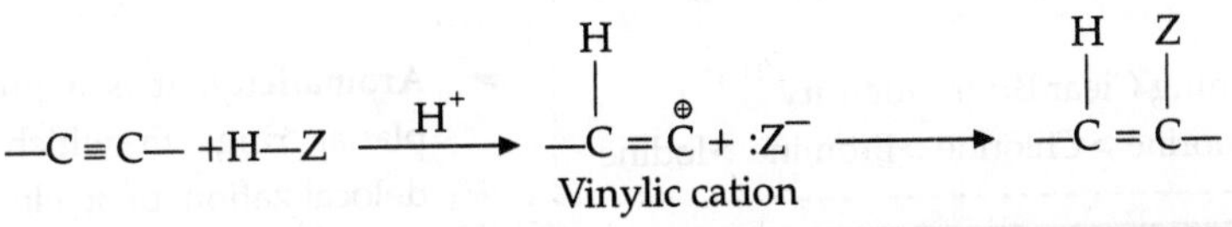

Alkynes undergo electrophilic addition reaction and addition to unsymmetrical alkynes takes place according to Markovnikov's rule. The addition product formed depends upon the stability of vinylic cation.

(a) Addition of dihydrogen:

$$\underset{\text{Propyne}}{CH_3—C \equiv CH} + H_2 \xrightarrow{Ni/Pd/Pt} \underset{\text{Propene}}{[CH_3—CH = CH_2]} \xrightarrow{H_2} \underset{\text{Propane}}{CH_3—CH_2—CH_3}$$

(b) Addition of halogens:

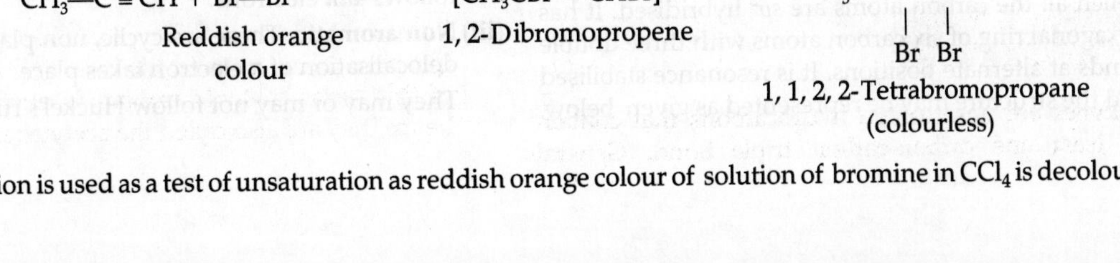

This reaction is used as a test of unsaturation as reddish orange colour of solution of bromine in CCl_4 is decolourised.

(c) Addition of hydrogen halides:

$$H—C \equiv C—H + H—Br \longrightarrow [CH_2 = CH—Br] \longrightarrow CH_3—CHBr_2$$

[$CH_2 = CH—Br$: Bromoethene; $CH_3—CHBr_2$: 1, 1-Dibromoethane]

(d) Addition of water:

$$\underset{\text{Ethyne}}{HC \equiv CH} + H—OH \xrightarrow[333\,K]{Hg^{2+}/H^+} CH_2 = C(OH)—H \xrightarrow{\text{isomerisation}} \underset{\text{Ethanal}}{CH_3-C(=O)—H}$$

$$\underset{\text{Propyne}}{CH_3—C \equiv CH} + H—OH \xrightarrow[333\,K]{Hg^{2+}/H^+} CH_3—C(O—H) = CH_2 \xrightarrow{\text{isomerisation}} \underset{\text{Propanone}}{CH_3-C(=O)—CH_3}$$

(e) Polymerization:

(1) Linear polymerization: Under suitable conditions, linear polymerisation of ethyne takes place to produce polyacetylene or polyethyne which is a high molecular weight polyene containing repeating units of $(CH = CH - CH = CH)$ and can be represented as $—(CH = CH - CH = CH)_n—$

Acetylene → Polyacetylene

(2) Cyclic polymerization: Ethyne on passing through red hot iron tube at 873K undergoes cyclic polymerization.

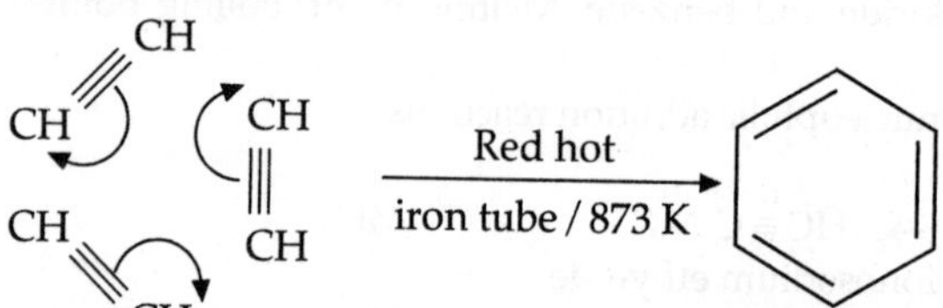

Acetylene Benzene

Concept: Order of Reactivity of Addition Halogens to Alkenes

Mnemonics: Flaming Clear Bright Identity

Interpretation: Fluorine >Chlorine >Bromine >Iodine

Aromatic Hydrocarbon

- These hydrocarbons are also known as 'arenes'. Most of the aromatic hydrocarbons were found to contain benzene ring. Aromatic compounds containing benzene ring are known as benzenoids and those not containing a benzene ring are known as non-benzenoids.
- Benzene molecule is a planar or flat molecule in which all the carbon atoms are sp^2 hybridised. It has hexagonal ring of six carbon atoms with three double bonds at alternate positions. It is resonance stabilised and the structure may be represented as given below.

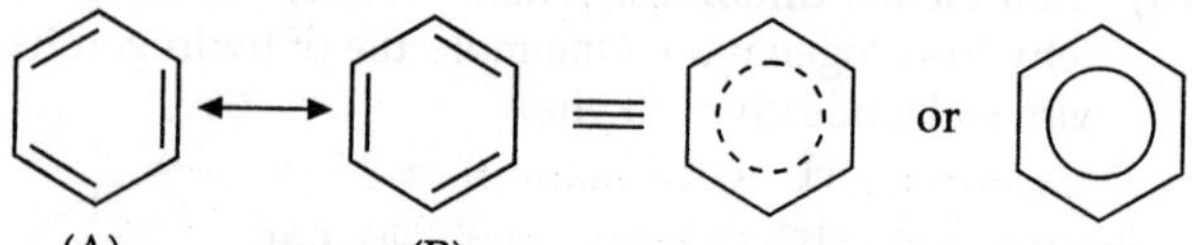

(A) (B) (C)

- **Isomerism:** When two hydrogen atoms in benzene are replaced by two similar or different monovalent atoms or groups, three different position isomers are possible. The 1, 2 or 1, 6 is known as the *ortho* (*o*–), the 1, 3 or 1, 5 as *meta* (*m*–) and the 1, 4 as *para* (*p*–) disubstituted compounds.
- **Structure of Benzene:** August Kekule in 1865 proposed benzene having cyclic arrangement of six carbon atoms with alternate single and double bonds and one hydrogen atom attached to each carbon atom.

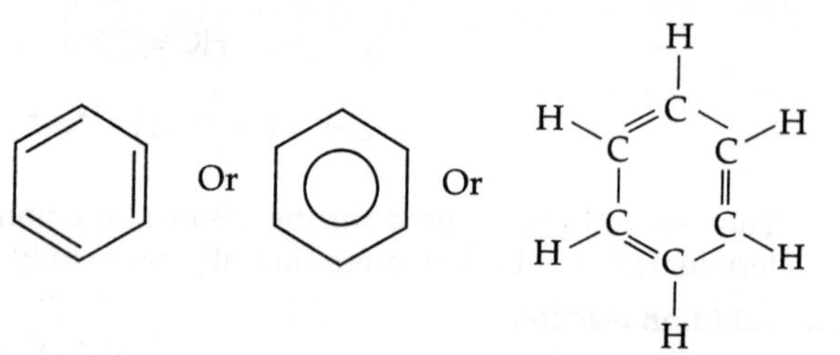

- **Aromaticity:** It is a property of the sp^2 hybridised planar rings in which the *p* orbitals allow cyclic delocalization of π electrons. Aromatic compounds have specific electronic structure in accordance with Huckel rule. The rule states that all planar cyclic conjugated polyenes containing $(4n + 2)\pi$ electrons where $n = 0, 1, 2, \ldots$ are aromatic in nature.

(i) Aromatic: They are cyclic, planar molecule where complete delocalisation of π electron takes place.
Huckle's rule $(4n + 2)$ π electrons

(ii) Anti aromatic: They are cyclic planar molecule which follows $4n\pi$ electrons.

(iii) Non aromatic: These are cyclic, non planar where no delocalisation of π electron takes place.
They may or may not follow Huckel's rule.

Mnemonics

Concept: Aromaticity
Mnemonics: A Police Car Drove near High Court
Interpretation: Polarity, Complete Delocalisation, Huckel Rule

- **Preparation of benzene:**

(i) **Cyclic polymerisation of ethyne:** Ethyne on passing through red hot iron tube at 873 K undergoes cyclic polymerisation. Three molecules polymerise to form benzene.

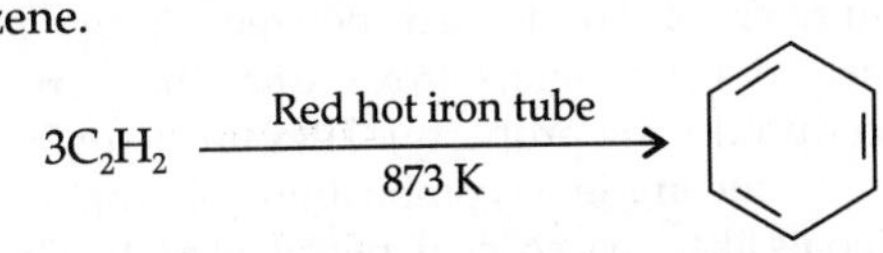

Benzene

(ii) **Decarboxylation of Aromatic acids:** Sodium salt of benzoic acid on heating with sodalime gives benzene.

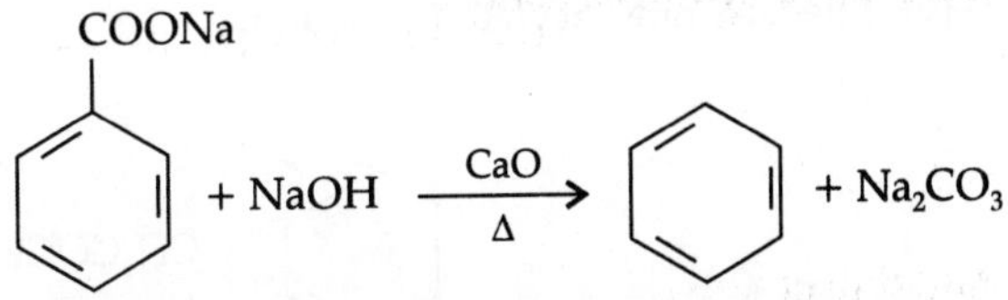

(iii) **Reduction of Phenol:** Phenol is reduced to benzene by passing its vapours over heated zinc dust.

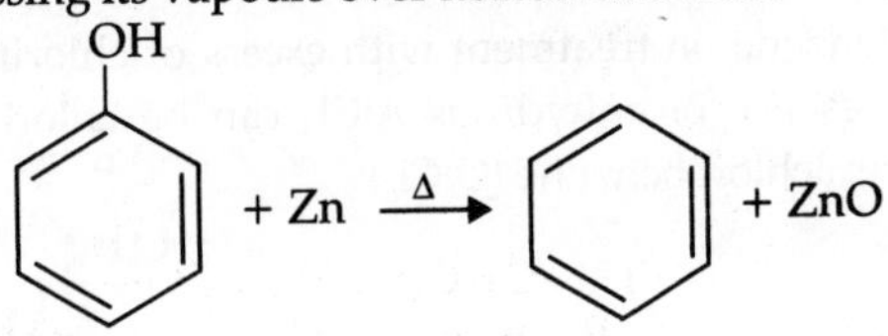

- **Physical Properties:** Aromatic hydrocarbons are non-polar molecules and are usually colourless liquids or solids with a characteristic aroma. Benzene itself is a good solvent for many organic and inorganic substances, e.g., fat, resins, sulphur and iodine. It burns with a luminous, sooty flame in contrast to alkanes and alkenes which usually burn with a bluish flame.

- **Chemical Properties:** Benzene undergoes following types of chemical reactions:
  (a) Electrophilic Substitution Reaction
  (b) Addition Reaction
  Electrophilic Substitution Reactions: Aromatic hydrocarbons undergo electrophilic substitution reactions, e.g., nitration, halogenation, sulphonation and Friedel-Craft alkylation/acylation.

(i) **Nitration:**

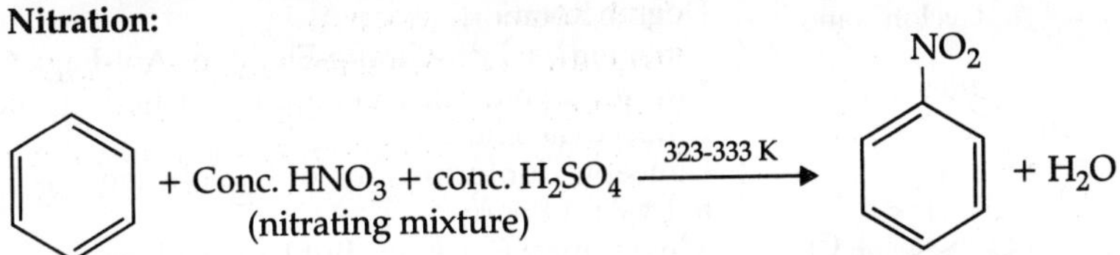

Nitrobenzene

(ii) **Halogenation:**

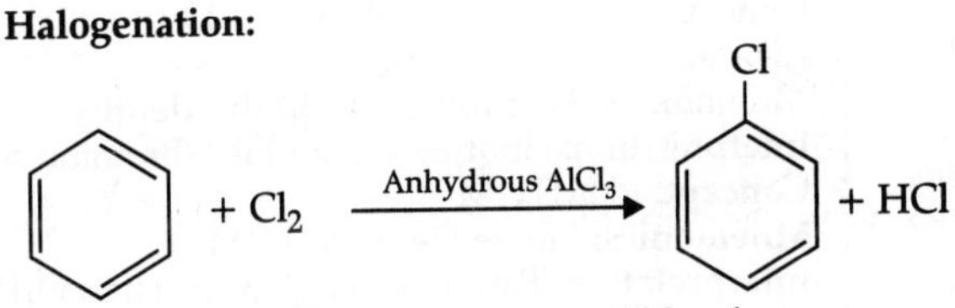

Chlorobenzene

(iii) **Sulphonation:**

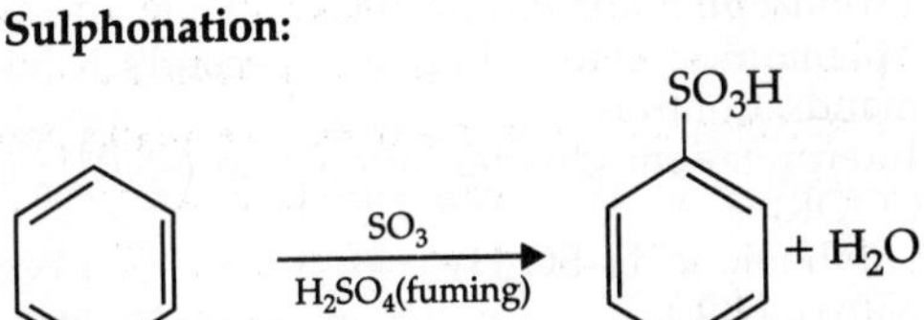

Benzene — Benzene sulphonic acid

(iv) **Friedel-Crafts alkylation reaction:**

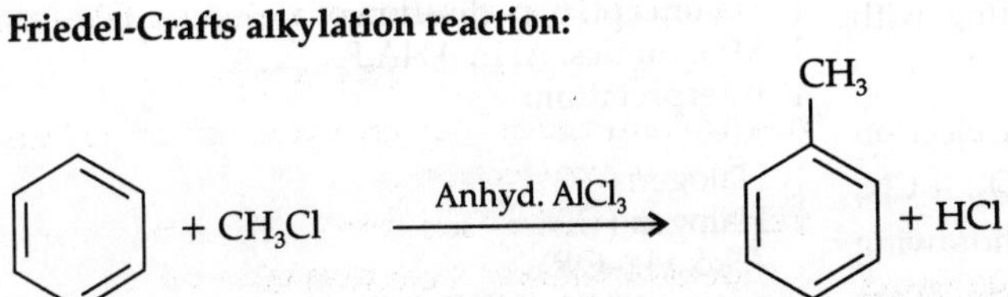

Toluene

(v) Friedel-Craft's acylation reaction:

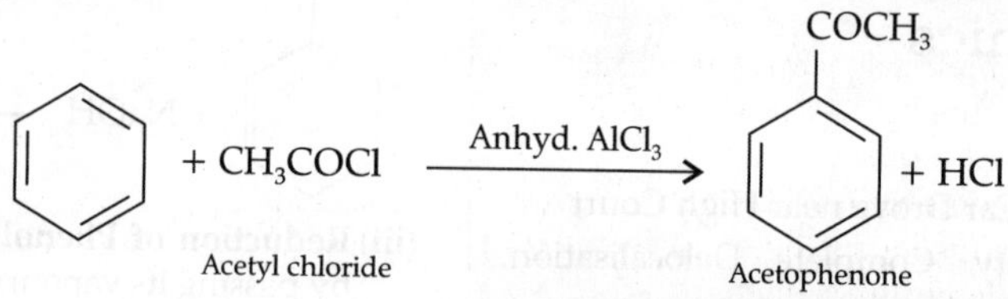

Benzene on treatment with excess of chlorine in the presence of anhydrous $AlCl_3$ can be chlorinated to hexachlorobenzene (C_6Cl_6)

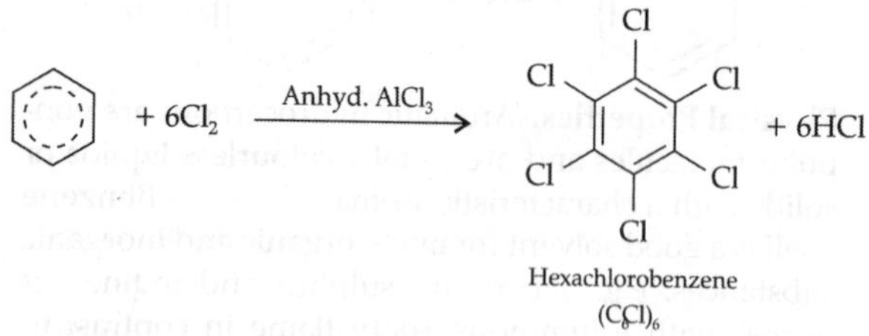

Addition reactions:

(a) Under vigorous conditions i.e. at high temperature and/or pressure in presence of nickel catalyst, hydrogenation of benzene gives cyclohexane.

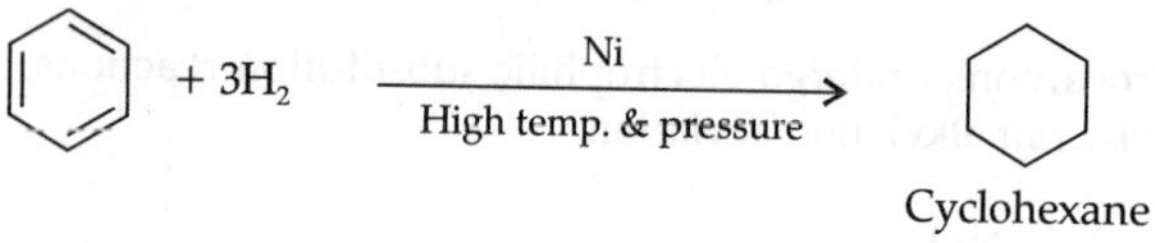

(b) Under UV light, three chlorine molecules add to benzene to produce benzene hexachloride, $C_6H_6Cl_6$.

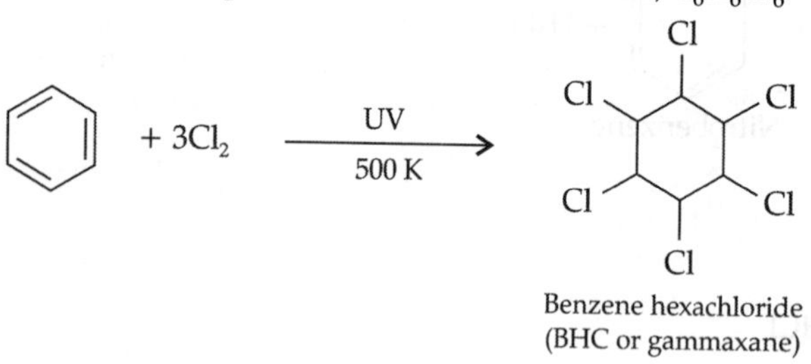

Combustion—When heated in air, benzene burns with sooty flame:

$$C_6H_6 + \frac{15}{2} O_2 \rightarrow 6CO_2 + 3H_2O$$

- The presence of substituent groups in aromatic ring activates/deactivates electrophilic substitution and also directs the orientation of incoming groups. Electron donating substituents facilitate further substitution with incoming groups at *o*- and *p*-positions while electron attracting groups deactivate the ring with substitution at *m*-position.

  $-CH_3$, $-OH$, $-OR$, $-NH_2$, $-NHR$, $-NR_2$ are electron donating (or activating groups) while $-NO_2$, $-CN$, $-CHO$, $-COOH$, $-SO_3H$ are electron withdrawing (or deactivating groups). Halogens ($-Cl$, $-Br$, $-I$) are *o*-, *p*-directing but moderately deactivating (due to strong $-I$ effect).

Carcinogenicity and Toxicity

- Polynuclear aromatic hydrocarbons (PAHs) have a number of condensed benzene rings and are suspected carcinogens (toxic and they are having cancer producing property). They are actually formed due to incomplete combustion of some organic materials like tobacco, coal, petroleum, etc. They enter into human body and undergo various biochemical reactions and finally damage DNA and cause cancer. For example : 1, 2-Benzanthracene, 1, 2-Benzpyrene, etc.

Mnemonics

Concept: Newmann Projection for Staggered and Eclipsed Conformations of *n*-Butane After Every 60 Degree Rotation.
Mnemonics: Fish-Giraffe-Elephant-Ant-EagleGoat
Interpretation: Fully eclipsed-Gauche-Eclipsed-Anti-EclipsedGauche
Concept: Conformations of Cyclohexane As Per Stability And Energy
Mnemonics: Cat Twigs But Horse-Clubs
Interpretation: Chair>Twist-boat>Boat>Half- Chair
Concept: Order of Reactivity of Addition Halogens to Alkenes
Mnemonics: Flaming Clear Bright Identity
Interpretation: Fluorine >Chlorine >Bromine >Iodine
Concept: PHMTOM
Mnemonics: Please Help Me,TOM
Interpretation: Para have High M.p. Than Ortho and Meta
1. Concept: m-directing Group
Mnemonics: Queen Elizabeth Second's Navy Commands, Controls
Interpretation: Quarternary amino ($-NR^{3+}$) Ester ($-COOR$)
Sulphonic acid ($-SO_3H$)
Nitro ($-NO_2$)
Carbonyl ($-CHO$)
Carboxyl ($-COOH$)
Cyano ($-CN$)
2. Concept: o, p–directing
Mnemonics: AHA AHA P
Interpretation:
Alkyl ($-R$)
Halogen ($-X$)
Halogen ($-X$)
Alkoxyl ($-OR$)
Amino ($-NH_2$, NHR, NR_2)
Hydroxyl ($-OH$)
Amide ($-CONH_2$)
Phenyl (C_6H_5)

Key Words

Cis-isomer: The geometrical isomer in which two identical atoms or groups lie on the same side of the double bond is called cis-isomer.

Trans-isomer: The geometrical isomer in which two identical atoms or groups lie on the opposite sides of the double bond is called trans-isomer.

Acidic Dehydration of Alcohols: The reaction in which a water molecule is eliminated from the alcohol molecule in the presence of an acid is called acidic dehydration of alcohols.

Polymerization: The process by which a long chain like molecule is obtained by the intermolecular combination of small molecules (monomers) is called polymerization.

Key Terms

- **Cycloalkanes:** Cyclic hydrocarbons having molecular formula C_nH_{2n}. These are isomeric with alkenes.
- **Cracking:** The process of breaking down less volatile higher molecular mass hydrocarbons from petroleum into different types of more volatile lower molecular mass hydrocarbons by heating in the presence of catalyst.
- **Reforming:** Cyclization followed by aromatization (or dehydrogenation of 6-8 C alkanes on heating to 773 K in the presence of Pt catalyst (e.g., *n*-heptane → methyl cyclohexane → toluene).
- **Knocking:** A sharp metallic rattling sound produced in an internal combustion engine.
- **Octane Number:** A scale for determining knocking quality in petrol. *n*-Heptane with very high knocking has octane number 0 while iso-octane has maximum value 100.
- **Cetane Number:** A scale for determining knocking quality of a diesel fuel. Cetane number of *n*-hexadecane (cetane) is 100 and that of α-methylnapthalene is zero.
- **Conformation isomerism:** the different arrangements of atoms in space that results from free rotation of groups about the carbon- carbon bond axes is known as conformation for rotational isomers and the phenomena is known as conformational or rotational isomerism

- **Aromaticity:** It is a property of conjugated cycloalkenes in which the stabilization of the molecule is enhanced due to the ability of the electrons in the π orbitals to delocalize. This acts as a framework to create a planar molecule.

Key Facts

- Iodination is a reversible reaction. So it is carried out by heating alkane in the presence of oxidising agent like iodic acid (HIO_3) or nitric acid (HNO_3) or mercuric oxide (HgO) which oxidises HI formed during the reaction.

$$CH_4 + I_2 \rightleftharpoons CH_3I + HI$$
$$HIO_3 + 5HI \longrightarrow 3I_2 + 3H_2O$$

- Fluorination of alkane takes place explosively resulting even in the rupture of C—C bond in higher alkanes.
- Petroleum is an important source of aliphatic hydrocarbons. It is refined in to several useful fractions and is a source of several petrochemicals. Coal tar is a rich source of aromatic hydrocarbons.
- LPG and CNG are petroleum products used as energy source in automobile industry and domestic fuel. Natural gas contains about 90% CH_4.
- The alkaline potassium permanganate solution is known as Baeyer's reagent. It has bright pink colour. It oxidises alkenes to glycols which is colourless. This reaction is used as a test for the presence of double bond in a molecule. This is also known as Baeyer test.
- Bromine water test and Baeyer's test are used to detect the presence of double bond while ozonolysis is used to detect the position of double bond.
- Originally fragrant substances were called aromatic compounds.
- In the laboratory, benzene was first prepared by heating benzoic acid or phthalic acid with calcium oxide.
- Most of the benzene is produced from petroleum.
- Compounds having atoms other than carbon in a ring system, which satisfies the conditions of aromaticity are called heteroaromatics.
- Those who follow neither Huckle's rule, i.e., $(4n + 2)$ π nor $4n\pi$ electrons are non aromatic.

NCERT CORNER

Q. 1. How do you account for the formation of ethane during chlorination of methane?

[NCERT Ex. Q. 9.1, Page 326]

Ans. Chlorination of methane proceeds through a free radical chain mechanism. The whole reaction takes place in the given three steps.

Step 1: Initiation: The reaction begins with the homolytic cleavage of Cl – Cl bond as:

$$Cl - Cl_2 \xrightarrow{hv} \dot{C}l + \dot{C}l$$

Chlorine free radicals

Step 2: Propagation: In the second step, chlorine free radicals attack methane molecules and break down the C–H bond to generate methyl radicals as:

$$CH_4 + \dot{C}l \xrightarrow{h\nu} \dot{C}H_3 + H-Cl$$
Methane

These methyl radicals react with other chlorine free radicals to form methyl chloride along with the liberation of a chlorine free radical.

$$\dot{C}H_3 + Cl-Cl \longrightarrow CH_3-Cl + \dot{C}l$$
Methyl chloride

Hence, methyl free radicals and chlorine free radicals set up a chain reaction. While HCl and CH_3Cl are the major products formed, other higher halogenated compounds are also formed as:

$$CH_3Cl + \dot{C}l \longrightarrow \dot{C}H_2Cl + HCl$$

$$\dot{C}H_2Cl + Cl-Cl \longrightarrow CH_2Cl_2 + \dot{C}l$$

Step 3: Termination: Formation of ethane is a result of the termination of chain reactions taking place as a result of the consumption of reactants as:

$$\dot{C}l + \dot{C}l \longrightarrow Cl-Cl$$

$$H_3\dot{C} + \dot{C}H_3 \longrightarrow H_3C-CH_3$$
(Ethane)

Hence, by this process, ethane is obtained as a by-product of chlorination of methane.

Q. 2. Write IUPAC names of the following compounds:

(a) $CH_3CH{=}C(CH_3)_2$

(b) $CH_2 = CH{-}C \equiv C{-}CH_3$

(c) 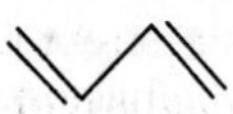

(d) 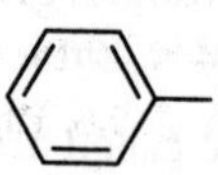 $-CH_2-CH_2-CH=CH_2$

(e) 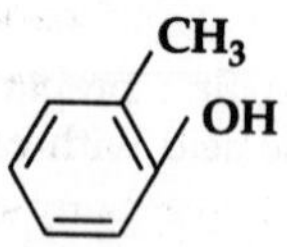

(f) $CH_3(CH_2)_4CH(CH_2)_3CH_3$ with $CH_2-CH(CH_3)_2$ on the CH

(g) $CH_3CH{=}CH{-}CH_2{-}CH{=}CH{-}CH{-}CH_2{-}CH{=}CH_2$ with C_2H_5 on the CH

[NCERT Ex. Q. 9.2, Page 326]

Ans. (a) 2-Methylbut-2-ene

(b) Pent-1-ene-3-yne

(c) 1, 3-Butadiene or Buta-1,3 diene

(d) 4-Phenyl but-1-ene

(e) 2-Methyl phenol

(f) 5-(2-Methylpropyl)-decane

(g) 4-Ethyldeca-1, 5, 8-triene

Q. 3. For the following compounds, write structural formulas and IUPAC names for all possible isomers having the number of double or triple bond as indicated:

(a) C_4H_8 (one double bond)

(b) C_5H_8 (one triple bond) [NCERT Ex. Q. 9.3, Page 326]

Ans. (a) The following structural isomers are possible for C_4H_8 with one double bond:

$$\overset{1}{H_2C} = \overset{2}{CH} - \overset{3}{CH_2} - \overset{4}{CH_3}$$
(I)

$$\overset{1}{CH_3} - \overset{2}{CH} = \overset{3}{CH} - \overset{4}{CH_3}$$
(II)

$$\overset{1}{CH_2} = \overset{2}{C}(CH_3) - \overset{3}{CH_3}$$
(III)

The IUPAC name of
Compound (I) is But-1-ene,
Compound (II) is But-2-ene, and
Compound (III) is 2-Methylprop-1-ene.

(b) The following structural isomers are possible for C_5H_8 with one triple bond:

$$\overset{1}{HC} \equiv \overset{2}{C} - \overset{3}{CH_2} - \overset{4}{CH_2} - \overset{5}{CH_3}$$
(I)

$$\overset{1}{H_3C} - \overset{2}{C} \equiv \overset{3}{C} - \overset{4}{CH_2} - \overset{5}{CH_3}$$
(II)

$$\overset{4}{H_3C} - \overset{3}{CH}(CH_3) - \overset{2}{C} \equiv \overset{1}{CH}$$
(III)

The IUPAC name of
Compound (I) is Pent-1-yne,
Compound (II) is Pent-2-yne, and
Compound (III) is 3-Methylbut-1-yne.

Q. 4. Write IUPAC names of the products obtained by the ozonolysis of the following compounds :

(i) Pent-2-ene (ii) 3,4-Dimethylhept-3-ene

(iii) 2-Ethylbut-1-ene (iv) 1-Phenylbut-1-ene

[NCERT Ex. Q. 9.4, Page 326]

Ans. (i) Pent-2-ene undergoes ozonolysis as:

$$CH_3-CH = CH_2-CH_2-CH_3 + O_3$$
Pent – 2 – ene   Ozone

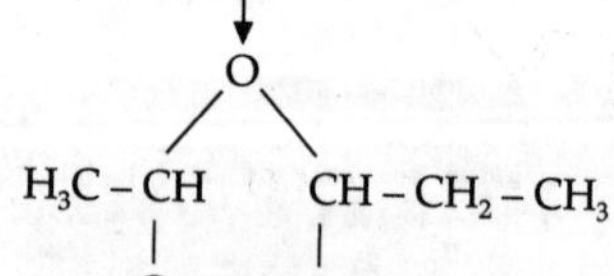

Pent – 2 – ene ozonide

$$\xrightarrow{Zn + H_2O}$$

$$H_3C-CHO + CH_3-CH_2-CHO$$
(I)   (II)

The IUPAC name of product (I) is ethanal and product (II) is propanal.

(ii) 3, 4-Dimethylhept-3-ene undergoes ozonolysis as:

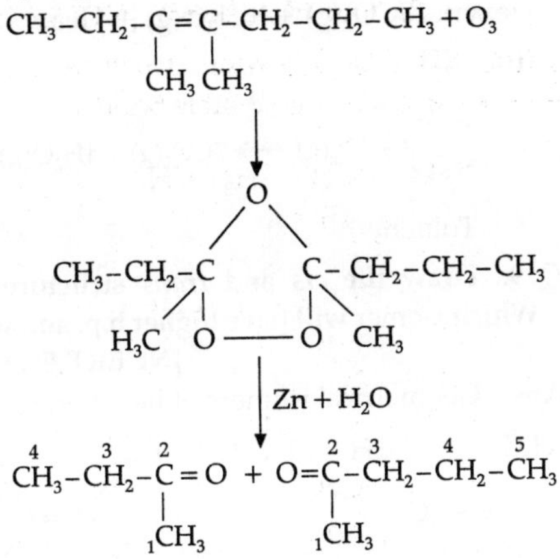

(I) (II)

The IUPAC name of product (I) is butan-2-one and product (II) is pentan-2-one.

(iii) 2-Ethylbut-1-ene undergoes ozonolysis as:

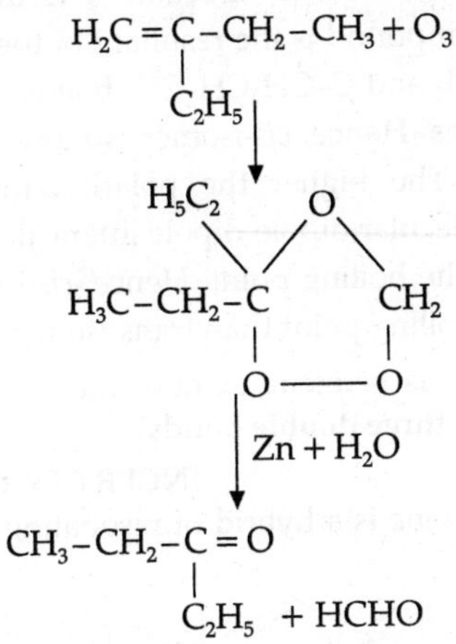

(I) (II)

The IUPAC name of product (I) is pentan-3-one and product (II) is methanal.

(iv) 1-Phenylbut-1-ene undergoes ozonolysis as:

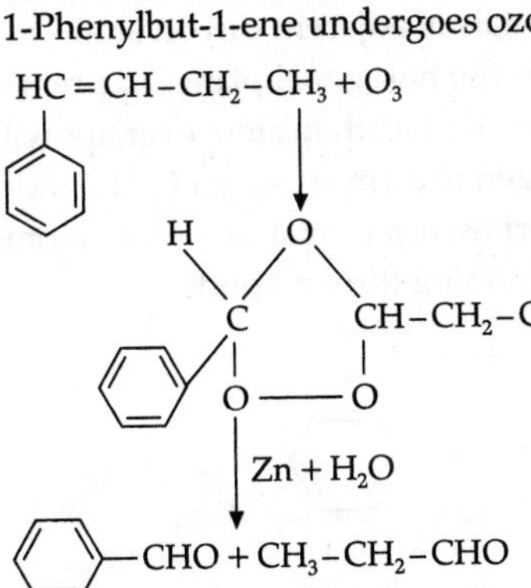

(I) (II)

The IUPAC name of product (I) is benzaldehyde and product (II) is propanal.

Q. 5. An alkene 'A' on ozonolysis gives a mixture of ethanal and pentan-3- one. Write structure and IUPAC name of 'A'. [NCERT Ex. Q. 9.5, Page 327]

Ans.

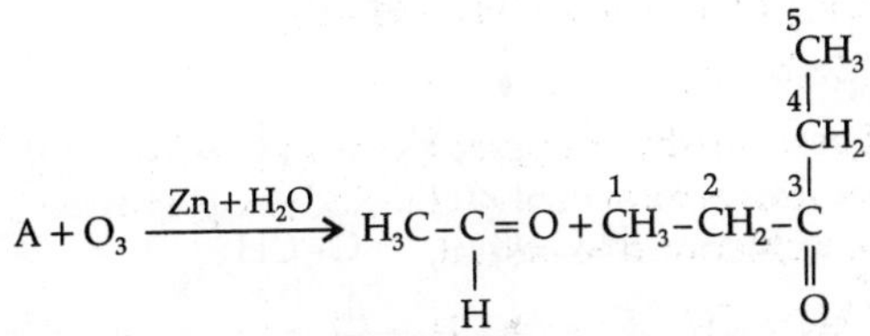

Ethanal Pentan – 3 – one

During ozonolysis, an ozonide having a cyclic structure is formed as an intermediate which undergoes cleavage to give the final products. Ethanal and pentan-3-one are obtained from the intermediate ozonide. Hence, the expected structure of the ozonide is:

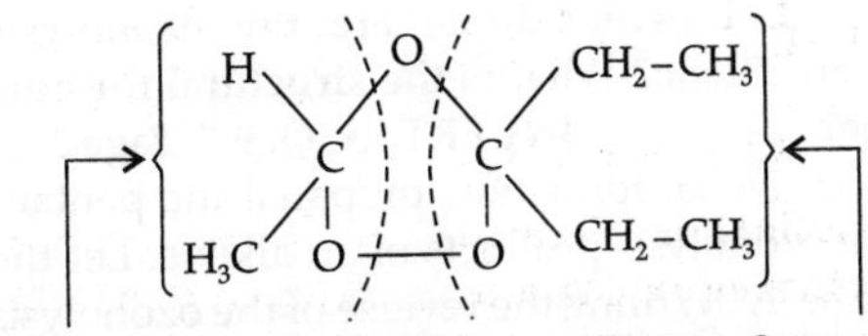

Ethanal Ozonide Pentan–3–one

This ozonide is formed as an addition of ozone to 'A'. The desired structure of 'A' can be obtained by the removal of ozone from the ozonide. Hence, the structural formula of 'A' is:

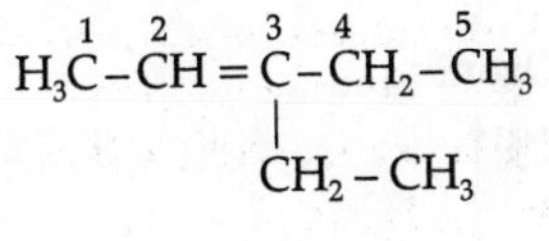

The IUPAC name of 'A' is 3-Ethylpent-2-ene.

Q. 6. An alkene 'A' contains three C – C, eight C – H σ bonds and one C – C π bond. 'A' on ozonolysis gives two moles of an aldehyde of molar mass 44 u. Write IUPAC name of 'A'. [NCERT Ex. Q. 9.6, Page 327]

Ans. As per the given information, 'A' on ozonolysis gives two moles of an aldehyde of molar mass 44 u. The formation of two moles of an aldehyde indicates the presence of identical structural units on both sides of the double bond containing carbon atoms. Hence, the structure of 'A' can be represented as:

$$XC = CX$$

There are eight C–H σ bonds. Hence, there are 8 hydrogen atoms in 'A'. Also, there are three C–C bonds. Hence, there are four carbon atoms present in the structure of 'A'. Combining the inferences, the structure of 'A' can be represented as:

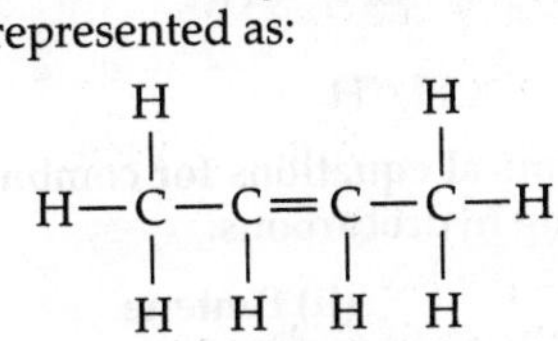

(A)

'A' has 3 C–C bonds, 8 C–H π bonds and one C–C π bond. Hence, the IUPAC name of 'A' is But-2-ene. Ozonolysis of 'A' takes place as:

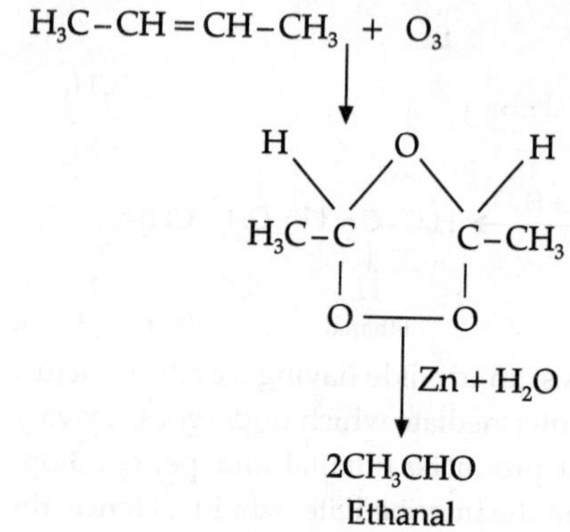

The final product is ethanal with molecular mass= 44u.

Q. 7. Propanal and pentan-3-one are the ozonolysis products of an alkene? What is the structural formula of the alkene? **[NCERT Ex. Q. 9.7, Page 327]**

Ans. As per the given information, propanal and pentan-3-one are the ozonolysis products of an alkene. Let the given alkene be 'A'. Writing the reverse of the ozonolysis reaction, we get:

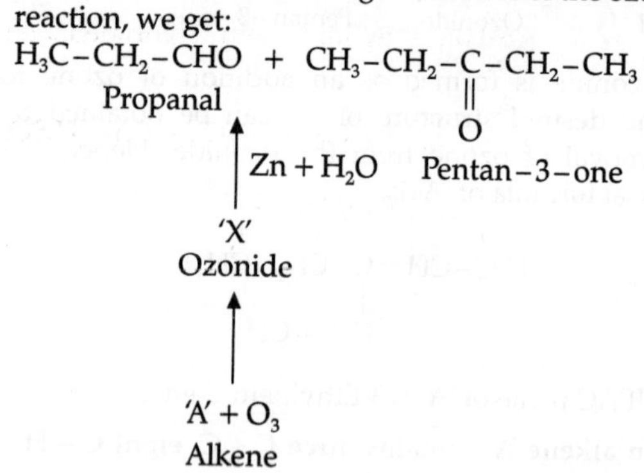

The products are obtained on the cleavage of ozonide 'X'. Hence, 'X' contains both products in the cyclic form. The possible structure of ozonide can be represented as:

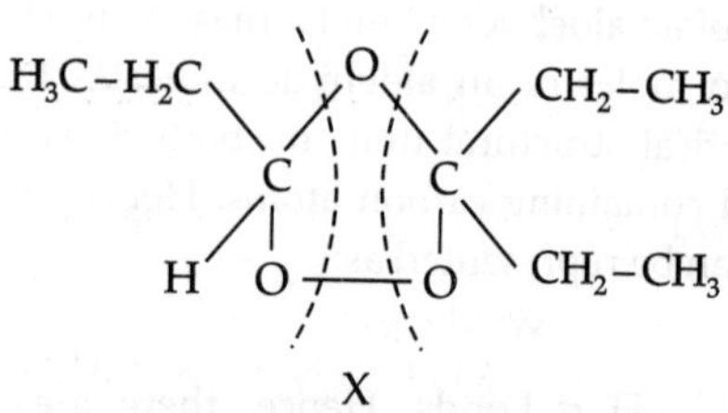

X

Now, 'X' is an addition product of alkene 'A' with ozone. Therefore, the possible structure of alkene 'A' is:

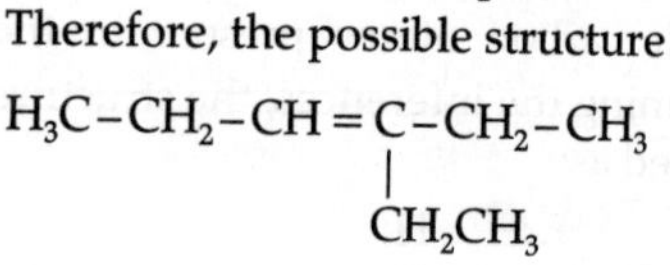

Q. 8. Write chemical equations for combustion reaction of the following hydrocarbons:

(i) Butane **(ii) Pentene**
(iii) Hexyne **(iv) Toluene**

[NCERT Ex. Q. 9.8, Page 327]

Ans. (i) $2C_4H_{10}(g) + 13O_2(g) \rightarrow$
Butane $8CO_2(g) + 10\ H_2O(g)$ + Heat

(ii) $2C_5H_{10}(g) + 15O_2(g) \rightarrow$
Pentene $10CO_2(g) + 10\ H_2O(g)$ + Heat

(iii) $2C_6H_{10}(g) + 17O_2(g) \rightarrow$
Hexyne$12CO_2(g) + 10H_2O(g)$ + Heat

(iv)

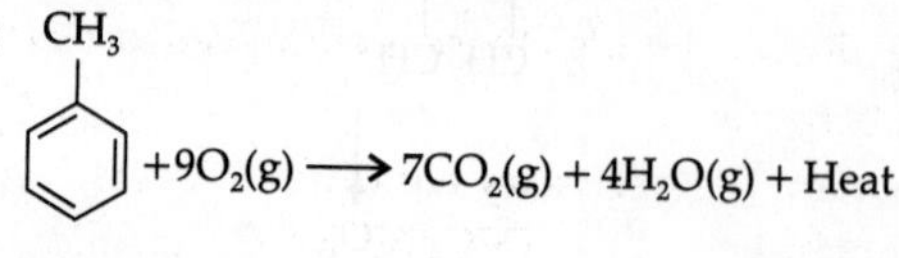

Toluene

Q. 9. Draw the *cis* and *trans* structures of hex-2-ene. Which isomer will have higher b.p. and why? **[NCERT Ex. Q. 9.9, Page 327]**

Ans. Geometrical isomers of hex-2-ene are :

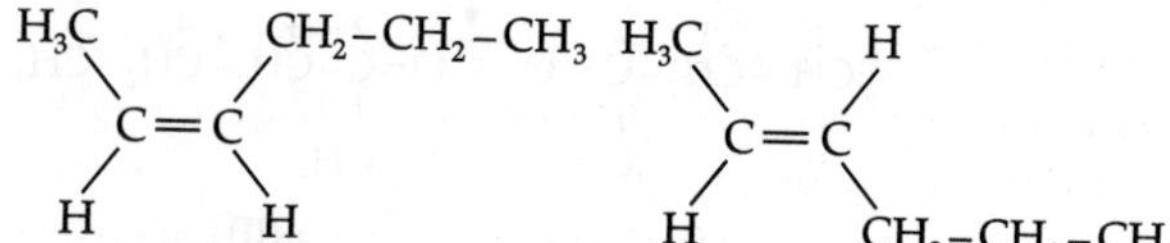

Cis – isomer *Trans* – isomer

The dipole moment of *cis*-compound is a sum of the dipole moments of C–CH_3 and C– $CH_2\ CH_2CH_3$ bonds acting in the same direction. The dipole moment of trans-compound is the resultant of the dipole moments of C–CH_3 and C–$CH_2CH_2CH_3$ bonds acting in opposite directions. Hence, *cis*-isomer is more polar than trans-isomer. The higher the polarity, the greater is the intermolecular dipole-dipole interaction and the higher will be the boiling point. Hence, *cis*-isomer will have a higher boiling point than trans-isomer.

Q. 10. Why is benzene extra ordinarily stable though it contains three double bonds?

[NCERT Ex. Q. 9.10, Page 327]

Ans. Benzene is a hybrid of resonating structures given as:

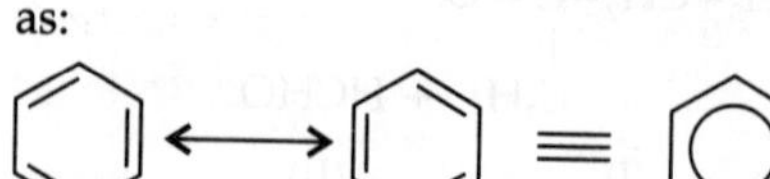

All six carbon atoms in benzene are sp^2 hybridised. The two sp^2 hybrid orbitals of each carbon atom overlap with the sp^2 hybrid orbitals of adjacent carbon atoms to form six sigma bonds in the hexagonal plane. The remaining sp^2 hybrid orbital on each carbon atom overlaps with the *s*-orbital of hydrogen to form six sigma C–H bonds. The remaining unhybridised *p*-orbital of carbon atoms has the possibility of forming three π bonds.

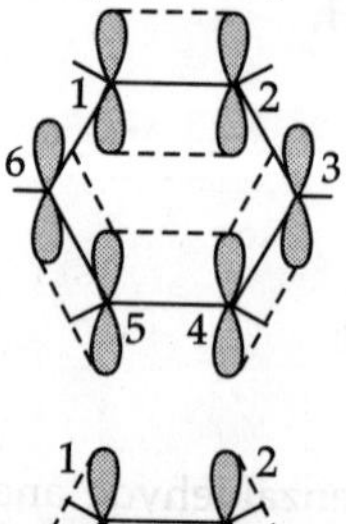

Or

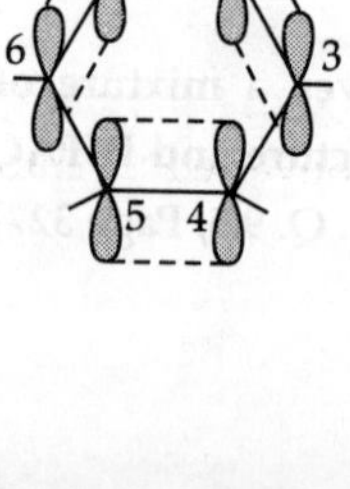

Or

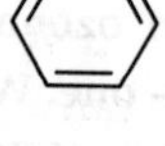

The six π-electrons are delocalized and can move freely about the six carbon nuclei. Even after the presence of three double bonds, these delocalized π-electrons stabilize benzene.

Q. 11. What are the necessary conditions for any system to be aromatic? **[NCERT Ex. Q. 9.11, Page 327]**

Ans. A compound is said to be aromatic if it satisfies the following three conditions:

(i) It should have a planar structure.

(ii) The π–electrons of the compound are completely delocalized in the ring.

(iii) The total number of π–electrons present in the ring should be equal to $(4n + 2)$, where $n = 0, 1, 2 ...,$ etc., This is known as Huckel's rule.

Q. 12. Explain why the following systems are not aromatic?

(i) 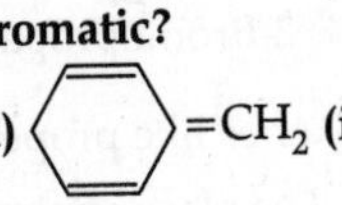 (ii)  (iii) 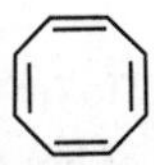

[NCERT Ex. Q. 9.12, Page 327]

Ans. (i) For the given compound, the number of π-electrons is 6.

By Huckel's rule,

$4n + 2 = 6$

$4n = 4$

$n = 1$

For a compound to be aromatic, the value n must be an integer ($n = 0, 1, 2...$). Since, the value of n is an integer, it should be aromatic However, for a compound to be aromatic p electron cloud should be equally distributed on all the ring, hence, it is non-aromatic in nature **(1)**

(ii) For the given compound, the number of π-electrons is 4.

By Huckel's rule,

$4n + 2 = 4$

$4n = 2$

$n = 1/2$

For a compound to be aromatic, the value of n must be an integer ($n = 0, 1, 2...$), which is not true for the given compound. Hence, it is not aromatic in nature.

(iii) For the given compound, the number of π-electrons is 8.

By Huckel's rule,

$4n + 2 = 8$

$4n = 6$

$n = 3/2$

For a compound to be aromatic, the value of n must be an integer ($n = 0, 1, 2...$). Since the value of n is not an integer, the given compound is not aromatic in nature.

Q. 13. How will you convert benzene into:

(i) *p*-nitrobromobenzene (ii) *m*- nitrochlorobenzene
(iii) *p* - nitrotoluene (iv) acetophenone?

[NCERT Ex. Q. 9.13, Page 327]

Ans. (i) Benzene can be converted into p-nitrobromobenzene as:

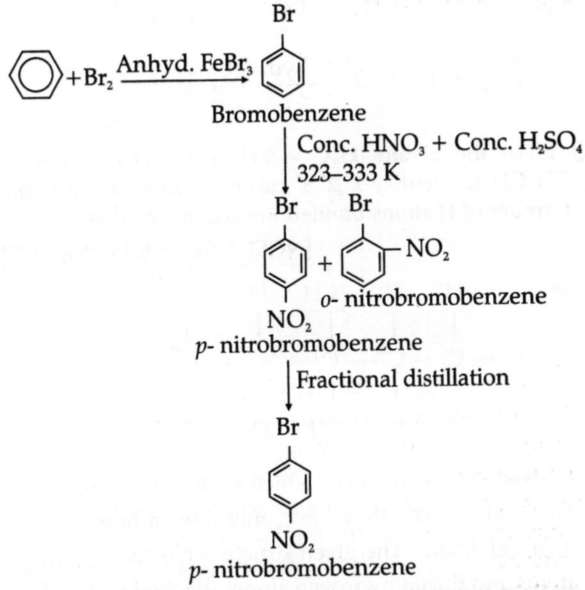

(ii) Benzene can be converted into m-nitrochlorobenzene as:

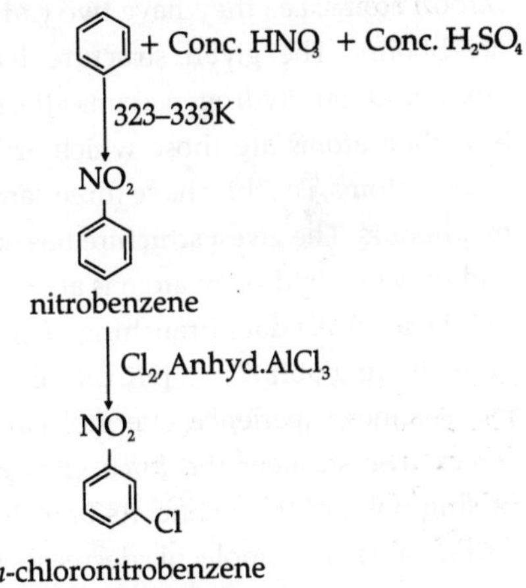

(iii) Benzene can be converted into *p*-nitrotoluene as:

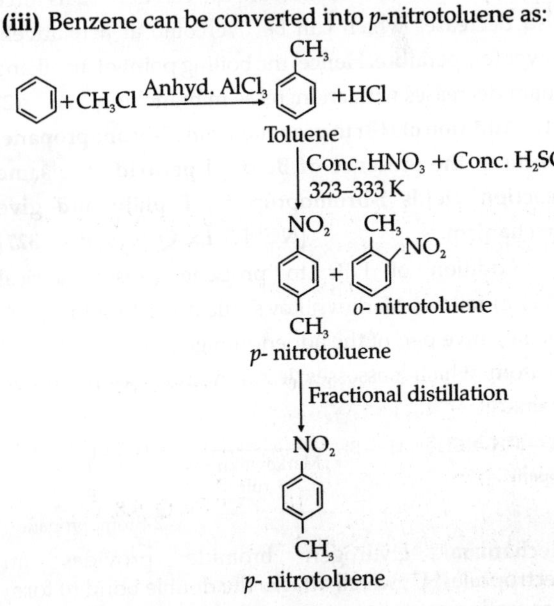

(iv) Benzene can be converted into acetophenone as:

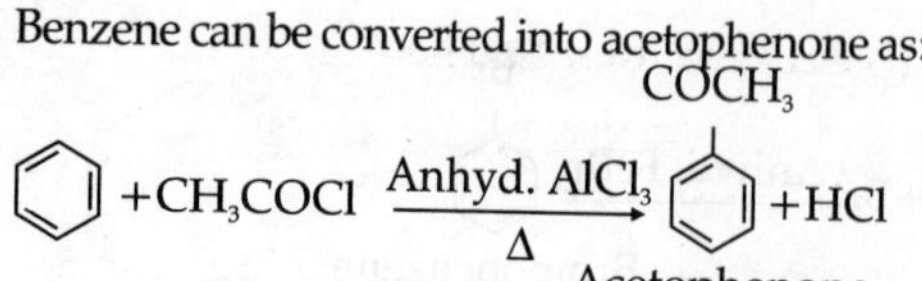

Acetophenone

Q. 14. In the alkane $H_3C - CH_2 - C(CH_3)_2 - CH_2 - CH(CH_3)_2$, identify 1°,2°,3° carbon atoms and give the number of H atoms bonded to each one of these.

[NCERT Ex. Q. 9.14, Page 327]

Ans.

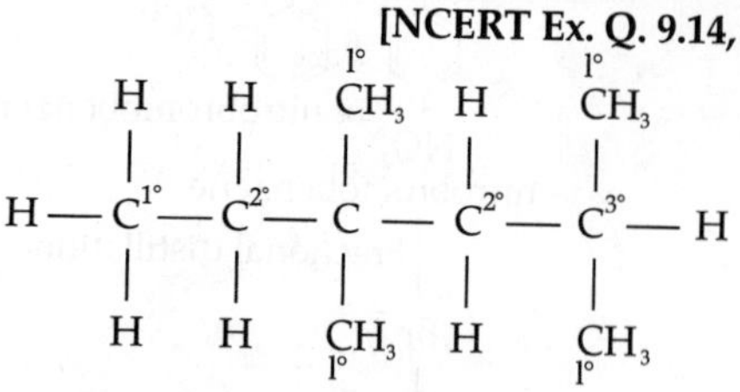

1° carbon atoms are those which are bonded to only one carbon atom, i.e., they have only one carbon atom as their neighbour. The given structure has five 1° carbon atoms and fifteen hydrogen atoms attached to it.

2° carbon atoms are those which are bonded to two carbon atoms, i.e., they have two carbon atoms as their neighbours. The given structure has two 2° carbon atoms and four hydrogen atoms attached to it.

3° carbon atoms are those which are bonded to three carbon atoms, i.e., they have three carbon atoms as their neighbours. The given structure has one 3° carbon atom and only one hydrogen atom is attached to it.

Q. 15. What effect does branching of an alkane chain has on its boiling point? [NCERT Ex. Q. 9.15, Page 327]

Ans. Alkanes experience intermolecular van der Waals forces. The stronger the force, the greater will be the boiling point of the alkane. As branching increases, the surface area of the molecule decreases which results in a small area of contact. As a result, the van der Waals force also decreases which can be overcome at a relatively lower temperature. Hence, the boiling point of an alkane chain decreases with an increase in branching. **(2)**

Q. 16. Addition of HBr to propene yields 2-bronopropane, while in the presence of Benzoyl peroxide the same reaction yields 1-bromopropane. Explain and give mechanism. [NCERT Ex. Q. 9.16, Page 327]

Ans. Addition of HBr to propene (unsymmetrical alkene) follows Markovnikov's rule according to which the negative part of the addendum gets attached to that C atom which possesses lesser number of hydrogen atoms.

$$\underset{\text{Propene}}{CH_3-CH=CH_3} + H-Br \xrightarrow[\text{rule}]{\text{Markovniknov's}} \underset{\text{2-Bromopropane}}{CH_3-\underset{\mathrm{Br}}{\underset{|}{CH}}-CH_3}$$

Mechanism: Hydrogen bromide provides an electrophile, H^+, which attacks the double bond to form carbocation as:

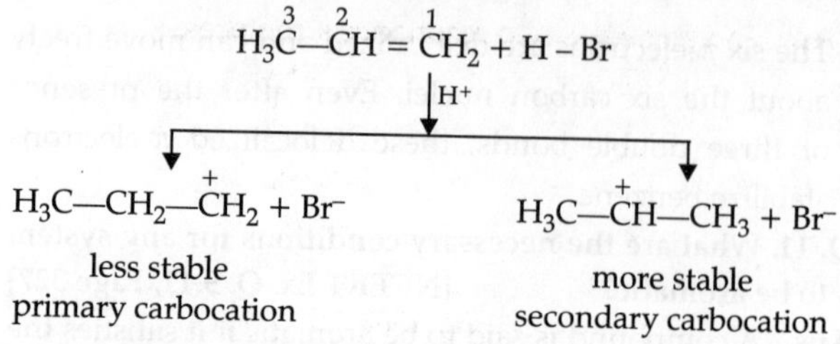

Secondary carbocations are more stable than primary carbocations. Therefore, the former predominates as it will form at a faster rate. Thus, in the next step, Br^- attacks the carbocation to form 2-bromopropane as the major product.

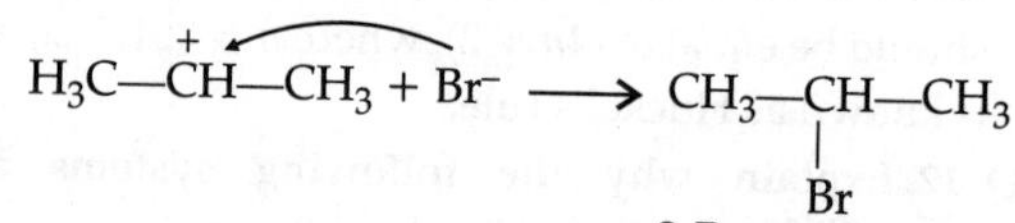

2-Bromopropane

Addition of HBr to unsymmetrical alkenes like propene in the presence of light or peroxide takes place contrary to the Markovnikov's rule. This so happens only with HBr but not with HCl and HI. This addition of HBr to propene in the presence of benzoyl peroxide follows anti-Markovnikov's rule or peroxide effect or Kharash effect.

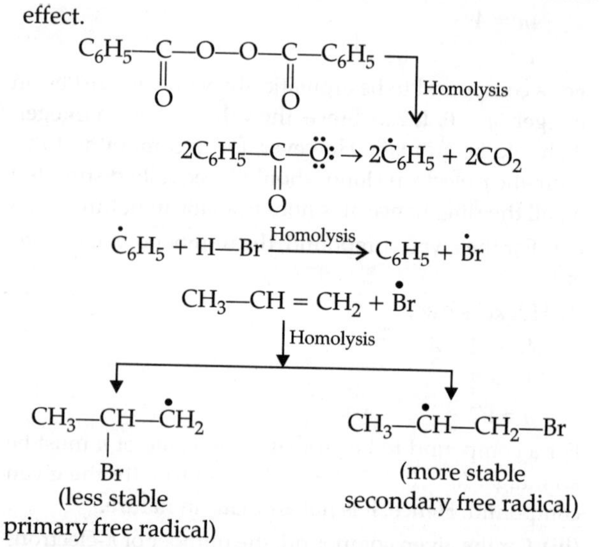

Secondary free radicals are more stable than primary radicals. Therefore, the former predominates since it forms at a faster rate. Thus, 1-bromopropane is obtained as the major product.

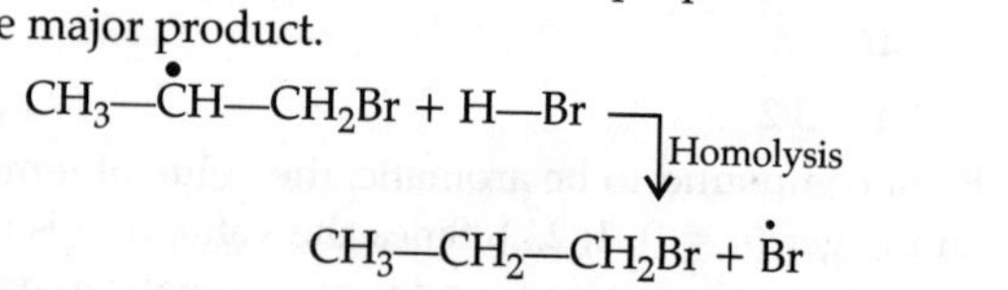

Q. 17. Write down the products of ozonolysis of 1,2-dimethylbenzene (*o*-xylene). How does the result support Kekulé structure for benzene?

[NCERT Ex. Q. 9.17, Page 327]

Ans. *o*-xylene has two resonance structures:

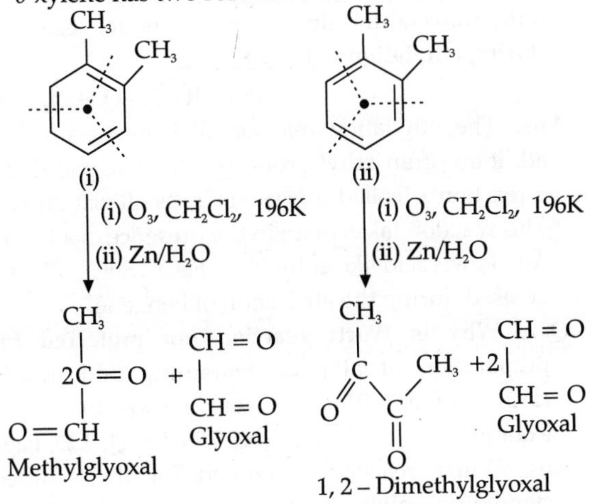

All three products, i.e., methyl glyoxal, 1, 2-dimethyl glyoxal and glyoxal are obtained from two Kekule structures. Since all three products cannot be obtained from any one of the two structures, this proves that *o*-xylene is a resonance hybrid of two Kekule structures.

Q. 18. Arrange benzene, *n*-hexane and ethyne in decreasing order of acidic behaviour. Also give reason for this behaviour. [NCERT Ex. Q. 9.18, Page 327]

Ans. Acidic character of a species is defined on the basis of ease with which it can lose its H– atoms. The hybridization state of carbon in the given compound is:

Benzene
sp^2

$CH_3-(CH_2)_4-CH_3$ $H-C\equiv C-H$
n-hexane sp^3 Ethyne sp

As the *s*–character increases, the electronegativity of carbon increases and the electrons of C–H bond pair lie closer to the carbon atom. As a result, partial positive charge of H– atom increases and H^+ ions are set free. The *s*–character increases in the order:

$$sp^3 < sp^2 < sp$$

Hence, the decreasing order of acidic behaviour is Ethyne > Benzene > *n*-Hexane.

Q. 19. Why does benzene undergo electrophilic substitution reactions easily and nucleophilic substitutions with difficulty? [NCERT Ex. Q. 9.19, Page 327]

Ans. Benzene is a planar molecule having delocalized electrons above and below the plane of ring. Hence, it is electron-rich. As a result, it is highly attractive to electron deficient species i.e., electrophiles. Therefore, it undergoes electrophilic substitution reactions very easily. Nucleophiles are electron-rich. Hence, they are repelled by benzene. Hence, benzene undergoes nucleophilic substitutions with difficulty.

Q. 20. How would you convert the following compounds into benzene?
(i) Ethyne (ii) Ethene (iii) Hexane
[NCERT Ex. Q. 9.20, Page 327]

Ans. (i) Benzene from Ethyne:

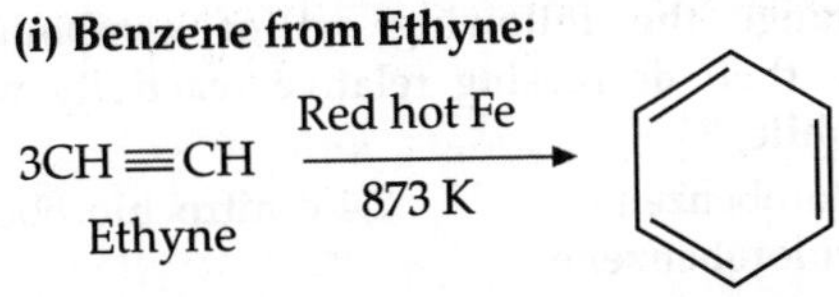

(ii) Benzene from Ethene:

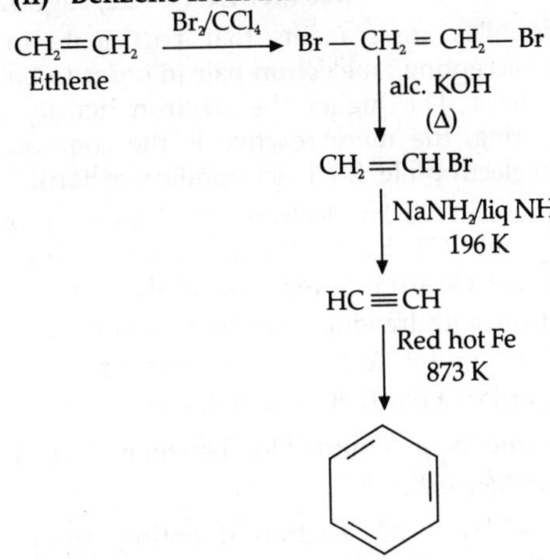

(iii) Hexane to Benzene:

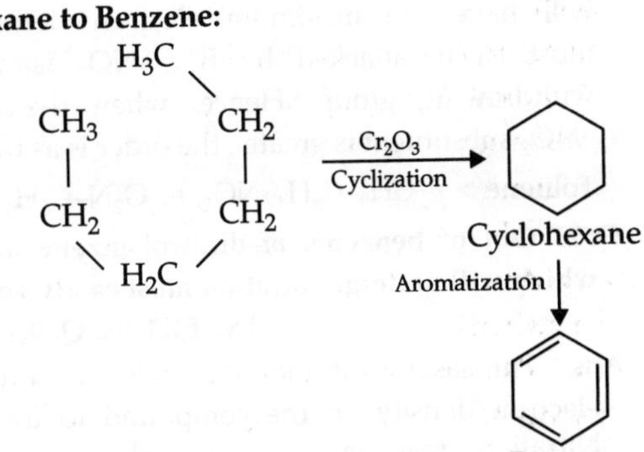

Q. 21. Write structures of all the alkenes which on hydrogenation give 2-methylbutane. [NCERT Ex. Q. 9.21, Page 327]

Ans. The basic skeleton of 2-methylbutane is shown below:

$$C^1-C^2-C^3-C^4$$
(with C attached to C^2)

On the basis of this structure, various alkenes that will give 2-methylbutane on hydrogenation are:

(a) $H_3C-CH(CH_3)-CH=CH_2$

(b) $H_3C-C(CH_3)=CH-CH_3$

(c) $CH_2=C(CH_3)-CH-CH_3$

Q. 22. Arrange the following set of compounds in order of their decreasing relative reactivity with an electrophile, E^+

(a) Chlorobenzene, 2,4-dinitrochlorobenzene, *p*-nitrochlorobenzene

(b) Toluene, *p*-$H_3C-C_6H_4-NO_2$, *p*-$O_2N-C_6H_4-NO_2$.

[NCERT Ex. Q. 9.22, Page 327]

Ans. Electrophiles are reagents that participate in a reaction by accepting an electron pair in order to bond to nucleophiles. The higher the electron density on a benzene ring, the more reactive is the compound towards an electrophile, E^+ (Electrophilic reaction).

(a) The presence of an electron withdrawing group (i.e., $-NO_2$ and $-Cl$) deactivates the aromatic ring by decreasing the electron density. Since $-NO_2$ group is more electron withdrawing (due to resonance effect) than the $-Cl$ group (due to inductive effect), the decreasing order of reactivity is as follows:

Chlorobenzene > *p* – nitrochlorobenzene > 2, 4 – dinitrochlorobenzene.

(b) While $-CH_3$ is an electron donating group, $-NO_2$ group is electron withdrawing. Hence, toluene will have the maximum electron density and is most easily attacked by E^+. $-NO_2$ is an electron withdrawing group. Hence, when the number of $-NO_2$ substituent is greater, the order is as follows:

Toluene > *p*–CH_3–C_6H_4–NO_2, *p* –O_2N–C_6H_4–NO_2

Q. 23. Out of benzene, *m*–dinitrobenzene and toluene which will undergo nitration most easily and why?

[NCERT Ex. Q. 9.23, Page 327]

Ans. The ease of nitration depends on the presence of electron density on the compound to form nitrates. Nitration reactions are examples of electrophilic substitution reactions where an electron-rich species is attacked by a nitronium ion ($-NO_2$). Now, $-CH_3$ group is electron donating and $-NO_2$ is electron withdrawing. Therefore, toluene will have the maximum electron density among the three compounds followed by benzene. On the other hand, m– dinitrobenzene will have the least electron density. Hence, it will undergo nitration with difficulty. Hence, the increasing order of nitration is as follows:

m–dinitrobenzene → benzene → toluene

Q. 24. Suggest the name of a Lewis acid other than anhydrous aluminium chloride which can be used during ethylation of benzene.

[NCERT Ex. Q. 9.24, Page 327]

Ans. The ethylation reaction of benzene involves the addition of an ethyl group on the benzene ring. Such a reaction is called a Friedel-Crafts alkylation reaction. This reaction takes place in the presence of a Lewis acid. Any Lewis acid like anhydrous $FeCl_3$, $SnCl_4$, BF_3, etc. can be used during the ethylation of benzene.

Q. 25. Why is Wurtz reaction not preferred for the preparation of alkanes containing odd number of carbon atoms? Illustrate your answer by taking one example.

[NCERT Ex. Q. 9.25, Page 327]

Ans. Wurtz reaction is limited for the synthesis of symmetrical alkanes (alkanes with an even number of carbon atoms). In the reaction, two similar alkyl halides are taken as reactants and an alkane, containing double the number of carbon atoms, are formed.

Example:

$$CH_3Br + 2Na + BrCH_3 \xrightarrow{\text{dry ether}} \underset{\text{Ethane}}{CH_3-CH_3} + 2NaBr$$

Bromomethane

Wurtz reaction cannot be used for the preparation of unsymmetrical alkanes because if two dissimilar alkyl halides are taken as the reactants, then a mixture of alkanes is obtained as the products. Since the reaction involves free radical species, a side reaction also occurs to produce an alkene. For example, the reaction of iodomethane and iodoethane gives a mixture of alkanes.

$$\underset{\text{Iodomethane}}{CH_3-I} + 2Na + \underset{\text{Iodoethane}}{I-CH_2CH_3} \xrightarrow{\text{Dry ether}} CH_3-CH_2-CH_3 + 2Na$$

$$CH_3-I + 2Na + I-CH_3 \xrightarrow{\text{Dry ether}} 2NaI + \underset{\text{Ethane}}{CH_3-CH_3}$$

$$CH_3CH_2-I + 2Na + I-CH_2CH_3 \xrightarrow{\text{Dry ether}} 2NaI + \underset{\text{Butane}}{CH_3CH_2-CH_2CH_3}$$

The boiling points of alkanes (obtained in the mixture) are very close. Hence, it becomes difficult to separate them.

□□